ANNUAL EDITIONS

Dying, Death, and Bereavement 12/13
Thirteenth Edition

EDITORS

George E. Dickinson, PhD
College of Charleston

George E. Dickinson, Professor of Sociology at the College of Charleston, received his Ph.D. in sociology from LSU in Baton Rouge (LA) and his M.A. in sociology and B.A. in biology from Baylor University (TX). He came to the College of Charleston in 1985, having previously taught in Minnesota and Kentucky. The recipient of both NSF and NEH grants, Dickinson has presented more than 70 papers at professional meetings and has been the author/co-author of over 80 articles in professional journals, primarily on end-of-life issues. In addition, he has co-authored/co-edited 22 books/anthologies (with Michael R. Leming), including *Understanding Dying, Death and Bereavement* 7th ed., Wadsworth/Cengage, 2011. His research and teaching interest in end-of-life issues goes back to 1974 when he taught a course on death and dying and in 1975 when he began research on medical schools and physicians. He is on the editorial boards of *Mortality* (UK) and the *American Journal of Hospice & Palliative Medicine* (US). He was the 2002 recipient of the Distinguished Teacher/Scholar Award and the 2008 Distinguished Research Award at the College of Charleston, a South Carolina Governor's Distinguished Professor Award in 2003 and 2008, and the Death Educator Award from the Association for Death Education and Counseling in 2009. In 1999 he was a Visiting Research Fellow in palliative medicine at the University of Sheffield's School of Medicine (UK) and in 2006 at Lancaster University's Institute for Health Research (UK). Earlier, Dickinson did postdoctoral studies at Pennsylvania State University(gerontology), at the University of Connecticut(medical sociology), and at the University of Kentucky's School of Medicine (thanatology).

Michael R. Leming, PhD
St. Olaf College

Michael R. Leming is Professor of Sociology and Anthropology at St. Olaf College. He holds degrees from Westmont College (B.A.), Marquette University (M.A.), and the University of Utah (Ph.D.) and has done additional graduate study at the University of California in Santa Barbara. Leming's research has primarily focused on the sociology of religion, the sociology of the family, and social thanatology. He has written or edited 27 books and numerous articles about cross-cultural and comparative studies of kinship, religion, death rituals, and bereavement behavior. The books he has worked on include *Understanding Families: Diversity, Continuity, and Change; Understanding Dying, Death, and Bereavement; The Sociological Perspective: A Value-Committed Introduction; Handbook of Death and Dying; and Encyclopedia of Death and the Human Experience.* Most of his publishing has been co-authored with George E. Dickinson.

Dr. Leming was the founder and former director of the St. Olaf College Social Research Center, former member of the board of directors of the Minnesota Coalition on Terminal Care and the Northfield AIDS Response, and has served as a hospice educator, volunteer, and grief counselor. Leming has also devoted much of his career to studying and teaching about the people of Asia, most notably Thailand and has produced a documentary film titled *The Karen of Musikhee: Rabbits in the Mouth of the Crocodile.* For the past eleven years Leming has directed the Spring Semester in Thailand(Amazing Thailand.org) program that is affiliated with Chiang Mai University and lives in Thailand during Minnesota's coldest months.

While teaching and research has been his vocation, community development and service to others has been Leming's passion and primary calling. He (and his Santa Claus persona) led efforts to raise money to build, water supplies, churches, and three schools in Karen, Lahu, and Akha villages in Thailand, and the success of these projects inspired him to work on bringing a performing and visual arts center for the disabled to Thailand. His tenacity was rewarded with a $6.9 million grant for the project from the Thai government.

The McGraw·Hill Companies

Mc Graw Hill

Connect
Learn
Succeed™

ANNUAL EDITIONS: DYING, DEATH, AND BEREAVEMENT, THIRTEENTH EDITION

Published by McGraw-Hill, a business unit of The McGraw-Hill Companies, Inc., 1221 Avenue of the Americas, New York, NY 10020. Copyright © 2012 by The McGraw-Hill Companies, Inc. All rights reserved. Previous edition(s) © 2011, 2010, and 2008. Printed in the United States of America. No part of this publication may be reproduced or distributed in any form or by any means, or stored in a database or retrieval system, without the prior written consent of The McGraw-Hill Companies, Inc., including, but not limited to, in any network or other electronic storage or transmission, or broadcast for distance learning.

Some ancillaries, including electronic and print components, may not be available to customers outside the United States.

This book is printed on acid-free paper.

Annual Editions® is a registered trademark of The McGraw-Hill Companies, Inc.
Annual Editions is published by the **Contemporary Learning Series** group within the McGraw-Hill Higher Education division.

1 2 3 4 5 6 7 8 9 0 QDB/QDB 1 0 9 8 7 6 5 4 3 2 1

ISBN: 978–0–07–805105–0
MHID: 0–07–805105–3
ISSN: 1096–4223 (print)
ISSN: 2162–1829 (online)

Managing Editor: *Larry Loeppke*
Developmental Editor: *Dave Welsh*
Permissions Coordinator: *Lenny J. Behnke*
Marketing Specialist: *Alice Link*
Project Manager: *Connie Oertel*
Design Coordinator: *Margarite Reynolds*
Cover Designer: *Kristine Jubeck*
Buyer: *Susan K. Culbertson*
Media Project Manager: *Sridevi Palani*

Compositor: Laserwords Private Limited
Cover Image Credits: Cherie Cullen/DoD (inset); Ingram Publishing/SuperStock (background)

Editors/Academic Advisory Board

Members of the Academic Advisory Board are instrumental in the final selection of articles for each edition of ANNUAL EDITIONS. Their review of articles for content, level, and appropriateness provides critical direction to the editors and staff. We think that you will find their careful consideration well reflected in this volume.

ANNUAL EDITIONS: Dying, Death, and Bereavement 12/13

13th Edition

Preface

In publishing ANNUAL EDITIONS we recognize the enormous role played by the magazines, newspapers, and journals of the public press in providing current, first-rate educational information in a broad spectrum of interest areas. Many of these articles are appropriate for students, researchers, and professionals seeking accurate, current material to help bridge the gap between principles and theories and the real world. These articles, however, become more useful for study when those of lasting value are carefully collected, organized, indexed, and reproduced in a low-cost format, which provides easy and permanent access when the material is needed. That is the role played by ANNUAL EDITIONS.

Dying, death, and bereavement have been around for as long as humankind, yet as topics of discussion they have been "offstage" for decades in contemporary American public discourse. In the United States, dying currently takes place away from the arena of familiar surroundings of kin and friends, with approximately 80 percent of deaths occurring in institutional settings such as hospitals and nursing homes. Americans have developed a paradoxical relationship with death: We know more about the causes and conditions surrounding death but have not equipped ourselves emotionally to cope with dying, death, and bereavement. The purpose of this anthology is to provide an understanding of dying, death, and bereavement that will assist in better coping with and understanding our own deaths and the deaths of others.

Articles in this volume are taken from professional/semiprofessional journals and from popular publications written for both special populations and a general readership. The selections are carefully reviewed for their currency and accuracy. Many of the articles have been changed from the previous edition through updating and responding to comments of reviewers. Most of the articles refer to situations in the United States, yet other cultures are represented. We strive to have current articles, although a few may be earlier than 2006, due to readers' requests to maintain them in this updated issue.

The reader will note the tremendous range of approaches and styles of the writers from personal, first-hand accounts to more scientific and philosophical writings. Some articles are more practical and applied, while others are more technical and research-oriented. If "variety is the very spice of life," this volume should be a spicy venture for the reader. Methodologies used in the more research-oriented articles range from quantitative (e.g., surveys/questionnaires) to qualitative (e.g., interviews/observation/content analysis). Such a mix should especially be of interest to the student majoring or minoring in the social sciences. If a particular article seems too technical for your background, do not bog yourself down with the statistical analysis, rather look ahead to the discussion and conclusions.

These articles are drawn from many different periodicals, thus exposing the reader to a variety of publications in the library. With interest stimulated by a particular article, the student is encouraged to pursue other related articles in that particular journal.

This anthology is organized into eight units to cover many of the important aspects of dying, death, and bereavement. Although the units are arranged in a way that has some logical order, one can determine from the brief summaries in the table of contents and the cross-references in the Topic Guide whether another arrangement would best fit a particular teaching situation. The first unit is on issues in dying and death. Unit 2 takes a life-cycle approach and looks at the developmental aspects of dying and death at different age levels. The third unit concerns the process of dying. Unit 4 is on the topic of suicide. The fifth unit is about animals and death. The sixth unit is on ethical issues of dying and death, whereas Unit 7 contains articles which deal with death rituals and funerals. Finally, Unit 8 contains articles on bereavement.

Annual Editions: Dying, Death, and Bereavement, 13/e is intended for use as a supplement to augment selected areas or chapters of textbooks on dying and death. The articles in this volume can also serve as a basis for class discussion about various issues in dying, death, and bereavement.

Annual Editions: Dying, Death, and Bereavement is revised periodically to keep the materials timely as new social concerns about end-of-life issues develop. Your assistance in the revision effort is always welcome. Please complete and return the postage-paid article rating form at the back of the book. We look forward to your input.

George E. Dickinson
Editor

Michael R. Leming
Editor

The Annual Editions Series

VOLUMES AVAILABLE

Adolescent Psychology

Aging

American Foreign Policy

American Government

Anthropology

Archaeology

Assessment and Evaluation

Business Ethics

Child Growth and Development

Comparative Politics

Criminal Justice

Developing World

Drugs, Society, and Behavior

Dying, Death, and Bereavement

Early Childhood Education

Economics

Educating Children with Exceptionalities

Education

Educational Psychology

Entrepreneurship

Environment

The Family

Gender

Geography

Global Issues

Health

Homeland Security

Human Development

Human Resources

Human Sexualities

International Business

Management

Marketing

Mass Media

Microbiology

Multicultural Education

Nursing

Nutrition

Physical Anthropology

Psychology

Race and Ethnic Relations

Social Problems

Sociology

State and Local Government

Sustainability

Technologies, Social Media, and Society

United States History, Volume 1

United States History, Volume 2

Urban Society

Violence and Terrorism

Western Civilization, Volume 1

Western Civilization, Volume 2

World History, Volume 1

World History, Volume 2

World Politics

Contents

UNIT 1
Issues in Dying and Death

UNIT 2
Dying and Death across the Life Cycle

The concepts in bold italics are developed in the article. For further expansion, please refer to the Topic Guide.

UNIT 3
The Dying Process

The concepts in bold italics are developed in the article. For further expansion, please refer to the Topic Guide.

UNIT 4
Suicide

UNIT 5
Animals and Death

The concepts in bold italics are developed in the article. For further expansion, please refer to the Topic Guide.

UNIT 6
Ethical Issues of Dying and Death

UNIT 7
Funerals

The concepts in bold italics are developed in the article. For further expansion, please refer to the Topic Guide.

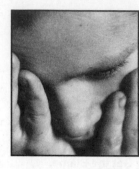

UNIT 8
Bereavement

The concepts in bold italics are developed in the article. For further expansion, please refer to the Topic Guide.

The concepts in bold italics are developed in the article. For further expansion, please refer to the Topic Guide.

Correlation Guide

The Annual Editions series provides students with convenient, inexpensive access to current, carefully selected articles from the public press. **Annual Editions: Dying, Death, and Bereavement 12/13** is an easy-to-use reader that presents articles on important topics such as the dying process, funerals, bereavement, and many more. For more information on *Annual Editions* and other *McGraw-Hill Contemporary Learning Series* titles, visit www.mhhe.com/cls.

This convenient guide matches the units in **Annual Editions: Dying, Death, and Bereavement 12/13** with the corresponding chapters in one of our best-selling McGraw-Hill Psychology textbooks by DeSpelder/Strickland.

Annual Editions: Dying, Death, and Bereavement 12/13	The Last Dance: Encountering Death and Dying, 9/e by DeSpelder/Strickland
Unit 1: Issues in Dying and Death	**Chapter 1:** Attitudes toward Death: A Climate of Change **Chapter 4:** Death Systems: Mortality and Society **Chapter 15:** The Path Ahead: Personal and Social Choices
Unit 2: Dying and Death across the Life Cycle	**Chapter 2:** Learning about Death: The Influence of Sociocultural Forces **Chapter 10:** Death in the Lives of Children and Adolescents **Chapter 11:** Death in the Lives of Adults **Chapter 13:** Risks, Perils, and Traumatic Death
Unit 3: The Dying Process	**Chapter 4:** Death Systems: Mortality and Society **Chapter 5:** Health Care Systems: Patients, Staff, and Institutions **Chapter 7:** Facing Death: Living with Life-Threatening Illness **Chapter 14:** Beyond Death/After Life
Unit 4: Suicide	**Chapter 12:** Suicide
Unit 5: Animals and Death	**Chapter 10:** Death in the Lives of Children and Adolescents
Unit 6: Ethical Issues of Dying and Death	**Chapter 5:** Health Care Systems: Patients, Staff, and Institutions **Chapter 6:** End-of-Life Issues and Decisions
Unit 7: Funerals	**Chapter 3:** Perspectives on Death: Cultural and Historical **Chapter 8:** Last Rites: Funerals and Body Disposition
Unit 8: Bereavement	**Chapter 9:** Survivors: Understanding the Experience of Loss

Topic Guide

This topic guide suggests how the selections in this book relate to the subjects covered in your course. You may want to use the topics listed on these pages to search the Web more easily.

On the following pages a number of websites have been gathered specifically for this book. They are arranged to reflect the units of this Annual Editions reader. You can link to these sites by going to www.mhhe.com/cls

All the articles that relate to each topic are listed below the bold-faced term.

Advance directives

Animals and death

Assisting grievers

Attitudes toward death

Bereavement and grief

Brain death

Caregivers

Children

Communication

Coping

Counseling

Internet References

The following Internet sites have been selected to support the articles found in this reader. These sites were available at the time of publication. However, because websites often change their structure and content, the information listed may no longer be available. We invite you to visit www.mhhe.com/cls for easy access to these sites.

Annual Editions: Dying, Death, and Bereavement 12/13

General Sources

An Introduction to Death and Dying
www.bereavement.org

This electronic book was created to help those who grieve and those who provide support for the bereaved. Sections include Grief Theories, Death Systems, Ritual, and Disenfranchised Grief.

Yahoo: Society and Culture: Death
http://dir.yahoo.com/Society_and_Culture/Death_and_Dying

This Yahoo site has a very complete index to issues of dying and a search option.

Unit 1: Issues in Dying and Death

Association for Death Education and Counseling, The Thanatology Association
www.adec.org

The Association for Death Education and Counseling, The Thanatology Association, is one of the oldest interdisciplinary organizations in the field of dying, death, and bereavement. Its nearly 2,000 members include a wide array of mental and medical health personnel, educators, clergy, funeral directors, and volunteers.

Bardo of Death Studies
www.bardo.org

Bardo of Death Studies assists in the development of discourse, discussion, and archival materials related to personal experiences in death and dying. We serve as a friendly net repository for these personal reflections (both from the professional and the lay public) and a crossroads resource for others who happen by in search for personal reflection in their own time of need.

Death and Culture
http://en.wikipedia.org/wiki/Death_and_culture

This article is about death in the different cultures around the world as well as ethical issues relating to death, such as martyrdom, suicide, and euthanasia. Death and its spiritual ramifications are debated in every manner all over the world. Most civilizations dispose of their dead with rituals developed through spiritual traditions.

Kearl's Guide to Sociology of Death and Dying
www.trinity.edu/~mkearl/death.html

An Internet resource on the Sociology of Death and Dying that includes issues of dying and death, such as death in the natural order, is found here.

Yahoo: Society and Culture: Death and Dying
http://dir.yahoo.com/Society_and_Culture/Death_and_Dying

This Yahoo site has a very complete index to issues of death and dying and a search option.

Unit 2: Dying and Death across the Life Cycle

American Academy of Child & Adolescent Psychiatry
http://aacap.org/page.ww?name=Children+and+Grief&section=Facts+for+Families

The American Academy of Child & Adolescent Psychiatry provides important information as a public service to assist parents and families in their most important roles. This article "Children and Grief" is one such resource, written in English, Spanish, and French.

Child Bereavement Charity
www.childbereavement.org.uk/home_page

The Child Bereavement Charity site provides support for families and educates professionals for bereaved families, including miscarriage, stillbirth, neonatal death, and termination for abnormality.

Children with AIDS Project
www.aidskids.org

The Children with AIDS Project offers a deeper understanding of children with, and at risk of, AIDS, including the medical, psychosocial, legal, and financial issues. The mission of the organization is to develop local and national adoptive, foster- and family-centered care programs that are both effective and compassionate.

The Compassionate Friends
www.compassionatefriends.org/resources/links.aspx

The Compassionate Friends site is a self-help organization for bereaved parents and siblings. There are presently hundreds of chapters worldwide.

Grief Net
http://rivendell.org

This website provides many links on the bereavement process, resources for grievers, and information concerning grief support groups.

Motherloss
www.freewebs.com/motherloss/front.htm

This site is a support group started to help with the grieving issues for women whose mothers have died.

Raindrop: Death Education for Children of All Ages
http://iul.com/raindrop

This site presents an explanation of "What happens when we die?" a question by children of all ages for the unexplainable phenomenon of life and death.

Yahoo: Society and Culture: Death and Dying
http://dir.yahoo.com/Society_and_Culture/Death_and_Dying

This Yahoo site has a very complete index to issues of death and dying and a search option.

Internet References

Unit 3: The Dying Process

Thanatolinks
http://netsociology.tripod.com/thanalinks.htm

This site contains links to some of the best sites related to death and dying on the Internet.

Yahoo: Society and Culture: Death and Dying
http://dir.yahoo.com/Society_and_Culture/Death_and_Dying

This Yahoo site has a very complete index to issues of death and dying and a search option.

Centers for Disease Control and Prevention
www.cdc.gov

Centers for Disease Control and Prevention (CDC) provide informational material to protect people and communities health, through health promotion, prevention, and preparedness.

Agency for Healthcare Research and Quality
www.ahrq.gov

Agency for Healthcare Research and Quality provides information on the dying process in the context of U.S. health policy.

The Natural Death Centre
www.naturaldeath.org.uk

This is a nonprofit charitable project launched in Britain in 1991, with three psychotherapists as directors. It aims to support those dying at home and their caregivers and to help them arrange funerals. It also has a more general aim of helping improve "the quality of dying."

Project on Death in America
www.soros.org/resources/articles_publications/publications/
pdia_20040101

Project on Death in America (PDIA) has the goal to help people understand and transform the dying experience in America.

Kearl's PARADIGM: Enhancing Life near Death
www.trinity.edu/~mkearl/paradigm.html

This Internet resource does not suggest that there is one particular way of dying well. However, it is possible to identify some general developmental tasks that the dying person can accomplish if dying well is the goal.

The Living Will and Values History Project
www.euthanasia.cc/lwvh.html

The Living Will and Values History Project was set up in response to an alarming growth and proliferation of living will documents that bore little correlation to academic and empirical data on their usefulness or effectiveness. It attempts to collate, analyze and apply research in this area, acting as an adviser and resource base, as well as publishing its own document.

Hospice Foundation of America
www.hospicefoundation.org

Hospice Foundation of America provides general information about hospice and specific information on the Foundation.

Hospice and Palliative Nurses Association
www.hpna.org

Hospice and Palliative Nurses Association (HPNA) is an international professional association with the mission of promoting excellence in hospice nursing.

National Prison Hospice Association
www.npha.org

National Prison Hospice Association promotes hospice care for terminally ill inmates and those facing the prospect of dying in prison. The goal of the association is to support and assist corrections professionals in their continuing efforts to develop high-quality patient care procedures and management programs.

Larson's Compilation of Great Ideas
www.scu.edu/Hospice/greatideas.html

Dale Larson's compilation of Great Ideas submitted from a wide variety of sources.

Hospice-Care
www.hospice-cares.com

The Hospice-Care website includes an extensive collection of links to hospice resources.

American Academy of Hospice & Palliative Medicine
www.aahpm.org

American Academy of Hospice and Palliative Medicine (AAHPM) is the only organization in the United States for physicians dedicated to the advancement of hospice/palliative medicine, its practice, research, and education.

The Zen Hospice Project
www.zenhospice.org

This site organizes programs dedicated to the care of people approaching death and to increasing the understanding of impermanence. The Zen Hospice Project also runs a small hospice in a restored Victorian house near the San Francisco Zen Center.

VNA of Hudson Valley, NY
www.vnahv.org

Visiting Nurse Association of Hudson Valley website provides quality healthcare to all people in their communities regardless of ability to pay, in a manner that recognizes the whole person and their environment. A primary focus is to maximize resources for the organization for the benefit of the patient. The VNAHV strives to foster independence and choice for all individuals with the overall goal of improving the quality of life by assuming a proactive advocate role.

The Connecticut Hospice
www.hospice.com

Founded in 1974 as the nation's first Hospice, today The Connecticut Hospice, Inc., offers a state-wide hospice home care program and the state's only 52-bed inpatient hospice care center that accepts referrals from throughout the United States and the world. Being a leader in palliative medicine, The Connecticut Hospice became the first and only accredited teaching hospice offering training and consultation to professionals from around the world through its teaching arm, the John D. Thompson Hospice Institute for Education, Training, and Research, Inc.

Houston Hospice
www.houstonhospice.org

The Houston Hospice website offers and provides, regardless of ability to pay, the highest quality of care for patients with life-threatening illnesses and their families through a well-qualified interdisciplinary team of professionals and volunteers.

Internet References

Hospice Service of Santa Barbara
www.hospiceofsantabarbara.org

The Hospice Service of Santa Barbara, Inc. is a program of the Santa Barbara Visiting Nurse Association.

Unit 4: Suicide

Thanatolinks
http://netsociology.tripod.com/thanalinks.htm

This site contains links to some of the best sites on the Internet related to death and dying.

Yahoo: Society and Culture: Death and Dying
http://dir.yahoo.com/Society_and_Culture/Death_and_Dying

This Yahoo site has a very complete index to issues of death and dying and a search option.

UNICEF
www.unicef.org/pon96/insuicid.htm

This website provides international suicide rates of young adults.

Suicide Awareness Voices of Education
www.save.org

Suicide Awareness Voices of Education (SAVE) is the most popular suicide site on the Internet; a well-kept and thorough site, with material on dealing with suicide both before and after, along with material from their many education sessions.

Light for Life Foundation
www.yellowribbon.org

The Yellow Ribbon Program of the Light for Life Foundation provides educational material for American youth aimed at preventing youth suicide through the provision of easy access to support services.

Centers for Disease Control and Prevention
www.cdc.gov

Centers for Disease Control and Prevention (CDC) provide informational material to protect people and communities health, through health promotion, prevention, and preparedness.

Suicide Prevention Action Network
www.spanusa.org

A more political site, that of a nonprofit organization whose aim is to have suicide treated as a national (and global) problem that must be solved as a priority.

Canadian Association for Suicide Prevention
www.suicideprevention.ca

Canadian Association for Suicide Prevention is a simple site with details on the organization, current suicide prevention research, electronic brochures, and upcoming conferences.

San Francisco Suicide Prevention
www.sfsuicide.org

The San Francisco Suicide Prevention website is a very well-presented website on suicide prevention with some interesting facts and details on local prevention programs.

Interactive Chat System: SuicideChat!
www.4-lane.com/supportchat/pages/suicidechat.html

This website is becoming more common these days, Internet chat is moving to the web. This interactive support system has a lot of potential, if only because it is more accessible (and reliable) than IRC (Internet Relay Chat).

Euthanasia Research & Guidance Organization
www.finalexit.org/index.html

Euthanasia Research & Guidance Organization (ERGO) provides links to right to die organizations worldwide.

Unit 5: Animals and Death

Association for Pet Loss and Bereavement (APLB)
www.aplb.org

This website is dedicated to helping people who grieve for a lost pet. APLB provides an international clearing house for information and direction on this subject.

In Memory of Pets
www.In-Memory-Of-Pets.Com

In Memory of Pets website includes poems, tributes, and resources.

Lightning Strike Pet Loss Support
www.lightning-strike.com

This website provides a cyber-shoulder for grieving owners of dead, dying, sick, or missing pets.

Chance's Spot Pet Loss and Support Resources
www.chancesspot.org

This site provides assistance to those who are grieving the death of pet as well as support programs to animal care professionals, animal shelters, and rescue groups.

Bereavement UK
www.bereavement.co.uk

Bereavement UK covers all aspects of death, dying, grief, and bereavement.

College of Veterinary Medicine Pet Loss Support
www.vetmed.wsu.edu/PLHL

Veterinary student volunteers can help you cope with grief and bereavement in the pending or past loss of a companion pet.

Pet Loss Support Page
www.pet-loss.net

Pet Loss Support Page features articles and resources for dealing with the death of a pet.

Best Friend Services
www.bestfriendservices.com

Best Friend Services offers best friend memorials for a lifetime of companionship, also offers pet urns and other pet loss memorials.

In Memory of Pets Cemetery
www.in-memory-of-pets.com

Open to all who are in grief after the loss of a pet and to pay tribute to all pets who, in their own way, gave love and happiness.

Rainbows Bridge
www.rainbowsbridge.com

Place a tribute for your pet, read others' stories and poetry, or visit the Pet Loss Grief Center and chat room.

Angel Blue Mist
www.angelbluemist.com

Portrait of an Angel is a website dedicated to the loss of a pet.

Internet References

Patsy Ann
www.patsyann.com

Bull terrier born deaf, that somehow managed to hear the whistles of ships approaching the harbor in Juneau, Alaska, and never missed greeting them during her 1929–1942 life. Today, her statue still greets visitors as they disembark their cruise ships.

Four Paws in Heaven
www.fourpawsinheaven.com

At this website you can read pet memorials from all over the world. Also features support forums, poetry for solace, and FAQs.

My Cemetery
www.mycemetery.com

My Cemetery is a website created for virtual remembrance, where those who have loss loved ones can post special words about them.

Tippie
www.tippie.com

Tippie's Place is a website dedicated to celebrating the life of Tippie the Shih Tzu.

Valor Rolls: Police Officers and Dogs Killed in Action
www.policek9.com/html/valor.html

The officers and dogs that worked the streets to make them safer for us all and gave their lives in the service of their respective communities.

Shaman
http://kimmurphy.net/shaman.html

The website is dedicated to Shaman, a Belgian shepherd who suffered from overwhelming fear and seizures.

Roadside America Pet Cemetery
www.roadsideamerica.com/pet

At this website, you can tour virtual grounds that feature humorous and touching stories of over 70 famous and heroic pets and animals. Plan to visit the real graves and stuffed tributes on your next vacation.

Gone to the Dog Star
www.gonetodogstar.com

Gone to the Dog Star is dedicated to our four-legged friends who await us at Dog Star. They are gone but not forgotten. A free memorial page open to all dogs.

Prince
www.catsdogs.com/prince.html

This website is dedicated to Prince, a sheltie companion of 14 1/2 years.

Odie
http://odiedog.com/

Odie's Homepage is full of memories and photos of this much-loved beagle. It is also a place to post photos, stories, and memories of your pet.

Bebe
www.bebemau.com

This website is in memory of the most beloved, cherished cat that lost his battle to an incurable cancer.

Justice for Junior
www.justiceforjunior.org

This website is dedicated to obtaining justice for Junior, gunned down in his prime because of his breed, by seeing that the confessed killer and his accomplices be tried for their crimes.

Unit 6: Ethical Issues of Dying and Death

Moral Debates of Our Times
www.trinity.edu/~mkearl/death-5.html#eu

Moral Debates of our Times is an Internet resource on biomedical issues.

Biomedical Ethics and Issues of Euthanasia
http://pwa.acusd.edu/~hinman/euthanasia.html

A website dedicated to biomedical ethics and issues of euthanasia.

Yahoo: Society and Culture: Death and Dying Euthanasia
http://dir.yahoo.com/Society_and_Culture/Death_and_Dying/Euthanasia

This Yahoo site has a very complete index to issues of euthanasia related to death and dying and a search option.

Deathnet
www.deathnet.com

Deathnet is an Internet searchable website containing many links to many biomedical topics including living wills, "how to" suicide, euthanasia, mercy killing, and legislation regulating the care for the terminally ill.

Thanatolinks
http://netsociology.tripod.com/thanalinks.htm

This site contains links to some of the best sites on the internet related to death and dying.

Living Will (Advance Directive)
www.mindspring.com/~scottr/will.html

Living Will contains the largest collection of links to living wills and other advance directive and living will information. Living wills (advance directives) and values histories help medical staff and others to make decisions about care and treatment of the seriously ill who are unable to speak for themselves. In some circumstances, living wills may become legally binding on healthcare staff. The Living Will and Values History Project was set up in response to an alarming growth and proliferation of living will documents that bore little correlation to academic and empirical data on their usefulness or effectiveness. It works on a nonprofit basis and attempts to collate, analyze, and apply research in this area, acting as an adviser and resource base, as well as publishing its own document.

Euthanasia Research & Guidance Organization
www.finalexit.org/index.html

Euthanasia Research & Guidance Organization (ERGO) provides links to right to die organizations worldwide.

Euthanasia in the Netherlands
www.euthanasia.com/netherlands.html

Website dedicated to the issues of euthanasia as practiced in the Netherlands.

Internet References

The Choice in Dying
www.choices.org

The Choice in Dying is an organization that provides information to patients interested in active and passive euthanasia.

Last Rights Organization
http://lastrights.info

Last Rights Organization publishes electronically the complete texts of many of the key legal documents concerning the dying patient's right to die.

Euthanasia and Christianity: Christian Views of Euthanasia and Suicide
www.religionfacts.com/euthanasia/christianity.htm

Roman Catholic perspective and view about euthanasia and suicide.

Not Dead Yet!
www.notdeadyet.org/pressrel.html

Americans with Disabilities have a website to mobilize American's against euthanasia and mercy killing. They say, "We don't want your pity or your lethal mercy."

Patients Rights Council
www.patientsrightscouncil.org

International Anti-Euthanasia Task Force that provides more links to internet resources which oppose euthanasia.

United Network for Organ Sharing
www.unos.org

The website of the United Network for Organ Sharing Transplantation Information SIte.

TransWeb
www.transweb.org

TransWeb is a website all about transplantation and organ donation.

Unit 7: Funerals

Personal Impacts of Death
http://www.trinity.edu/~mkearl/death-6.html#funerals

Personal Impacts of Death is an internet resource regarding funeral guides and planning.

Willed Body Program
www.utsouthwestern.edu/utsw/home/pcpp/willedbody

The Willed Body Program is a universal program in which people can donate their body for medical science, after death. The program is a division of the Department of Anatomy and Neurobiology at the University of California, Irvine's College of Medicine.

Mortuary Science
www.alamo.edu/sac/mortuary/mortuarylinks.htm

A list of some Internet links.

Funerals: A Consumer Guide
www.ftc.gov/bcp/edu/pubs/consumer/products/pro19.shtm

Funerals: A Consumer Guide presents facts for consumers produced by the Federal Trade Commission.

Funeral Net
www.funeral.net/info/notices.html

Funeral Net's intention is to provide an avenue to the general public to gain a basic understanding of the funeral and grief process so that they may be better equipped, emotionally, psychologically, and mentally to deal with the closure of significant relationships in their lives.

The Internet Cremation Society
www.cremation.org

The Internet Cremation Society contains statistics on cremations and links to funeral industry resources.

Cremation Consultant Guidebook
www.funeralplan.com/funeralplan/cremation/options.html

The Cremation Consultant Guidebook provides information to families who are interesting in cremation and memorial services.

National Academy of Mortuary Science
www.drkloss.com

The National Academy of Mortuary Science informs how you can enroll in funeral school to gain mortuary service employment.

Alcor
www.alcor.org

Alcor is the world's largest cryonics organization.

CyroCare
www.cyrocare.org

CyroCare is a website dealing with cryonics.

Funerals and Ripoffs
www.funerals-rIpoffs.org

Funerals and Ripoffs is a website that is very critical of the funeral industry and specializes in exposing funeral home financial fraud.

The Making of a Classic
www.monitor.net/monitor/decca/death.html

The Making of a Classic is an Internet resource that provides a critical perspective on the funeral industry in America.

The End of Life: Exploring Death in America
http://www.npr.org/programs/death/index.html

The End of Life: Exploring Death in America provides assistance for families who want a "do-it-yourself" funeral. They assist families in providing in conducting their own legal, uncomplicated, dignified, and inexpensive funeral without advanced planning or professional help.

Forensic Entomology
www.forensic-entomology.com

Forensic Entomology provides information concerning what happens to the human body after death and the process of body decomposition.

Hospice: A Guide to Grief Bereavement, Mourning, and Grief
www.hospicenet.org/html/grief_guide.html

Hospice: A Guide to Grief Bereavement, Mourning, and Grief is an informational resource to learn about the different ways people cope with the loss of a loved one.

Internet References

Growth House
www.growthhouse.org

Growth House is a nonprofit organization working with grief, bereavement, hospice, and end-of-life issues.

Directory of Grief, Loss and Bereavement: Support Groups
www.dmoz.org/Health/Mental_Health/Grief,_Loss_and_Bereavement/Support_Groups

The death of a loved one is an emotionally devastating time for survivors. But not knowing what to expect can often lead to unnecessary additional pain. To alleviate some of the confusion, to begin to examine the many issues that are often hard to discuss and to find all the help bereaved individuals need as they begin this journey, we created the most comprehensive book, the first of its kind, to assist them with resources and answers—all in one place.

Bereaved Families of Ontario
www.bereavedfamilies.net

Bereavement self-help resources guide indexes resources of the center along with over 300 listings to other resources and information.

Death Notices
www.legacy.com/NS

Death Notices is a placement of death notices for information purposes.

Burial Insurance
www.burialinsurance.org

Burial Insurance is a website that informs about final expense insurance standard policy that many use to cover the cost of a funeral.

Unit 8: Bereavement

After Death Communication Research Foundation
www.adcrf.org

This website includes information and resources regarding after death communication, bereavement, grief, life after death.

Thanatolinks
http://netsociology.tripod.com/thanalinks.htm

This site contains links to some of the best sites on the Internet related to death and dying.

Hospice: A Guide to Grief Bereavement, Mourning, and Grief
www.hospicenet.org/html/grief_guide.html

Hospice: A Guide to Grief Bereavement, Mourning, and Grief is an informational resource to learn about the different ways people cope with the loss of a loved one.

Growth House
www.growthhouse.org

Growth House Is a nonprofit organization working with grief, bereavement, hospice, and end-of-life issues.

Grief in a Family Context
www.indiana.edu/~famlygrf/sitemap.html

Grief in a Family Context is an internet resource provided with links to various grief issues.

Directory of Grief, Loss and Bereavement: Support Groups
www.dmoz.org/Health/Mental_Health/Grief,_Loss_and_Bereavement/Support_Groups

The death of a loved one is an emotionally devastating time for survivors. But not knowing what to expect can often lead to unnecessary additional pain. To alleviate some of the confusion, to begin to examine the many issues that are often hard to discuss and to find all the help a bereaved individuals need as they begin this journey, we created the most comprehensive book, the first of its kind, to assist them with resources and answers—all in one place.

Bereaved Families of Ontario
www.bereavedfamilies.net

Bereavement self-help resources guide indexes resources of the center along with over 300 listings to other resources and information.

Grief Net
http://rivendell.org

This website provides many links on the bereavement process, resources for grievers, and information concerning grief support groups.

Child Bereavement Charity
www.childbereavement.org.uk/home_page

The Child Bereavement Charity site provides support for families and educates professionals for bereaved families, including miscarriage, stillbirth, neonatal death, and termination for abnormality.

Core Principles for Helping Grieving Children
www2.cfalls.org/hs_pdf/core_principles_for_helping_grieving_children.pdf

Core Principles for Helping Grieving Children provides core principles for helping grieving children.

The Compassionate Friends
www.compassionatefriends.org/resources/links.aspx

The Compassionate Friends site is a self-help organization for bereaved parents and siblings. There are presently hundreds of chapters worldwide.

American Academy of Child & Adolescent Psychiatry
http://aacap.org/page.ww?name=Children+and+Grief&section=Facts+for+Families

The American Academy of Child & Adolescent Psychiatry provides important information as a public service to assist parents and families in their most important roles. This article "Children and Grief" is one such resource; written in English, Spanish, and French.

Children with AIDS Project
www.aidskids.org

The Children with AIDS Project offers a deeper understanding of children with, and at risk of, AIDS, including the medical, psychosocial, legal, and financial issues. The mission of the organization is to develop local and national adoptive, foster- and family-centered care programs that are both effective and compassionate.

Rites of Passage: Our Fathers Die
www.menweb.org/daddie.htm

The Men Web-M.E.N. Magazine posts an article "Rites of Passage: Our Fathers Die" written by Bert H. Hoff

Internet References

Motherloss

www.freewebs.com/motherloss/front.htm

This site is a support group started to help with the grieving issues for women whose mothers have died.

Widow Net

www.widownet.org

Widow Net is an information and self-help resource for, and by, widows and widowers. Topics covered include grief, bereavement, recovery, and other information helpful to people of all ages, religious backgrounds and sexual orientations who have suffered the death of a spouse or life partner.

Web Healing

www.webhealing.com

Tom Golden of the Crisis, Grief, and Healing Page brings you A Place to Honor Grief. This is a website where people write concerning the grief they are experiencing at the death of a loved-one.

Dearly Departed

http://dearlydprtd.com

Dearly Departed is a free service, dedicated to the memory of those loved ones who passed away from this life, but not from our hearts—a virtual Internet mausoleum.

In Memory of Pets

www.In-Memory-Of-Pets.Com

In Memory of Pets website includes poems, tributes, and resources.

Burial Insurance

www.burialinsurance.org

Burial Insurance is a website that informs about final expense insurance standard policy that many use to cover the cost of a funeral.

UNIT 1

Issues in Dying and Death

Unit Selections

1. **Grief in the Age of Facebook,** Elizabeth Stone
2. **The Proliferation of Postselves in American Civic and Popular Cultures,** Michael C. Kearl
3. **Roadside Memorial Policies in the United States,** George E. Dickinson and Heath C. Hoffmann
4. **Brain Death Guidelines Vary at Top US Neurological Hospitals,** Susan Jeffrey
5. **Criteria for a Good Death,** Edwin Shneidman

Learning Outcomes

After reading this unit, you should be able to:

- Better explain how Facebook has contributed to grief to today's world.

- Discuss how brain death guidelines vary in hospitals.

- Wrestle with the issue of a good death.

- Identify how the different states in the United States deal with the issue of roadside memorials.

- Give reasons as to why some states in the United States have roadside memorial policies and others do not.

- Discuss the general attitude of Americans regarding an afterlife.

- Explain the latest research regarding individuals in different parts of the world having "contact" with deceased persons.

- Indicate the roles of dead people in popular media such as movies.

- Describe the enhanced status of dead people in the U.S. society.

Student Website

www.mhhe.com/cls

Internet References

Association for Death Education and Counseling, The Thanatology Association
    www.adec.org
Bardo of Death Studies
    www.bardo.org
Death and Culture
    http://en.wikipedia.org/wiki/Death_and_culture
Kearl's Guide to Sociology of Death and Dying
    www.trinity.edu/~mkearl/death.html
Yahoo: Society and Culture: Death and Dying
    http://dir.yahoo.com/Society_and_Culture/Death_and_Dying

Death, like sex, is a rather taboo topic. British anthropologist Geoffrey Gorer's writing about the pornography of death in the mid-20th century seemed to open the door for publications on the subject of death. Gorer argued that death had replaced sex as contemporary society's major taboo topic. Because death was less common in the community, with individuals actually seeing fewer corpses and being with individuals less at the time of death, a relatively realistic view of death had been replaced by a voyeuristic, adolescent preoccupation with it. Our modern way of life has not prepared us to cope any better with dying and death. Sex and death have "come out of the closet" in recent decades, however, and now are issues discussed and presented in formal educational settings. Baby Boomers are aging and changing the ways we handle death. In fact, end-of-life issues are frequently discussed in the popular media, as evidenced by the recent popular television shows *Six Feet Under* and *Family Plots* and numerous documentaries and other drama series about hospitals and emergency rooms. Yet, we have a long way to go in educating the public about these historically taboo subjects.

We are beginning to recognize the importance of educating youth on the subject of dying and death. Like sex education, death education (thanatology, literally "the study of death") is an approved topic for presentation in elementary and secondary school curricula in many states, but the topics (especially death and dying) are optional and therefore rarely receive high priorities in the classroom or in educational funding. With terrorist attacks around the world, the war in Afghanistan, and various natural disasters such as in Japan in 2011, an increased interest on death and dying in the curricula could have a positive impact on helping to cope with these various megadeath-related situations.

Just what is a "good death"? "Criteria for a Good Death" addresses this topic as Edwin Shneidman discusses criteria for a good death, although it will vary significantly between cultures and individuals within cultures.

When is a person dead? The "brain death" definition of death is one of the more definitive definitions of death, yet brain death guidelines vary in U.S. hospitals, as noted in "Brain Death Guidelines Vary at Top U.S. Neurological Hospitals." Sociologist Michael Kearl writes about the increased interest in the dead, the afterlife, and memorialization of the dead.

Other issues discussed in this section include the impact of technology, particularly the Internet and Facebook, on how

© Ingram Publishing/SuperStock

death and grief are handled. Roadside memorials began to appear in the late 20th century in the United States. Just how the various states have dealt with this issue is presented in "Roadside Memorial Policies in the United States."

Grief in the Age of Facebook

ELIZABETH STONE

On July 17 last year, one of my most promising students died. Her name was Casey Feldman, and she was crossing a street in a New Jersey resort town on her way to work when a van went barreling through a stop sign. Her death was a terrible loss for everyone who knew her. Smart and dogged, whimsical and kind, Casey was the news editor of the *The Observer,* the campus paper I advise, and she was going places. She was a finalist for a national college reporting award and had just been chosen for a prestigious television internship for the fall, a fact she conveyed to me in a midnight text message, entirely consistent with her all-news-all-the-time mindset. Two days later her life ended.

I found out about Casey's death the old-fashioned way: in a phone conversation with Kelsey, the layout editor and Casey's roommate. She'd left a neutral-sounding voice mail the night before, asking me to call when I got her message, adding, "It's OK if it's late." I didn't retrieve the message till midnight, so I called the next morning, realizing only later what an extraordinary effort she had made to keep her voice calm. But my students almost never make phone calls if they can help it, so Kelsey's message alone should have raised my antenna. She blogs, she tweets, she texts, and she pings. But voice mail? No.

Paradoxically it was Kelsey's understanding of the viral nature of her generation's communication preferences that sent her rushing to the phone, and not just to call boomers like me. She didn't want anyone to learn of Casey's death through Facebook. It was summer, and their friends were scattered, but Kelsey knew that if even one of Casey's 801 Facebook friends posted the news, it would immediately spread.

So as Kelsey and her roommates made calls through the night, they monitored Facebook. Within an hour of Casey's death, the first mourner posted her respects on Casey's Facebook wall, a post that any of Casey's friends could have seen. By the next morning, Kelsey, in New Jersey, had reached *The Observer*'s editor in chief in Virginia, and by that evening, the two had reached fellow editors in California, Missouri, Massachusetts, Texas, and elsewhere—and somehow none of them already knew.

In the months that followed, I've seen how markedly technology has influenced the conventions of grieving among my students, offering them solace but also uncertainty. The day after Casey's death, several editorial-board members changed their individual Facebook profile pictures. Where there had been photos of Brent, of Kelsey, of Kate, now there were photos of Casey and Brent, Casey and Kelsey, Casey and Kate.

Now that Casey was gone, she was virtually everywhere. I asked one of my students why she'd changed her profile photo. "It was spontaneous," she said. "Once one person did it, we all joined in." Another student, who had friends at Virginia Tech when, in 2007, a gunman killed 32 people, said that's when she first saw the practice of posting Facebook profile photos of oneself with the person being mourned.

Within several days of Casey's death, a Facebook group was created called "In Loving Memory of Casey Feldman," which ran parallel to the wake and funeral planned by Casey's family. Dozens wrote on that group's wall, but Casey's own wall was the more natural gathering place, where the comments were more colloquial and addressed to her: "casey im speechless for words right now," wrote one friend. "i cant believe that just yest i txted you and now your gone . . . i miss you soo much. rest in peace."

Though we all live atomized lives, memorial services let us know the dead with more dimension than we may have known them during their lifetimes. In the responses of her friends, I was struck by how much I hadn't known about Casey—her equestrian skill, her love of animals, her interest in photography, her acting talent, her penchant for creating her own slang ("Don't be a cow"), and her curiosity—so intense that her friends affectionately called her a "stalker."

This new, uncharted form of grieving raises new questions. Traditional mourning is governed by conventions. But in the age of Facebook, with selfhood publicly represented via comments and uploaded photos, was it OK for her friends to display joy or exuberance online? Some weren't sure. Six weeks after Casey's death, one student who had posted a shot of herself with Casey wondered aloud when it was all right to post a different photo. Was there a right time? There were no conventions to help her. And would she be judged if she removed her mourning photo before most others did?

As it turns out, Facebook has a "memorializing" policy in regard to the pages of those who have died. That policy came into being in 2005, when a good friend and co-worker of Max Kelly, a Facebook employee, was killed in a bicycle accident. As Kelly wrote in a Facebook blog post last October, "The question soon came up: What do we do about his Facebook profile? We had never really thought about this before in such a personal way. How do you deal with an interaction with someone who is no longer able to log on? When someone leaves us, they don't leave our memories or our social network. To reflect that reality, we created the idea of 'memorialized' profiles as a place where people can save and share their memories of those who've passed."

Casey's Facebook page is now memorialized. Her own postings and lists of interests have been removed, and the page is visible only to her Facebook friends. (I thank Kelsey Butler for making it possible for me to gain access to it.) Eight months after her death, her friends are still posting on her wall, not to "share their memories" but to write to her, acknowledging her absence but maintaining their ties to her—exactly the stance that contemporary grief theorists recommend. To me, that seems preferable to Freud's prescription, in "Mourning and Melancholia," that we should detach from the dead. Quite a few of Casey's friends wished her a merry Christmas, and on the 17th of every month so far, the postings spike. Some share dreams they've had about her, or post a detail of interest. "I had juice box wine recently," wrote one. "I thought of you the whole time: (Miss you girl!" From another: "i miss you. the new lady gaga cd came out, and if i had one wish in the world it would be that you could be singing (more like screaming) along with me in my passenger seat like old times."

It was against the natural order for Casey to die at 21, and her death still reverberates among her roommates and fellow editors. I was privileged to know Casey, and though I knew her deeply in certain ways, I wonder—I'm not sure, but I wonder—if I should have known her better. I do know, however, that she would have done a terrific trend piece on "Grief in the Age of Facebook."

Critical Thinking

1. How can Facebook serve as a therapeutic device for grieving individuals?

2. Facebook makes the grief process more public. How is this helpful and how might it not be therapeutic?

3. How does grief via Facebook differ from traditional ways of grieving?

ELIZABETH STONE is a professor of English, communication, and media studies at Fordham University. She is the author of the memoir *A Boy I Once Knew: What a Teacher Learned From Her Student* (Algonquin, 2002).

The Proliferation of Postselves in American Civic and Popular Cultures

Michael C. Kearl

Introduction

The Gershwin Centennial Celebration of the San Antonio Symphony was a remarkable event as it featured Gershwin himself. Though dead since 1937, he 'performed' in a 1912 concert grand player piano, flown in from Denver, with rolls that precisely preserved his keystrokes. As the music was about to begin, a spotlight moved across stage as if following Gershwin as he was taking his seat. An attendant even brought a glass of wine, placing it above the keyboard for him to drink.

Gershwin was neither the first nor last deceased person in recent years to engage with the living. Prime-time television is full of programmes and commercials featuring spirits, channeling mediums, angels, and dissected corpses. Annually rank ordered is the earnings of deceased celebrities by *Forbes* and their recognisability and likeability 'Dead Q' scores by Marketing Evaluations Inc. Halls of fame proliferate. James Dean and Marilyn Monroe achieve the philatelic immortality previously reserved for founding fathers, victorious military figures, and Presidents. And concurrent with the screening of Tim Burton's 'Corpse Bride' was the national tour of Gunther von Hagen's 'Body Worlds', featuring skinned and variously dissected plastinated cadavers.

The intent here is to speculate on the interrelationships between these and other apparently unrelated phenomena. From the only country to put men on the moon and park a spacecraft on an asteroid 196 million miles away, whose scientists have mapped the human genome and who investigate the most elemental components of matter, we find a population with renewed interests in immortality and novel connections with its deceased members.

The Presumed Disappearance of the Dead in Late Modern Life

There is an irreversible evolution from savage societies to our own: little by little, the dead cease to exist. They are thrown out of the group's symbolic circulation. They are no longer beings with a full role to play, worthy partners in exchange, and we make this obvious by exiling them further and further away from the group of the living (Baudrillard, 1993, p. 126).

Reflected in the Baudrillard passage above is the thesis that late modernity has banished the dead from everyday life. One inference is that the dead do not exist because humanity eventually outgrows its needs to believe in the illusions of an afterlife and to attribute unintended or inexplicable events to ancestral meddling. In addition, there is a sense of disconnect with a perceived irrelevant past, accounting for the profound degree of historical ignorance (Kearl, 2001). Memories of the deceased evaporate within a generation or two along with their traditional statuses as role models and reference groups.

Further, the modern adult mind, programmed with the scientific insights of inevitable extinction of not only all life forms but of the post-Big Bang universe itself, has reached psychologists' final developmental stage of death understandings, when one maturely grasps the inevitability, irreversibility, and finality of finitude—particularly with increasing education, decreasing religion, and the here-and-now orientation fostered by materialism.

Finally, the supposed disappearance of the dead also owes to the changing nature and visibility of death itself. With the longevity revolution, death increasingly arrives with advance warning only to the oldest segments of society, to those who have lived full and completed lives and who now live largely segregated from other, younger age groups. With lives no longer ending 'prematurely' to the unprepared, the ghostly embodiments of social frustrations occasioned by incompletely lived lives have largely disappeared. The dead, like the contemporary old, supposedly occupy a 'roleless role'.

The Transcendence Motive and Its Cultural Shapings

Man cannot live without a continuous confidence in something indestructible within himself

—Franz Kafka. (cited in Choron, 1964, p. 15)

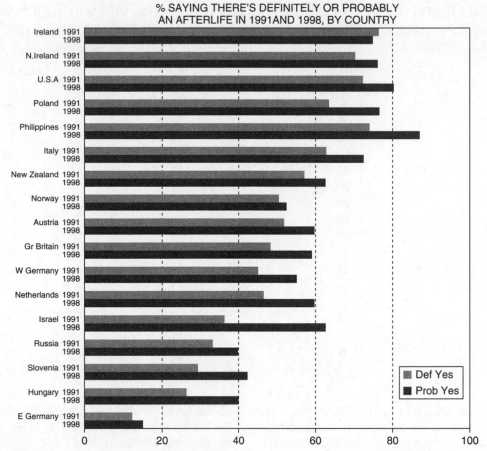

% SAYING THERE'S DEFINITELY OR PROBABLY
AN AFTERLIFE IN 1991AND 1998, BY COUNTRY

Figure 1 International differences in the percentage of the adult public believing in life after death.

On the other hand, there are various psychological, sociological, and cultural forces at work that continue to keep the dead very much alive. The human primate has always been infested with lice and ghosts—the former the consequence of our biological nature, the latter because of our symbolic essence. For the only creature aware of its inevitable demise, its death-transcending drive is seen not only to underlie its psychic health but also the creation and maintenance of entire cultural orders (Bauman, 1992; Becker, 1973; Lifton, 1979).

The quest for immortality runs deeply throughout the earliest known Western stories (Hentsch, 2004), whose themes involve not speculation of the existence of an afterlife but rather how to keep the dead in their place (Walter, 1996, p. 13). Underlying Western civilization is Christianity's synthesis of these stories, featuring its grand assumption of immortal existence. The cultural consequences of challenging and possibly voiding this basic assumption are profound. St. Paul observed 'if the dead are not raised . . . our Gospel is null and void . . . and your faith has nothing in it' (1 Corinthians 15:13). What have changed are the array of death-transcending strategies and the proliferation of *postselves.* Here Shneidman's (1973) concept of the postself is expanded to include all engagements between deceased individuals and the living, whether based on their intended legacies or the designs of others. Since the time of the concept's coinage,

technological innovations, legal expansion of posthumous rights, and capitalism's commodification of symbolic immortality have expanded considerably the roles of the dead in everyday life.

American Exceptionalism
If we follow our reading of Baudrillard's line of reasoning, it would seem logical to conclude that the death ethos of the United States—one of the most economically advanced, scientifically inclined, and materialistic of nations—should resemble those of other highly developed Western cultures. However, as is evident in Figure 1, such is not the case. Various surveys show that more than seven out of 10 Americans fully expect an afterlife. This proportion has been on the increase at least over the past three decades, particularly among Catholics, Jews, and those with no religious affiliation (Greeley & Hout, 1999)—a proportion unexplained by demographic changes (e.g. the ageing of the population).

Not only do Americans lead the developed world in confidence in an afterlife but, according to this cross-national study of religious beliefs (ISSP, 1998), they led all surveyed countries in the percentage believing in the existence of heaven (86%) and are basically tied with Cypriots for the greatest percentage believing in hell (74%, compared to 14% of Swedes, 22% of French, 33% of British, and 59% of Italians). Further, when

Table 1 'How Often Have You Felt as Though You Were Really in Touch with Someone Who Had Died'? Percentage Saying at Least Once—with DKs Omitted (ISSP, 1991).

	Men	Women	Total Once+
USA	37	42	40
New Zealand	30	37	34
Slovenia	26	36	32
Israel	27	34	31
Ireland	26	33	29
Austria	35	32	28
Poland	24	32	28
Great Britain	23	33	28
Philippines	28	27	27
Netherlands	23	25	24
West Germany	21	26	23
Italy	15	27	21
Hungary	16	23	20
East Germany	12	21	17
Northern Ireland	15	17	16
Russia	11	16	14
Norway	9	17	13

asked if one has felt personally in touch with someone who had died, Americans again top the chart of international respondents with four in 10 having experienced such connection (see Table 1). Such findings prompted George Gallup Jr. to observe how 'one of the most dramatic—yet perhaps least noticed—developments of the late 20th and early 21st century has been the explosion of interest among the U.S. populace in spiritual matters' (Gallup, 2001).

The American story is unique in its cultural challenges to death's finality. For Europeans, the New World was the place for second chances, for personal rebirths, and quests for immortality. It was where Ponce de León searched for the fountain of youth and the current home of the anti-ageing Methuselah Foundation. It was from where sprouted the Church of Latter Day Saints with its certitude in the continuation of familial relations through eternity, Scientology with its belief in an immortal soul that undergoes countless reincarnations, and from where emerged the Spiritualism movement with its conviction that the dead could communicate with the living (Braude, 2001).

The immortalist zeitgeist was to nurture and be nurtured by American ingenuity. Thomas Edison, the epitome of American inventiveness, wrote of dying bodies being deserted by a swarm of highly charged energies that enter into space and another cycle of existence, detectable by 'an instrument so delicate as to be affected by our personality as it survives in the next life' (Lescarboura, 1920). Eighty-five years later, Raymond Kuzweil, recipient of the Lemelson-MIT prize and the 1999 National Medal of Technology Award, predicted immortality to be but a few decades away for a software-based humanity. He envisions cybernetically enhanced humans genetically improved through Internet downloads and through whose bodies course billions of 'nanobots', molecular-level robots, that reverse the ageing process by continuously modifying brain cells, muscles, arteries, and bone (Kurzweil, 2005).

In recent years, quantum physicists have demonstrated a phenomenon called 'entanglement', where particles can be at two places at once and change in one simultaneously alters the other. Researchers have not only slowed light to the speed of a train but have brought it to a dead stop, stored it and then released it as if it were an ordinary material particle. Certainly, such activities are no more mystical than a person's essence surviving in some form after death. The present era holds considerable parallels to the mid-nineteenth century and the 1920s (periods Swatos & Gissurarson [1997] argue are one and the same epoch, the golden age of Western spiritualism), when pseudo-science flourished as prestige in science grew, together producing then and now an anything-is-possible mindset. If dead pets can be cloned and perhaps woolly mammoths be resurrected, why cannot deceased loved ones continue to live?

We should note the relative non-exclusivity of most Americans' criteria for eternal life. In this religious country without a state-sanctioned faith, according to a 2008 Pew national survey, two-thirds of the religiously affiliated believe many religions can lead to eternal life, with a majority of Christians understanding that this includes non-Christian faiths (Pew Forum on Religion and Public Life, 2008). The individualist creed underlying this unrestrictive mindset has engendered a do-it-yourself approach to both material and spiritual matters, at times viewing the two as interrelated. During the nineteenth century, for instance, subscribers of spiritualism included many leaders of the abolitionist, feminist, Temperance, and labour reform movements (Buescher, 2003). For

Table 2 The Effects of Party Identification and Beliefs in an Afterlife on Culture War Battleline Issues among Those Strongly and Not Strongly Religious (Davis & Smith, 2007).

	Democrats[1]		Independents		Republicans[1]	
Believe in Afterlife?	**Yes**	**No/ Undecided**	**Yes**	**No/Undecided**	**Yes**	**No/Undecided**
Strongly religious						
% Favouring abortion[2]	54.2	58.6	36.3	39.3	34.5	54.9
% Favouring euthanasia[3]	56.9	66.7	46.0	66.7	46.8	81.3
% Saying homosexuality not wrong at all[4]	28.1	25.0	14.8	5.0 (n.s.)	12.3	29.4
Not strongly religious						
% Favouring abortion[2]	54.2	58.6	36.3	39.3	34.5	54.9
% Favouring euthanasia[3]	79.8	78.6	70.7	76.0	72.0	83.5
% Saying homosexuality not wrong at all[4]	47.2	47.4	34.9	33.0	30.8	42.9

[1]Responses to 'Generally speaking, do you usually think of yourself as a Republican, Democrat, Independent, or what?' Category 'independent lean Democrat' combined with 'strong Democrat' and 'Democrat'. Category 'independent lean Republican' similarly combined with 'strong Republican' and 'Republican'.

[2]'Do you think that a woman should have the right to a legal abortion if she wants it for any reason'?.

[3]'When a person has a disease that cannot be cured, do you think doctors should be allowed by law to end the patient's life by some painless means if the patient and his family request it'?.

[4]'What about sexual relations between two adults of the same sex—do you think it is always wrong, almost always wrong, wrong only sometimes, or not wrong at all'?

both Spiritualists and Mormons, the dead were to be liberated by the living (leading to the latter's difficulties with various Jewish groups in 1995 over its postmortem baptisms of Holocaust victims).

Finally, Americans' belief in an afterlife plays an underlying role in the so-called 'culture wars'. In 2006, the difference in afterlife expectations between Democrats and Republicans was greater than any year since 1973, with Republicans 13 percentage points more likely to believe. To control for the fact that 10% of Republicans were more likely also to be strongly religious. Table 2 shows the party differences among those not strongly religious in the correlation between afterlife beliefs and attitudes towards abortion (agreeing that women should have the right to a legal abortion if she 'wants it for any reason'), euthanasia, homosexuality, and belief in evolution. With the exception of evolution, afterlife beliefs have little or no effect on the attitudes of Democrats and Independents. Among Republicans, however, the effects are considerable, with the afterlife non-believers closely resembling the Democrats. And while beliefs in an afterlife have little correlation with agreement about Darwinian tenets among Independents, sizable differences are produced in the minds of Republicans and Democrats. In the Discussion, I will return to the significance of these correlations.

In sum, in contradiction to the claim that late modern secular cultures have extinguished the role of the dead in everyday life, I argue that extreme individualism, capitalism, and technological innovations together have increased their number, visibility, and influence. My proposal is that American culture can best be understood in terms of its core salvific goal of death control and its embracement of the hereafter: its *immortalist ethos*.

The Proliferation of Postselves

With these points in mind, I turn to current death transcending trends in American popular and civic cultures as well as their commodification in the service economy.

Postselves in Popular Culture

Popular culture is often where deep cultural trends are crystallised and given clear expression. The 'success' of an artistic motif owes as much to public receptivity towards its message as to the work's artistic merits. Consider the socio-cultural context producing the audience receptivity to the immortalist ethos in mass media. In cinema, the spiritual genre of popular movies has grossed hundreds of millions of dollars, with such blockbusters as the 'Star Wars' trilogy capturing and restoring to American culture the archetypal sacred sense. Over the past two decades not only are there more roles for the dead in mainstream productions but their task in the plotline has largely shifted from instilling terror to becoming guardians of the living: 'Field of Dreams' (1989), 'Ghost' (1990), 'Ghost Dad' (1990), 'Casper' (1995), 'City of Angels' (1998), 'What Dreams May Come' (1998), 'Meet Joe Black' (1998), 'Jack Frost' (1999), 'City of Angels' (1998), 'Sixth Sense' (1999), 'The Gift' (2000), 'What Lies Beneath' (2000), and 'Dragonfly' (2002). In addition, the deceased now perform with the living, perhaps beginning with Woody Allen's 'Zelig' (1983) and perfected in 'Forrest Gump' (1994), wherein John Kennedy, George Wallace, Lyndon Johnson, John Lennon, and Elvis Presley are put to work from the grave.

Cinematic success leads to television imitations and no longer in the latter medium are attempts made by the living to connect with the dead limited to Shirley MacLaine New Age cable specials, but rather, these attempts have become prime-time fare. Almost nightly, one can watch John Edward reunite 'people in the physical world with their loved ones who have crossed over'. Facing plummeting ratings in the Spring of 2002, ABC television aired 'Contact: Talking to the Dead', featuring psychic George Anderson's interviews with the deceased loved ones of Vanna White and Mackenzie Phillips as well as the murdered wife of Robert Blake. In the Fall of that year appeared spiritual medium James Van Praagh's 'Beyond', following his CBS miniseries 'Living With the Dead'. The central message from the great beyond: one never dies. In 2005, NBC premiered its 'Medium' series, 'inspired by the non-fictional story of research medium Allison Dubois, . . . who begins to suspect that she can talk to dead people, see the future in her dreams and read people's thoughts' (nbc.com).

Deceased celebrities have proven to be great pitchmen as they are highly regarded and never embarrass the sponsors. The trend in television began in 1991 when Elton John performed for Louis Armstrong, James Cagney, and Humphrey Bogart in a Diet Coke commercial. By the mid 1990s, Babe Ruth was receiving 100 endorsement deals a year and was, followed by James Dean, the most popular client of the Curtis Management Group.

This Indianapolis firm markets 'late greats' on behalf of the descendants (who, in some states, own the rights to the deceased's image for seventy years). Its website opens with an image of James Dean with the quotation 'If a man can bridge the gap between life and death . . . if he can live on after he's dead, then maybe he was a great man'. Clients of 2009 include such disparate individuals as Gen. George Patton, Mark Twain, Jean Harlow, Ed Sullivan, Malcolm X, Oscar Wilde, Amelia Earhart, Will Rogers, and Tiny Tim. In 1997, 25 years after his death and 50 years after his debut with the Brooklyn Dodgers, Jackie Robinson became the first deceased athlete to adorn Wheaties cereal boxes. So great had the earnings of the dead become that in 2000 Forbes began its annual rankings of the 'top-earning dead celebrities' (see Table 3).

Though the dead have released albums since at least the 1970s, there is a new twist: their songs are no longer simply remastered archival retrievals but rather are postmortem performances made with the living. Natalie Cole sings with her long-deceased father Nat; the surviving Beatles reunite with John Lennon to perform 'Free As a Bird' and 'Real Love'.

Postselves in Civic Culture

To fortify the illusion of our own immortality, the deathlessness of others must be acknowledged—and of the groups responsible for maintaining their memories and those of one's self. For most, the chief hope for being remembered after death was by one's descendants. With changes in modern family systems, however, that assumption has often been invalidated. Modern repressions of death terror are now made possible through identifications with the death-defying powers of other social groups.

Increasingly, organizations are rescuing from oblivion the memories of their deceased members. Halls of fame multiply as social groups attempt to affirm their sovereign status (hence the national-, state-, city-, organisational- and professional-levels of halls) by conferring immortality to their elect. Of the 213 halls of fame identified from Danilov's (1997) detailed inventory, the web, and contacts from a local newspaper, all but four were founded after World War II and roughly one-half since 1980. Through time-transcending rituals for their special (and often deceased) members, groups establish special claims to legitimacy and respect in part by their ability to protect their members' identities and deeds from time's oblivion. Cities and towns are always willing to host these halls of fame, hoping for increased revenues from tourist dollars—especially during the annual ceremonies for new inductees.

Such affirmations of sovereign status through death-transcending capacities are most evident with the nation-state, the broadest of social integrators. Consider the Social Security Administration's creation of an online deceased Americans database, the Social Security Death Index, which totalled over 83 million individuals in 2009. In addition, beyond its

Table 3 Forbes Richest Deceased Celebrities

Forbes richest deceased celebrities			
2000 Rank	**Name**	**2000 Earnings**	**2007 Earnings**
1	Elvis Presley	$35 million	$49 million
2	Charles Schulz	$20 million plus	$35 million
3	John Lennon	$20 million	$44 million
4	Theodor 'Dr. Seuss' Geisel	$17 million	$13 million
5	Jimi Hendrix	$10 million plus	(did not make top 13)
6	Bob Marley	$10 million	$ 4 million
7	Andy Warhol	$ 8 million	$15 million
8	J.R.R. Tolkien	$ 7 million	(did not make top 13)
9	Frank Sinatra	$ 6 million	(did not make top 13)
10	Jerry Garcia	$ 5 million	(did not make top 13)
	(Fong & Lau, 2001; Goldman & Paine, 2007).		

monuments and other memorialisations for the political saints, there's the federal funding of various genealogical resources such as the Statue of Liberty-Ellis Island Foundation's online passenger arrival records, whose database contains information on over 25 million immigrants.

Consider also, how political immortality is conferred philately. Between 1847 and 2000, the United States issued nearly 3500 distinct stamps. Generally, such symbolic immortality was reserved for a select group of the politically elite, typically featuring the busts or heads of the founding fathers, Presidents, and generals. In the last quarter of the twentieth century, I have observed a veritable explosion in the number and backgrounds of Americans so honored—even those from such historically disenfranchised groups as women (with only 19 so commemorated through 1970) and African Americans (the first appearing in 1940).

Since 1980, the number and diversity of individuals so honoured reflects an affirmative action programme for a political afterlife, featuring the likes of Elvis Presley, Marilyn Monroe, James Dean, and Malcolm X (one of the Black Heritage series). Through the 1990s nine sets of the 'Legends of American Music' series were issued, along with 'Legends of the West', 'Legendary Football Coaches', 'Comedians', 'Legends of Hollywood', and 'Stars of the Silent Screen'.

In addition to halls of fame, electronic databases, and postage stamps, other death-transcending activities of civic groups have included political rituals of resurrection and immortalisation. As evidenced by attempts to recover identifying DNA from long-fallen unknown warriors from WW II and Vietnam, the Justice Department's reopening of Emmitt Till's case one-half century after his infamous murder, and the political debates of the 1970s over the restoration of citizenship to Robert E. Lee and Eugene V. Debs as well as the current attempts to grant a presidential pardon for Jack Johnson (the country's first black heavyweight boxing champion who was convicted in 1913 for violating the Mann Act by having consensual relations with a white woman), the American government has long been in the business of preserving the identities, rights, and citizenship status of its deceased members (Kearl & Rinaldi, 1983). Three days following the 9/11 terrorist attacks on America, Representative Serrano introduced HR 2897 to 'provide for the granting of posthumous citizenship to certain aliens lawfully admitted for permanent residence who died as a result of the hijackings of four commercial aircraft, the attacks on the World Trade Center, or the attack on the Pentagon, on September 11, 2001, and for other purposes'.

The nation-state has no monopoly over such bestowals of symbolic immortality. A historically recent trend of professional groups, particularly in the arts, is the 'Lifetime Achievement Awards' ritual. Here simultaneously acknowledged and fused are the ways individuals' biographies contribute to the illusion of immortality of the group. Unlike funerals, recipients are often alive for the celebrations of their lives—albeit proximate to death. Examples (year founded: first recipient) include Grammy (1962: Bing Crosby), American Film Institute (1973: John Ford), and the Horror Writers Association (1987: Fritz Leiber; Frank Belknap Long; Clifford D. Simak).

From Columbine High School to the sprouting of roadside memorials across the nation attempts to personalise death and

to preserve the identities of the deceased can be observed. The Oklahoma City National Memorial Center features a field of 168 empty chairs, placed in nine rows according to the floor on which one died, each seat etched with the name of a victim. The AIDS Memorial Quilt comprises over 44,000 individualised 3-by-6 foot panels to individualise each and every victim of the epidemic.

The growing reaffirmations of the rights of the dead were dramatised by the Native American Graves Protection and Repatriation Act. In August 1989, the World Archaeological Congress, in association with The International Indian Treaty Council, the World Council of Indigenous Peoples, and American Indians Against Desecration, held at the University of South Dakota the first inter-congress on 'Archaeological Ethics and the Treatment of the Dead', all framing the issue in terms of human rights. The same year, the Smithsonian Institution agreed to return the skeletal remains of thousands of American Indians to their tribes for reburial in their homelands.

Finally, in addition to simply being remembered, the dead are also being accorded greater social powers in the worlds of the living. Consider the political lengthening of the rights accorded to postselves. The Constitution authorised Congress to give authors and inventors the exclusive right to their works for a 'limited' time. In 1790, copyrights lasted 14 years. Two centuries later in 1998 the Sonny Bono Copyright Term Extension Act lengthened protection by 20 years, to 70 years after the death of the inventor or author if known. (Works owned by corporations are protected for 95 years.)

Commodifications of the Afterlife

Given the increasing visibility of postselves in the public realm, especially those who continue to make money posthumously, it should come as little surprise that this demand would be recognised by the private sector. Capitalism has not been oblivious to ways in which to profit from this metaphysical zeal. Indeed, full-blown *transcendence markets* have come into existence to enhance individuals' prospects for being remembered—and for the living to profit from their existence. To protect the persona of the deceased, the first postmortem celebrity rights law was passed in California (Civil Code § 990) in 1984. Presently, 28 states extend the right of publicity past death, allowing the deceased's image and likeness to be inherited (the descendible right of publicity) like property for up to one century. In Indiana, the inheritable extends to name, voice, gestures, distinctive appearances, signature, and mannerisms.

In addition to the preservation of personas, new industries have arisen to preserve individuals' physical essence. Companies like Geneternity (whose mission is 'to serve humanity's interest in immortality') preserve DNA samples of the departed. Kentucky bookbinder and printer, Timothy Hawley Books, offers a line of what it calls ;bibliocadavers'—bound volumes whose blank or printed pages are created from a pulp containing the ashes of a loved one. The cremains of loved ones are also transformed into living coral reefs by Eternal Reefs, Inc., high-quality diamonds by LifeGem, and into customised granite-like slabs by Relict Memorials.

Some desire not only the preservation of their personas but the actual resurrection of their selves after crossing over. Since 1967, over 90 Americans have been cryonically suspended at the moment of death, for possible renascence in the distant future when a cure has been found for their demise. For those who cannot afford full body freezing, discount cryonics centres like Alcor Life Extension Foundation have come into existence that just preserve heads, which await eventual body transplants.

Such commodifications of the dead are not limited to one's self or family members, illustrated by the international publicity in 1987 given to Michael Jackson's attempts to buy the remains of Joseph Merrick, the so-called 'Elephant Man'. One can now purchase a biological connection with those already immortalised. For instance, consider one of the collector pen lines of the Krone Company, the Lincoln pen, which contains a molecule of the President's DNA from an authenticated snippet of his hair. When Ed Headrick, the inventor of the modern Frisbee, died during the summer of 2002, his son reported that his father's wish was for his ashes to be moulded into commemorative Frisbees. The family observed his request and now markets the 'Steady' Ed Memorial Discs'.

Symbolic immortality is less macabre and more easily marketable. Americans are a charitable people but not all can afford having a building or major charity named after them. Fundraisers for schools, municipal facilities, and a myriad of causes have discovered that such illusions of immortality can be broken down into numerous parts. For the new $165.5 million Seattle Central Library, for instance, donors contributed $45 million to have their monikers affixed to 24 named spaces. Two decades ago at the Ann Arbor Michigan Theater, one could have one's name on a concession stand for $12,000, a light fixture for $250, or an aisle sign for $100 (Fuchsberg, 1987).

There are growing desires to design postselves that remain active players in the world of the living. In the early 1990s, *Cards From Beyond,* a Fairport, N.Y. Company, offered deceased individuals the ability to send cards to loved ones for holidays and anniversaries. A decade later, Loving Pup Productions provided 'Timeless Mail', a posthumous email service: 'You care about your family, friends, and loved ones, show you care by leaving them each an e-mail to be delivered after you pass on'. How about receiving a phone call from a deceased relative? With AT&T Labs' Natural Voices speech software, voice cloning is now a reality.

For those wishing not only to connect with but to exercise control over the living along the lines of their values, the legal institution provides opportunities. Estate lawyers report growing numbers of clientele desiring to control posthumously the life plans of the living, motivating Time magazine to publish 'Ruling from The Grave: Through incentive trusts, you can lead wayward young heirs to fruitful lives' (Kadlec, 2002).

The Post-9/11 Politics of the Afterlife

> The faithful shall enter paradise, and the unbelievers shall be condemned to eternal hellfire.
>
> —Koranic verse

The above quotation portrays the cultural context of 9/11/01. With the terrorists' attacks on the American symbols of financial and military might—on the day matching the nation's emergency telephone number followed by the first year of the West's new millennium—Americans were shaken to the core. Within moments, thousands of living beings simultaneously entered the spirit world, leaving little corporeal evidence of their existence seconds earlier. Never had so many Americans simultaneously perished in such compressed space, let alone in their homeland.

Evidence of American immortalism can be seen in the speed with which the press gravitated to the afterlife component of the zealot's motivations, how these individuals were motivated by the promise of a glorious afterlife in exchange for giving up their lives to exterminate infidels. There were many interpretative frames available, such as capitalism's injustices in the Third World (i.e. Bhopal) or the ways in which western powers carved up their colonial holdings into self-defeating states. Instead, the American press focused on stories like that of West Bank suicide bomber Raed Barghouti, who reportedly told his family how he would spend eternity with great Islamic leaders and be tended to by 72 virgins (Caldwell, 2001), and how other *shahids*-to-be anticipated their actions would allow them to bring 70 relatives with them to heaven.

A Republican was at the helm of power. Much has been made about the rise of the Religious Right and its influence over the Republican Party and the national agenda during the administration of George W. Bush. According to a national survey conducted the year following the attacks (Pew Research Center for the People and the Press, 2002), belief in one's faith's exclusivity in providing eternal life ranged from 32% among conservative Republicans (53% among Republican Evangelicals) to 11% of liberal Democrats. In Table II one can see the potency of belief in an afterlife in shaping Republicans' positions towards the major battlelines in America's 'culture wars'. Looking at those strongly religious, observe how afterlife beliefs have little effect on Democrats' support for abortion while Republican disbelievers are two-thirds more likely to support women's rights to an abortion for any reason than Republicans believing in an afterlife. Similarly, only among Republicans does belief in an afterlife produce significant differences in support for homosexual relations. Finally, the more conservative the party identification the larger the effect of afterlife beliefs on support for euthanasia.

Such effects of afterlife beliefs on these core moral issues are even more interesting among those who are not strongly religious (which is the case for 65% of Democrats and 53% of Republicans). Among these individuals, the belief in life after death has virtually no effect neither on Democrats' nor Independents' support of abortion, euthanasia, or homosexual relations. For Republicans, on the other hand, afterlife beliefs suppress support for these issues by 11 to 20 percentage points.

Given the increased presence of the dead in American civic and popular cultures prior to 9/11/01, the publicity given to the terrorists' immortal motivations strengthened the Republican Party's hand in the country's culture wars. Afterlife beliefs assumed a dramatic increase in political saliency; Christian notions of desirable eternal lives being reserved for those having lived morally worthy lives had to be reaffirmed. And given the cognitive connections between this fundamental outlook with the moral issues of the time, we have better insight into why Terri Schiavo, gay marriage, and the administration's restrictions on stem cell research and attempts to redefine 'abortion' to include birth control received the considerable cultural attention that they did.

Discussion

Contrary to the thesis that late modern selves have outgrown the need for immortality beliefs and that there is no place for the dead in late modern societies, it is argued that an immortalist *zeitgeist* now permeates American civic and popular cultures, underlying a number of curious and seemingly disparate phenomena. It is not unique but rather an extreme case of trends occurring throughout much of the West (Figure 1 revealed how afterlife beliefs increased during the 1990s in all but one of the countries surveyed), prompting Howarth's (2000) observation of the blurring of boundaries between the living and the dead.

There are a number of factors accounting for American exceptionalism to the culture's pursuits towards death transcendence. These include the religious foundations underlying the nation's founding and the New World symbolising the possibilities for personal rebirth and spatialising mythic associations with the West's hyperborean and fountain themes of superlongevity (Gruman, 2003, pp. 30, 32–33). Additionally, the ethos of individualism, self-sufficiency, and personal responsibility for salvation was unleashed upon a rare frontier. Analysts of the American character often cite the implications of not being bogged down by history; here fates were no longer preprogrammed by the legacies of feudalism, aristocracy, or by ancestral deeds and rivalries. In this land bereft of reminders of the accomplishments of scores of generations past, the proverbial slate was clean for leaving one's own mark on time.

American militarism adds to this cultural chemistry. Wars produce an abundance of spirits and postlife beliefs. High water marks in the American spiritualism movement, for instance, followed the Civil War, World War I, and the Vietnam War. A spiritual realm is required to overcome the natural death fears of the combatants. As Bertrand Russell observed one-half century ago:

> ... as the Mohammedans first proved, belief in Paradise has considerable military value as reinforcing natural pugnacity. We should therefore admit that militarists are wise in encouraging the belief in immortality, always supposing that this belief does not become so profound as to produce indifference to the affairs of the world (1957, p. 91).

Attempting to counter the finality of death, from this perspective, the Bush administration censored photographs of military coffins being returned to the United States from the conflicts in Iraq and Afghanistan (Milbank, 2003).

Much of the evidence of the recent growth in American zeal for death transcendence began in the late 1970s and early 1980s. At the time, connections were already being made linking Americans' extreme individualism with their rejuvenated defiant stance against death. Christopher Lasch observed how the 'irrational terror of old age and death is closely associated with the emergence of the narcissistic personality ... giving rise to attempts to abolish old age and to extend life indefinitely' (1979, p. 211). In 'The Me Decade and the Third Great Awakening', Tom Wolfe, noted the dissolution of 'man's age-old belief in serial immortality', where most generations 'have lived as if they are living their ancestors' lives and their offspring's lives and perhaps their neighbors' lives as well' (1976, p. 39). Such framing of existence no longer sufficed for the new predominant personality type. Neither did science's insights that cells and creatures are programmed to die nor that extinction is the fate of all species provide compensation for primates who think about timelessness and eternity. In sum, the death consolation of the genetic form of symbolic immortality was waning, being replaced by mimetic immortality to shore up the transcendent reaffirmations of religion.

It was also during this era that the human environment was increasingly becoming a McLuhanian electronic envelope, whose lineaments became understood as various information systems and whose essence was increasingly one of Baudrillard's simulacra. Given the interwoven nature of self and society, the understood essence of selfhood was to be profoundly changed as well. Instead of being corporeal mechanisms, modern selves are becoming seen as attention- and identity-seeking social algorithms whose distinctive 'programs' influence the programming of others' lives and the logics of institutional systems. And, just as individuals cannot erase their residues in cyberspace, neither does their existence conclude with physical extinction. One's images, behaviours, words, beliefs, and accomplishments exist indefinitely in this new electronic world, available to be paused, reversed, and fast forwarded.

These cultural solutions to the problem of transcendence fit well with American capitalism's need to counter the scientific materialism of its chief twentieth-century ideological rival, communism. One highly publicised battle line during the Cold War was drawn when the Soviet Union officially proclaimed the finality of death (Kluckhohn, 1962), even banning Sir Arthur Conan Doyle's 1892 *The Adventures of Sherlock Holmes* because of its references to occultism and spiritualism. Nevertheless, Communist regimes were to embalm and place on public display the physical remains of founding fathers (e.g. Vladimir Lenin, who used to have the companionship of Josef Stalin in the Red Square Mausoleum; Mao Tse-tung [who had wished cremation] in Beijing; Hồ Chí Minh in Hanoi; Georgi Dimitrov, founder of Communist Bulgaria [until cremated in 1990 after regime overthrow]; Kim Il Sung in Pyongyang, North Korea). It turned out to be an interesting balancing act of the United States, supposedly a secular nation, walking the tight rope when immortalising its elite and to do so without the non-putrefying saints of the Catholic Church and the Communist Party.

Conclusion

Four decades after Toynbee (1969, p.131) observed how 'Death is un-American' ethicist Arthur Caplan proclaimed 'It's not immoral to want to be immortal' (MSNBC, 2008). Crystallised between the pronouncements, two fronts in the culture's war against death were drawn: one in the here-and-now and the other in the hereafter. With regards to the former, the USA has witnessed growing public demands for the nation–state to kill (or at least give forewarning to) whatever kills us, whether Taliban fighters, lethal microbes, stray asteroids, dangerous chemicals or foods, death genes, or unexpected earthquakes and tsunamis. This has led to further expansion of the medical-military-industrial complex, the proliferation of warning labels, demands for risk-free environments and dramatic improvements in life expectancy. Well over three quarters of the American federal budget is currently devoted to military and medical endeavours and to assisting those most likely to die (e.g. the old; in 2003, the portion of the federal budget going just to Social Security, Medicare, and Medicaid was 42%). Like the classical Egyptians, this high civilisation has become increasingly oriented towards conquering the finality of death through new death-transcending technologies.

This contrasts with Americans' deep faith in being able to transcend death. Like Maslow's needs-based hierarchy of motivations of the living, there exists a hierarchy of post-mortem objectives that range across simply being a part of others' DNA (or genetic immortality), being remembered (mnemetic immortality), being able to influence others' behaviours and beliefs (mimetic immortality), and finally, being able to continue as a fully conscious social actor (sentient immortality). Though traditional religious beliefs offer hope for the latter, a growing multitude of secular symbolic forms have demonstrably delivered all the others. For this reason, Shneidman's (1973) concept of the postself is broadened to include these other forms, not just individuals' anticipations of and actions towards how they will be posthumously remembered. Since its coinage, so many laws and industries have emerged around the social status and commodification of deceased individuals that the concept requires broadening. The extreme individualism of the American character rejects death's finality and its consignment to oblivion. In the new market-driven and media-saturated culture, even revisionist biographical memories and infamy can be preferable to being forgotten.

References

Baudrillard, J. (1993). *Symbolic exchange and death.* (I. GRANT, Trans.). London: Sage.

Bauman, Z. (1992). *Morality, immortality, and other life strategies.* Stanford, CA: Stanford University Press.

Becker, E. (1973). *The denial of death.* New York: The Free Press.

Braude, A. (2001). *Radical spirits: Spiritualism and women's rights in nineteenth-century America.* Indianapolis, IN: Indiana University Press.

Buescher, J. B. (2003). *The other side of salvation: Spiritualism and the nineteenth-century religious experience.* Boston, MA: Skinner House Books.

Caplan, A. (2008). It's not immoral to want to be immortal. Msnbc .com (April 25). Retrieved 29 December, 2009 from: www .msnbc.msn.com/id/23562623/

Caldwell, J. (2001). Suicide bombings tear at the heart of Islam. *Irish Examiner,* September 18. Retrieved 29 December, 2009, from http://archives.tcm.ie/irishexaminer/2001/09/18/ story12963.asp

Choron, J. (1964). *Death and modern man.* New York: Collier Books.

Danilov, V. J. (1997). *Hall of Fame Museums: A reference guide.* Westport, CT: Greenwood Press.

Davis, J. A., & Smith, T. W. (2007). *General social surveys, 1972– 2006.* [machine-readable file]. Principal Investigator, James A. Davis; Director and Co-Principal Investigator, Tom W. Smith; Co-Principal Investigator, Peter V. Marsden. Sponsored by the National Science Foundation. Chicago, IL: National Opinion Research Center [producer]. Storrs, CT: The Roper Center for Public Opinion Research Center, University of Connecticut [distributor].

FONG, M., & Lau, D. (2001). Earnings from the Crypt. *Forbes,* February 28. Retrieved 29 December, 2009 from www.forbes .com/2001/02/28/crypt.html

Fuchsberg, G. (1987). For the right price, just about anything can bear your name. *The Wall Street Journal,* (Sept. 21), pp. 1, 14.

Gallup, G., Jr. (2001). Tuesday briefing: Religion update. Forbes. com, July 31.

Goldman, L., & Paine, J. (2007). Top earning dead celebrities. *Forbes.* October 29. Electronic Edition. Retrieved 29 December, 2009 from www.forbes.com/media/2007/10/26/top-dead-celebrity-biz-media-deadcelebs07-cz_lg_1029celeb.html

Greeley, A., & Hout, M. (1999). Americans' increasing belief in life after death: Religious competition and acculturation. *American Sociological Review, 64,* 813–835.

Gruman, G. (2003). *A history of ideas about the prolongation of life: Classics in longevity and aging.* New York: Springer.

Hentsch, T. (2004). *Truth or death: The quest for immortality in the Western narrative tradition.* Vancouver, BC: Talonbooks.

Howarth, G. (2000). Dismantling the boundaries between life and death. *Mortality,* 5(2), 127–138.

International Social Survey Program (ISSP). (1994). *International Social Survey Program: Religion, 1991. [CUMULATIVE FILE] [Computer File].* Koeln, Germany: Zentralarchiv fuer empirische Sozialforschung [Producer]. 1993. Koeln, Germany: Zentralarchiv fuer empirische Sozialforschung/Ann Arbor, MI: Inter-university Consortium for Political and Social Research [Distributors].

Kadlec, D. (2002). Ruling from the Grave. *Time,* April 22.

Kearl, M., & Rinaldi, A. (1983). The political uses of the dead as symbols in contemporary civil religions. *Social Forces, 61,* 693–708.

Kearl, M. (2001). An investigation into collective historical knowledge and implications of its ignorance. *Texas Journal of Ideas, History and Culture, 23,* 4–13.

Kluckhohn, R. (Ed.). (1962). *Culture and behavior: Collected essays of Clyde Kluckhohn.* New York: The Free Press.

Kurzweil, R. (2005). *The singularity is near: When humans transcend biology.* New York: Viking.

Lescarboura, A. C. (1920). Edison's views on life and death. *Scientific American,* 123, 446.

Lifton, R. J. (1979). *The broken connection: On death and the continuity of life.* New York: Simon & Schuster.

Milbank, D. (2003). Curtains ordered for media coverage of returning coffins. *The Washington Post,* October 21, p. A23.

Pew Forum on RELIGION AND PUBLIC LIFE. (2008). Many Americans say other faiths can lead to eternal life. (Dec. 18). Retrieved April 26, 2009, from http://pewforum.org/ docs/?DocID=380

Pew Research Center for the People and the Press. (2002). Americans struggle with religion's role at home and abroad. (March 20). Retrieved on May 4, 2009 from: http://people-press.org/ reports/display.php3?ReportID=150

Russell, B. (1957). *Why I am not a Christian.* London: George Allen & Unwin.

Safire, W. (2001). For a Muslim legion. *New York Times,* October 1, p. A23.

Shneidman, E. S. (1995). The postself. In J.B. WILLIAMSON & E.S. Shneidman (Eds.), *Death: Current perspectives,* Fourth Edition. Menlo Park, CA: Mayfield. Adopted from Death of Man by Edwin S. Shneidman (Quadrangle: NY), 1973.

Swatos W. H., Jr. & Gissurarson, L. R. (1997). *Icelandic spiritualism: mediumship and modernity in Iceland.* New Brunswick, NJ: Transaction.

Thiessen, M. (2004). Jewish group: Mormons still Baptize dead. *AP online,* Retrieved 9 April, 2009 from http://story.news .yahoo.com/news?tmpl=story&cid=519&ncid=519&e=6 &u=/ap/20040410/ap_on_re_us/baptizing_the_dead

Toynbee, A. (1969). *Man's concern with death.* St. Louis, MO: McGraw-Hill.

Walter, T. (1996). *The eclipse of eternity: A sociology of the afterlife.* New York: St. Martin's Press.

Wolfe, T. (1976). The me decade and the third great awakening. New York (August 23), pp. 26–40.

Word, R. (2003). *Abortion doctor's killer expects reward. AP Online,* September 2. Retrieved 29 December, 2009 from www.encyclopedia.com/doc/1P1-79097390.html

Critical Thinking

1. What are some indications of an increasing presence of the dead in everyday life?

2. Do you agree with the author's argument that extreme individualism, capitalism, and technological innovations have together increased the number, visibility, and influence of postselves?

3. What is meant by "postselves" in modern culture?

MICHAEL C. KEARL is a Professor of Sociology at Trinity University, San Antonio, Texas. His current research focuses on the coalescing of attitudes towards abortion, euthanasia, immortality, same sex marriages, and evolution in the American culture wars.

Roadside Memorial Policies in the United States

GEORGE E. DICKINSON AND HEATH C. HOFFMANN

Introduction

As one drives across the United States, it is not unusual to see a roadside memorial such as a cross, an official state sign, or some other secular reminder that death occurred on or near that spot. Roadside memorials often consist of a plaque with the name of the deceased, the date of birth and death, and sometimes messages from the deceased's close friends or family. The memorial may be decorated with flowers, a teddy bear, a football jersey, a toy, photograph, or some other personal item of the deceased person. Memorial decorations may also change with anniversaries and holidays. The practice of erecting a marker or placing a grave along roadways can be traced back to prehistoric traders of amber and flint in Central Europe who buried their dead along trailways (Clark & Cheshire, 2004). Various roadside cross memorials to mark an accident or crime scene stand throughout England, dating from 1290 to the present (Everett, 2002). In the United States, the phenomenon of roadside memorialisation is often considered to have originated in the Southwest reflecting Hispanic customs and the influence of Catholicism after the arrival of Spanish conquistadors in the sixteenth century (Petersson, 2009). The religious symbols of a cross mark the sites as 'sacred', or 'micro sacred sites', as Weisser (2004) notes, and have been the predominant structure chosen for memorials (Collins & Rhine, 2003). The small white crosses were used to mark the rest areas for funeral procession pallbearers travelling by foot from the church to the graveyard, thus in this sense was influenced by religion. These sanctified holy rest areas called *Descansos* (Spanish for 'resting place') have since evolved into markers of the location of traffic fatalities (Nance, 2001).

Despite the deep historical roots of roadside memorials, it has only been within the last 15 years that roadside memorials have become a common practice in Australia, Central America, Japan, New Zealand, North America, Northern and Southern Europe, and South America (Churchill & Tay, 2008; Clark & Cheshire, 2004; Clark & Fransmann, 2002; Petersson, 2009). Today's commemorative sites represent a shift in the way that western societies regard death, funerals, and mourning rituals; death-negating practices seem to gradually give way to greater expressiveness in public mourning (Klaassens, Groote, & Huigen, 2009). Memorials typically appear when there has been a sudden and violent death of a younger person. Such a memorial placed by an accident site could enable a connection between the deceased's personal life and the impersonal site, reinforcing it as a memorial space (Petersson, 2005). Memorials serve as a means of engaging the issue of death and afterlife. Folklorist George Monger (1997, p. 114) suggested two primary reasons for roadside memorials, memorialisation and warning, describing the action of maintaining the site of the fatality as a 'private and individual pilgrimage'. Everett (2002) observed that roadside memorials symbolically represent on-going grief work. For example, as a relative or friend passes the memorial, there is the reminder of the life, and death, of that person. Roadside memorials differ from cemeteries where death is kept 'in order' (Petersson, 2005). Yet, a cemetery is not where individuals previously lived. Petersson observed that roadside memorials may be seen as an additional way of expressing the deceased person's identity and social person rather than as a replacement for the grave lot in the cemetery. A roadside marker located 'outside' the cemetery may allow the deceased to continue to exist in the world of the living. In this sense, as cultural geographers Kate Hartig and Kevin Dunn (1998) proposed, roadside memorials may be filling a gap in the trend towards gardens of remembrance and plaque-gardens, leaving the survivors with no personalised space to visit.

In America, Clark and Cheshire (2004) show that the Department of Transportation (DOT) in several states used crosses in the mid-twentieth century to indicate dangerous stretches of road where previous fatalities had occurred. These crosses were used to warn drivers, not to commemorate a lost life, and often included warnings such as 'Drive slow, one killed' (Clark & Cheshire, 2004). To this day, many states sponsor programmes that allow the deceased's name to be placed along the highway as part of an Adopt-A-Highway programme or, in the case of drinking and driving-related fatalities, special signs are erected with the victim's name placed underneath a message like, 'Please Don't Drink and Drive. In memory of . . .' However, these memorials usually appear in the form of large, rectangular highway signs, not crosses, and thus usually attract little controversy. Yet the placement of crosses on public property has been controversial in a number of American states. For example, the Utah Highway Patrol Association erected a separate 12-foot cross for each of 14 fallen Utah patrolmen. The crosses were placed on public property and included a plaque describing the life of the deceased. In 2005, American Atheists, Inc., a group that advocates for the separation of church and state, sued the state of Utah in federal court for allowing the group to post the memorial crosses on public land, arguing that the cross is a religious symbol. In *American Atheists, Inc. v. Duncan,* the federal District Court of Utah sided with the defendants, asserting that the cross is not exclusively a religious symbol but is also a secular representation of death and burial (Roberts & Shurtleff, 2006). American Atheists, Inc. appealed to the 10th Circuit Court of Appeals in Denver, Colorado, where the appeal was heard on 10 March 2009. A decision is pending and has implications for similar memorials in the states of Colorado, Kansas, New Mexico, and Oklahoma (Coakley, 2009).

The use of the cross to memorialise roadside fatalities is only one of the concerns to emerge from the proliferation of roadside memorials across America's roads and highways. In recent years, roadside memorials have been banned by states, counties, and city governments because they may constitute a safety hazard to maintenance crews and drivers passing the memorial (Coakley, 2009; Madigan, 2003; Ross, 1998). This is somewhat ironic since, as noted above, roadside markers were used by several states in the 1940s and 1950s to warn of dangerous roadways where drivers had previously died. In addition to safety concerns, some individuals oppose roadside memorials because they are 'macabre eyesores' (Urbina, 2006) that serve as unwanted reminders of tragic loss (Grabbe, 2008), which is why some states require family approval before friends can erect a memorial for the deceased (Ross, 1998). Memorials are often removed by state personnel as a matter of policy or by citizens who are offended by a cross or the reminder of death. The desecration and/or unauthorised removal of roadside memorials spurred the New Mexico state legislature to pass legislation in 2007 making it a misdemeanor to destroy a memorial that has been placed in the public right-of-way in memory of victims of fatal traffic accidents (New Mexico Legislative Finance Committee, 2007).

As is evident in the above discussion, roadside memorials carry tremendous diversity in style and origin. There are the roadside memorials created by the friends and family members of the deceased which has been the dominant focus of the published literature to date. However,

there are also state-sanctioned memorials created by the state as part of Adopt-A-Highway or drinking and driving awareness programmes which conform to state regulations in terms of design, height, and location. For both lay and state-sanctioned memorials, the 50 American states have apparently employed an inconsistent patchwork of policies and practices that control how state personnel handle roadside memorials. US Federal laws prohibit placement of anything along interstate highways except highway-related signs and devices, yet it is state maintenance crews that are responsible for managing America's highways. Despite prohibitions of and opposition to roadside memorials in jurisdictions throughout America, these memorials proliferate. Thus, as Ross (1998, p. 50) notes, 'in probably no other area of public life does public practice diverge so dramatically from official policy' as is the case with roadside memorials. Having the right memorial policy is important for each state because transportation agencies need to balance safety and maintenance considerations with the needs of the public to grieve for the loss of their significant other (Tay, 2009). So, while lay and/or state-sanctioned roadside memorials can be found in all 50 states, as we report below, scholarship on American roadside memorials has been limited to county (Barrera, 1991; Zimmerman, 1995) or state-level (Everett, 2002; Reid & Reid, 2001) analyses that focus primarily on the appearance, symbolic meaning, and/or purpose of memorials. Any discussion of state policies toward those memorials has been secondary. The purpose of this research, therefore, is to ascertain the current status and content of roadside memorial policies in the 50 states in the US.

Methodology

Through the Internet, we obtained the mailing addresses of the Director of the Department of Transport (DOT) in each of the 50 states. A survey, accompanied by a cover letter and self-addressed stamped envelope, was mailed on 23 June 2008 to all 50 DOT Directors. We then twice mailed follow-up reminders to the states that had yet to respond. Several respondents requested and completed an electronic version of the survey, an option made available to all participants. We received completed surveys from 47 of the 50 states. Massachusetts returned a letter and Montana returned a description of its policy but did not complete any questions on the survey. The respondent from Massachusetts reported that the state has no formal policy regarding roadside memorials. With safety their primary concern, Massachusetts officials were working on a policy but the current practice allows 'small, temporary, unobtrusive memorials to remain, as long as they do not present a public safety hazard . . . [and] maintenance forces have been instructed to remove any permanent or hazardous memorials in the course of general highway maintenance activity'. Montana endorses the American Legion's Highway Fatality Marker Program, but did not respond about how the state manages private memorials not installed through the Fatality Marker Program. Using the information provided in those materials, we were able to code parts of a survey for both states.

Alaska was the only state not to respond after three surveys were mailed to that state's transportation department. After consulting Alaska's website, we were able to identify some details regarding its roadside memorial policy (Alaska Department of Transportation, 2003a, 2003b, 2004). Since Alaska's policy went into effect in 2003 and was valid at the time data were collected for this study, we have included Alaska in the results presented below.

We sought to determine whether states had a formal policy for roadside memorials and, if they did, what that policy entailed, including the following items:

- Are memorial markers required to be uniform in terms of size dimensions, design and/or materials (e.g., aluminium)?
- How do family members and friends apply for the erection of a memorial?
- Are state-sanctioned memorials limited to fatalities related to driving under the influence of alcohol and other drugs?
- What guidelines exist for the placement of state-sanctioned and private markers and are they allowed to face traffic?
- Does the state keep a record of the names of those memorialised?
- Is there a specific time limit for how long the roadside memorials can remain standing?
- What percent of roadside memorials contain religious symbols?
- What action does the state take if memorials fall into disrepair, if complaints about specific memorials are received, and/or if memorials are erected in defiance of the law?
- Does the DOT maintain an annual budget for the erection and maintenance of memorials?
- Do counties, cities, and other jurisdictions within the state have their own regulations governing roadside memorials?
- Are 'green' or natural memorials available (e.g., planting a tree in honour of the deceased)?

Findings

In this section, we summarise the aggregate findings from our survey, highlighting examples from states to illustrate important aspects of states' roadside memorial policies.

States with Roadside Memorial Policies[1]

Twenty-three states (46%) adopted a policy regarding the placement of roadside memorials along state highways. Two other states (Iowa and Minnesota) reported not having a policy but included with their returned survey a 'statement' or 'guidelines' that spelled out how private memorials would be handled in the absence of state legislation. The Montana DOT also reported not having a roadside memorial policy. However, Montana formally recognises the Montana American Legion Highway Fatality Marker Program which, since 1953, places a white cross at the site of a fatal traffic accident. Thus, we include Montana among those states with a formal roadside memorial policy.

Five of those states with a policy also said that 'counties, cities, or precincts' in their state have their own regulations regarding roadside memorials and four additional states without an official state policy indicate that counties, cities, or other jurisdictions have their own policies. Twenty-seven states report no existing policies at the county or city level and the remaining 14 states either did not respond or did not know whether policies existed at the local level. A number of respondents indicated that the DOT was also responsible for county roads throughout the state, suggesting a broader reach of the state's roadside memorial policy. We did not specifically ask respondents if the DOT was responsible for county roads so we cannot say how widespread the practice is.

Some states, such as Illinois and Washington, have a Driving Under the Influence (DUI) Memorial Sign Program. For example, a sign may read 'Please Don't Drink and Drive' which is posted 'In Memory of' the deceased. At least five states have Adopt-A-Highway (AAH) programmes for volunteer participation in roadside litter removal along designated roads. These AAH groups are recognised with a sign, which in some cases acknowledges the deceased person for the stretch of road that has been adopted.

In South Dakota, the DOT erects a sign near the right-of-way adjacent to where a fatal crash occurred. The sign will include words like 'X Marks the Spot—Why Die? Drive Safely' or 'X Marks the Spot—Think! Drive Safely'. These signs are placed at the scene of the fatality unless opposed by the family of the deceased. Ten states' policies require that the memorials be erected by the state, with an average cost of US$414 per memorial. When asked if the state charges the family/friends for the memorial erection, eight states answered in the affirmative, with an average charge of US$419.

Of the 23 states with a formal policy for roadside memorials, 11 states (48%) require that roadside memorials be applied for by submitting a paper application and two states accept paper applications or an on-line electronic application. Respondents in three other states accept written requests from family members (e.g., paper letters or e-mails) but have no formal application for roadside memorials. While Washington State has a formal paper application process, the DOT representative who completed this survey reports that the DOT receives roadside memorial referrals from Mothers Against Drunk Driving and county level DUI Victim Information Panels. Eleven states' (48%) policies require that friends who wish to erect a memorial for the deceased must first obtain permission from the deceased's family. Six states (26%) permit memorials for drinking and driving fatalities only, whereas 14 states (61%) allow memorials for all highway fatalities.

In terms of location, 17 of the states with a policy (74%) require memorials to be placed in the right-of-way, whereas three states require placement on the 'edge of the right-of-way but not on it.' Eleven states require that the memorial face oncoming highway traffic. Other states, such as Texas, specifically place the markers so that they cannot be read by drivers passing by, except in special cases designated by the Texas Legislature. Instead, memorials erected by the Texas DOT are placed in rest areas or turnouts and are designed to be read by individuals on foot.

A particular size dimension must be adhered to in 15 states (65%), with variations ranging from a 15-inch round sign to 60" × 48" rectangular signs. Fifteen states (65%) require that memorials be made of specific materials (e.g., aluminium, wood, or natural vegetation), whereas six states (26%) do not specify the materials (the remaining states with a policy reported that this question was not applicable to their policy). Asked whether or not the states keep a record of the name(s) of the individual(s) honoured by the memorial, 14 states (70%) keep such records and five states (25%) do not.

Thirteen states (62%) have a particular time limit as to how long a memorial can stay up. The time limit ranged from 30 days to 10 years with 4.5 years being the average time limit for respondents who reported this information. Other states permit memorial signs to remain standing 'until sign is faded', 'deteriorated', or for the 'life of sign'. Six states (29%) report having no time limit for roadside memorials but, as the data below suggest, many of these states would remove the signs if they fell into disrepair or otherwise posed a safety hazard for maintenance crews and/or drivers.

States with and Without Roadside Memorial Policies

None of the states allocates specific funds in their annual DOT budget for the erection, maintenance, and/or removal of memorials: managing roadside memorials is a cost that is absorbed by the general DOT budget. When asked what action the DOT takes if roadside memorials fall into disrepair, 29 respondents (63%) said they remove it and five states (11%) leave the memorial. Seven respondents report that all private memorials are removed regardless of their condition. This was not a question specifically asked in our survey but this response was usually included in the 'other' response category. Respondents reported a range of 'other' actions taken against memorials in disrepair including removing the memorial 'with [the] next

work activity in the area', making an 'attempt to contact the family', or 'remove [the memorial] within 30 days after notification of family'. These quotes generally reflect a common theme among respondents in our survey who explicitly acknowledged trying to balance safety concerns while simultaneously respecting a family's need to grieve for the loved one. This is an important finding given that 70% of respondents say roadside memorials are considered a safety hazard in their state (30% said memorials were not a safety hazard).

When asked whether the DOT receives complaints about roadside memorials, regardless of whether the memorials have been placed legally, or not, the majority of respondents indicated receiving complaints rarely (45%) or occasionally (41%). Four states (9%) report never receiving complaints and only Tennessee reports receiving frequent complaints. After receiving a complaint, 91% of the respondents said the DOT removes the memorial in response to the complaint and 9% leave the memorial as is. Of those states that remove the memorial following a complaint, 7% said that they destroy the memorial and 76% try to return it to the person who erected it. The remaining respondents either said the question was not applicable to their state (7%) or marked 'other' (10%), reporting a range of responses including storing the memorial and returning it to the person who erected it, or 'work with [the] person who erected it and try to get it relocated or removed'. Vandalism of roadside memorials is one means by which memorials would become unsightly and require DOT action. However, only Maryland reported that vandalism of roadside memorials was a problem.

A number of states have adopted 'green memorials' where, instead of erecting metal or concrete memorials, trees, bushes, and/or gardens are planted to memorialise the site of the deceased. Green memorials were reported by 11 states (24%) where the DOT allows a tree to be planted near where a highway fatality occurred. Delaware was the first state to build a memorial garden dedicated to those who lost their lives in all types of traffic fatalities. The garden was created specifically to provide a safe, legal alternative for those families and friends who wish to place a roadside memorial. Similarly, Maryland has started a Living Memorial Program in which a grove of trees will be planted each year to memorialise the individuals killed in highway automobile accidents during the year. The Maryland programme includes a dedication ceremony in honour of the previous year's victims. Tennessee had not yet developed a 'green' memorial programme but that state's DOT representative reported that they are 'kicking off a tree planting programme this fall to try and cut back on roadside memorials'.

We asked respondents to estimate the percentage of roadside memorials in their respective states that contained religious symbols or secular content. Thirty-seven states answered this question, each indicating that religious memorials (e.g.,

17

the cross) were more common than secular memorials, which is consistent with previous research in other countries (see Clark & Cheshire, 2004). Overall, respondents estimated that 73% of memorials contained religious symbols and 27% were secular.

States Where Roadside Memorials Are Not Legal

We asked respondents what the DOT does if roadside memorials are posted in defiance of the state's law and/or the DOT policy. Only Nebraska reported doing nothing. Twenty-seven states take down illegal memorials if they pose a safety hazard and 15 states report removing memorials if they interfere with the work of road maintenance crews (e.g., mowers). Three states take down illegal memorials only if they are considered an eyesore and eight states always remove illegal memorials. Respondents offered additional details to explain their state's response to illegal memorials which include removing the memorial 'after a 10–14 day grieving period', 'remove them in two months or so', and/or 'remove only if severely damaged or in disrepair'. Several states gave more than one response to this query, thus the total number of responses exceeds the number of states where roadside memorials are not legal.

Discussion

Roadside memorials overall are relatively new to the scene on US highways, yet they do not seem to be going away. These memorials may serve as a reminder of the deceased individual each time a family member or friend passes by. To others, it may be a reminder that they do not wish to encounter on a regular basis. The construction of memorials may fit within a larger context of decreasing interest in church-based rituals and an increasing tendency to view spiritual authority resting with the individual conscience (Clark & Franzmann, 2002). Individuals may feel that they have the right to establish roadside memorials which function outside of official burial grounds. Such roadside markers offer a meeting place for communication, remembrance, and reflection (Everett, 2002).

In addition to serving as an enhancement to coping with grief for some individuals, roadside memorials are beginning to be viewed as serving a range of other positive functions. First, state-sponsored drinking and driving memorials may be a possible deterrent against drinking and driving as the deceased's name is placed beneath a sign that warns drivers not to drink and drive. Similarly, AAH programmes, where the victim's name appears on an official state sign, allow family members to take responsibility for picking up litter along a mile stretch of a highway which helps to maintain the cleanliness of the right-of-way. Defenders of family-constructed roadside memorials have even suggested that, rather than constituting a road hazard, memorials actually prevent traffic accidents by providing

drivers with stimulating scenery along stretches of highway that might otherwise induce sleep and result in an accident (Ross, 1998). Whether this is true cannot be verified but roadside memorials can also help to improve the landscape, as is evidenced through 'green memorials' in the planting of a tree (or numerous trees as in Maryland) or the construction of memorial gardens to honour all who have died in roadway accidents. The centralised natural memorials also attempt to address safety concerns raised by the placement of individual memorials along the highway. However, it is unlikely that memorial gardens will replace individual memorials constructed by friends and family, given the importance the latter place on the specific location at which the death occurred (Klaassens, Groote, & Breen, 2007).

While only 23 of the states have officially adopted a roadside memorial policy, virtually all states report taking action against memorials if the circumstances warrant it (e.g., a complaint is made or safety is jeopardised). Memorials devoted specifically to fatalities related to drinking and driving are found in only five states. The DOTs in 13 states erect the roadside memorials themselves and 12 states require that an application be completed in order to put up a memorial. However, even when a state officially prohibits roadside memorials (i.e., 'all' lay memorials are unauthorised and will be removed) and/or the state has an official programme through which families can apply for a state-constructed memorial, there remains a discrepancy between policy and practice. For example, Ross (1998) recalls receiving conflicting information from two separate Nevada transportation officials regarding their roadside memorial policy. One person said that memorials are not permitted for safety reasons while another said that memorials are 'a positive marker in life—a grim reminder that we all need to watch out for each other' (Ross, 1998, p. 50). We found similar discrepancies in our survey. Slightly over half of the states said that roadside memorials present a safety hazard and are removed accordingly. Yet the states are generally sensitive to the grief of the survivors by balancing these concerns with the responsibility to maintain public safety. For example, the respondent from a western state said, 'We try to take into consideration the sensitivity of this issue during a time when families are grieving. By contacting them directly, we can offer condolences and explain the safety issues [the memorials pose] for other drivers'. A similar sentiment was communicated by the respondent of a southern state who wrote, 'Roadside memorials are illegal but we try to be sympathetic during the initial grieving period. These are mostly funeral wreaths or flower baskets, occasionally a small cross. If the grieving person moves the memorial to the right-of-way line we will not bother it'. Finally, a respondent from a southern state said, 'Though we do not allow the permitting of these types of memorials, we are sympathetic to the families affected by these tragic accidents, and therefore do not actively pursue removing these types of memorials when they first appear, unless they are potential safety hazards or affect our routine maintenance operations'.

Confrontations sometimes develop, however, over the removal of a memorial, as it is a private symbol located in a public place (Kong, 1999). A recent case in Massachusetts exemplifies this potential for conflict (Grabbe, 2008). A cross, carved by the deceased man's father, was erected to commemorate the fatality of his 17-year-old son. The home owners who live near the site where the cross is erected want it removed because it reminds them of the horror of the accident and the night they went to the aid of the accident victims. The parents of the deceased teen are going through mediation with the neighbours with the hope that negotiation, in contrast to an adversarial civil court process, will help the opposing parties arrive at a solution amenable to all. In an earlier situation in Florida, the DOT began to receive complaints about the display of religious symbols after the state approved a programme to memorialise traffic fatalities with small crosses (DOT won't, 1998). The Florida DOT later replaced the state-constructed crosses with small disks printed with the accident information (Porter, 2001). This public space may be regulated by the state but it is for the use of the wider community, thus the non-grieving may see roadside memorials as an intrusion upon their space (Clark & Franzmann, 2006). While complaints about roadside memorials are not frequent occurrences, according to respondents in our study, the overwhelming majority of states report removing the memorials when complaints are received. Further, the majority of DOTs that remove memorials in a state of disrepair complies with their mission of keeping roadsides beautiful as a shared public space. In addition, a shabby roadside memorial does not show respect for the deceased.

The one universal theme among roadside memorials, if indeed any exists, is that the cross is a dominant feature of most roadside memorials, perhaps a carryover of the Catholic influence in earlier days. Larson-Miller (2005) suggests that the establishment of roadside memorials is a type of popular religious activity. The cross is typically the memorial when a religious symbol is displayed. There is a belief among some individuals that the soul tends to linger on for some time after death and has the power to trouble the living if necessary precautions are not taken (Petersson, 2009). The construction of the cross, therefore, could help persuade the dead soul not to haunt or harm passers-by. That the symbol of the cross is often found in cemeteries, either carved into the grave marker or is itself the marker, further explains why the cross is so common among roadside memorials.

French sociologist Emile Durkheim (1915) said that the essence of religion is to divide the world into profane and sacred spheres or dimensions. Whatever a group designates as 'sacred', whether a totem animal or a roadside memorial, is to be approached and treated with respect and reverence.

The spot where the roadside memorial is placed may be considered sacred, holy ground, yet not all members of the public recognise the location of the memorial as sacred (Klaassens et al., 2009). Moreover, the individuals choosing the cross may not do so because the cross has a religious connotation but rather out of a cultural tradition going back many years. As Clark and Franzmann (2006) note, the roadside memorial is a private expression of grief that turns a public place into sacred space, its sacredness directly constructed by individuals who would typically make no claim to such civil or religious authority. Collins and Rhine (2003) concluded that the expression of faith ranked low on the purposes of a memorial, suggesting that the use of a cross, which has been the source of so much controversy, is in most cases not a religious expression, but a cross-cultural symbol of death (Clark & Cheshire, 2004). This, too, was the legal opinion of the US District Court in Utah in *American Atheists, Inc. v. Duncan*. Though we have no data regarding this, several studies (Clark & Cheshire, 2004; Reid & Reid, 2001) have found that, while the cross was the prominent feature in nearly all of the roadside memorials analysed, a smaller number of memorials added a crucifix to the memorial, suggesting an attempt to overtly express religious belief not otherwise reflected by the cross. It is also possible, as Collins and Rhine (2003) found, that the location of the death may be more important than the memorial itself and that the purpose of the memorial is to mark the place which is now considered sacred, whatever the 'mark' may be.

It has been suggested that contemporary society is 'deritualised' regarding matters of death as such assignments are given over to professionals (Freedman, 1997). Additionally, roadside memorials indicate a desire to reconstruct new forms of ritualised mourning because traditional mourning practices are old fashioned and inadequate (Haney, Leimer, & Lowery, 1997). Accordingly, in discussing grief work, Kamerman (1988) and Rosenblatt, Walsh, and Jackson (1976) link the inability of many bereaved individuals to accomplish grief work to the limited availability of meaningful death-related rituals. They argue that, whether grounded in formal religious or civil culture or not, individuals and groups have developed for themselves death-related rituals in order to work through loss in a more timely and successful fashion. Thus, an increasing number of individuals have adapted a custom with roots from Europe into their way of life (Everett, 2002). Everett suggests that roadside crosses may not always reach a state of closure, regarding grief work. Nonetheless, such adaptations apparently have been helpful to many as evidenced by the proliferation of roadside memorials.

Roadside memorials can provide solace to grieving families and also serve as a reminder of the potential consequences of inattention at the wheel (Grabbe, 2008). To others, however, these memorials are seen as distractions to motorists or as eyesores. Sometimes roadside memorials are seen as private expressions of grief located in public places (Everett, 2000), much to the dislike of individuals who do not like seeing these on public land, especially when they contain religious symbols. Variation in how roadside memorials are viewed by the general public are reflected in the diverse state policies and practices regarding roadside memorials. The 50 American states, however, are seriously addressing this issue as they continue to debate and produce policies/statements on how to manage roadside memorials.

Note

1. A state by state breakdown of the results can be obtained by emailing Heath Hoffman hoffmannh@cofc.edu

References

Alaska Department of Transportation. (2003a). A primer for roadside memorials. Retrieved April 30, 2010, fromhttp://www.dot.state. ak.us/stwddes/dcsrow/assets/pdf/roadsidememorials.pdf.

Alaska Department of Transportation. (2003b). Memorials sign program. Retrieved April 30, 2010, fromhttp://www.dot.state. ak.us/stwddes/dcsrow/assets/pdf/memorialsign.pdf.

Alaska Department of Transportation. (2004). Application for participation in memorial sign program. Retrieved April 30, 2010, fromhttp://dot.alaska.gov/stwddes/dcsrow/assets/pdf/forms/25ar977.pdf.

Barrera, A. (1991). Mexican-American roadside crosses in Starr County. In J. S. Graham (Ed.), *Hecho en Tejas: Texas-Mexican folk arts and crafts*. Publications of the Texas Folklore Society (Vol. 50). Denton, TX: University of North Texas Press.

Churchill, A., & TAY, R. (2008). An assessment of roadside memorial policy and road safety. *Canadian Journal of Transportation, 2*(1), 1-12.

Clark, J., & Cheshire, A. (2004). RIP by the roadside: A comparative study of roadside memorials in New South Wales, Australia, and Texas, United States. *Omega, 48*(3), 203-222.

Clark, J., & Franzmann, M. (2002). 'Born to eternal life': The roadside as sacred space. *Pointers, 12*(3), 14-16.

Clark, J., & Franzmann, M. (2006). Authority from grief, presence and place in the making of roadside memorials. *Death Studies, 30,* 579-599.

Coakley, E. (2009, March 11). Roadside memorials spark debate over religious symbolism in Utah. Retrieved October 28, 2009, fromhttp://www.findingdulcinea.com/news/Americas/2009/March/Roadside-Memorials-Spark-Debate-Over-Religious-Symbolism-in-Utah.html.

Collins, C. O., & Rhine, C. D. (2003). Roadside memorials. *Omega, 47*(3), 221-244.

DOT won't install roadside crosses. (1998). Retrieved April 28, 2008, fromhttp://www.adl.org/Regional/Miami/DOTWontInstallRoadsideCrosses.html.

Durkheim, E. (1915). *Elementary forms of religious life*. New York: George Allen and Unwin.

Everett, H. (2000). Roadside crosses and memorial complexes in Texas. *Folklore, 111*(1), 91–102.

Everett, H. (2002). *Roadside crosses in contemporary memorial culture*. Denton, TX: University of North Texas Press.

Freedman, D. (1997, June 27). Driving reminders. *Anchorage Daily News*. p. El.

Grabbe, N. (2008, June 27). Leverett neighborhood wrestles with weight of a cross. *Amherst Bulletin.* p. Al. Retrieved April 30, 2010, from www.amherstbulletin.com/story/id/98909/.

Haney, C. A., Leimer, C., & Lowery, J. (1997). Spontaneous memorialization: violent death and emerging mourning rituals. *Omega: Journal of Death and Dying, 35,* 159–171.

Hartig, D. V., & Dunn, K. M. (1998). Roadside memorials: Interpreting new deathscapes in Newcastle, New South Wales. *Australian Geographical Studies, 36*(1), 5–20.

Kamerman, J. B. (1988). *Death in the midst of life*. Englewood Cliffs, NJ: Prentice Hall.

Klaassens, M., Groote, P., & Breen, V. (2007). Roadside memorials: public places of private grief. Unpublished manuscript, Department of Spatial Sciences, University of Groningen, Groningen, Netherlands.

Klaassens, M., Groote, P., & Huigen, P. P.P. (2009). Roadside memorials from a geographical perspective. *Mortality, 14,* 187–201.

Kong, L. (1999). Cemeteries and columbaria, memorials, and mausoleums: Narrative and Interpretation in the study of deathscapes in geography. *Australian Geographical Studies, 37*(1), 1–10.

Larson-Miller, L. (2005). Holy ground: Roadside shrines and sacred space. *America, 192*(18), 11.

Madigan, E. (2003, June 10). Safety concerns fail to curb roadside memorials. Retrieved April 30, 2010, from www.stateline.org/live/printable/story?contentId=15276.

Monger, G. (1997). Modern wayside shrines. *Folklore, 108,* 113-114.

Nance, D. (2001). Roadside memorials on the American highway. Retrieved June 18, 2008, from http://photo.net/photodb/presentation?presentatoin_id=97863.

New Mexico Legislative Finance Committee. (2007). *Fiscal impact report*. Retrieved March 15, 2009, from http://legis.state.nm.us/sessions/07%20Regular/firs/HB0333.pdf.

Petersson, A. (2005, September). The production of a proper place of death. Paper presented at the conference on Social Context of Death, Dying and Disposal, Bath, England.

Petersson, A. (2009). Swedish Offerkast and recent roadside memorials. *Folklore, 120*(1), 75–91.

Porter, K. (2001). Debate rekindles on safety of roads. *The News Herald,* May 30. Retrieved January 22, 2005, from www.newsherald.com/articles/2001/05/30/lo053001a.htm.

Reid, J. K., & Reid, C. L. (2001). A cross marks the spot: A study of roadside death memorials in Texas and Oklahoma. *Death Studies, 25*(4), 341–356.

Roberts, T.D., & Shurtleff, M.L. (2006). Memorandum in opposition to plaintiff's motion for partial summary judgment RE: Christian cross as religious symbol. Retrieved April 30, 2010, from www.atheists.org/upload/050506.Dk.pdf.

Rosenblatt, P. C., Walsh, R. P., & Jackson, D. A. (1976). *Grief and mourning in cross-cultural perspective,* n.c: HRAF Press.

Ross, C. (1998, May). Roadside memorials: Public policy vs. private express. American City & County. Retrieved April 30, 2010, from http://americancityandcounty.com/mag/government_roadside_memorials_public/.

Tay, R. (2009). Drivers' perceptions and reactions to roadside memorials. *Accident Analysis and Prevention, 41,* 663-669.

Urbina, I. (2006, February 6). As roadside memorials multiply, a second look. Retrieved April 30, 2010, from www.nytimes.com/2006/02/06/national/06shrine.html.

Weisser, J. (2004). Micro sacred sites: The spatial pattern of roadside memorials in Warren County, Ohio. Unpublished master's thesis, University of Cincinnati, Cincinnati, Ohio.

Zimmerman, T. A. (1995). Roadside memorials in five south central Kentucky counties. Masters Thesis, Western Kentucky University.

Critical Thinking

1. What are some of the pros and cons of roadside memorials?

2. What is the history of roadside memorials in the United States?

3. How do roadside memorial policies differ in the 50 states? Which one(s) do you personally believe to be the most appropriate?

GEORGE E. DICKINSON is Professor of Sociology at the College of Charleston, Charleston, SC (USA). His research interests include death education in healthcare professional schools in the US and UK. HEATH C. HOFFMANN is Associate Professor of Sociology at the College of Charleston, Charleston, SC (USA). His research interests include policies and practices affecting prisoner reentry in the US.

From *Mortality*, vol. 15, no. 2, May 2010, pp. 154–167. Copyright © 2010 by Association for Death Education and Counseling. Reprinted by permission of Taylor & Francis via Rightslink.

Brain Death Guidelines Vary at Top US Neurological Hospitals

SUSAN JEFFREY

A new survey shows wide variation in brain death guidelines among leading neurological institutions in the United States, differences that may have implications for the determination of death and initiation of transplant procedures, the researchers say.

Under the Uniform Determination of Death Act, guidelines for brain death determination can be developed at the institutional level, leading to potential variability in practice, David M. Greer, MD, from Massachusetts General Hospital, in Boston, and colleagues report. Although there are guidelines on brain death determination from the American Academy of Neurology (AAN), they are not binding at the local level.

Results of this survey, published in the January 22 issue of *Neurology,* now suggest that substantial variation is in fact present even among top US hospitals.

"It was very concerning that there was a huge mismatch between what is set forth in the practice parameters from the AAN and what is actually being stipulated at local hospitals," Dr. Greer told *Medscape Neurology & Neurosurgery* when their findings were first presented in October 2007 at the 132nd Annual Meeting of the American Neurological Association.

Although it is possible that actual performance at these hospitals is better than what is suggested by the protocols, he noted, "We have no evidence of that."

Top 50 Hospitals

For the study, the authors requested the guidelines for determination of death by brain criteria from the *US News and World Report* top 50 neurology/neurosurgery institutions in 2006. There was an 82% response rate to their request, from 41 institutions, but 3 did not have official guidelines, leaving protocols from 38 hospitals for evaluation.

The guidelines were evaluated for 5 categories of data: guideline performance, preclinical testing, clinical examination, apnea testing, and ancillary tests. They compared the guidelines directly with the AAN guidelines for consistencies and differences.

"Major differences were present among institutions for all 5 categories," the authors write. "Variability existed in the guide-lines' requirements for performance of the evaluation, prerequisites before testing, specifics of the brain-stem examination and apnea testing, and what types of ancillary tests could be performed, including what pitfalls and limitations might exist."

For example, with regard to preclinical testing, it was surprising to find that the cause of brain death was not stipulated in a large number of guidelines, they note. "Of concern was the variability in the apnea testing, an area with the greatest possibility for inaccuracies, indeterminate testing, and potentially even danger to the patient," they note. "This included variability of temperature, drawing of an [arterial blood gas sample] ABG prior to testing, the proper baseline [partial pressure carbon dioxide] pCO_2, and technique for performing the test. Although a final pCO_2 level was commonly stated (most often 60 mm Hg), specific guidelines in a situation of chronic CO_2 retention, clinical instability, or inconclusive testing were commonly lacking. A surprising number (13%) of guidelines did not specify that spontaneous respirations be absent during the apnea test."

In the category of guideline performance, there was a "surprisingly low rate of involvement of neurologists or neurosurgeons in the determination." Further, the requirement that an attending physician be involved was "conspicuously uncommon."

"Given a technique with some complexity as well as potential medical-legal implications, we find it surprising that more institutions did not require a higher level or more specific area of expertise," they write.

Their findings suggest that stricter AAN guidelines may be in order, they conclude. "Given the fact that the guidelines put forth by the AAN are now 13 years old, perhaps now is the time that they be rewritten, with an emphasis on a higher degree of specific detail in areas where there is greater variability of practice. Furthermore, perhaps now there should be standards by which individual institutions are held more accountable for their closeness to, or variability from, national guidelines."

Coauthors on the study were Panayoitis Varelas, MD, PhD, and Shamael Haque, DO, from Henry Ford Hospital, in Detroit, Michigan, and Eelco Wijdicks, MD, PhD, from the Mayo Clinic, in Rochester, Minnesota.

A "Disturbing Pattern of Nonuniformity"

In an editorial accompanying the paper, James L. Bernat, MD, from Dartmouth-Hitchcock Medical Center, in Lebanon, New Hampshire, points out that Greer and colleagues have shown that "physicians declaring brain death in leading neurology departments in the United States practice with a disturbing pattern of nonuniformity."

Some of these variations are inconsequential, he notes, but some could make a serious difference in outcomes. "Practices that do not require demonstrating an anatomic lesion sufficient to explain the clinical findings, do not rigorously exclude potentially reversible metabolic and toxic factors, do not properly test brain-stem function, or do not require proper apnea testing are consequential because they could yield an incorrect determination of death," he writes.

Although brain death has to be determined correctly to maintain confidence in high-quality medical care and the organ-procurement enterprise, he writes, in addition to accuracy, "it is desirable to achieve a uniformity of practice using the optimal guidelines."

"I suggest that the AAN, the American Neurological Association, and Child Neurology Society jointly empanel a task force to draft evidence-based guidelines, including specific recommendations for conducting the clinical and confirmatory tests for brain death," Dr. Bernat continues. "Once these guidelines have been accepted and published, neurologists should act as envoys to ensure that they become incorporated into hospital policies throughout the country and help implement them locally."

This task force could also update the guidelines at intervals to accommodate emerging technologies as they are validated, such as noninvasive neuroimaging tests measuring the absence of intracranial blood flow, he writes. "The most daunting global problem of establishing worldwide uniformity of brain death guidelines is a task for the World Federation of Neurology."

Critical Thinking

1. How do the guidelines for brain death vary in U.S. hospitals?
2. Why would a uniformity of hospital practice in brain death guidelines be useful?
3. What is the Uniform Determination of Death Act? Was this a wise act to pass?

Dr. Greer reports receiving speaker honoraria from Boehringer-Ingelheim Pharmaceuticals Inc. Disclosures for coauthors appear in the paper.

Criteria for a Good Death

This brief paper advances the concept of a "good death," outlines ten specific criteria for a good death, and proposes a simple golden rule for optimal dying.

EDWIN SHNEIDMAN, PhD

By almost universal common consent, death has a bad reputation. Words like awful and catastrophic are practically synonymous with death. Good and death seem oxymoronic, incompatible, mutually exclusive. Given all this, what then can it mean to speak of a good death? Are some deaths better than others? Can one plan to improve on one's death? My answer to these questions is yes, and that is what this brief paper is about.

In a previous article about a related topic (Shneidman, 1998), I discussed how *suicide*—the meaning and connotations of the A good death is one word—had palpably changed over the last 230 years. The entries on suicide traced in fifteen different editions of the *Encyclopedia Britannica* indicate that suicide has mutated from being a sin and a crime (involving the punishment of the corpse and the survivors) to being a mental health issue meriting the therapeutic and sympathetic response of others. Death is the over-arching topic of suicide and is more culturally gyroscopic, slower to change, yet subject to shifts in the cultural zeitgeist. If one begins, somewhat arbitrarily, in the Middle Ages with another related topic—courtly love, specifically courtship (DeRougemont, 1940)—one sees that there were elaborate rules for courtly love and for courtly deportment in general. The goal was to be able to do admittedly difficult tasks with seeming effortlessness and without complaint (Castiglione, 1528/1959); in other words, with grace.

The challenge for this paper is to propose some criteria for a good death—a sort of report card of death, a fantasied optimal dying scenario—and to provide a chance to debate what a good death ought to be.

There is no single best kind of death. A good death is one that is appropriate for that person. It is a death in which the hand of the way of dying slips easily into the glove of the act itself. It is in character, on camera, ego-syntonic. It, the death, fits the person. It is a death that one might choose if it were realistically possible for one to choose one's own death. Weisman (1972) has called this an appropriate death.

A decimal of criteria of a good death can be listed. The ten items include (see also Table 1):

1. *Natural.* There are four modes of death—natural, accident, suicide, and homicide (NASH). Any survivor would prefer a loved one's death to be natural. No suicide is a good death.
2. *Mature.* After age 70. Near the pinnacle of mental functioning but old enough to have experienced and savored life.
3. *Expected.* Neither sudden nor unexpected. Survivors-to-be do not like to be surprised. A good death should have about a week's lead time.
4. *Honorable.* Filled with honorifics but not dwelling on past failures. Death begins an ongoing obituary, a memory in the minds of the survivors. The Latin phrase is: *De mortuis nil nisi bonum* (Of the dead [speak] nothing but good).
5. *Prepared.* A living trust, prepaid funeral arrangements. That the decedent had given thought and made arrangements for the necessary legalities surrounding death.
6. *Accepted.* "Willing the obligatory," that is, accepting the immutables of chance and nature and fate; not raging into the night; acceding to nature's unnegotiable demands.
7. *Civilized.* To have some of your loved ones physically present. That the dying scene be enlivened by fresh flowers, beautiful pictures, and cherished music.
8. *Generative.* To pass down the wisdom of the tribe to younger generations; to write; to have shared memories and histories; to act like a beneficent sage.
9. *Rueful.* To cherish the emotional state which is a bittersweet admixture of sadness, yearning, nostalgia, regret, appreciation, and thoughtfulness. To avoid depression, surrender, or collapse; to die with some

Table 1   Ten Criteria for a Good Death

Natural
A natural death, rather than accident, suicide, or homicide

Mature
After age 70; elderly yet lucid and experienced

Expected
Neither sudden nor unexpected; some decent warning

Honorable
Emphasis on the honorifics; a positive obituary

Prepared
A living trust; prearranged funeral; some unfinished tasks to be done

Accepted
Willing the obligator; gracefully accepting the inevitable

Civilized
Attended by loved ones; with flowers, pictures, and music for the dying scene

Generative
To have passed the wisdom of the tribe to younger generations

Rueful
To experience the contemplative emotions of sadness and regret without collapse

Peaceable
With amicability and love; freedom from physical pain

---

projects left to be done; by example, to teach the paradigm that no life is completely complete.

10. *Peaceable.* That the dying scene be filled with amicability and love, that physical pain be controlled as much as competent medical care can provide. Each death an ennobling icon of the human race.

I end with a sweeping question: Is it possible to formulate a Golden Rule for a good death, a maxim that has the survivors in mind? I would offer, as a beginning, the following Golden Rule for the dying scene: Do unto others *as little as possible.* By which I mean that the dying person consciously try to arrange that his or her death—given the inescapable sadness of the loss-to-be—be as little pain as humanly possible to the survivors. Along with this Golden Rule for dying there is the copperplated injunction: Die in a manner so that the reviews of your death speak to your better self (as a courtier distinguished by grace) rather than as a plebian marked by coarseness and complaint. Have your dying be a courtly death, among the best things that you ever did. It is your last chance to get your neuroses under partial control.

References

Castiglione, B. (1959). *The book of the courtier.*, trans. Charles S. Singleton. Garden City, NY: Anchor Books. Originally published in 1528.

DeRougemont, D. (1940). *Love in the western world.* Princeton, NJ: Princeton University Press.

Shneidman, E. S. (1980). *Voices of death.* New York: Harper & Row.

Shneidman, E. S. (1998). Suicide on my mind; Britannica on my table. *American Scholar,* 67(3), 93–104.

Weisman, A. (1972). *On dying and denying.* New York: Behavioral Publications.

Critical Thinking

1. Are there any of the ten criteria that you disagree with? Why?
2. What criteria would you add to the list in this article?

EDWIN S. SHNEIDMAN is professor of Thanatology Emeritus, UCLA and founder of the American Association of Suicidology.

Address correspondence to Edwin S. Shneidman, 11431 Kingsland St., Los Angeles, CA 90066.

UNIT 2

Dying and Death across the Life Cycle

Unit Selections

Learning Outcomes

After reading this unit, you should be able to:

- Discuss what societal steps can be taken to help children better cope with the death of an individual.

- Explain how animated characters in Disney films can help in a child's understanding of death.

- Describe how death is depicted in Walt Disney films.

- Discuss sources that exist to aid with the trauma of death in one's life.

- Describe what the stress is like for small children to have a mother or father fighting in the military overseas.

- List at-risk behaviors for children after a traumatic death event.

- Enumerate how caregivers can be helped to lessen their assignment of dealing with a dying family member and what kinds of support are available for caregivers.

- List particular needs of elderly persons in a palliative care unit.

Student Website
www.mhhe.com/cls

Internet References

American Academy of Child & Adolescent Psychiatry
http://aacap.org/page.ww?name=Children+and+Grief&section=Facts+for+Families

Child Bereavement Charity
www.childbereavement.org.uk/home_page

Children with AIDS Project
www.aidskids.org

The Compassionate Friends
www.compassionatefriends.org/resources/links.aspx

Grief Net
http://rivendell.org

Motherloss
www.freewebs.com/motherloss/front.htm

Raindrop: Death Education for Children of All Ages
http://iul.com/raindrop

Yahoo: Society and Culture: Death and Dying
http://dir.yahoo.com/Society_and_Culture/Death_and_Dying

Death is something that we must accept, although no one really understands it. We can talk about death, learn from each other, and help each other. By better understanding death conceptualization at various stages and in different relationships within the life cycle, we can help each other. It is not our intent to suggest that age should be viewed as the sole determinant of one's death concept. Many other factors influence this cognitive development such as level of intelligence, physical and mental well-being, previous emotional reactions to various life experiences, religious background, other social and cultural forces, personal identity and self-worth appraisals, and exposure to or threats of death. Indeed, a child in a hospital for seriously ill children is likely more sophisticated regarding death, as she or he may be aware of dying and death, more so than an adult who has not had such experiences. Nonetheless, we discuss dying and death at various stages from the cradle to the grave or, as some say, the womb to the tomb.

The death of a child and the death of a spouse are both in the top five list of 100 stresses that an individual has in life. The death of a child is so illogical, because the child has not lived through the life cycle. One can anticipate attending the funeral of a grandparent and then a parent. We do not, however, anticipate attending the funeral of a child, since the adult is expected to die before the child. Such is the rational sequence of the life cycle.

Research on very young children's conceptions of death does not reveal an adequate understanding of their responses. Adults, many decades later, recall vivid details about their first death experiences, whether a pet or a person, and for many it was a traumatic event filled with fear, anger, and frustration. How might we help with such situations? "Death in Disney Films" might aid in working with children trying to understand dying and death. Additionally, "Helping Military Kids Cope with Traumatic Death" and "Teaching Children about Death and Grief" address these issues.

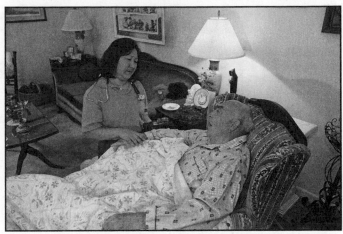

© The McGraw-Hill Companies, Inc./Rick Brady, photographer

As individuals move into the "autumn" of their lives and are classified as "elderly," death surrounds them, and they are especially made aware that they are reaching the end of the tunnel. Although old age is often pictured as gloom and doom, it can be viewed as "the best is yet to be," as poet Robert Browning noted. The aging professional athlete Satchel Paige observed years ago that aging is really mind over matter—as long as you don't mind, it really doesn't matter. You are as old (or young) as you feel. Research suggests that the elderly are accepting of death, having lived a normal life span, and are grateful for the life they have had. Some of these issues are addressed in "Needs of Elderly Patients in Palliative Care" and in "End-of-Life Concerns and Care Preferences: Congruence Among Terminally Ill Elders and their Family Caregivers."

Death in Disney Films: Implications for Children's Understanding of Death

Meredith Cox, Erin Garrett, and James A. Graham

Introduction

Death is an aspect of life that is not only inevitable but also painful, especially for children. Children do not have the knowledge or experience that adults have; thus, they are often unprepared to deal with the death of a loved one or even of a beloved cartoon character in a movie. Furthermore, it is not until about 10 years of age that healthy children achieve an understanding that death is irreversible, permanent, and inevitable (Brent, Speece, Lin, Dong, & Yang, 1996).

If death is a concept that many young children do not have a working understanding of, then why is it such a prominent theme in children's media, specifically in Disney movies? Do Disney's portrayals influence children's comprehension of death? The current content analysis describes and analyzes the portrayal of death in selected animated Disney films. In order to examine the possible affect that death scenes in Disney films might have for children, it is necessary to understand how children conceive of death.

Children's Understanding of Death

Many of the classic Disney movies target young audiences who do not have very developed or accurate concepts of death. For instance, many children younger than five years old do not understand that death is final, and inevitable (Grollman, 1990; Speece & Brent, 1984). Between the ages of five and nine, children who do acknowledge the permanence and inevitability of death see death as something that only applies to older adults (Grollman, 1990; Speece & Brent, 1984). Some children who do not have a complete understanding of death often will fill in gaps in understanding with fantasy elements (Baker, Sedney, & Gross, 1992), which may be taken from the media that children view, such as Disney movies. If the media, specifically some Disney films, convey unrealistic messages about death, then aspects of those portrayals are likely to be internalized by children. These less than desirable notions about death may have an impact on how children will view later instances of death.

In general, children's comprehension of death depends on two factors: experience and developmental level. First, children's experiences with death (i.e., actual experience and what they have been told about death) are critical to their understanding of death (Speece & Brent, 1984). Second, the developmental level of the child also must be taken into account when examining the comprehension of death (Brent et al., 1996; Willis, 2002). For example, Willis pinpointed four aspects of death that children and adults do not view in the same way: irreversibility, finality, inevitability, and causality. Children may not understand that death is permanent and that it cannot be "fixed" or reversed. They also do not have enough life experience to realize that death is inevitable for all living things. Furthermore, because they do not think abstractly, some young children do not understand the causality of death.

There is much support to the idea that children have a very limited understanding of death (e.g., Baker et al., 1992; Brent et al., 1996; Grollman, 1990; Speece & Brent, 1984; Willis, 2002), and the partial understanding they do have is often based on fuzzy logic (Brent et al., 1996). Brent et al. found that most children do not fully understand that death is a universal, irreversible, and nonfunctional state (meaning that dead beings cannot do the things that the living do) until the age of 10 years. Interestingly, it was also found that even after children reach this level of understanding they might continue to struggle with the idea that death is final, possibly because of certain religious beliefs. However, this may suggest a more mature understanding of death rather than a less mature one (Brent et al., 1996). Children with immature, binary concepts of death see people as either alive or dead, and do not consider the idea that there may be any other options based on religious values and ideas about afterlife.

According to Baker et al. (1992), the process of grieving after a loss and coming to understand death is a process that consists of psychological tasks that children progress through to eventually overcome their grief. The first stage involves *understanding what death is,* knowing its characteristics, and being able to recognize when it has happened. At this stage, it is important for children to feel self-protected, meaning that they need to know that just because someone or something has died does not mean the child or his or her family is in any immediate danger.

The middle phase involves *understanding that death is a reality and accepting the emotions that come along with that realization*. This may include reflecting on times spent with the deceased loved one and coming to terms with the fact that he or she is gone while still maintaining memories and an internal connection to that person. Thus, we should not give children the false hope that a loved one may "come back" after death, and we should not discourage them from remaining emotionally attached to the deceased individual (Baker et al., 1992). This phase shows a marked difference in the way that children and adults grieve. Many adults move through the process more quickly than children do because they may understand and have more actual experience with the concept of death. Thus, many adults do not have to spend as much time figuring out what has happened when a loved one is suddenly gone, as would a child.

The last phase of this process involves a *reorganization of a child's sense of identity and his or her relationships with others and with the environment*. The child will also be able to invest emotionally him- or herself in relationships with others without being overly afraid of losing that person to a death. At this stage, a well-adjusted child still remembers the loved one without fearing excessively that others will die and is able to cope with those memories and any sadness associated with them (Baker et al., 1992).

Parents' Role in Children's Comprehension of Death

There are other reasons why children may misunderstand death beyond the obvious cognitive limitations. Many children tend not to discuss death with their parents or friends because they think the subject is too unpleasant, frightening, or even unnecessary (Wass, Raup, & Sisler, 1989). The manner in which some parents communicate with their children about death may influence the child's comprehension of it. When it comes to talking about death, a lot of parents do so in a way that is very confusing and potentially harmful to children (Ryerson, 1977; Willis, 2002). It seems that some parents' main objective shifts from explaining and teaching to *protecting*. For instance, rather than telling children why and how people die they may focus on downplaying the emotionality, seriousness, and reality of death.

Though their intentions are good, many adults often hinder children's understanding of death by using confusing terms and abstract language to explain the concept to them. They may say that someone has "passed away," which does not convey a realistic portrayal of death to children (Willis, 2002). They may use euphemisms (such as "sleeping for a long time" or "taken a long trip") in an attempt to downplay the impact of death in order to protect children, which only serves to confuse them. These phrases convey to the young child that the loved one who has "passed away" may "wake up" from their long nap or "come home" from their voyage (Willis, 2002). Furthermore, describing death to children as a long "sleep" is not only confusing but may foster a fear of going to sleep among children (Grollman, 1990).

Ryerson (1977) points out that sometimes parents avoid the topic of death altogether and are very awkward about discussing it with children. Many parents' hesitation to talk to children about death in a straightforward way likely stems from their own fears of death, which may have origins in the way that their own parents spoke to them about it. The implication is that this matter-of-fact manner of explaining death is likely to perpetuate a cycle of faulty communication between parents and children. Ryerson describes the mourning process in children as well as ways to help children cope with death. The use of fairy tales may be a source of identification and interest for children, and they can be used to facilitate discussion between children and adults about death and grieving.

The fairy tale has served as the most honest and clear-cut managing of death available to children over the ages (Dobson, 1977). According to Dobson (1977), its main purpose is to stimulate children's intellect and help them tackle their "darkest and scariest thoughts about separation, rejection, abandonment, and death" (p. 175). Fairy tales often contain non-threatening references to death, which makes them appropriate for use with children. Fairy tales, many of which have inspired many Disney films, present interesting and somewhat controversial portrayals of death and grieving.

Popular Children's Films, Children's Grieving Processes, and Death Education

The present study is an exploratory analysis of death from animated Disney movies. In general, there is limited research that examines the relationship between popular children's films and children's comprehension of death. For instance, Sedney (1999) examined the portrayal of grief in young characters in children's films. The films all had hopeful messages showing the possibility for a happy life following the death of a loved one. However, the films showed differing degrees of grieving. Sedney points out that sometimes deaths are unacknowledged completely, which is an aspect that is common to children's films, especially among those with missing parents. In other cases, there is an acknowledgment of death, but it is not grieved, as in *Bambi*. In contrast, in *The Lion King,* death *is* acknowledged and the young character grieves and displays a gamut of typical grieving emotions ranging from self-blame and anger to profound sadness. Sedney describes the merits of *The Lion King's* grief portrayal because it offers a realistic view of grief as well as a resolution to sadness. For this reason, this particular film has the potential to be an effective teaching tool to serve as a basis of discussion on the topic of death with children.

In contrast with Sedney (1999, 2002) who found positive aspects of portrayals of death in children's films, Schultz and Huet (2001) examined the highest grossing American films and Academy Award nominees and concluded that the majority of portrayals of death are unrealistic and sensational, and are rarely accompanied by realistic and normal grief reactions. This was true about some children's films as well. Many of the films did not either acknowledge death or use "death terminology," lending further support to the idea that our culture has taboos about discussing death in a straightforward manner

(Schultz & Huet, 2001). Interestingly, Schultz and Huet point out that the Motion Picture Association of America (MPAA) does not distinguish between types of violence and death when considering ratings, which also affects audiences, and most notably children.

As previously emphasized, the amount of research done on the media's influence on children's understanding of death is very limited. Many death educators propose some form of death education for children (Wass et al., 1989). How is this education to be initiated? We propose that using popular animated Disney films may be one way to intervene and may provide a foundation for discussion between children and adults about death. Specifically, we examined the portrayal of death and grieving in Disney films geared toward children, focusing on five factors: character status, depiction of death, death status, emotional reaction, and causality.

Method
Film Selection
The analyzed content consists of 10 Disney Classic animated full-length feature films. The movies were selected only if a death occurred or was a theme in the plotline. The movies were chosen from various decades in order to sample the portrayal of death across time in Disney films. The first animated Disney full-length feature film was released approximately 60 years ago; thus, films were selected from both the first 30 years of production (pre-1970s) and from the last 30 years (post-1970s). Due to a lack of full-length films with death scenes released before the 1970s, only three movies were selected from that period, whereas seven were selected from more recent decades. This limited selection could also be attributed to the fact that full-length animated Disney movies were released on an average of three per decade in the past, whereas 14 were released in the 1980s and 1990s. The films were not chosen haphazardly; rather, the researchers went through the plot outlines of all animated Disney Classic films and chose from that list, being careful to select both older classics and more modern films that children are familiar with today. The movies examined for this study were: *Snow White and the Seven Dwarfs* (1937), *Bambi* (1942), *Sleeping Beauty,* (1959), *The Little Mermaid* (1989), *Beauty and the Beast* (1991), *The Lion King* (1994), *The Hunchback of Notre Dame* (1996), *Hercules* (1997), *Mulan* (1998), and *Tarzan* (1999).

Coding Categories
Two coders watched the movies together and coded the data individually. Each character's death was analyzed by the following five coding criteria.

Character Status
This category refers to the role the character that died played in the plot. We coded for two different types of characters. First, a *protagonist* is a character that is seen as the "good guy," hero/heroine of the movie, or the main character whom the story revolves around. An *antagonist* is a character who is seen as the "bad guy," villain, nemesis, or enemy of the protagonist.

Depiction of Death
Refers to how the character's death was shown in the film. In an *explicit death* the audience sees that the character is definitely dead because the body is shown being physically damaged/killed and/or the dead, motionless body is shown on screen. An *implicit death* refers to one in which the audience can only assume that the character is dead based on the fact that they do not appear again in the film and/or that they have encountered something that would presumably result in death. Examples include seeing a shadow of a dead body or a character falling off a cliff. *Sleep death* refers to an instance in which a character falls into a state of prolonged sleep. Generally, this is the result of a spell due to an original intent to kill.

Death Status
This category refers to if a death was a true end of life or if it was shown as something negotiable that does not necessarily represent the absolute end of life. A *permanent/final* death is one in which the character does not return in any form. A *reversible* death is one where a character returns in one of two ways. A *reversible-same form* death is one in which the character seemingly comes back from a dead or seemingly dead state in his or her original body. In a *reversible-altered form* death, the character returns either in a physically transformed state or in the form of a spirit.

Emotional Reaction
Refers to how the other characters in the movie responded to or dealt with death. *Positive emotion* refers to a character or characters being visibly happy (e.g., smiling, cheering) or showing signs of relief. *Negative emotion* refers to a character or characters reacting with frustration, remorse, anger, or with general signs of sadness (e.g., crying). *Lacking emotion* refers to characters reacting to death as if it is inconsequential or the death is not dealt with or acknowledged by all characters.

Causality
Causality refers to what led to or caused the death and whether the death was portrayed as being justified or unjustified. In a *purposeful* death, a character dies as the result of another character's intent to harm or kill him or her. An *accidental* death refers to one where the death was unintentional and was the result of an unplanned event. In addition to being either purposeful or accidental, death events were also coded as being either *justified* or *unjustified*. *Justified* deaths were ones in which the character who died had done something that warranted punishment; the general message conveyed was that they "deserved" to die. *Unjustified* deaths were ones in which the character did not do anything wrong; there was a sense that they did not deserve to die.

Intercoder Reliability
Two coders rated the selected films. Intercoder reliability was judged as acceptable if the raters achieved more than 70% agreement on all categories, using Cohen's Kappa. The reliability between coders was tested on a randomly selected subsample of

Table 1 Depiction of Death by Character Type

Depiction of Death	Protagonist	%	Antagonist	%	Total
Explicit death	7	63.64	4	36.36	11
Implicit death	3	30.0	7	70.0	10
Sleep death	2	100.0	0	0	2
Total	12	52.17	11	47.83	23

Note. Percentages are row percentages.

Table 2 Death Status by Character Types

Death Status	Protagonist	%	Antagonist	%	Total
Reversible/Same	4	100	0	0	4
Reversible/Altered	2	100	0	0	2
Permanent/Final	7	41.18	10	58.82	17
Total	13	56.52	10	43.48	23

Note. Percentages are row percentages.

four films (40% of the sample). Intercoder reliability was computed for each of the five categories of interest: character status ($K = 1.00$), depiction of death ($K = 0.92$), death status ($K = 1.00$), emotional reaction ($K = 1.00$), and causality ($K = 0.87$).

Results

Our study examined the portrayal of death and grieving in Disney films geared toward children, and focused on five factors.

Character Status

A total of 23 death scenes occurred in the 10 Disney films analyzed. Protagonists and antagonists were portrayed nearly equally in those scenes. Out of the 23 characters who died, 52% were protagonists ($n = 12$) and 48% ($n = 11$) were antagonists (see Table 1).

Depiction of Death

Implicit death accounted for 43% of total deaths ($n = 10$) and explicit death ($n = 11$) accounted for 48%. We found that 64% of explicit deaths occurred among protagonists ($n = 7$) while only 36% of explicit deaths were the deaths of antagonists ($n = 4$). In contrast, implicit deaths occurred more among antagonists: 70% of antagonists died in implicit death scenes ($n = 7$), whereas only 30% of protagonists did ($n = 3$). Sleep death was not nearly as common as "real" death portrayals, occurring in 9% of death instances ($n = 2$). Both sleep deaths occurred among protagonists (see Table 1).

Death Status

A large majority of deaths (74%) were portrayed as permanent, final, and irreversible ($n = 17$). Out of the permanent deaths, 59% were those of antagonists ($n = 10$) and 41% were

protagonists ($n = 7$). Reversible death occurred in 26% of death scenes ($n = 6$). Of the six reversible deaths, 67% ($n = 4$) of characters returned in their same form and 33% ($n = 2$) reappeared in altered forms. All of the reversible deaths were among protagonists (see Table 2).

Emotional Reaction

In terms of reactions to a character's death, the most prevalent type of emotion displayed by characters was negative emotion, which occurred in 48% of death scenes ($n = 11$). Negative emotions included typical grieving responses such as fear, crying, and expressing anger or frustration over a loss. Out of the negative emotional responses, 91% ($n = 10$) were for the deaths of protagonists, whereas only 9% ($n = 1$) resulted from the death of an antagonist. Positive emotion, indicated by happiness, relief, or celebration of a loss, occurred in only 13% of deaths ($n = 3$). Positive emotion resulted solely from the deaths of antagonists.

Interestingly, neutral or lacking emotion occurred in 39% of death scenes ($n = 9$), which is nearly as frequently as grieving/negative emotion did. The majority of instances of lacking emotion (78%) were associated with the deaths of antagonists ($n = 7$), whereas only 22% of protagonist deaths resulted in neutral or lacking emotion ($n = 2$) (see Table 3).

Causality

Purposeful deaths occurred most frequently, i.e., 70% ($n = 16$) of all deaths. Out of these purposeful deaths, 38% ($n = 6$) were justified and 62% ($n = 10$) were unjustified. Accidental deaths made up 30% of total deaths ($n = 7$). Out of accidental deaths, 71% ($n = 5$) were justified and 29% ($n = 2$) were seen as unjustified. When justification was considered, regardless of motivation or cause of death, it was found that the respective prevalences of justified and unjustified deaths were nearly

31

Table 3 Emotional Reactions by Character Type

Emotional Reaction	Protagonist	%	Antagonist	%	Total
Positive emotion	0	0	3	100	3
Negative emotion	10	90.9	1	9.1	11
Lacking emotion	2	22.22	7	77.78	9
Total	12	52.17	11	47.83	23

Note. Percentages are row percentages.

Table 4 Cause of Death by Character Type

Cause of Death	Protagoniste	%	Antagonist	%	Total
Accidental–justified	0	0	5	100	5
Accidental–unjustified	2	100	0	0	2
Purposeful–justified	0	0	6	100	6
Purposeful–unjustified	10	100	0	0	10
Total	12	52.17	11	47.83	23

Note. Percentages are row percentages.

equal: justified deaths accounted for 48% of all deaths ($n = 11$) and unjustified deaths accounted for 52% of deaths ($n = 12$).

When both aspects of the causality category were considered together (purposeful/accident and justified/unjustified), the following was found: all purposeful, justified deaths resulted in the death of an antagonist ($n = 6$), and all purposeful, unjustified deaths were those of the protagonists ($n = 10$). All of the accidental, justified deaths were to antagonists ($n = 5$) and the accidental, unjustified deaths were to all protagonists ($n = 2$) (see Table 4).

Discussion

The purpose of our content analysis was to examine the depiction of death in Disney movies. Based on the content analysis of 23 death scenes in 10 Disney films, several trends were observed. Each of the five aspects of death portrayals is discussed separately.

Character Status

The deaths shown in the films were comprised of almost equal numbers of protagonists and of antagonists. This demonstrates a fair distribution of the portrayal of "good" and "bad" characters, showing that both character types are susceptible to death. Many children viewing these scenes receive the message that even good characters that we care about may also die (Brent et al., 1996; Willis, 2002).

Depiction of Death

The depictions of explicit and implicit deaths were fairly equal. Explicit deaths were seen more in scenes where protagonists died. This can be viewed as a positive point because these scenes demonstrate real, explicit deaths of characters to whom the viewer has developed an attachment. However, this can be potentially traumatic for some children because they actually must witness a death. An example is seen in *The Lion King*, where a child must watch as Mufasa is thrown to his death.

The fact that implicit deaths occurred mostly among antagonists may send the message that their deaths are inconsequential in comparison to those of the protagonists. This can perhaps be seen as negative due to the fact that the antagonists' deaths are often merely implied (rather than being explicitly described).

Though sleep deaths only occurred twice out of 23 total deaths, it is important to discuss the implications of this type of portrayal. The sleep deaths occurred in two older films: *Sleeping Beauty* and *Snow White,* which is likely due to the fact that before the 1970s presenting death to audiences in animated films was not considered as big of an issue as it is today. Instead, the issue was dealt with through the use of the sleep deaths, in which spells meant to incur death were magically altered to produce only sleep in characters, rather than death. The fact that sleep deaths did not occur in Disney films released post-1970s may be an indication that children's exposure to death has increased and is now a somewhat less taboo issue in our society.

Death Status

The majority of deaths shown in the selected Disney films were permanent. This is a positive message because it enforces the idea that death is a permanent phenomenon, a concept that many young children do not fully grasp (Baker et al., 1992; Brent et al., 1996; Grollman, 1990; Willis, 2002). Seeing this in Disney films might help some children develop this understanding sooner. However, if they are left unaided in understanding these scenes, they may be upset at the permanence of death. Therefore, because many young children lack the cognitive abilities and experiences required to comprehend the concept of death fully, it is important for parents or teachers to guide them through the processes of learning about death.

Of the deaths that occurred, only six were shown as reversible. All of these reversible deaths occurred among protagonists, showing that antagonists or "bad guys" do not get a second chance at life, at least in some Disney films. Protagonists, on the other hand, fare much better. Half of the protagonists that had died in all 10 films "came back" in some way. An example of a scene that represents this concept is one in which Mufasa returns to communicate with Simba in *The Lion King*. This shows many children that loved ones can always be a part of them, even after death. However, young children may confuse this idea with the notion that the deceased may actually return (Worden & Silverman, 1996).

Emotional Reaction

In terms of emotion shown over death, almost all of the negative emotion was shown as a result of protagonist's deaths. This may provide some children who lack experience with death with a model of grieving (Baker et al., 1992). Presumably, when children see characters grieve and show sadness or frustration over the deaths of loved ones, they may learn that these are acceptable and normal behaviors.

Positive emotional reactions to death occurred solely for antagonists. However, this was not common; the deaths of only three "bad guys" resulted in positive emotion such as visible happiness and relief over their deaths. Most of the deaths that lacked any real emotional reactions were those of antagonists. This shows that the death of a character that is disliked may not warrant clapping and cheering but that it is not worth recognizing it at all. In addition, when one of these deaths *is* acknowledged, it is done in a positive and celebratory manner.

Causality

It was found that all of the justified deaths within the 10 Disney films were those of antagonists. This further demonstrates the trend in Disney films to vilify the antagonists to a point where they are seen as deserving their death. Along the same lines, all unjustified deaths were those of protagonists, showing that good characters never deserve to die.

The deaths of antagonists often result from accidents. However, we are made aware by the films that the antagonists deserve to die because they have done negative things, usually to a protagonist. The fact that they die accidentally allows them to "get what they deserve" while still allowing the protagonists to look good. In other words, protagonists are too good to kill others; thus, the antagonists must die accidentally. For example, in *Beauty and the Beast*, Gaston (the antagonist) stabs the Beast (the protagonist). The Beast, writhing in pain, "accidentally" causes Gaston to lose his balance on the castle tower, which results in Gaston falling to his implied death. When protagonists died, antagonists most often purposely killed them. This further demonstrates the evil of the antagonists.

Conclusions

The purpose of this content analysis was to examine how death is depicted in Disney films. This study is limited in scope, but it serves as a good starting point for the work of others in the area of animated film and children's understanding of death. We are not making conclusive statements about the effects of media on actual children; however, we are suggesting possibilities worth further examination. Our conclusions, based on the content analysis of 10 Disney films containing 23 death scenes, indicate that Disney's portrayal of death may be both good and bad; yet they can serve as effective learning tools for children. Some portrayals of death in Disney films send ambiguous messages about death and may be confusing to many young children. As stated earlier, some young children do not have the cognitive ability or experience to understand death fully (Brent et al., 1996; Speece & Brent, 1984; Willis, 2002). Furthermore, many animated Disney films contain moral implications. The results from this content analysis indicate that the antagonists ("bad guys") deserve to die. These aspects of death in the film may serve as discussion points for parents to talk about their own family's beliefs and morality.

These films may give children something to relate to when they are experiencing a loss. Watching films in which characters die may help children understand real death in a way that is less traumatic and threatening. Based on many of the movie scenes, children may better learn how to deal with death in terms of grieving and understanding what has happened when someone or something dies.

Depictions of death may also serve as springboards for discussion between children and adults about death. As previously mentioned, many parents try to downplay the severity and reality of death when discussing it with children (Grollman, 1990; Ryerson, 1977; Willis, 2002). However, using Disney movies may be a more comfortable way of discussing this difficult topic for both parents and children. Even films with unrealistic messages about death can be used as tools for pursuing discussion about death. Parents can watch Disney films with their children and verbally walk them through a death scene, deconstructing aspects that may be unrealistic and clarifying points that are exaggerated or confusing. This idea of using Disney films to discuss death can be extended to educational and counseling settings as well.

Though our content analysis provides interesting insight into the portrayal of death in Disney films, there are some limitations of this study that should be addressed. First, because the current study focused solely on Disney movies that were known to contain death, our sampling method was one of convenience. Future research may benefit from examining a wider variety of children's media. In addition, due to the small sample of films, the results may not generalize to other animated features. Continuing studies should be done on other types of animated films besides Disney movies.

Further studies may be done utilizing concrete hypotheses based on current findings. The findings from this and future studies can be used to implement new ways of educating children about death, both in home and counseling settings, possibly using Disney films as springboards for discussion. It may also be interesting to examine the next wave of Disney films, as they are released, to determine whether Disney's past and current trends in death portrayals remain the same. Although findings in this area may someday enlighten the creators of Disney movies to their potential to impact children's conceptions of death.

References

Baker, J. E., Sedney, M. A., & Gross, E. (1992). Psychological tasks for bereaved children. *American Journal of Orthopsychiatry, 62,* 105–116.

Brent, S. B., Speece, M. W., Lin, C., Dong, Q., & Yang, C. (1996). The development of the concept of death among Chinese and U.S. children 3–17 years of age: From binary to "fuzzy" concepts? *Omega: The Journal of Death and Dying, 33,* 67–83.

Dobson, J. (1977). Children, death, and the media. *Counseling and Values, 21*(3), 172–179.

Grollman, E. A. (1990). *Talking about death: A dialogue between parent and child* (3rd ed.). Boston: Beacon Press.

Ryerson, M. S. (1977). Death education and counseling for children. *Elementary School Guidance and Counseling, 11,* 165–174.

Schultz, N. W., & Huet, L. M. (2001). Sensational! Violent! Popular! Death in American movies. *Omega: The Journal of Death and Dying, 42,* 137–149.

Sedney, M. A. (1999). Children's grief narratives in popular films. *Omega: The Journal of Death and Dying, 39,* 315–325.

Sedney, M. A. (2002). Maintaining connections in children's grief narratives in popular film. *American Journal of Orthopsychiatry, 72,* 279–288.

Speece, M. W., & Brent, S. B. (1984). Children's understanding of death: A review of three components of a death concept. *Development, 55,* 1671–1686.

Wass, H., Raup, J. L., & Sisler, H. H. (1989). Adolescents and death on television: A follow-up study. *Death Studies, 13,* 161–173.

Willis, C. A. (2002). The grieving process in children: Strategies for understanding, educating, and reconciling children's perceptions of death. *Early Childhood Education Journal, 29,* 221–226.

Worden, J. W., & Silverman, P. R. (1996). Parental death and the adjustment of school-age children. *Omega: The Journal of Death and Dying, 33,* 91–102.

Critical Thinking

1. Think back to Disney films you saw as a child. How do you recall that they impacted on your own thinking about dying, death and grief?

2. How sensitive do you feel that Walt Disney was when producing films on death for children? For example, how did you react to Bambi's death (assuming you saw it as a child)?

3. What is your thinking regarding the importance of an adult always watching films (Disney or otherwise) with a small child, rather than letting the child view them alone?

From Omega: *Journal of Death and Dying,* vol. 50, no. 4, 2004–2005, pp. 267–280. Copyright © 2005 by Baywood Publishing Co., Inc. Reprinted by permission via the Copyright Clearance Center.

Teaching Children about Death and Grief

Children Can Learn about Grief and Dying from Teachable Moments

KIRSTI A. DYER

For a child learning how to cope with loss, with death and with grief are some of the most important life lessons that parents, grandparents, teachers can teach them.

For many children, the first loss they may experience is the death of a grandparent or a pet. The death of a treasured pet may be more real for many children than the death of a distant grandparent.

One simple way for children to learn about death before they may be exposed to a death is for parents to take advantage of the teachable moments in life that present themselves, like discovering a dead bird or dying plant.

Using Teachable Moments to Teach Children about Death

A teachable moment is a brief instant when something happens that causes a child to be uniquely and specifically interested in a particular thing or idea and more likely to learn something. A teachable moment is a special educational opportunity.

Teachable moments occur unexpectedly. Children's grief expert Phyllis R. Silverman points out in her 1999 book, *Never Too Young to Know* [Oxford University] "We cannot always choose our moments. Children raise questions as they think of them and when they are ready. They ask questions about things for which we have not answers, such as what is death."

According to Silverman, "If these moments are utilized well, children learn to be respected as mourners and that they have a legitimate role as part of their community."

Examples of Teachable Moments

Opportunities for teaching children about death may arise when parents least expect it. Parents should be ready to use teachable moments that occur in conversations about news, watching television, or reading books to talk to your child about death. Teachable moments can be used to explain the parents' beliefs about death and how they may feel when something or someone dies.

There may be a news story in the newspaper, a dying person on a television program, in a movie or a book. Seeing a dead lizard, butterfly or bird in the yard can be used to explain to children how death comes to all living creatures.

Many children struggled to understand death when the beloved Crocodile Hunter, Steve Irwin died suddenly or when some of the more popular Harry Potter characters were unexpectedly killed. Older parents may remember learning about death by watching *Bambi* or reading *Charlotte's Web*.

The death of a family pet is often very traumatic for a child. Parents can talk about how death has ended the pet's life. Being exposed to a death helps children see that death is final and irreversible and that their pet will not come back to life the way it does on television. Parents can encourage the child, plan and carry out a pet burial to cope with the loss.

Teaching with "The Circle of Life" or Life Cycles

Elton John and Tim Rice helped parents to explain living with loss and death and the circle of life to their children by bringing up the topic in their song, "The Circle of Life" written for the 1994 movie, *The Lion King:*

> *"Some of us fall by the wayside
> And some of us soar to the stars
> And some of us sail through our troubles
> And some have to live with the scars"*

Animals and nature can be one of the best tools for teaching children about the circle of life and death providing a wide variety of teachable moments. When out in nature, one becomes more aware of the life cycle, by seeing decay and death, but also by seeing renewal and rebirth. Birth and death are a part of the life cycle.

The changing seasons can be used as a concept to explain life cycles. Parents can talk about what happens with the changing seasons, how plants grow or animal babies are born in spring.

Leaves wither and fall in the autumn and plants hibernate in the winter. When spring returns again there is evidence of new life growing from the dust and decay of the old plants.

Create a Safe Environment to Teach about Death

Fortunately, most children, even those exposed to loss and death, are quite resilient. Teachable moments that present themselves can be a good way for parents to explain death and their family's death beliefs to children.

By creating a safe, open environment where children feel free to ask questions and talk about feelings, parents can help their children learn about loss, death and grief.

Resource

Dyer KA. Help a Child Cope with Loss or Death: Helping Children Deal with Life's Losses and Tragedies. Suite 101.

Critical Thinking

1. Recall your first childhood death experience. Was it a pet or a person? How old were you? How did you react? How did your parents/guardians relate to this experience?

2. What "teachable moments" regarding death did you have as a child? How well do you recall that your "teacher" (mom/dad/whoever) handled this?

3. How might the death of a pet differ from that of a person (e.g., your grandfather)?

Helping Military Kids Cope with Traumatic Death

Linda Goldman, MS, LCPC, FT

Ordinary fears are a normal part of a child's developmental growth, and children create internal and external mechanisms to cope with these fears. But a child's ordinary fears can be transformed into very real survival fears in the face of severe trauma. After children experience the death of a parent, they often feel alone and different. Frightened because their once comfortable world now seems unpredictable and unsafe, they may react in ways that we as adults can truly not judge, understand, or anticipate. The impact of a dad's or mom's death in the military can be so traumatically disturbing that the terror involved with the death and the way the parent died may override a child's ability to grieve in a natural way, and share sadness and frustration.

Events can cause panic, stress, and extreme anxiety in kids' lives, and the feelings are heightened with each new instance reported in the media. The terror that grips our children in these circumstances emerges from situations that suddenly overwhelm them and leave them feeling helpless, hopeless, and unable to cope. Trauma is defined by the Encarta® World English Dictionary as "an extremely distressing experience that causes severe emotional shock and may have long-lasting psychological effects." This unexpected and shocking event destroys a child's ability to cope and function in a normal way.

Children can suffer from a state of trauma that can develop into Post-Traumatic Stress Disorder, in which present events trigger memories of trauma resulting in panic, anxiety, disorientation, fear, and all the psycho-physical feelings associated with the traumatic memory.

Signs of Traumatized Children

Seven-year-old Joey's dad was killed in Iraq. He constantly questioned Mom. "Tell me exactly what happened. Did my Dad suffer?" Joey had nightmares and regressed to bedwetting. Tyler's dad was killed by a stray bullet during military combat. His father would always tell him "Nothing can stop me from coming home." Tyler constantly worries about where the bullet hit him, did it hurt him, was he unprotected, and did he die instantly. He began having stomachaches and panic attacks, worrying his mom could get killed too. Jonathan's dad was killed in a firefight in Iraq. Instead of being honored as the son of a military hero, he was often victimized on the playground by a school bully. Jonathan kicked him and both boys were punished. His grades dropped from straight A's to F's after his dad died.

Many young people may experience physical, emotional, cognitive, and behavioral symptoms. These signals range from stomachaches and nightmares to poor grades, isolation, depression, regression, and hostility.

Caring adults need to recognize the signs of grieving and traumatized children, and they need to be aware of the techniques and resources available to help bring safety and protection back to the child's inner and outer world. For example, listening to children's thoughts and feelings, and providing a safe means of expression helps teachers, parents, and educators reinforce their ability to ensure a safe and protected environment.

Traumatized children tend to recreate their trauma, often experiencing bad dreams, waking fears, and recurring flashbacks. Young children have a very hard time putting these behaviors into any context of safety. Many withdraw and isolate themselves, regress and appear anxious, and develop sleeping and eating disorders as a mask for the deep interpretations of their trauma. Young children engage in post-traumatic play by compulsively repeating some aspect of the trauma.

The most common identifying factors that children are re-experiencing the event are play reenactment, nightmares, waking memories, and disturbing thoughts and feelings about the event. Sometimes kids avoid reminders of the traumatic event and show little conscious interest.

Many traumatized children exhibit hyper arousal by increased sleep problems, irritability, inability to concentrate, startle reactions, and regressive behaviors.

When caring adults can identify traumatized kids, they can normalize grief and trauma signs and develop ways kids can express their feelings and emotions. Parents, educators, and other caring professionals can model, present, and support comfortable ways to bring safety and protection back into kids' lives.

Young children developmentally live in an egocentric world filled with the notion that they have caused and are responsible for everything. George's dad was deployed to Iraq twice. Over and over George explained to his teacher. "It's my fault my dad died. I should have made him stay home from Iraq." Some kids may also feel survival guilt. They may think, "Why am I living when so many others have died?" Adults can reframe guilt and magical thinking from "What could I have done?" to "What can I do now?"

At-Risk Behaviors

Children may begin to exhibit at-risk behaviors after a traumatic event. The frequency, intensity, and duration of these behaviors are important factors to consider. Children may experience post-traumatic stress, revisiting the traumatic event through outside stimulus like photos, music, and the media, or by reliving the sights and sounds of the tragedy in their minds. Expect children to re-experience a degree of their original trauma on the anniversary of their parent's death.

The following behaviors may be indicators that a child may benefit from professional help:

- Sudden and pronounced change in behavior
- Threat of suicide or preoccupation with suicide, evidenced through artwork or writing
- Harmful acts to other children or animals
- Extreme confusion or incoherence
- Evidence of substance abuse—drugs, alcohol, etc.
- Sudden change of grades
- Avoidance or abandonment of friends
- Angry or tearful outbursts
- Self-destructive behavior
- Inability to eat or sleep
- Over-concern with own health or health of a loved one
- Giving away important possessions
- Sudden unexplained improvement in behavior or schoolwork
- Depression, isolation, or withdrawal

Activities That Help Kids Express Thoughts and Feelings

Helping children to establish a sense of order in an ever-changing and chaotic world is important. Not only do we want our kids to realize they are survivors of a difficult event, but they also need to know that their life still has continuity and meaning. Parents and educators working with traumatized children should keep to the daily routine as much as possible. This allows kids to feel a renewed sense of security.

Establishing family activities also has a reassuring effect on children. Preparing meals together, eating dinner as a family,

reading stories aloud, or playing family games can help to reestablish a sense of normalcy to kids' lives. It is important to initiate safe places for kids to express their ideas. This can be done by finding quiet times at home, in the car, or on a peaceful walk. Being with children without distractions can produce a comfortable climate to begin dialogue. Bedtime should be a reassuring time, too. Often, this is the time children choose to talk about their worries. Parents can consider an increase in transition time, storytelling, and book reading to create a peaceful, uninterrupted nighttime environment.

Hope for the Future

The sudden death of a mom or dad in military service can shatter a child's emotional and physical equilibrium and stability. Too many boys and girls experience fear, isolation, and loneliness after a parent's traumatic death. Faced with a myriad of losses ranging from parental death, moving, change of school, reduced income level, and public mourning, many children are left in a world where they see no future and no protection.

One goal of trauma work with children is to restore safety and protection to children who have experienced the loss of a parent in combat. Another goal is to provide parents and youth workers with information, understanding, and skills related to the issues creating trauma. With these tools we can help our children become less fearful and more compassionate human beings, thereby increasing their chances of living in a future world of increased inner and outer peace.

Critical Thinking

1. How might the media contribute to a heightened anxiety in children's lives, when a parent(s) is serving in the military? Should such "exposure" be limited or do you feel the reality of traumatic death for children is helpful toward a mature attitude about death?

2. What are some at-risk behaviors for children that may follow a traumatic death experience?

3. What activities might help children express their thoughts following a traumatic death experience?

LINDA GOLDMAN is the author of *Life and Loss, Children Also Grieve, Raising Our Children to Be Resilient,* and *Breaking the Silence: A Guide to Help Children with Complicated Grief.* She works with traumatized children in her practice near Washington, D.C. Email: Linda. goldman@verizon.net, Web: www.childrensgrief.net

Needs of Elderly Patients in Palliative Care

Helle Wijk, RN, PhD and Agneta Grimby, PhD

Europe's population is aging and more people are dying from chronic diseases. Still, the range and quality of palliative care services remain rather limited and inadequate. According to the World Health Organization, many Europeans who are terminally ill die in unnecessary pain and discomfort because their health systems lack skilled staff and do not widely offer palliative care services.

Even though evidence may be lacking and the empirical studies characterized by a high degree of heterogeneity, some important areas seem to stand out considering the elderly patient's views and needs in the terminal phase of life.[1] Assessments of quality of life have shown that the lowest scores are related to the physical domain, followed by the existential, supportive, and social domains.[2] A similar trend can be observed among people wishing to hasten death.[3] Actions to avoid nutritional and pain problems are also crucial at the end-of-life stage, as are avoiding inappropriate prolongation of dying and having a sense of control.[4]

To be able to provide high-quality palliative care, it is important for the health care staff to see and understand the special needs and wishes of the patients; however, knowledge, methods, and programs for this are sparse. The patients themselves seem not to be the one to blame.[5] On the contrary, studies have demonstrated that older people are willing to talk about death and dying in a rather spontaneous way.[6]

Existing empirical evidence on elderly patients' thoughts about death and dying has so far mostly been collected after cross-sectional, quantitative, or qualitative designs, mainly using personal interviews. Open conversations are considered the optimal way of learning about needs at the end-of-life stage. The method, however, is time consuming for daily practice, where somewhat more fixed estimates of needs may be preferred.

Identifying desires and needs of the palliative patient may provide increased quality of care. This pilot study about needs at the end of life aims at describing the individual reports from 30 elderly palliative patients on their needs and their ranking of these needs by degree of concern.

Method
Participants
Thirty consecutively chosen patients, admitted for palliative care at the Geriatric Department, Sahlgrenska University Hospital in Gothenburg, Sweden, were willing to join the study. Inclusion criteria were strength enough to perform an interview and Swedish mother tongue. Exclusion criteria were aphasia, dementia, or lack of strength. The respondents (15 men and 15 women) were an average age of 79 years (75 for men, 81 for women) and had a 50:50 background of manual labor and white-collar jobs.

The primary diagnosis was different types of cancer, with a variation of length of illness of 1 month to several years. All but 1 of the patients were admitted to the palliative unit from another health care institution. All patients signed an informed consent before they participated in the study. The study was approved by the Ethics Committee of the Faculty of Medicine, University of Gothenburg, Sweden.

Procedures
The survey included demographic data and information about reason for admittance and state of health at the time of admittance, reactions to the admittance, and awareness of illness. The information was retrieved partly through patients' files and partly through patient interviews.

Individual needs were identified by semistructured interviews by a research nurse (PhD student) at the palliative unit of the Geriatric Department at Sahlgrenska University Hospital. Most of the interviews were conducted, if possible, once a week and at daytime between 9:00 AM and 2 PM. Interview length was 20 to 30 minutes in 50%; 30% lasted 30 to 60 minutes, 2 interviews lasted for more than an hour, and 2 were very short due to the patient's fatigue.

The introductory question was "How do you feel today?" This was followed by questions about (1) the patient's ranking of important needs for the moment, (2) things in particular that the patient wanted help with at the moment, and

(3) things in particular that the patient wanted to speak about at the moment. The patient was asked to try to rank the different needs by the degree of concern. The answers were categorized according to physical, psychologic, social, and spiritual needs.

Statistical Analysis

For statistical trend tests, the Fisher exact test and permutation trend tests were used.[7] All results given refer to $P < .05$ unless otherwise stated.

Results

Most patients (61%) wanted to spend their last days in their own home, whereas the rest preferred to stay at an institution where "one would receive the best help." The most common symptoms before admission were pain, lack of appetite, anxiety, sleeplessness, fatigue, vomiting, cough, and shortness of breath (Table 1). At admission, more than 50% of the patients were not quite sure of their diagnosis; of the transition from curative to palliative care, 30% were completely sure, and 20% were completely unsure. The figures were very similar among the relatives. This was mostly due to incomplete former information, not to language or communication problems.

Before admission, 11% of the patients needed practical help with most daily services, but 20% had not been in need of any help at all. The helpers were next of kin (63%), a close friend (10%), and different people (11%). Most patients considered the help to be pretty good or good, but 5 of the patients were less satisfied. More than 50% of the patients considered it pleasant to receive professional care. A few patients felt it as a relief not being a burden to their family; 4 felt resigned or depressed.

Most interviews were experienced as less strenuous. All of the patients reported some type of need. If only 1 kind of need was reported, this was rated as a primary one. More patients ranked the physical needs as primary compared with the psychologic needs, which in turn were more important than the social needs (Table 2). Spiritual needs were only mentioned by 1 person. In the first interview, 14 patients ranked their physical needs as primary, 6 as secondary, and 2 as tertiary. Ten patients ranked their psychological needs as primary, 8 ranked them as secondary, and 1 as tertiary. Social needs were ranked as primary by 6 patients; just as many patients ranked them as secondary as well as tertiary. The rankings were equal in interviews II and III.

In the continued interviews, which comprised a reduced number of patients, the ranking changed in favor of the nonphysical dimensions of need. There was no significant trend related to the kind of need; they varied extensively from 1 interview to another. Correlation analysis on primary needs and symptoms/troubles resulted in no significant outcomes apart from nausea, which was related to physical need ($P < .025$). No significant correlations were found

Table 1 Reported/Registered Symptoms and Problems at the First Interview with 30 Patients

Symptom	Patients, n	Little	Some	Much	Missing Data
Pain	12	3	7	8	0
Shortness of breath	21	1	3	5	0
Cough	23	2	1	4	0
Vomiting	9	7	4	11	0
Loss of appetite	4	5	12	8	1
Diarrhea	20	4	4	2	0
Obstipation	15	3	7	5	0
Incontinence, fecal	25	2	3	—	0
Incontinence, urinary	21	—	2	4	3
Fever	27	—	2	1	0
Bleeding	28	1	1	—	0
Pressure sores	30	—	—	—	0
Bad smells	29	1	—	—	0
Lack of energy	16	2	4	8	0
Depression	21	6	3	—	0
Nervousness	10	10	8	2	0
Sleeplessness	17	7	3	3	0
Confined to bed	12	9	6	3	0
Caring need	4	15	7	4	0
Comatose	29	1	—	—	0
Other[a]	20	3	2	5	0

[a]unsteadiness, 5 patients; infection, cramps, swollen legs, personality change, 1 patient.

between the remaining primary needs (psychologic, social, and spiritual) and symptoms or troubles.

Physical Needs

Many of the physical needs ranked as primary were related to pain. Quotes from different patients reveal a fear of pain, which for many patients seemed to be equal to the experience of pain itself. Other types of needs of a physical character ranked as primary were often related to severe nausea or feebleness. Shortness of breath and a feeling of choking resulted in agony of death. Cough, phlegm, and oral hygiene problems were a recurrent source of irritation for some patients. The lack of opportunities for taking care of personal hygiene made some of the men and women feel in physical decay. Others complained about being cold, that they didn't get any better, or that they wanted to get well and be discharged. A few of the patients had more unusual requests of a physical character.

Table 2 Reported Primary, Secondary, and Tertiary[a] Needs of Patients at the Geriatric Palliative Ward

Interview	Respondents	Physical Needs	Psychologic Needs	Social Needs	Spiritual Needs
I	30	14-6-2	10-8-1	6-6-6	0-0-0
II	20	10-6-3	6-5-1	4-3-2	0-0-0
III	10	6-0-0	3-2-1	1-2-1	0-0-0
IV	4	2-0-1	1-2-0	1-1-0	0-0-0
V	2	2-0-0	0-1-0	0-0-0	0-0-0
VI	2	1-1-0	0-0-0	0-1-0	1-0-0
VII	1	0-0-0	1-0-0	0-1-0	0-0-0
VIII	1	0-1-0	1-0-0	0-0-1	0-0-0

[a]The combinations of figures refer to the number of patients reporting primary, secondary, and tertiary types of needs, respectively.

The physical needs of a secondary nature (ie, the second most important need) were often similar to the primary ones, which may or may not have been attended to.

Tertiary physical needs mainly concerned the feeling of feebleness. A few patients emphasized the importance of appearance and getting good food.

"I suffer from such perspirations, sometimes I'm soaking wet. To remain without any pain the rest of my days! Shortness of breath and pain make me scared. Spare me this feebleness, feels awful, may as well finish the old man."

"Don't want to be so tired [falls asleep several times during the conversation], that's the only thing!"

"I want to feel cleaner, don't even have the strength to care for my personal hygiene! My only wish is that I get to lie comfortably, but now I have been given a comfortable mattress."

"There is a draft from the fan. I get cold easily, at the same time I perspire a lot. I suffer a lot from it. The nausea is troublesome, but it comes and goes. I want my hair to grow back. The scalp is itchy from the wig and it is so hot. Some people say that the hair may turn blond and curly when it grows out, we'll have to wait and see [laughs]."

Psychologic Needs

Anxiety, uncertainty, and security were explicit and frequent primary psychologic needs among many of the patients. A feeling of longing was often directed towards their home environment, belongings, and "the ordinary" and "freedom." But at the same time, staying at home was associated with anxiety and worry. The wish for taking 1 day at a time and not having to contemplate the future occurred quite frequently.

There was a need for seclusion to get some peace and quiet, maybe to have the opportunity to see relatives, and to be freer to express emotions and reactions to the situation.

A common wish was to think back on their lives, maybe to recapitulate. Some of the patients pointed to psychosocial needs, for example, to restore broken relationships and becoming reconciled before it was too late.

Physical and psychologic fatigue often went hand-in-hand, and they often seemed to have a reciprocal effect. The power of initiative sometimes fell short, but if conquered, there was a feeling of great victory. For example, a patient who had been lying in a draft found the greatest triumph (primary need) when he succeeded at closing the vent. "I knew I could make it. One should never give up!" Worries could also be directed towards variations in psychologic functions such as memory and cognitive functioning.

The psychologic needs to find a meaning in life, feel security, or have opportunities to go out were ranked as second most important (secondary). So were also worries about the future for the spouse and other relatives. Pleasurable needs could include the opportunity to have a good meal. Moreover, there were also expressed needs for contemplating, thinking over their life and to summing up things, and finally, to having their life substantiated by telling others of what their life had been like.

Quite a few psychologic needs were given a tertiary ranking, for example, a mixed anxiety and expectation when awaiting a move to a nursing home or feeling the need to keep their private room.

"What is it going to be like? Where will I end up? What if I didn't have to worry about what the future is going to look like. Want to avoid the anxiety of feeling nauseous and vomiting all the time, don't dare to go anywhere, not even to the hairdresser."

"Want to avoid thinking ahead, just want to relax, take it easy, one day at a time."

"There is no point in wishing to see what the future holds; how my grandchildren will do in life or what is going to happen to the world. No use in worrying; better to live in the present and to take one day at a time."

"I only want to be left in peace."

"I lack the strength to both think and do things now. It's a shame."

"If only I didn't have to wait for answers about everything and being worried about people at home!"

Social Needs

The primary needs of a social nature were often associated with visits from family and close friends, reunions, and practical and economical tasks when moving back home or to a nursing home.

Social needs of a secondary nature often included, as did the primary ones, contact with or care for the family. For a few of the patients, that meant reunion or reconciliation. Practical tasks related to finances or accounting also came up as well as being given some privacy.

Social needs, which had been ranked as tertiary, were also similar to primary and secondary wishes; that is, they comprised troubles about family and finances, the longing for their relatives and privacy, but also retrieving parts of their former way of life.

"Mostly I wish to come home to friends and family. I do have to think about my wife, to help each other and to be together!"

". . . to see my brother, never told you that I have a brother, did I? I regret not staying in contact with him during all these years. But I do hear from my son now. It made me happy and moved me. But is it too late now?"

"I need to have someone to talk to about anything but illness all the time!"

"I want the caravan to be ready, cleaned and connected to the car. I need to sort my finances. I don't have a will, do I?"

"Mostly, I'm worried about the boy; what's going to happen when I'm gone. How will he do in school?"

"Want to be able to handle my bills and finances."

Spirituality

One person had a primary need of a spiritual nature. However, spiritual needs of secondary and tertiary rank did not occur.

"I've started to ponder. Ask myself if I'm religious. I've never thought about those things before, but I do now."

Discussion

During the 4 months of observation, the initial (at admission) general state seemed to be dominated by a rather extensive need for care, bad physical condition with nausea, emaciation, pain, anxiety, and feebleness. The palliative care, however, appeared to have had a rapid and intended effect on the physical troubles. Because the observations were made only at the ward, the state and needs of the patients were recorded most thoroughly during the first period after admission. A small portion of the patients could be interviewed for a longer period, a few of them until their deaths.

To have the opportunity to speak about one's fear of being in pain and to have it confirmed that pain relief could be guaranteed seemed to dominate the physical picture of need and was just as prominent as the need of pain relief itself. These findings may suggest that adequate pain relief was accomplished but that the memory of the pain itself was very dominating and strong. Perhaps it points to a need for assurance of relief of recurrent pain. However, the frequent wishes of reduced nausea and increased energy were more difficult to fulfil because of type and course of illness.

Successful pain relief and other types of palliative care may be behind the fact that a great number of psychologic needs were reported. The relief of physical needs may have facilitated the expression of needs of security when being cared for in the hospital. One patient did even admit of pleasurable aspects of life, for example, to allow oneself to long for something or somebody, or maybe to have that feeling of longing fulfilled. It could mean having satisfied the need to come back home to well-known things or being offered a good meal. Many of those who had been uneasy at the time of admission later seemed to have improved their abilities to better specify needs and wishes of psychologic nature, particularly if symptoms of the disease did not stand in the way.

Social needs bore a clear socioeconomic touch. Many patients wished to be with their life partner or children, as well as to look over and secure their future lives. To make sure there were enough pension benefits and savings for continuous care also seemed be important. Moreover, patients expressed a longing for having things taken care of. Issues that had been ignored for a lifetime were now of highest priority, maybe because the patient suspected that not much time was left.

Very few of the patients were interviewed when they were in the very final stage of their lives. Maybe that was one of the reasons why only 1 patient expressed a wish to talk about existential issues and their relation to divine powers (spiritual-existential needs). Great psychologic torment, remorse over the past, and a wish for forgiveness or understanding from significant individuals was also expressed.

Interpreting and describing a strict mapping or preference of needs in the terminal stage of life is risky, however. Depending on the state of illness, identifying and reporting needs can be difficult. Boundaries between categories of needs can become blurry, and the intensity of wishes can be hard to perceive. There may be rapid and wide variations in needs, and individual and unstable preference on wishes can vary under different circumstances.

Conclusion

Despite the limitations of the study, considering the small number of patients, certain tendencies could be noticed in the outcome. Physical pain overshadows everything, at least in the very last stage of life. Furthermore, pain seems to hinder the recognition of other psychologic, social, and spiritual needs. Merely the fear of physical pain, originating from prior experiences of pain, may be the most common feeling to be relieved from. Other important needs appear when pain and other health problems, for example, vomiting and shortness of breath, no longer generate fear of death. The feeling of security mediated by the presence of loved ones, as well as worries about their future, seems to occupy a severely ill person's mind even during the last days of his or her life.

The study was small, and the results may not be accurate for all types of palliative units; however, it did seem to confirm former, unrecorded observations of the priorities of needs among our patients. We intend to repeat the study including a larger number of patients to further investigate end-of life needs.

Notes

1. Hallberg, RI. Death and dying from old people's point of view. A literature review. *Aging Clin Exp Res.* 2004;16:87–103.
2. Lo RS, Woo J, Zhoc KC, et al. Quality of life of palliative care patients in the last two weeks of life. *J Pain Symp Man.* 2002;24:388–397.
3. Kelly B, Burnett P, Pelusi D, Badger S, Varghese F, Robertson M. Terminally ill patients' wish to hasten death. *Palliat Med.* 2002;16:339–345.
4. Singer PA, Martin DK, Kelner M. Quality end-of-life care: patients' perspectives. *JAMA.* 1999;281:163–168.

5. Ottosson JO. *The Patient-Doctor Relationship* [Swedish]. Stockholm, Sweden: *Natur och Kultur.* 1999:282–308.
6. Thomé B. *Living with Cancer in Old Age: Quality of Life and Meaning.* Thesis. Lund University, Faculty of Medicine; 2003.
7. Cox DR, Hinkley DV. *Theoretical Statistics.* London: Chapman & Hall; 1974.

Critical Thinking

1. Just what is palliative care all about? How might this holistic approach to relating to the elderly (or anyone else) be beneficial to the patient?

2. What are the four needs of geriatric patients as discussed in the article? How does palliative care attempt to satisfy these needs?

3. What are some limitations of this study (how it might have been improved)?

From the Institute of Health and Care Sciences, Sahlgrenska Academy, University of Gothenburg and Sahlgrenska University Hospital (HW) and Department of Geriatric Medicine (AG), Sahlgrenska University Hospital, Gothenburg, Sweden.

Address correspondence to: Helle Wijk, Sahlgrenska University Hospital, Röda stråket 8, 413 45 Göteborg, Sweden; e-mail: helle.wijk@vgregion.se.

Acknowledgments—This study was facilitated by grants from the Coordinating Board of Swedish Research Councils, the Swedish Medical Research Council, Medical and Social Services Administrations, the Helge Axson Johnson Foundation, and the Hjalmar Svensson Foundation. Thanks are due to Valter Sundh, BSc, for statistical discussions and invaluable help with the data processing.

End-of-Life Concerns and Care Preferences: Congruence Among Terminally Ill Elders and their Family Caregivers

DANIEL S. GARDNER, PhD AND BETTY J. KRAMER, PhD

Introduction

In the past several decades, it has become clear that there are substantial disparities between the way older Americans wish to die and the way their last days are realized. This discrepancy is due, in part, to well-documented gaps in the quality of care that people receive at the end of life (Field & Cassel, 1997; SUPPORT, 1995). Although most people prefer to die in their own homes (Higginson & Sen-Gupta, 2000; Tang & McCorkle, 2003; Thomas, Morris, & Clark, 2004), a majority of deaths occur in hospitals or nursing homes (Gallo, Baker, & Bradley, 2001; Pritchard, Fisher, Teno, Sharp, Reding, Knaus, et al., 1998). And despite considerable advances in medical and supportive approaches to pain management, a significant number of older adults with advanced and terminal illness experience serious pain and discomfort (SUPPORT, 1995; Teno, Clarridge, Casey, Welch, Wetle, Shield, et al., 2004). In an effort to better understand the needs and enhance the care of dying individuals and their families, end-of-life researchers have explored these and other disparities between end-of-life preferences and outcomes.

Barriers to quality end-of-life care include the unpredictable nature of terminal illness, communication difficulties in familial and social relationships, and the complex care needs of dying patients and their families (Kramer & Auer, 2005). Quality care is also hindered by systemic-level factors, including the emphasis on curative and life-sustaining intervention over quality of life and supportive care, health care financing and service delivery structures that move patients between multiple care settings with minimal coordination and poor continuity of care, a lack of providers trained in the fundamentals of palliative care (e.g., biopsycho-social-spiritual aspects of grief and loss, effective clinical communication, attention to family systems), and the absence of evidence-based practice knowledge in this area (Emanuel, von Gunten, & Ferris, 2000; Field & Cassel, 1997; Morrison, 2005). Further, end-of-life care models that represent the standard of care—hospice and palliative care—are underutilized and often inaccessible to the poor, racial and ethnic minorities, and elders with uncertain disease pathways.

Less is known about the subjective end-of-life experiences, concerns, and preferences of older patients and their family members (Cohen & Leis, 2002; Singer, Martin & Kellner, 1999; Vig, Davenport, & Pearlman, 2002). Recently there have been calls for research to better understand factors that affect patients' and families' perceptions of quality of life and quality of care at the end of life (Field & Cassel, 1997; Kramer, Christ, Bern-Klug, & Francoeur, 2005; NIH, 2004; SUPPORT, 1995). This study explores the challenges, concerns, and preferences of low-income elders receiving palliative care, and focuses on congruence and incongruence between the elders and their primary family caregivers.

Quality of Life and Care at the End of Life

The Institute of Medicine defined a "good death" as one with minimal suffering, which satisfies the wishes of dying patients and their families, while adhering to current medical, cultural and ethical standards (Field & Cassel, 1997). Researchers often operationalize a good death as the degree to which an individual's dying experiences correspond with their preferences for quality of life and quality of care at the end of life (Engelberg, Patrick, & Curtis, 2005). A growing literature has sought to shed light on the aspects of care that are most important to terminally ill elders and their family members (Heyland, Dodek, Rocker, Groll, Gafhi, Pichora, et al., 2006; Laakkonen, Pitkala, & Strandberg, 2004).

When faced with advanced life-threatening illness, most people wish to be free of pain and symptoms (Heyland et al., 2006; Vig & Pearlman, 2004), to be treated with dignity and respect (Chochinov, Hack, Hassard, Kristjianson, McClement,

& Harlos, 2002; Steinhauser, Christakis, Clipp, McNeilly, McIntyre, & Tulsky, 2000), and to maintain a sense of autonomy and control over their last days (Singer et al., 1999; McSkirmning, Hodges, Super, Driever, Schoessler, Franey, et al., 1999; Vig & Pearlman, 2004). Nearly all prefer to be informed of their prognoses and have time to put their affairs in order (Heyland et al., 2006; McCormick & Conley, 1995; Terry, Olson, Wilss, & Boulton-Lewis, 2006). Dying elders hope to avoid becoming burdens to their families (McPherson, Wilson, & Murray, 2007; Vig & Pearlman, 2004) and typically eschew the use of artificial means to prolong life (Heyland et al., 2006; Singer, et al., 1999; see Steinhauser et al., 2000 for divergent findings). There is, however, a great deal of heterogeneity in what constitutes a "good death." Ultimately, end-of-life preferences are individual, dynamic and multidimensional, and vary across contexts such as age, gender, disease course, care setting, financial resources, and social and familial relationships (Thomas et al., 2004).

Congruence in Patient and Family Perspectives

During the course of advanced and terminal illness, elders increasingly rely on family members to identify and communicate their emotional and physical needs and concerns (McPherson, Wilson, Lobchuk, & Brajtman, 2008; Waldrop, Kramer, Skretny, Milch, & Finn, 2005). Much of the research on patients' end-of-life care preferences is also based on the report of family surrogates or healthcare proxies (Teno et al., 2004). However, the accuracy of family members' assessments of dying patients' concerns and preferences is uncertain. Studies have documented significant incongruence between patients and family members on their evaluations of quality of life (Farber, Egnew, Herman-Bertch, Taylor, & Guldin, 2003; McPherson & Addington-Hall, 2003), frequency and severity of pain and other physical and psychological symptoms (McPherson et al., 2008; Mularski, Curtis, Osborne, Engelberg, & Ganzini, 2004; Sneeuw, Sprangers, & Aaronson, 2002), and end-of-life preferences (Engelberg et al., 2005; Moorman & Carr, 2008; Shalowitz, Garrett-Myer, & Wendler, 2006; Steinhauser et al., 2000). Farber and colleagues (2003) describe these differences as reflecting the often highly divergent "cultural perspectives" of patients and their formal and informal caregivers around death and dying.

Although findings have been inconsistent, congruence in the end-of-life preferences and perceptions of elders and their family caregivers has been found to range from moderate to poor. There is some evidence of greater agreement around objective and measurable factors such as patient functioning and mobility, and less regarding subjective factors such as pain and depression (Desbiens & Mueller-Rizner, 2000; Engelberg et al., 2005; McPherson & Addington-Hall, 2003; Tang & McCorkle, 2003). Congruence may be more likely when surrogate decision-makers are younger and female (McPherson & Addington-Hall, 2003; Zettel-Watson, Ditto, Danks, & Smucker, 2008), family income is higher (Desbiens & Mueller-Rizner, 2000), the illness is of longer duration, or the patient is closer to death (Sneeuw et al., 2002). Notably, there is evidence that families who have

had explicit discussions about dying and the patient's wishes are more likely to agree with each other about end-of-life care preferences (Engelberg et al., 2005; Sulmasy, Terry, Weisman, Miller, Stallings, Vettese et al., 1998).

Despite gaps in our understanding of the correspondence between individual and family experiences of dying and preferences for end-of-life, very few studies have focused on congruence among paired patient-family caregiver dyads (Engelberg et al., 2005). And there remains a critical lack of knowledge about the shared and distinct challenges, concerns, and preferences of older adults and their family caregivers at the end of life (Vig et al., 2002). Empirical inquiry in this area may help to enhance familial understanding of older patients' concerns and the accuracy of surrogate decision-making, and to ultimately improve the quality of life at the end of life. The study described here uses qualitative methods to delve more deeply into the subjective experiences of terminally ill elders and their family caregivers, describe their end-of-life preferences and identify areas of congruence and incongruence.

Methods
Study Design

These data were collected as part of a larger longitudinal research study exploring the process and experience of end-of-life care provided to frail elders with advanced chronic disease enrolled in an innovative, fully "integrated" managed care program (Kramer & Auer, 2005). The design was an embedded case study (Scholz & Tietje, 2002), involving in-depth data collection with multiple sources of data. Case study research design makes it possible to examine processes, perceptions and outcomes regarding naturalistic phenomena of which the researcher seeks multiple perspectives (Yin, 2003). The results reported here address the congruent and incongruent end-of-life perceptions, challenges, concerns, and care preferences of elders and their primary family caregivers.

Research Site and Sample

Elder Care of Dane County, a not-for-profit organization, has provided community-based health and social services for older adults since 1976. The Elder Care Partnership (ECP) program, the largest program offered by this organization, provides comprehensive, fully integrated health, psychosocial, and long-term care to low-income frail elders. The program integrates practices that are consistent with clinical practice guidelines for quality palliative care (National Consensus Project, 2004). Detailed descriptions of the study and site can be found elsewhere (Kramer & Auer, 2005).

Study participants were purposively selected by interdisciplinary team members from the pool of elders (aged 65 years or older) enrolled in ECP. Enrollees had annual incomes below $10,000, seven to eight chronic medical conditions, and functional limitations in three or more Activities of Daily Living. Team members were asked to identify elders who were likely to die within 6 months, spoke English, were cognitively able to understand and respond to interview questions, and had a family member involved in their care. Once the elder completed consent procedures and agreed to participate, team members invited the identified primary family caregiver to participate in an interview with the Principal Investigator (PI; second author).

Data Collection

In-depth, semi-structured, face-to-face interviews, which ranged from 1 to 2 hours long, were conducted by the project PI, a university professor and Project on Death in America Social Work Leader. Elders and their identified family care-givers were interviewed separately at a time and place selected by the participant, most often in the participant's home. The interviews were not standardized in order to facilitate greater exploration of issues deemed most important to respondents (Padgett, 2008). Instead, each interview was structured around open-ended questions reflecting the study aims, including questions designed to explore the perceived challenges and concerns of the participants, their end-of-life preferences, and the extent to which they had discussed these issues with family members:

- What has been most difficult or challenging to you and your family members at this time?
- What are your [your family member's] concerns or worries?
- What is most important to you about the care you [your family member] receive[s] in your [their] last days?
- If you could plan it perfectly, what kind of death would you hope for [for the patient]? What would make a "good" death?

Additional questions and probes were used to explore participant preferences about the location of death, the desire for family members to be present, and the importance of family communication and saying "goodbye" during the elder's last days. In addition, the interviewer asked about the extent to which they had talked about the elders' end-of-life preferences, and their comfort or difficulty in doing so.

Data Analysis

All of the interviews were recorded on audiotape and transcribed verbatim, with participant consent. The researchers employed qualitative methods that entailed detailed readings and re-readings of each transcript, team coding, and thematic and conceptual analysis. Data analysis followed a form of *template analysis* (Crabtree & Miller, 1999) that begins with an a priori set of coding categories (i.e., a "template") based on the researchers' domains of interest (end-of-life challenges and worries or fears, care concerns, preferences, and family communication). Two researchers independently read the transcripts, identified segments that were relevant to the research domains, and used the preliminary coding template to search for and identify patterns and themes in the data. These themes were then tested within and across cases, and refined in order to generate broader and more integrated conceptual domains. Upon reaching theoretical saturation, a thematic conceptual matrix (Patton, 2002) was developed to examine the congruent (i.e., like) and incongruent (distinct) themes relevant to the domains of elder and family caregiver end-of-life challenges, concerns, and care preferences.

While no tests were conducted of inter-rater reliability, the research team employed several strategies to ensure analytic rigor. The protocol included: extended engagement, or the use of long interviews with extensive probing and clarification; independent team coding and peer debriefing; deviant case analysis in the development and testing of a final thematic schema; and careful auditing that involved documentation (including verbatim transcripts, field notes, and analytic memos) of the data collection and analytic process (Padgett, 2008).

Findings
Study Participants

Ten elders (five women and five men) and ten family caregivers (six women and four men) completed face-to-face interviews (see *Table 1*). The mean age of the elders was 85 years-old (range: 64-101), and family members were a mean 53 years-old

Table 1 Elder and Family Caregiver Dyads

Elder	Family Caregiver
97-year-old African-American female with heart disease	47-year-old African-American grandson; single, live-in caregiver
86-year-old white female with lung disease	50-year-old white daughter; lives separately
89-year-old white male with heart disease	56-year-old white son; married, lives separately
82-year-old white female with lung cancer	52-year-old white daughter; single, lives separately
101-year-old white female with heart disease	67-year-old white son; single, live-in caregiver
84-year-old white male with heart disease	47-year-old white daughter; divorced, lives separately (in same town)
80-year-old white male with heart disease and accident-related injuries	48-year-old white daughter-in-law (married to step-son); lives separately
86-year-old white male with prostate cancer	56-year-old daughter; single, live-in caregiver
82-year-old white female with lung disease and accident-related injuries	48-year-old white son; married, lives with elder
64-year-old white male with lung disease	55-year-old white wife; live-in

Table 2 Congruence & Incongruence among Elders & Family Caregivers

Domain	Themes	Incongruent		Congruent
		Elder	**Family**	**Both**
Challenges	Experiencing decline			X
	Accepting dependence	X		
	Providing adequate care		X	
	Living with uncertainty			X
Worries	Pain & suffering			X
	Meeting elders' care needs		X	
	Becoming a burden	X		
	Anticipating the impact on survivors			X
Concerns about EOL Care	Receiving competent, consistent & responsive care			X
	Managing pain			X
	Being treated with dignity and respect			X
	Living while dying			X
A "Good Death"	Dying at home			X
	Dying quickly, without suffering			X
	Avoiding life support			X
	Being prepared	X		
	Addressing spiritual needs addressed		X	

(range: 47-67). Family caregivers included four daughters, three sons, one daughter-in-law, one grandson, and one wife. Nine of the dyads were non-Hispanic white, and one was African American. Elders were enrolled in the program an average of 2.6 years (range: 1.5-4), and all had multiple chronic health conditions. The most debilitating diagnoses included serious heart disease ($n = 5$), lung disease ($n = 3$), and cancer ($n = 2$). Five of the elders lived alone and five lived with their family caregivers (four with an adult child and one with a spouse).

Domains of Care

Four domains of end-of-life care framed the results of our analysis: a) the *challenges* or day-to-day difficulties related to the patient's terminal illness; b) participants' *worries* or fears about the patient's death and dying; c) *care concerns* regarding the patient's end-of-life care by formal and informal caregivers; and d) participants' hopes and preferences for a *good death*. These domains reflect a range of end-of-life concerns and preferences that were expressed and elaborated on by study participants, some of which are shared or congruent, and others which are distinct to either elders or their family members (see *Table 2*).

Challenges

Elders and their family caregivers identified four primary illness-related challenges they struggled with on a daily basis.

Experiencing Physical and Functional Decline

Elders spoke articulately about their efforts to participate in normal daily activities in the face of decreased energy and declining physical and functional capacities, as is illustrated here:

> I like to walk. I can't get out and walk. I have to have a walker so sometimes the kids take me in a wheelchair and we can walk around the campgrounds, or we'll go down by the lake. I'd like to be able to walk, too. But I can't do it. I can't go up and down the stairs so I have to stay here and let somebody else go down and do my laundry. I haven't been down the stairs in the basement for two years. (83 year-old female elder)
>
> I can't do the things I want to do, like mow the lawn or walk down the block. It's hard to breathe . . . Yeah, feels like you're ready to die—takes your breath right away from you. (64-year-old male elder)

Family caregivers also struggled with the changes in their loved ones' functioning, often within the context of lifelong relationships:

> It's just that I can't be with him like I'd like to be . . . we've been married almost 37 years so it's a long time, and, just to see him going downhill like he is. (55-year-old wife)

Accepting Increasing Dependence

Closely associated with physical and functional decline, many elders struggled to contend with the diminished autonomy and increasing dependence on others:

> I miss driving . . . I have to depend on other people and I was always so independent. It bothers me when I have

to ask people to haul me around and pick me up, but they don't care, they don't say anything, but I—that's one thing that bugs me but I can't change it so I'll just go on the way it is. (80-year-old male elder)

Some family caregivers were aware that decreased autonomy could be challenging for the elders, but rather than viewing dependence as a challenge they emphasized the benefits of relying on others:

He was able to take his own baths and do everything and then wham-o, here he is. He's in bed all the time and somebody has to help him bathe or whatever . . . although I tell him it's *teamwork,* that we're doing this as a team. (56-year-old daughter)

Providing Adequate Care

Family caregivers spoke at length about caring for the elders, often emphasizing the challenges and responsibilities inherent in the role of family caregiver.

Basically, I'm her number one health advocate. I've had to deal with these situations where people didn't want [her] to go to the hospital and I knew she had to, or just on and on with different things that have happened. So, I just kind of focus on her. (48-year-old son)

The challenge of providing care was often experienced as stressful by family members, given the elder's changing medical needs and the complex nature of family history and relationships:

Part of my life is on hold right now because I'm staying here to take care of her. . . . I'm married and I have a wife and we want to enjoy our life together, so as painful as it is to see your parent leave your life, it's also going to be a big transition when I finally get on with my life . . . it's really a dichotomy because you feel selfish when you think about yourself and your own situation and what your preferences are and what you'd do if you were just living in your own house with your own family versus taking care of a parent. So, it's pretty hard. (48-year-old son)

Living with Uncertainty

Both elders and family caregivers talked about the difficulties they had in coping with their uncertain futures. Although all participants were aware that the elders had limited prognoses, many struggled with not knowing how and when their terminal decline would occur:

About death? I've had pains and stuff, you know, and I had to go to the hospital and all that. I don't know if I'm gonna come home again or not. You don't know that—if you're that bad—and these blood clots can move. They can hit you just like that and you're gone. (64-year-old male elder)

For me, it's never knowing when he's going into an attack, and if I'm at work . . . I told them at work—I said there'll be days when I can't come in because he isn't

good, or I'll have to leave because something's gone wrong. (55-year-old wife)

Worries or Fears about Dying

Elders and family caregivers were encouraged to talk about their concerns, worries, and fears related to dying. In response to direct questions, most of the elders initially denied any fears of death or dying. As the interviews progressed, however, elders and family caregivers raised a variety of concerns about the future. Four areas of concern or worry were expressed by a majority of the participants.

Pain and Suffering

The principal concern shared by elders and family caregivers was that the elder would experience unmanageable pain or physical discomfort as they were dying.

I'm concerned about pain and cancer, I never had anyone in my family that's had cancer, my ideas of it are strictly from novels or movies, so they give you enough pain medication to control the pain then you're going to be nauseated and sleepy and even [lose] your mind, hallucinating even, so that's not something I look forward to. (82-year-old female elder)

I guess I'm . . . afraid of the pain, if she might have a lot of pain. I don't know, it really is kind of terrifying. I don't know what it's going to be like when the, if the cancer really hits. The best thing would be if she would die from some secondary, related, symptomatic illness like pneumonia or something. (52-year-old daughter)

Meeting Elders' Increasing Needs

Family caregivers were particularly worried about their capacity to respond to the intensifying needs of the elders, and that they might lack the necessary supports and resources to continue providing care at home. Several participants feared having to place elders in long-term care institutions in the future:

I suppose my biggest concern . . . is that he will regress and have a physical deterioration that will make it virtually impossible for him to be able to continue in that apartment, making a full time placement in a nursing home type facility necessary. That's going to be hard in a lot of ways. There's the physical move and taking care of all the stuff that will need to be moved over there, and then there's just the emotional aspect for [Elder] in terms of being in a place where he just damn well doesn't want to be. (48-year-old daughter-in-law)

A related concern was that the elder might not be aware of—or might hide—signs of his or her decline.

I think probably one of my biggest concerns with my mother is whether or not she'll be totally honest and recognize when something is really wrong. And so that, that's got me some concern to the point when she did fall the last time and she was in the nursing home . . . she had fallen a couple of times earlier in the week and hadn't told anybody that she had been dizzy and that she had fallen and if she, if she had told anybody either her home nurse or us, that that was going on, then we would have intervened, so it raised questions about whether or not she could be on her own or not. (50-year-old daughter)

Family caregivers often feared a sudden decline in the elder's health, and, in particular, "something happening with no one around." Several family members expressed anxiety and guilt about going to work or returning to their own homes, and leaving the elder in the care of others.

Well, I worry every single day about her falling down and stuff like that, and what's going to be the next trigger that sends her back to the hospital for the next surgery that she can barely tolerate or not at all—that whole thing (48-year-old son)

Becoming a Burden

A major concern of most of the elders was the fear of experiencing a long trajectory of decline, and becoming a burden on their families:

Well, I'd like to go fast. I don't want to suffer a lot and make everybody else suffer a lot. That would be important. My husband had Alzheimer's and that was just pathetic, watching him for ten years go downhill . . . most families now-a-days are half crazy with trying to make a living . . . they have to spend so much time with the woman working and the man working, and then to add the care of an elderly patient is just too much for them, it overburdens them so that they, the parent or the aunt or grandmother, whoever it is, begins to feel well I don't want to bother my children with this, I'll just let it go which is what I do to some extent. (82-year-old female elder)

Family caregivers did not share the concern that their elders were becoming burdens; most did not question their responsibility to provide care and support for the elders.

Anticipating Survivors' Wellbeing

Many elders worried about the needs and wellbeing of their families after their impending death. They were primarily concerned about family members' grief and ability to cope with the loss:

Just to keep my daughter as calm as possible—that's the main thing. I don't want to upset her any more than I have to. What can you do? Your parents die, that's going to happen, so . . . there is nothing to be done about it but I want to, want her to be as calm as possible. (82-year old female elder)

One elder was also specifically anxious about the spiritual wellbeing of her children and grandchildren after she died:

Well, to know that they're taken care of—their health and they're able to—their religion—stay with that. And then I hear about some of them giving up religion and they're all becoming atheists—it makes me feel kind of blue. I don't like to hear that. (101-year-old female elder)

Some elder participants worried more about practical concerns (e.g., medical bills, taxes, or loss of income) that would affect their loved ones. Many expressed regrets that they would not be around to look out for family members after death.

Well, the thing I'd be concerned about is my wife and the kids, and the house and stuff, you know? All the bills should be paid, or whatever. Well, she'd be living here by herself, you know? And if she was taken care of, or whatever she has to do—I don't think she'd ever get remarried again, but I imagine it'd be tough for her to keep on rolling, keeping the house maybe. The taxes ain't cheap. (64-year-old male elder)

I just hope that the kids will get along fine, and the grandkids, that's it. And hope the world straightens out a little bit better. All this terrorism and stuff, I don't like that but that's way beyond my help. (80-year-old male elder)

Family caregivers echoed these concerns with their own worries about life after the elder's death. Some concerns were about their anticipation of grief and loss, but several caregivers worried about pragmatic matters such as arranging funeral plans and paying bills.

[My fears are] stupid. [Laughs]. My worries are about her funeral, okay? That it will come at a really bad time, like when I'm in the middle of three hundred and forty report cards and my house is a mess, you know, and that kind of stuff that, that I won't know what to do. That there will be a division, and fighting like over the paintings and things like that [Laughs]. I want her to write people's names on the backs of the paintings so I won't have to deal with it. (50-year-old daughter)

Concerns about End-of-Life Care

In addition to their worries about dying, elders and family caregivers articulated their concerns and care preferences regarding the care the elders would receive from healthcare team members in their last days. Specifically, they reported four major preferences.

Receiving Competent, Consistent and Responsive Care

Elders and family caregivers felt that quality care required the involvement of skilled healthcare professionals who were competent, "consistent and responsive" to the elders' needs. For elders, it was of critical importance to feel they could depend on reliable caregivers that met their basic needs:

Well [hospice] volunteers means that no one person would come every week, instead you would probable get a stream of people coming in, none of whom you knew and I don't like that idea at all . . . . Just that whoever takes care of me shows me respect . . . taking good care of me. You know, keeping me clean and fed and whatever. If I can't eat—well that's another thing but . . . I just think to take good care of me, see that my needs were taken care of. (82-year-old female elder)

For family members, these concerns seemed to be associated with their anxieties about meeting the elders' escalating needs as death approached (see above). Their descriptions of adequate care often emphasized the medical and concrete aspects of care (e.g., keeping the elder safe and clean, and ensuring their adherence to medication regimens):

I think hygiene is way up on the scale as for as her, granny's is. Her body is so fragile and her skin is so, you know, tender, so I mean for them making sure she's gets the proper hygiene. And medical, um, well granny won't take a lot of medical, but I mean, but they're there for any medical needs. But, I think, just trying to make her comfortable as possible. (48-year-old grandson)

Managing Pain

Elders and family caregivers were concerned that the elders receive good pain control and prompt alleviation of physical discomfort at the end of their lives. For several participants, this was a primary reason for choosing hospice or palliative care services:

Well that, the hospitals, they never used to give you enough painkiller to make enough difference because they said you were going to become addicted. Well what difference does it make at that point? And so I would want someone managing that and I . . . I think I would want to go to hospice and let them handle it. (86-year-old female elder)

I happen to be a big proponent of hospice-type transitions from life to death. And, I'm a big believer in you make the person comfortable. At that point, I don't care if he gets hooked on a particular drug. It's irrelevant. But if he could have his needs tended to, the pain alleviated, and the transition as smooth as possible, I'd rather see that—except to go quickly. (48-year-old daughter-in-law)

Being Treated with Dignity and Respect

Elders and family caregivers also agreed that respectful treatment was of paramount concern in end-of-life care. For elders, this meant appreciating their need for autonomy and control, and being cared for in a courteous, compassionate manner. Family members also articulated the importance of having providers who treated the elders with dignity and valued each patient as a unique, "whole person":

Just that, that whole, you know, just having respect and beauty and concern around. . . . But a nursing home staff in all fairness is totally overloaded, I mean so it's not like totally all their fault. It's our system's fault, it's like, we don't value that so much. (50-year-old daughter)

To try to meet the person on their own level. In my mother's case, in other words, to try and find out what is important to that person and take an interest in those things with them. Share with them those things. If someone thinks clipping coupons is important, than the social worker who's coming says look at all these coupons

I found, we can go get such and such at so and so or if the person is a musician and the social worker would come and say well I have a new recording of so and so's orchestra doing such and such. (52-year-old daughter)

Living While Dying

Many of the elders thought it was important to continue living as they had their entire lives. "Focusing on living" instead of dying included eating the foods they loved, participating in activities they enjoyed (e.g., walking, sewing, card-playing, and socializing) with friends and family.

Just comradeship. . . . [Having] people that are around that I will talk with, or will talk with me, and you would miss them if you don't see them at least once a week, or more than that. (84-year-old male elder)

This concern was associated with the desire to be treated with dignity and respect, and to die at home in the context of intimate surroundings, people, and routines! Elders emphasized the critical importance of having a measure of control over their lives and choice in their care during the dying process.

Well, if I could eat—to get some decent food—and they wouldn't cut me off my martinis or beer. That's about all. (80-year-old male elder)

Although not often a primary concern, most family caregivers expressed an understanding of how important it was for the elder to continue "living while dying," and sought to provide them with opportunities to enjoy their cherished activities.

Well, I think she wants to maintain a sense of normalcy, that things are still the way they used to be as much as possible. So even if life is slipping away, she still can enjoy it. She can still feel at home. So little things, like being able to watch her favorite television shows. . . . Being able to get out—she likes to get out and drive around. You know, just anything that would make her feel normal. So eating the types of things that she's enjoyed in the past, being able to go to a movie with us, go for a drive with the relatives. All the types of things like that. (48-year-old son)

A "Good Death"

In response to a being asked to describe a good death, participants expressed their fundamental end-of-life preferences for the elders' final days.

Dying at Home

Almost all participants expressed a preference for the elder to die at home. Dying at home was viewed as a more "natural death," where elders could more easily be surrounded by friends and family, and their final wishes could be best met. Several family caregivers worried that the patient's needs might outstrip the supports and resources necessary to keep the elder at home until death, but preferred that the death take place at home if at all possible.

Dying Quickly, Without Suffering

For elders and family members, the ideal death was seen as one where the elder dies swiftly, "peacefully, and without pain." One patient summed this perspective up memorably:

> Just let me die. Quickly. Fast. And painlessly. . . . Stand out there and have lightening strike me, or anything that would do me in like that! (84-year-old male elder)

Many imagined a "natural" death, spending their last moments comfortably ensconced in a favorite chair or sitting in a garden surrounded by natural beauty. Some hoped they would simply be able to "go to sleep and not wake up":

> Good death would be able to roll out in a wheelchair onto a garden patio and be surrounded by beautiful flowers, you know, I mean that would be all right. Just that . . . having respect and beauty and concern around you. (50-year-old daughter)
>
> He would sit down in his chair and he wouldn't wake up. That would be ideal. (48-year-old daughter-in-law)

Avoiding High-tech Life Support

For most elders, the desire to die naturally meant not having to accept unwanted intervention, and not taking advantage of feeding or breathing "tubes," or other medical technologies meant to prolong their lives.

> Well, I don't want this—I don't want to be resuscitated. If I'm going I want to go, and that's supposed to prevent them from putting me on any machines. I don't want to wake up a lunatic or something, you know, be alive—breathing but not knowing what's going on. I don't want that. . . . I want to go—no life saving treatments for me. It might be a terrible thing to say. . . . It's my life. (80-year-old male elder)

For the most part, family caregivers reported that they respected these concerns and believed it important to follow their elders' preferences, even if they did not share them:

> Um yes, we, we talked, we talked about it and she just basically wants to be at home, not hooked up to any machines um, you know, just to die naturally, you know, just go. She don't want to go to a revival or resuscitory thing, you know, she dies, she just wants to die, you know. (47-year-old grandson)

Being Prepared

The elders expressed a preference to be made aware of their impending death so that they could "get things in order." Many worked to develop a sense of completion in their lives, had arranged their financial and other affairs, and felt to some extent prepared to die. Those who did not feel a sense of completion or closure reported that having time for preparation was quite important to them.

> Well, I wouldn't want to go in my sleep. I'd want to prepare better. I'd want some doctor to say "[Name], you only have two days, three days, six days," whatever and then I can prepare myself better—get things straightened out with the kids, get my will set, and just have a priest with me and that's all. I don't want to die in my sleep. (80-year-old male elder)

Family caregivers were not aware of and did not share the elders' desire to be prepared for death, although some shared regrets that they had not talked enough or spent enough time with elders when they were still "able to do things."

Addressing Spiritual Needs

Many family members hoped their loved ones would achieve "peace of mind" at the end of their lives, and felt this was an important component of a good death. This sense of peace was most often expressed in spiritual or religious terms; several family members hoped that elders would achieve "spiritual closure" through faith and prayer, and wanted them to have access to clergy to talk with about their spiritual concerns.

> I guess it's um, being taken care of spiritually . . . contacting the people at the church. And have somebody come talk to him, and um, give him a peace of mind. (56-year-old son)

Although we asked questions about faith, spirituality, and religion, there was a great deal of variability in the extent to which faith was important to the elders. Most denied that having their spiritual or faith needs addressed were essential to a "good death" in the way they were to family caregivers.

Communication about End-of-Life Care Preferences

As part of our analysis, the researchers examined the ways in which families talked about death and dying, and how family communication influenced the congruence between participants in expressed challenges, concerns, and preferences. When asked about the extent to which they had discussed dying or their care preferences with family members, the majority of elders and family members—six of the ten dyads—indicated they had not done so. Three elders believed the lack of communication was due to their own lack of desire to talk about dying or end-of-life care with family members. Two others reported that it was difficult to talk about these subjects with family, either due to their own or their family members' discomfort.

> It doesn't make me feel uncomfortable but I can't think of anything that I could, that I can add to it that I haven't already thought about. . . . No, I think I'd like to talk to them about that. They don't seem to want to talk about it—'cause it's an unpleasant thing and they don't always go for it—kind of push it back. But I want to talk a little more about this. (82-year-old male elder)

Four families indicated that they had talked about dying and discussed the elders' care preferences. Even though she had talked with her husband, one caregiver indicated that she found these conversations about dying and his care preferences extremely uncomfortable.

Table 3   Communication Patterns and Congruence in End-of-Life Care Preferences

Communication Pattern	Congruence	Incongruence
Communication Constraints	3	3
Open Communication	4	0

In order to examine the relationship, if any, between participants' communication patterns and congruence in end-of-life care preferences, we compared the responses of families who reported communication constraints with those who reported open communication. As illustrated in Table 3, the level of congruence was much higher among families reporting open communication regarding dying and end-of-life care. None of the four families with open communication and half of the six families with communication constraints shared end-of-life concerns or preferences that were not congruent. Examples of the latter include: the 84-year-old male elder who stated a preference to be alone at the time of death, and his 47-year-old daughter who reported he wished to be surrounded by family; the 101-year-old female elder who expressed a strong desire to be kept informed of her evolving health status whose 67-year-old son preferred her not to be informed of these changes; and the 64-year-old male elder who expressed a strong desire to die at home without the use of life-sustaining machines, contrasting his 55-year-old wife's preference for him to die at the hospital, with full access to medical and technological resources.

Discussion

The findings of this study were generally consistent with the empirical literature on congruence between patients and surrogate decision-makers, which suggests that agreement about dying and end-of-life care ranges from poor to moderate (Engelberg et al., 2005; Moorman & Carr, 2008; Mularski et al., 2004). Elder participants acknowledged their need for support and care as their illnesses progressed, but—in contrast to family caregivers—most strongly valued their independence, and wanted to maintain control over their lives and continue to participate in activities they enjoyed. This parallels the finding that family members often underestimate the patient's need for autonomy and control over their own care (Farber et al., 2003; McSkimming et al., 1999; Singer, et al., 1999; Vig & Pearlman, 2004). Elders were greatly concerned about becoming a burden on their families, echoing another well-documented finding, particularly with older patients (McPherson et al., 2007; Vig & Pearlman, 2004).

The lack of apparent spiritual or religious needs on the part of the elders may be due, in part, to the lack of minority elder participants; a wealth of prior research suggests spirituality is of primary importance to African Americans and Latinos at the end of life (Born, Greiner, Sylvia, & Ahluwalia, 2004; Waters, 2001). One African-American elder shared that she spent all of her waking hours in prayer, but she too denied a desire to talk with others about her faith. This may reflect a perception that spiritual needs are felt to be intrinsic, and not as something that requires intervention from others.

Family caregivers felt most challenged by the responsibilities of managing and providing adequate care, and were concerned about their capacity to meet their loved ones' physical and spiritual needs as the illness progressed. The preeminence of these concerns is consistent with the literature (Terry et al., 2006) and reflects the high level of cognitive, emotional, and physical investment made by family caregivers at the end of life (Waldrop et al., 2005). Although other researchers have found strong congruence around the importance of preparation and a sense of completion in determining a good death (Engelberg et al., 2005; Steinhauser et al., 2000), in this study only elder participants identified this as a significant preference. Unlike the elders, family caregivers were concerned about elders' spiritual wellbeing, and felt that achieving "peace of mind" was essential to experiencing a good death.

Despite these differences, elders and family caregivers reported many congruent concerns and preferences. Consistent with the literature on quality of life at the end of life, most elders and family caregivers preferred that the elder die at home (Tang & McCorkle, 2003; Steinhauser et al., 2000), and for death to come swiftly, without pain or suffering (Heyland et al., 2006; Vig & Pearlman, 2004). Experiencing loss related to the elders' physical, functional, and cognitive decline, and managing advanced illness in the face of an uncertain and unpredictable future were among the most difficult challenges reported by the elders and their care-givers. Accepting the inherent uncertainty and ambiguity of the dying process may indeed be one of the more significant challenges for terminally ill patients and their families (Bern-Klug, 2004; Gardner, 2008; McKechnie, Macleod & Keeling, 2007). Elders and family caregivers also shared concerns about the wellbeing of survivors following the patient's eventual death.

There was particularly consistent agreement regarding end-of-life care preferences, specifically around the importance of reliable, high-quality care, and the avoidance of life-sustaining treatment. Another shared concern was that elders be treated with dignity and respect by formal caregivers, and would be allowed to continue living until death, a finding echoed in the literature (Chochinov et al., 2002). A finding not compatible with prior literature was the shared preference of elders and family caregivers to avoid using life-sustaining treatment. Many studies suggest that family members are less likely than older patients to prefer life-support, and that surrogates often underestimate elders' preference for aggressive measures at the end of life (Hamel, Lynn, Teno, Covinsky, Wu, Galanos et al., 2000; Pruchno, Lemay, Field, & Levinsky, 2005). The present finding may be another artifact of a sample that includes few minority elders, who are more likely than white patients to prefer life-sustaining medical treatment (Phipps, True, Harris, Chong,

Tester, Chavin et al., 2003; Steinhauser et al., 2000). Nonetheless, the findings suggest the need for further exploration of patients and family preferences for life-sustaining treatment.

Replicating findings from prior research (Parker, Clayton, Hancock, Walder, Butow, Carrick et al., 2007; Teno, Lynn, Wenger, Phillips, Murphy, Connors et al., 1997), a minority of families had communicated with each other about end-of-life concerns and preferences. Despite the advantages of open family communication (Metzger & Gray, 2008), the literature on advance care planning and family communication suggests that less than 20% actually talk about dying and their preferences for care (Bradley & Rizzo, 1999; Rosnick & Reynolds, 2003; Teno et al., 1997). Lack of communication can contribute to family conflict between the elder and family surrogates, difficulties in decision-making and advance care planning, and ultimately to poorer quality end-of-life care (Kramer, Boelk, & Auer, 2006). This corroborates our finding that a lack of communication was associated with greater incongruence, and suggests the importance of future research on the impact of family conflict on end-of-life experiences and outcomes.

Conclusions & Implications

While many of these findings were consistent with the literature on congruence in patient and caregiver perceptions, the current study is unusual in that it compared the subjective experiences of older chronically and terminally ill patients with those of their matched family caregivers. This study confirms that end-of-life concerns and care preferences found with broader populations also apply to frail elders and their caregivers. The findings further suggest that there may be more family congruence around preferences for end-of-life care than around challenges, concerns, and wishes related to dying. Open family communication was associated with greater congruence in patient and family preferences, which supports prior findings that open communication is associated with better adjustment in family caregivers after the death of their loved ones (Kramer, 1997; Metzger & Gray, 2008). These results have important implications for intervention and research, as they highlight potential sources of unmet needs and conflict among dying elders and their family members.

Although there were more areas of congruence than incongruence among family members, the findings of this study suggest that healthcare professionals providing end-of-life care would be prudent to view family reports as imperfect proxies for elder's concerns, challenges, and preferences. Principle domains of incongruence included the elders' difficulties in accepting dependence, their fears of becoming a burden, and desire to be prepared for death. Unlike the elders, family caregivers were primarily concerned with providing adequate care to meet the elders' physical and spiritual care needs. The study highlights the need for more focused and comprehensive assessment of terminally ill elders and their family caregivers, and for sensitivity to potential differences in preferences and concerns.

It is perhaps not surprising that elders and family caregivers viewed the end-of-life experience somewhat differently, given their different ages, roles, and perspectives. Incongruence presents difficulties only when patients and caregivers with different views are unable to communicate openly and resolve differences with each other (de Haes & Teunissen, 2005). Family conflict and communication constraints can present significant barriers to the provision of quality care, the completion of advance directives, and the attainment of a "good death" (Covinsky, Fuller, Yaffe, Johnston, Hamel, Lynn et al., 2000; Kramer et al., 2006). Terminally ill elders and their families may therefore derive particular benefit from interventions that address congruent and incongruent experiences, and teach communication and family problem-solving skills around the end-of-life and end-of-life care. Working to enhance families' efforts to talk about and resolve differences, and to make informed decisions about care is fundamental to facilitating advance care planning, and reducing inappropriate procedures and hospitalizations.

There were some limitations to this study, which involved a small, non-representative sample of primarily white, low-income elders, recruited purposely from a unique comprehensive health and long-term care program in the Midwest. Casual generalizations should not, therefore, be made to other populations of terminally ill elders and family caregivers. The sample lacked heterogeneity in terms of race/ethnicity, and cultural factors have been shown to be important variables in end-of-life preferences (Phipps et al., 2003). There was also a good deal of variability in medical diagnosis, elders' living situations, and family caregivers' relationships to the elder, all of which may have influenced the findings.

Despite these limitations, this qualitative study identifies subjective concerns and care preferences of terminally ill elders and their family caregivers at the end of life. The findings highlight the need for more focused and comprehensive assessment of terminally ill elders and their family caregivers, and attention to potential differences in patient and family preferences and concerns. Further research into this population's unique needs and perceptions, including the dynamics of family communication and decision making at the end of life, is necessary to further healthcare efforts to better meet elders' psychosocial needs, enhance their wellbeing, and facilitate a "good death." Understanding elders' experiences and preferences, identifying areas of congruence and incongruence, and improving communication in families are essential to providing quality end-of-life care to all dying patients and their families.

References

Bern-Klug, M. (2004). The Ambiguous Dying Syndrome. *Health and Social Work, 29*(1), 55–65.

Born, W., Greiner, K., Sylvia, E., & Ahluwalia, J. (2004). Knowledge, attitudes, and beliefs about end-of-life care among inner-city African Americans and Latinos. *Journal of Palliative Medicine, 7*(2), 247–256.

Bradley, E., & Rizzo, J. (1999). Public information and private search: Evaluating the Patient Self-Determination Act. *Journal of Health Politics, Policy and Law, 24*(2), 239–273.

Chochinov, H., Hack, T., Hassard, L., Kristjianson, S., McClement, S., & Harlos, M. (2002). Dignity in the terminally ill: A cross-sectional, cohort study. *The Lancet, 360,*(9350), 2026–2030.

Cohen, S. R., & Leis, A. (2002). What determines the quality of life of terminally ill cancer patients form their own perspective? *Journal of Palliative Care, 18*(1), 48–58.

Covinsky, K., Fuller, J., Yaffe, K., Johnston, C., Hamel, M., Lynn, J., et al. (2000). Communication and decision-making in seriously ill patients: Findings of the SUPPORT project. *Journal of the American Geriatrics Society, 48*(5), S187–S193.

Crabtree, B., & Miller, W. (1999). Using codes and code manuals: A template organizing style of interpretation. In B. F. Crabtree & W.L. Miller (Eds.), *Doing qualitative research* (2nd ed., pp. 163–178). Thousand Oaks, CA: Sage.

de Haes, H., & Teunissen, S. (2005). Communication in palliative care: A review of recent literature. *Current Opinion in Oncology, 17*(4), 345–350.

Desbiens, N., & Mueller-Rizner, N. (2000). How well do surrogates assess the pain of seriously ill patients? *Critical Care Medicine, 28,* 1347–1352.

Emanuel, L., von Gunten, C., & Ferris, F. (2000). Gaps in end-of-life care. *Archives of Family Medicine, 9,* 1176–1180.

Engelberg, R., Patrick, D., & Curtis, J. (2005). Correspondence between patients' preferences and surrogates' understandings for dying and death. *Journal of Pain and Symptom Management, 30*(6), 498–509.

Farber, S., Egnew, T., Herman-Bertch, J., Taylor, T., & Guldin, G. (2003). Issues in end-of-life care: Patient, caregiver, and clinician perceptions. *Journal of Palliative Medicine, 6*(1), 19–31.

Field, M. J., & Cassel, C. K. (Eds.). (1997). *Approaching death: Improving care at the end of Life.* Institute of Medicine. Washington, DC: National Academy Press.

Gallo, W., Baker, M., & Bradley, E. (2001). Factors associated with home versus institutional death among cancer patients in Connecticut. *Journal of the American Geriatrics Society, 49,* 771–777.

Gardner, D. (2008). Cancer in a dyadic context: Older couples' negotiation of ambiguity and meaning in end-of-life. *Journal of Social Work in End-of-life and Palliative Care, 4*(2), 1–25.

Hamel, M., Lynn, J., Teno, J., Covinsky, K., Wu, A., Galanos, A., et al. (2000). Age-related differences in care preferences, treatment decisions, and clinical outcomes of seriously ill, hospitalized adults: Lessons from SUPPORT. *Journal of the American Geriatrics Society, 48*(5/Supplement), S176–S182.

Heyland, D., Dodek, P., Rocker, G., Groll, D., Garni, A., Pichora, D., et al. (2006). What matters most in end-of-life care: perceptions of seriously ill patients and their family members. *Canadian Medical Association Journal, 174*(5), 627–633.

Higginson, I., & Sen-Gupta, G. (2000). Place of care in advanced cancer: a qualitative systematic literature review of patient preferences. *Journal of Palliative Medicine, 3*(3), 287–300.

Kramer, B. J., & Auer, C. (2005). Challenges to providing end-of-life care to low-income elders with advanced chronic disease: Lessons learned from a model program. *The Gerontologist, 45,* 651–660.

Kramer, B. J., Boelk, A., & Auer, C. (2006). Family conflict at the end of life: Lessons learned in a model program for vulnerable older adults. *Journal of Palliative Care 9*(3), 791–801.

Kramer, B. J., Christ, G., Bern-Klug, M., & Francoeur, R. (2005). A national agenda for social work research in palliative and end-of-life care. *Journal of Palliative Medicine 8,* 418–431.

Kramer, D. (1997). How women relate to terminally ill husbands and their subsequent adjustment to bereavement. *Omega: Journal of Death and Dying, 34*(2), 93–106.

Laakkonen, M., Pitkala, K., & Strandberg, T. (2004). Terminally ill elderly patients' experiences, attitudes, and needs: A qualitative study. *Omega: Journal of Death and Dying, 49*(2), 117–129.

McCormick, T., & Conley, B. (1995). Patients' perspectives on dying and on the care of dying patients. *Western Journal of Medicine, 163*(3), 236–243.

McKechnie, R., Macleod, R., & Keeling, S. (2007). Facing uncertainty: The lived experience of palliative care. *Palliative and Supportive Care, 5,* 367–376.

McPherson, C., & Addington-Hall, (2003). Judging the quality of care at the end of life: Can proxies provide reliable information? *Social Science and Medicine, 56,* 95–109.

McPherson, C., Wilson, K., & Murray, M. (2007). Feeling like a burden: Exploring the perspectives of patients at the end of life. *Social Science & Medicine, 64*(2), 417–427.

McPherson, C., Wilson, K., Lobchuk, M., & Brajtman, S. (2008). Family caregivers' assessment of symptoms in patients with advanced cancer: Concordance with patients and factors affecting accuracy. *Journal of Pain Symptom Management, 35*(1), 70–82.

McSkimming, S., Hodges, M., Super, A., Driever, M., Schoessler, M., Franey, S. G., et al. (1999). The experience of life-threatening illness: Patients' and their loved ones' perspectives. *Journal of Palliative Medicine, 2*(2), 173–184.

Metzger, P., & Gray, M. (2008). End-of-life communication and adjustment: Pre-loss communication as a predictor of bereavement-related outcomes. *Death Studies, 32*(4), 301–325.

Moorman, S., & Carr, D. (2008). Spouses' effectiveness as end-of-life surrogates: Accuracy, uncertainty, and errors of overtreatment or undertreatment. *Gerontologist, 48*(6), 811–819.

Morrison, S. (2005). Health care system factors affecting end-of-life care. *Journal of Palliative Medicine, 8*(Supplement 1), S79–S87.

Mularski, R., Curtis, R., Osborne, M., Engelberg, R., & Ganzini, L. (2004). Agreement among family members and their assessment of the quality of dying and death. *Journal of Pain and Symptom Management, 28*(4), 306–315.

National Consensus Project (2004). *Clinical practice guidelines for quality palliative care.* Brooklyn, NY.

National Institutes of Health (NIH). (2004). *State-of-the-science conference on improving end-of-life care: Conference statement.* Bethesda, MD: National Institutes of Health.

Padgett, D. K. (2008). *Qualitative methods in social work research: Challenges and rewards* (2nd ed.). Thousands Oaks, CA: Sage Publications, Inc.

Parker, S., Clayton, J., Hancock, K., Walder, S., Butow, P., & Carrick, S. et al. (2007). A systematic review of prognostic/end-of-life communication with adults in the advanced stages of a life-limiting illness: Patient/care-giver preferences for the content, style, and timing of information. *Journal of Pain and Symptom Management, 34*(1), 81–93.

Patton, M. (2002). *Qualitative research and evaluation methods* (3rd ed.). Thousands Oaks, CA: Sage Publications, Inc.

Phipps, E., True, G., Harris, D., Chong, U., Tester, W., Chavin, S., et al. (2003). Approaching the end of life: Attitudes, preferences, and behaviors of African-American and white patients and their family caregivers. *Journal of Clinical Oncology, 21*(3), 549–554.

Pritchard, R., Fisher, E., Teno, J., Sharp, S. Reding, D., Knaus, W., et al. (1998). Influence of patient preferences and local health system characteristics on the place of death. (SUPPORT Investigators: Study to Understand Prognoses and Preferences for Risks and Outcomes of Treatment). *Journal of the American Geriatrics Society, 46*(10), 1242–1250.

Pruchno, R., Lemay, E., Field, L., & Levinsky, N. (2005). Spouse as health care proxy for dialysis patients: Whose preferences matter? *Gerontologist, 45*(6), 812–819.

Rosnick, C., & Reynolds, S. (2003). Thinking ahead: Factors associated with executing advance directives. *Journal of Aging & Health, 15*(2), 409–429.

Scholz, R. and Tietje, R. (2002). *Embedded case study methods: Integrating quantitative and qualitative knowledge.* Thousand Oaks, CA: Sage Publications.

Shalowitz, D., Garrett-Meyer, E., & Wendler, D. (2006). The accuracy of surrogate decision makers: A systematic review. *Archives of Internal Medicine, 166,* 493–497.

Singer P., Martin D., & Kellner M. (1999). Quality end-of-life care: patients' perspectives. *Journal of the American Medical Association, 281,* 163–168.

Sneeuw, K., Sprangers, M., & Aaronson, N. (2002). The role of health care providers and significant others in evaluating the quality of life of patients with chronic disease. *Journal of Clinical Epidemiology, 55*(11), 1130–1143.

Steinhauser A., Christakis N., Clipp E., McNeilly M., McIntyre L., & Tulsky J. (2000). Factors considered important at the end of life by patients, family, physicians, and other care providers. *Journal of the American Medical Association, 284*(19), 2476–2482.

Sulmasy, D., Terry, P., Weisman, C., Miller, D., Stallings, R., Vettese, M., et al. (1998). The accuracy of substituted judgments in patients with terminal disease. *Annals of Internal Medicine, 128*(8), 621–629.

SUPPORT Principal Investigators (1995). A controlled trial to improve care for seriously ill hospitalized patients: The study to understand prognosis and preferences for outcomes and risks for treatments (SUPPORT). *Journal of the American Medical Association, 274*(20), 1591–1598.

Tang, S., & McCorkle, R. (2003). Determinants of congruence between the preferred and actual place of death for terminally ill cancer patients. *Journal of Palliative Care 19*(4), 230–237.

Teno, J., Clarridge, B., Casey, V., Welch, L., Wetle, T., Shield, R., et al. (2004). Family perspectives on end-of-life care at the last place of care. *Journal of the American Medical Association, 291*(1), 88–93.

Teno, J., Lynn, J., Wenger, N., Phillips, R., Murphy, D., Connors, A., et al. (1997). Advance directives for seriously ill hospitalized patients: Effectiveness with the patient self-determination act and the SUPPORT intervention. SUPPORT Investigators. *Journal of the American Geriatric Society, 45*(4), 500–507.

Terry, W., Olson, L., Wilss, L., & Boulton-Lewis, G. (2006). Experience of dying: Concerns of dying patients and of carers. *Internal Medicine Journal, 36*(6), 338–346.

Thomas, C., Morris, S., & Clark, D. (2004). Place of death: Preferences among cancer patients and their carers. *Social Science & Medicine, 58,* 2431–2444.

Vig, E., Davenport, N., & Pearlman, R. (2002). Good deaths, bad deaths, and preferences for the end of life: A qualitative study of geriatric outpatients. *Journal of the American Geriatric Society, 50*(9), 1541–1548.

Waldrop, D., Kramer, B.J., Skretny, J., Milch, R., & Finn, W. (2005). Final transitions: Family caregiving at the end of life. *Journal of Palliative Medicine, 8*(3), 623–638.

Waters, C. (2001). Understanding and supporting African Americans' perspectives of end-of-life care planning and decision making. *Qualitative Health Research, 11,* 385–398.

Vig, E., & Pearlman, R. (2004). Good and bad dying from the perspective of terminally ill men. *Archives of Internal Medicine, 164*(9), 977–981.

Yin, R. (2003). *Case study research: Design and methods* (3rd ed.). Thousand Oaks, CA: Sage Publications.

Zettel-Watson, L., Ditto, P., Danks, J., & Smucker, W. (2008). Actual and perceived gender differences in the accuracy of surrogate decisions about life-sustaining medical treatment among older spouses. *Death Studies, 32*(3), 273–290.

Critical Thinking

1. What are the barriers to quality end-of-life care?

2. What were the major worries and fears about dying expressed by the elders and their family caregivers?

3. What were the end-of-life preferences for the elders in their final days?

Acknowledgements—The authors' extend their appreciation to Elder Care Partnerships staff and administration, and to End-of-Life committee members who provided ongoing support and consultation. Special thanks to the elders and their family members who offered their valuable insights.

UNIT 3
The Dying Process

Unit Selections

Learning Outcomes

After reading this unit, you should be able to:

- Know something about homeless persons' concerns and desires about end-of-life care.

- Relate to what nurses cross-culturally and via different religious backgrounds need to know in order to deal with persons at the end of life.

- Discuss the spirit hypothesis regarding deathbed and near-death visions.

- Point out weaknesses of the spirit hypothesis regarding deathbed and near-death visions.

- Present the benefits of hospice care in addition to some of the problems currently faced by hospice programs.

- Talk with knowledge about sudden unexpected death in epilepsy.

Student Website
www.mhhe.com/cls

Internet References

Thanatolinks
http://netsociology.tripod.com/thanalinks.htm

Yahoo: Society and Culture: Death and Dying
http://dir.yahoo.com/Society_and_Culture/Death_and_Dying

Centers for Disease Control and Prevention
www.cdc.gov

Agency for Healthcare Research and Quality
www.ahrq.gov

The Natural Death Centre
www.naturaldeath.org.uk

Project on Death in America
www.soros.org/resources/articles_publications/publications/pdia_20040101

Kearl's PARADIGM: Enhancing Life near Death
www.trinity.edu/~mkearl/paradigm.html

The Living Will and Values History Project
www.euthanasia.cc/lwvh.html

Hospice Foundation of America
www.hospicefoundation.org

Hospice and Palliative Nurses Association
www.hpna.org

National Prison Hospice Association
www.npha.org

Larson's Compilation of Great Ideas
www.scu.edu/Hospice/greatideas.html

Hospice-Care
www.hospice-cares.com

American Academy of Hospice & Palliative Medicine
www.aahpm.org

The Zen Hospice Project
www.zenhospice.org

VNA of Hudson Valley, NY
www.vnahv.org

The Connecticut Hospice
www.hospice.com

Houston Hospice
www.houstonhospice.org

Hospice Service of Santa Barbara
www.hospiceofsantabarbara.org

While death comes at varied ages and in differing circumstances, for most of us there will be time to reflect on our lives, our relationships, our work, and what our expectations are for the ending of life. This is called the dying process. In recent decades, a broad range of concerns has arisen about that process and how aging, dying, and death can be confronted in ways that are enlightening, enriching, and supportive. Efforts have been made to delineate and define various stages in the process of dying so that comfort and acceptance of our inevitable death will be eased. The fear of dying may heighten significantly when actually given the prognosis of a terminal illness by one's physician. Awareness of approaching death allows us to come to grips with the profound emotional upheaval that will be experienced. Fears of the experience of dying are often more in the imagination than in reality. Yet, when the time comes and death is forecast for the very near future, it is reality, a situation that may be more fearful for some than others.

Perhaps you know someone who has communicated with and even "seen" a deceased family member or friend. What is really happening here? Is such an experience an hallucination or is it real? Stafford Betty looks into this "twilight zone" to determine if such is real or a mere hallucination.

Homeless individuals seem somewhat segregated from the rest of the population, yet what are their feelings regarding death not at home, as dying in one's home seemingly is the all-American way to die? John Song and colleagues address this issue in their article regarding homeless persons' concerns about end-of-life issues.

Death across cultures and religions, in terms of what nurses need to know, is presented by ElGindy. Nurses are on "the front line" on their eight-hour shifts in the hospital relating to patients, thus they see patients as their health improves or deteriorates. Nurses, therefore, are pivotal in helping patients cope with the dying process.

The article by Hannon addresses hospice care and the benefits of such. Hospice programs came into existence in healthcare in the US in the early 1970s and have expanded rapidly, especially in the twenty-first century. Hospice typically relates to individuals literally in the last few weeks/months of life. Yet, not everyone dies a lingering death; some individuals die

© Liquidlibrary/Dynamic Graphics/Jupiterimages

rather unexpectedly. Such is the case of a rather sudden death, as described by Jennifer Couzin as she addresses the devastating effect of epilepsy and sudden death.

Dying on the Streets

Homeless Persons' Concerns and Desires about End-of-Life Care

Background: There is little understanding about the experiences and preferences at the end of life (EOL) for people from unique cultural and socioeconomic backgrounds. Homeless individuals are extreme examples of these overlooked populations; they have the greatest risk of death, encounter barriers to health care, and lack the resources and relationships assumed necessary for appropriate EOL care. Exploring their desires and concerns will provide insight for the care of this vulnerable and disenfranchised population, as well as others who are underserved.

Objective: Explore the concerns and desires for EOL care among homeless persons.

Design: Qualitative study utilizing focus groups.

Participants: Fifty-three homeless persons recruited from agencies providing homeless services.

Measurements: In-depth interviews, which were audiotaped and transcribed.

Results: We present 3 domains encompassing 11 themes arising from our investigation, some of which are previously unreported. Homeless persons worried about dying and EOL care; had frequent encounters with death; voiced many unique fears, such as dying anonymously and undiscovered; favored EOL documentation, such as advance directives; and demonstrated ambivalence towards contacting family. They also spoke of barriers to EOL care and shared interventions to improve dying among the very poor and estranged.

Conclusions: Homeless persons have significant personal experience and feelings about death, dying, and EOL care, much of which is different from those previously described in the EOL literature about other populations. These findings have implications not only for homeless persons, but for others who are poor and disenfranchised.

JOHN SONG, MD, MPH, MAT[1,2], DIANNE M. BARTELS, RN, MA, PHD[1,2], EDWARD R. RATNER, MD[1,2], LUCY ALDERTON, MPH[4], BRENDA HUDSON, MS[3], AND JASJIT S. AHLUWALIA, MD, MPH, MS[2,3]

[1]*Center for Bioethics, University of Minnesota, N504 Boynton, 410 Church Street S.E., Minneapolis, MN 55455, USA;*
[2]*Medical School, University of Minnesota, Minneapolis, MN, USA;*
[3]*Academic Health Center, University of Minnesota, Minneapolis, MN, USA;*
[4]*Worldwide Epidemiology, GlaxoSmithKline, Mail Stop UP4305, Collegeville, PA 19426-0989, USA.*

Background

There remain many deficiencies in how society addresses the needs of dying individuals.[1] One shortcoming is the fundamental assumptions behind end-of-life (EOL) care: it focuses on individuals with loved ones, health care, and a home. Society has not considered homeless persons, who often die without these resources. It is necessary to address EOL care in this population for several reasons. First, the high prevalence of homelessness in the United States, with estimates ranging up to several million,[2] and the disproportionate amount and severity of illness in this population[3,4] is a public health crisis. Homeless persons also suffer high mortality rates—several times the rate of domiciled populations[5–7]—and premature mortality (average ages of death in Atlanta, San Francisco, and Seattle are 44, 41, and 47).[8,9] In addition, homeless persons encounter many barriers to health care[10–12] and, it may be hypothesized, to EOL care. Homeless persons, for example, die with little medical care immediately prior to their deaths.[13] Finally, additional concerns are raised by the unique personal, cultural, and medical characteristics of homelessness. Given the immediacy of basic human needs while living without shelter, homeless persons' concerns beyond daily survival may be different from those of persons who do not worry about food or shelter.

Few studies have addressed EOL care for underserved or disenfranchised persons,[1] and existing work is limited as it reflects the concerns of people with health care and personal resources and relationships. Three studies have previously examined homeless persons and EOL care. One demonstrated that homeless persons are eager to address EOL issues,[14] and a second explored EOL scenarios among homeless persons.[15] A third study addressed ICU care preferences.[16] The first 2 studies, however, are limited by their small and homogeneous samples, and the third focused on one specific aspect of EOL care.

This work represents the first in-depth exploration of a homeless population and their attitudes towards EOL care. We hypothesized that they would have concerns different from those of other previously studied populations. We previously reported how life on the streets influences attitudes towards death and dying (Song et al. submitted for publication) The present paper's objective was to examine how homelessness influences concerns and desires about care at the time of death.

Design

We conducted a qualitative investigation utilizing focus groups of homeless individuals. The study was funded by the NIH/National Institute of Nursing Research and approved by the University of Minnesota Institutional Review Board.

Participants

Participants were recruited from 6 social service agencies that serve homeless persons in Minneapolis and St. Paul, MN. These agencies provide a variety of services, including food, shelter, and health care. Participants were required to be at least 18 years old, speak English, and able to give informed consent. Participants were required to have been homeless at least once in the last 6 months, ascertained by a demographic questionnaire consistent with the federal guidelines.[17]

Participants were recruited through a mixture of random and purposive sampling, utilizing key informants[18]; details of this procedure are detailed elsewhere (Song et al. submitted for publication). Six focus groups were held, with an average of 9 participants per group. Participants were compensated $20. Interim analyses were conducted, and interviews were held until theme saturation was achieved.

Table 1 Interview Guide for Focus Groups

Questions

General questions

Do you have any experience with a serious illness or injury or a close friend or relative who had a serious illness or injury or who has died?

Are you concerned about dying?

Do you think about dying, care while dying, or death? Is this an issue that concerns you?

Is this an issue that you would like to talk about more?

Specific questions

Do you have any one that you can talk to about these issues?

Probes: Do you have family that you are in contact with? Do you have friends that you trust? Do you know any social workers, service providers, or health care providers whom you trust?

What concerns do you have regarding dying, care at the end of life, and death?

Probes: Are you concerned about what happens to your body? Your health care? Pain, symptom management, discomfort? Are you concerned about being stuck on life support? Are you concerned about dying alone?

If you were sick or dying, are there people you trust or love that you can get support from? Who can make decisions for you?

Probes: Do you have family that you are in contact with? Do you have friends that you trust? Do you know any social workers, service providers, or health care providers whom you trust? Have you ever heard of a living will or durable power of health attorney?

Describe a "good death."

Probes: Where would you like to die? Who would you like to have by your side? Who do you need to make peace with? What would you like to have happen to your body? What are you afraid of when dying?

What stands in the way of you having a good death?

Probes: What stands in the way of good health care? What would you need to die in comfort and dignity? What are some problems with services that you have encountered?

What kind of services would you say would be needed so that homeless people might die in comfort and with dignity?

Measurement

Interviews were conducted between July 2003 and January 2004. A semistructured interview guide consisting of open-ended questions was developed through a pilot study,[14] community consultants, and the EOL and homelessness literature (Table 1).

The sessions were audio-taped and investigators took field notes on the group process and nonverbal communication, which served to contextualize the interviews and verify congruence of verbal and nonverbal communication.[18] Audiotapes were transcribed, and Atlas ti software was used to facilitate analysis.

Analysis

Investigators utilized a modified consensual qualitative research (CQR) approach to analyze data, which has proven effective in evaluating complex psychosocial phenomena.[19] This method involves an inductive analytic process to identify themes, which the team derives by consensus and verifies by systematically checking against the raw data.[19] This CQR approach incorporates a 3-step process to identify salient themes; details of CQR utilized by this team are provided elsewhere (Song et al. submitted for publication).

Results

Fifty-three people participated in the 6 focus groups. The mean age of participants was 47, and 35% were female. Thirty-six percent were identified as Native American, 8% reported an advanced degree, and 40% responded that they experienced more than one living situation during the last 6 months (Table 2).

Main outcomes were participants' concerns about and wishes for EOL care. We found 11 themes grouped into 3 domains, by locus of concern: personal themes, relational concerns, and environmental influences (Table 3).

Personal Themes

This domain involves participants' experiences with and attitudes towards EOL care. These results represent internal dynamics and considerations—the experiences that have influenced participants' conceptions about EOL care, including their wishes and concerns about their own care. Within the "personal theme" domain, we found 6 themes: experience with EOL care, fears and uncertainties, advance care planning, preferences/wishes/hopes, spirituality/religion, and veteran status (Table 3).

Experience with End of Life Care

Participants consistently had experiences with serious illnesses and deaths of loved ones or acquaintances, or their own encounters with serious illness. These experiences influenced their beliefs and attitudes towards EOL care. Past experiences with death and EOL care were frequently poor and frightening:

When she (my mom) got sick, they put her in a nursing home, and they denied me access . . . she deteriorated, she lost her hair, she was almost comatose . . . I never got to see her. What they did to her I'll never know. One thing I knew—when she saw me she said, 'Call a taxi; get me out of here.' . . . So everything right now is in a nightmare. I'm trying to find out how she

Table 2 Participant Demographics

Characteristics	%
Age, years	
<35	15
36–45	25
46–55	45
56–65	9
>65	6
Gender	
Female	35
Race	
Hispanic or Latino	2
Not Hispanic or Latino	2
American Indian or Alaskan Native	36
Asian	2
Black or African American	27
Native African	2
Hawaiian/other Pacific Islander	0
White	22
Not reported	7
Years of education	
5–8	8
9–11	39
12–15	32
16+	8
Not reported	13

died . . . nobody told me . . . In my mind I'm thinking she's still alive . . . I never thought I'd lose my mom, or not in this way, not this hideous mess that happened that I can't understand.

This perception of EOL care as being out of the control of patients and family was common: "My mother lacked two weeks being 94 years old when she passed away. She was forced into a nursing home . . . She lost her freedom . . ." So, too, was the feeling that EOL care was unresponsive to the suffering party: "It was a situation where he didn't want to come out of there, living off the machine. When the time came for him to start to die, they wanted us to resuscitate him . . . That kind of weighed heavy on me because I thought I was letting him down. The last of his hours, he was kind of in pain. I just kept asking the doctor to give him something for his pain. They never did."

Because experiences contributed to an attitude that care is imposed, most interventions are seen as an unwanted and invasive: "After I saw my mom die, I'm almost thinking alone would be better. I don't want to be hooked up to tubes and all that crap when it comes time for me to go." Loss of control was a common concern, "Once I got real sick and got [put] in a nursing home. I don't care how old I was, I can't deal with not

Table 3 Domains and Themes of EOL Care Expressed by Homeless People

Domain	Definitions	Representative quote(s)
Personal themes		
Experience with EOL care	Experience with deaths of loved ones, friends, and acquaintances on the streets or personal experiences with illness or injury, and the care received	I've had a lot of tragedy. My girlfriend died in my arms with my baby. She was four months pregnant at the time . . . and she comes back in my dreams.
		He had a stroke and was on dialysis. Me and him, being about the same age, it made me fear for my life.
Fears and uncertainties	Concerns and fears about dying and EOL care	Me? I'd just like to be remembered by somebody.
		The only thing I'm worried about is that I don't want to die on the streets.
		After I've passed, my biggest fear would be not making it back home to Canada and my reservation.
		. . . they'll throw you in a pauper's grave someplace and nobody's going to mourn you.
Preferences/ wishes/hopes	Possibilities related to what would be a "good death"	If that was to happen, I would want it to happen some place where it was noticeable. Yeah, you may be dead there for three, four years . . . I'll be somewhere where nobody could find me.
		But also, once you see the doctor, the doctor should spend a little more time and get to know you a little bit better and show a little more compassion.
Advance care planning/ documentation	Strategies to influence outcomes in the event of death or serious illness	You gotta have it wrote down, or else they'll do just what they want.
		I'm going to have one of those made out, a living will, because if I end up in the hospital, I don't think I'd want no life support keeping me alive.
		My will says that if I go into a diabetic coma or if I get hit by a car, they can start life-saving techniques, and then my brother Bob's name is on that. They are to call him and say John's in the hospital, doesn't look good; do you want to come down and sign the papers to pull the plug; we will try to keep him going for some time to see if he improves. If he doesn't improve, then come down. That is exactly how it's worded.
Spirituality/religion	Influence and role that an individual's spirituality or religious convictions has on dying and EOL care	Personally, death comes like peace, but like John said, we look forward to it if we're Christian because I can go and get my reincarnate body and dance without this one.
Veteran status	Thoughts about death and EOL care related to having served in the armed forces	Even though I'm a serviceman, if I was buried in a national cemetery, I feel that my soul would be lost.
		I went to get medical care, something that they guaranteed me for life. They looked at me and said, 'OK, you have an honorable discharge.' As a matter of fact, I have two. 'Do you have insurance on your job?' and I'm like, whoa. The insurance on my job, OK, when I signed these contracts you didn't say that my insurance would be primary. You said that you would take care of it. So the VA does nothing.
Relational themes		
Relationships with known people	How current relationships with family, friends, and peers affect desires and fears about dying and EOL care	Most of these guys, they don't want their family to know. They ask you what happened. Why are you homeless? What's the problem?
		But I notice that homeless people, or street punks, whatever you call them, whatever is right for them, prostitutes or whatever, sometimes these type of people, another street person they have known for years and seems more like a family member than their own family. For me that is considered a family member.
		They'd be there for me, but I wouldn't want them to make all them changes. It takes a lot of money to travel and I don't want them wasting money. Not because I ain't worth the money, but I don't want them.

Table 3 Domains and Themes of EOL Care Expressed by Homeless People (*continued*)

Domain	Definitions	Representative quote(s)
Relationships with strangers	How individuals' relationship with institutions and its representatives influence their views of dying and EOL care	Have a doctor, an intern, or even have a medical student for a doctor, come and work at a shelter for a week to two weeks, just to see how it is, to get woke up at 6:00 in the morning and booted out, and getting a cold bowl of cereal from the branch for breakfast, and just shadowing somebody that has been homeless or is homeless, just to feel what it's like to, if just to say 'I know this guy; he's homeless and this needs to be taken care of right away' and not making him wait. Then they will have an idea of what it's like being homeless.
		The doctor called me a goddamn drug addict and told me to get the hell out of his office.
Communication tools/ strategies	The communication between the subjects and their loved or valued ones, and strategies homeless persons have to communicate with loved ones during a health care crisis or if unable to communicate directly	My sister, I put her name on everything that I have. There can be contact with her and she will communicate with my daughter.
		My living will says my family will have no say or discussion of what is done. Basically, they don't know me, so why should they have a say in whether I live or not.
		I made sure to talk to him (nephew) on the telephone. It just came into my mind. I said, 'I'm going to leave this in your hands. I'm going down hill now.
Environmental		
Environmental barriers/facilitators to good EOL care	Barriers or facilitators identified by subjects to good EOL care	They don't give you proper medical care because they know you are homeless.
		They think because we live in the streets, we're all junkies that don't feel no pain.
		Even if your family is not around at the hospital, there are these great hospice people. If you could spend your last time talking with them . . . that would be a good death.
		Living without life insurance, who's going to put me away—stuff like that?
		I had cancer just last year. My fear was being alone because my children ain't here. But I had support from the people at Listening House, friends.
Participant-suggested interventions	Interventions suggested by participants to improve dying and EOL care for homeless persons	What we do need is a shelter somewhere between Minneapolis and St. Paul that would be fully staffed 24/7 . . . and if you came out and just had surgery, you could go there . . .

EOL end of life.

having my freedom. There's no way. I need to be free . . . once you're in a nursing home or hospital you lose control."

Fears and Uncertainties

Participants expressed many fears and uncertainties similar to those of domiciled people: "Don't prolong my life. I don't want to carry on laying there as a vegetable . . ." However, the derivation of these fears may be different in this population—a combination of experience and the impotence and indignity of homelessness: "I was thinking of my friend Jeff wound up under the bridge. They look at it like another junkie guy, but he was trying really, really hard to work every day. And just to see him treated with little dignity was [not] right . . ."

Another common fear was dying anonymously, which may be unique to this population: "It makes a difference when you're homeless and you're dying by yourself. You're

here by yourself, no one to care"; and, "Me? I just want to be remembered by somebody." A dreaded consequence expressed by many was that their passing, and life, would go unnoticed and without memorialization. Similar fears include not being found and dying in a public place: "I wouldn't want to be under a bridge. If you die somewhere and not be found."

Participants also expressed many misconceptions and uncertainties about surrogate decision-making, persistent vegetative states and heroic treatments, and advance care planning: "A good buddy of mine that used to be a street person . . . fell out and ended up in a coma . . . There [were] doctors and nurses . . . calling, asking anybody to come down and say you were his family, just so you could sign a waiver to pull the plug." This was one of many urban EOL myths expressed by participants.

Another common concern was the final disposal of their body, a fear that appears unique to this population; they believed a homeless, disenfranchised person's body would be anonymously cremated, buried in a common grave, or used in medical experimentation: "I don't know if the city will just take me to the furnace down there and burn me." Participants were not aware of Minnesota state law that forbids cremation without consent of patient or family.

Preferences, Wishes, and Hopes

Participants expressed preferences and hopes, many echoing those articulated in the mainstream EOL literature, such as a wish for reconciliation with loved ones or avoiding heroic interventions. However, the wish for companionship had a unique twist in this disenfranchised population. While some desired reunion with their families, many more simply wanted anyone compassionate at the time of death, whether homeless friends or even anonymous care providers: "I would wish someone to be there, especially since I know my folks won't be."

Given the misconceptions and fears about body disposal, there were explicit and detailed desires that participants' bodies be laid to rest in a personally and culturally acceptable manner. Native Americans, for example, often stated a preference that their body be taken to native lands for proper burial.

Another common desire expressed was that EOL care focus on symptom management, particularly pain control. At the end of a long dialogue on pain control, one participant summed up the prevailing mood: "I'm kind of on the same page as him . . . if I'm dying, just give me my drugs. Make sure I'm loaded; then I'm cool. I'm not going to sell it to anybody; I just want to . . . Let me go in peace."

Finally, participants desired simply to be treated with respect: "deal with us not as some sleaze bag out for trouble, but we are just homeless." A lack of respect fostered fear of dying among subjects: "Right now I'm afraid of dying mostly because I don't have nothing. It's like a disgrace or shame to me to die that way . . . Even though I can't hear it and I won't know it, talking about, 'He was a tramp. He was a no-good tramp.'"

Advance Care Planning

A major finding is the importance of advance care planning and documentation for this isolated population: "My fear is being found on the street, but no one knowing how to help me or who I am." It appears that this desire for advance care planning arises from several concerns. One is, as reflected above, anonymity and estrangement. Given the belief that EOL care is paternalistic and unresponsive, advance care planning was also seen as a way to maintain control: "In '73, I was actually declared brain dead . . . I regained consciousness . . . my only real fear about death is that the doctor tried too aggressively to keep me alive, and because of this, I created a living will."

For some participants advance care planning meant discussion with significant others and/or appointment of a proxy; however, the most cited forms of advance care planning included written documentation of wishes or contact information, personal identification, or written directive or other advance care planning document. One participant voiced a typical strategy to dictate circumstances of his death: "In my wallet, I have a card with my sister's name and a phone number. Do I want to be buried in Minnesota? Hell no!"

When speaking of surrogate decision-makers, nearly all who had thought of this issue or who had appointed one chose surrogates who were not related; they were most often service providers; friends; and, occasionally, romantic partners.

Sprituality/Religion

Spirituality and religion were means of finding comfort and solace when confronting death while homeless: "Can you die alone? I remember when Bill Cosby's son died on the street . . . nobody came to touch him and hold him, but if he's a child of God, then God was holding him and taking him home." Despite the physical reality of dying alone, religion made it possible to believe that, spiritually, one was not alone.

Veteran Status

Many opinions about EOL care related to prior military experience. Participants identified veteran status as either a positive or negative factor. Some, for example, felt reassured they would have care or even a grave provided by the U.S. government: "If I drop dead or die or get my head blown off, if my parents don't do it or my family, put me in the national cemetery, too, with other veterans, my brothers." Others feared poor VA care or did not want burial in a veteran's cemetery.

Relational Themes

A second major domain was "relational themes," which we organized into 3 categories: relationships with known people, relationships with strangers, and communication tools/strategies. This domain captures how current personal and institutional relationships affect attitudes towards EOL care.

Relationships with Known People/Burden to Others

Relationships were described as complex, fractured, or nonexistent. Many were estranged from their family of origin. Some homeless persons viewed dying as an opportunity for reconciliation, though they were uncertain whether this would happen: "Truthfully, I couldn't honestly say who would and who wouldn't [be there]. I'll just have to see when I get there . . . Sometimes when they say they'll be there, they're never there."

A majority of participants did not want contact with their families while dying or after their deaths. There were several reasons for this preference, including the assertion that their families, "abandoning" them in life, had no right to claim a relationship or authority in death: "I got 6 sisters and five brothers . . . but, dead is dead. So don't cry; help me while I breathe, not when I'm stiff and frozen." This rejection extended into surrogate decision-making: "My living will says my family will have no say or discussion of what is done. Basically, they don't know me, so why should they have a say in whether I live or not." Others feared that their families would not be compassionate: "They'd be saying, 'bury him like he lived,' or 'we don't want nothing to do with him.'" Some did not want to be a burden on their families, either emotionally or financially, or feared revealing their circumstances and homelessness: "When I die, don't tell them. I don't want them to know that I'm homeless." Finally, many others did not want their families contacted because they had found, while living on the streets, trusted friends and service providers to serve as surrogates.

Relationships with Strangers

Most respondents commented that society, including police, medical professionals, and social service agency staff, does not treat them with respect or compassion. When discussing physicians, one respondent insisted: "We are homeless. They say, 'well this guy's homeless . . . You ain't got to worry about it.'" They cited slow and poor service at health care facilities, and felt betrayed by the social services system. Based on these experiences, they expected poor care at the EOL: "He'd a died more dignified if they [the counselors] actually sat down and listened to him, instead of saying, 'we're too busy; get out of here . . .'"

However, not all comments were negative. Compassionate providers were described gratefully. Several respondents claimed a particular social service provider as their most trusted confidant and indicated that this individual should be contacted as a surrogate decision-maker. "John," said one respondent, referring to a street case manager, "knows what I want. I trust him."

Communication Tools/Strategies   Those who did wish communication or reconciliation at the EOL had different strategies to insure that this occurred. These strategies were often inventive and adapted to the disenfranchised lives many led. Many, for example, carried phone numbers of loved ones or left them with various social service providers. Although in jest, this comment demonstrates how difficult communication may be: "If I was going to die in three months, I'd probably rob a bank . . . I figure if I robbed a bank, I would get caught. [My family] heard about it in the newspaper and call me up . . ."

Environmental Factors

Our final domain's common thread is the environment in which dying occurs and the structural boundaries of EOL care. We organized it into 2 categories: barriers/facilitators to good EOL care and participant-suggested interventions.

Barriers/Facilitators to Good EOL Care

Health care professionals' attitudes were most often cited as a barrier to good EOL care, while others found care inaccessible or inadequate because of financial or insurance insufficiencies. Because of poverty, even the simplest aspects of EOL care cause worry in this population: "My goal is to get me some type of burial plan. $300 won't bury nobody at this table. Then I wouldn't mind it so much, but right now I'm afraid of dying mostly because I don't have nothing." Inappropriate care also resulted because of preconceptions about homeless persons, such as the denial of pain medication for fear of abuse. Respondents also complained about the lack of respite or hospice facilities and programs; once discharged from the hospital, they only have shelters to go to.

Participant-Suggested Interventions

Finally, participants suggested many interventions to improve care for dying homeless people. Some were educational, directed towards both health care providers and homeless people. Another frequently suggested intervention was some form of advance care planning or document to preserve autonomy: "It's a legal document. Let's say that's your wish, but it's not written anywhere, and someone says, 'keep him on the respirator.' They [would] . . . unless you written it down." Indeed, any kind of identification was considered essential and encouraged for a disconnected population. Finally, homeless participants demanded special accommodations to facilitate dying among this population.

Discussion

In our study, homeless participants demonstrated more differences than similarities in their attitudes and beliefs towards EOL care compared to other populations studied.[20–25] First, many participants have had personal experiences with death, dying, and EOL care. These experiences led them to view EOL care as paternalistic, unresponsive, and poor. Other unique concerns expressed include fear of dying anonymously, without memorialization or remembrance; fear of not being found or identifiable in death; and worry about the final resting place of their bodies. These concerns are all new to the EOL literature.

Another unexpected finding is participants' advocating advance care planning, especially the appointment of surrogate decision-makers and the preparation of advance care documents, such as living wills. These findings are interesting, given the current disfavor toward advance care documents[1] and the intuition that homeless individuals would not value or utilize documentation. According to participants, documents serve different functions among a population that is anonymous, voiceless, or lacks obvious surrogate decision-makers.

Important relational findings were also expressed. Though some participants wished reconcilement and contact, a greater number did not want their families contacted when seriously ill, when dying, or after death. These desires derived from several different reasons, including avoiding emotional and financial burdens on their families, shame, and anger over abandonment. Many had made surrogate decision-making plans that did not include family.

Relationships with institutions also figured prominently in the EOL experiences and desires of homeless persons—which is expected given the role institutions play in the daily lives of homeless persons, providing food, shelter, and other necessities. These relationships were occasionally positive. Participants spoke of trusted service providers, such as shelter personnel, some of whom were even designated as surrogate decision-makers. Most often, though, relationships with systems of care were described as poor, and contributed to give views of dying.

Participants spoke of "environmental" contexts or contributors to EOL care, noting multiple barriers to EOL care, including poor relationships, lack of insurance or finances, poor health care, lack of respect, and lack of knowledge of available resources or rights. Some participants, though, cited factors that led to satisfactory health care experiences or positive expectations of EOL care, such as advance care planning, facilitation of health care by social service workers, and physician advocacy.

Finally, subjects suggested interventions for improving EOL care for homeless or underserved persons. These included patient and provider education, advance care planning, living wills and other documentation, and special programs and facilities for dying or seriously ill homeless persons. A Medline and web search yields no reports of specific efforts focused on dying homeless individuals. Clearly, interventions are needed to serve this population.

The recent NIH state-of-science statement on improving EOL care reported that insufficient research has focused on individuals from different cultural and socioeconomic backgrounds.[1] While there is a growing body of evidence that these individuals may experience disparities in EOL care,[23–29] relatively little attention has been paid to the desires of these populations or interventions to improve their care.[1] Our study provides new and important information on EOL issues among homeless persons, among the most unfortunate of overlooked populations.

Our study's limitations include the selection of subjects from one urban area, a high number of Native Americans represented, and potential selection bias, as our participants are those who accessed service providers. The findings of our study are not necessarily generalizable. Rather, our data are exploratory, examining a previously unknown health-related phenomena: we are among the first to characterize in-depth the EOL concerns and desires of a vulnerable and disenfranchised population from their perspective.

Conclusions

Our study demonstrates that homeless persons have extensive, and often unique, concerns about dying and EOL care. The experiences and circumstances of homelessness inform and influence a view of death and EOL care unlike previously reported findings in the study of EOL care. Our work has implications for further study of this population, as well as study of other underrepresented and underserved populations. This work also suggests examining interventions to improve care for this and other vulnerable populations.

Notes

1. National Institutes of Health State-of-the-Science Conference Statement on Improving End-of-Life Care December 6–8, 2004. Available at www.consensus.nih.gov/2004/2004EndOf LifeCareSOS024html.htm. Accessed March 16, 2006.
2. Burt MR. Homelessness: definitions and counts. In: Baumohl J, ed. Homelessness in America. Phoenix, AZ: Oryx Press, 1996:15–23.
3. Breakey WR, Fischer PJ, Kramer M. Health and mental problems of homeless men and women in Baltimore. *JAMA* 1989; 262:1352–7.
4. Gelberg L, Linn LS. Assessing the physical health of homeless adults. *JAMA* 1989; 262:1973–9.
5. Barrow SM, Herman DB, Cordova PBA. Mortality among shelter residents in New York City. *Am J Public Health* 1999; 89:529–34.
6. Hibbs JR, Benner L. Mortality in a cohort of homeless adults in Philadelphia. *N Engl J Med* 1994; 331:304–9
7. Cheung AM, Hwang SW. Risk of death among homeless women: a cohort study and review of the literature. *CMAJ* 2004; 170(8):1243–7.
8. Hwang SW, Orav EJ, O'Connell JJ, Lebow JM, Brennan TA. Causes of death in homeless adults in Boston. *Ann Intern Med* 1996; 126:625–8.
9. King County Public Health 2004. Available at www.metrokc. gov/HEALTH/hchn/2004-annual-report-HD.pdf. Accessed January 20, 2006.
10. Gallagher TC, Andersen RM, Koegel P, Gelberg L. Determinants of regular source of care among homeless adults in Los Angeles. *Med Care* 1997; 35(8):814–30.
11. Gelberg L, Andersen RM, Leake BD. Healthcare access and utilization. *Health Serv Res.* 2000; 34(6):1273–1314.
12. Gelberg L, Thompson L. Competing priorities as a barrier to medical care among homeless adults in Los Angeles. *Am J Public Health* 1997; 87:217–20.
13. Hwang SW, O'Connell JJ, Lebow JM, Bierer MF, Orav EJ, Brennan TA. Health care utilization among homeless adults prior to death. *J Health Care Poor Underserved* 2001 Feb; 12(1):50–8.
14. Song J, Ratner E, Bartels D. Dying while homeless: Is it a concern when life itself is such a struggle? *J Clin Ethics.* Fall 2005; 16(3):251–61.
15. Tarzian A, Neal M, O'Neil J. Attitudes, experiences, and beliefs affecting end-of-life decision-making among homeless individuals. *J Palliat Med.* Feb 2005, Vol. 8, No. 1: 36–48.
16. Norris W, Nielson E, Engelberg R, Curtis JR. Treatment preferences for resuscitation and critical care among homeless persons. *Chest* 2005; 127(6):2180–7.
17. Stewart B. McKinney Homeless Assistance Act (42 U.S.C. 11431 et seq.)
18. Bernard HR. Reseach Methods in Cultural Anthropology. Beverly Hills, CA: Sage Publications 1988.
19. Hill CE, Thompson BJ, Williams EN. A guide to conducting consensual qualitative research. *Couns Psychol* 1997; 25:517–72.

20. Singer PA, Martin DK, Kelner M. Quality end of life care: patients' perspectives. *JAMA* 1999; 281:163–8.

21. Steinhauser KE, Clipp CC. In search of a good death: observations of patients, families, and providers. *Ann Intern Med.* 2000; 132:825–31.

22. Vig EK, Pearlman RA. Quality of life while dying: a qualitative study of terminally ill older men. *J Am Geriatr Soc* 2003 Nov; 51(11):1595–601

23. Born W, Greiner KA, Sylvia E, Butler J. Ahluwalia JS. Knowledge, attitudes, and beliefs about end-of-life care among inner-city African Americans and Latinos. *J Palliat Med.* 2004 7(2): 247–56.

24. Blackhall LJ, Murphy ST, Frank G. Ethnicity and attitudes toward patient autonomy. *JAMA* 1995;274:820–5.

25. Caralis PV, Davis B, Wright K, Marcial E. The influence of ethnicity and race on attitudes toward advance directives, life-prolonging treatments, and euthanasia. *J Clin Ethics* 1993;4(2):155–65.

26. Carrese JA, Rhodes LA. Western bioethics on the Navajo reservation. *JAMA* 1995;274:826–9.

27. Daneault S, Labadie J. Terminal HIV disease and extreme poverty: a review of 307 home care files. *J Palliat Care* 1999; 15:6–12.

28. Degenholtz HB, Thomas SB, Miller MJ. Race and the intensive care unit: disparities and preferences for end-of-life care. *Crit Care Med.* 31(5 Suppl):S373–8, 2003 May.

29. Cleeland CS, Gonin R, Baez L et al. Pain and treatment of pain in minority patients with cancer. *Ann Intern Med* 1997;127:813–6.

Critical Thinking

1. Because homeless individuals do not have a "home," what would you expect their attitudes to be toward end-of-life issues: similar to or rather different from a population with a "home?"

2. What were the six personal themes that related to homeless individuals' attitudes toward end-of-life care?

3. What were the two relational themes that impacted on homeless persons' attitudes toward end-of-life care?

Corresponding Author: JOHN SONG, MD, MPH, MAT; Center for Bioethics, University of Minnesota, N504 Boynton, 410 Church Street S.E., Minneapolis, MN 55455, USA (e-mail: songx006@umn .edu).

Acknowledgments—The authors would like to thank the clients and staff of St. Stephen's shelter; Holy Rosary Church; Listening House; Hennepin County Outreach Services; Health Care for the Homeless, Minneapolis; and Our Saviors Church who were so generous with their time, thoughts, and dedication to serving others. We would also like to thank LeeAnne Hoekstra for administrative support, Tybee Types for transcription, and Karen Howard for manuscript preparation. This study was funded by the National Institute of Nursing Research, National Institutes of Health, grant RO3 NR008586-02.

Death and Dying across Cultures

GIHAN ELGINDY, RN, MSN

Death and dying is a universal human experience throughout the globe. Yet human beings' beliefs, feelings and practices in regard to this experience vary widely between different religions and cultures. As nurses, it is amazing how much we need to learn in order to incorporate sensitivity to unique religious and/or cultural needs into our daily practice. For patients from diverse cultures, quality of care means culturally appropriate care. We need to remember that dying is difficult enough; no one needs to undergo additional stress or suffering as a result of cultural misunderstanding.

As we all learn in nursing school, the patient is the focus of our care. Therefore, patients—and their families—from cultures we may not be familiar with should be viewed as a source of knowledge about their special religious/cultural needs and norms. In many cases, accommodating these needs in a hospital setting is not that difficult, but it definitely requires creativity and just a few extra minutes of our time.

Often, just being aware of our own perceptions and religious/cultural practices, and possessing a degree of openness toward other individuals' unique needs, is more than enough to lead our basic common sense in caring competently for dying patients from diverse cultural backgrounds during this difficult time.

However, we must resist the temptation to make generalizations or assumptions that all individuals from the same cultural, ethnic or religious background are exactly alike. Within many ethnic populations, such as Hispanics/Latinos, there is a great deal of diversity in terms of cultural practices, geographic origin, etc. Above all, it's important to realize whether you are dealing with recent immigrants to the U.S. or with first- or second-generation individuals.

Q: As an ICU nurse, I care for dying patients every shift. Often when there is a Hispanic or Latino patient dying or deteriorating, I have to face a crowd of family and friends all day, regardless of the visible visiting hours sign, posted in Spanish. The frustration is mutual. In addition, sometimes the families request to place a special food item in a special location next to the patient's bed. I know how much this item must mean to them but many of our inflexible unit policies do not promote such practices. What is the best approach to resolve this issue?—Mary John, RN

A: Yes, it is true that America's health care facilities have many inflexible polices that do not allow much room for promoting diverse cultural/religious rituals or practices. This is a conflict that we nurses face every day and need to work on through ongoing dialog. It can often be difficult to accommodate a patient's wishes without changing these old, dry polices that ignore many individuals' needs, even during their last minutes of life.

In the situation you have described, to fully understand these families' requests we need to understand their culture, too. Hispanics/Latinos are predominantly Christians, yet they encompass varied cultural backgrounds and traditions. Sometimes when a Hispanic/Latino person is sick or dying, close family members such as the spouse, children, parents, etc. may all sit in a circle around a carefully selected food item, such as a fruit dish, placed in the middle of the room. They may spend most of the night praying and conducting special religious practices around this fruit dish. As a result, it becomes a holy dish that holds a great religious significance; the family believes that the holy object can assist their sick or dying loved one. At the end of the night, the family carries the holy fruit dish to the nurse or other care providers, expecting their full compliance in placing it next to the patient to facilitate healing, recovery or a peaceful death.

A simple discussion with the family explaining hospital and unit policies will usually lead nowhere. To please everyone and maintain a positive environment—including compliance with unit policies—the best approach is to place the holy fruit dish or food item in a sealed plastic bag, placing it exactly as the family specifies and explaining to them the perishable item's time limitation depending on fermentation status and weather conditions. Allowing the item to remain in place for several hours—such as only eight, 10 or 24 hours—will be very much appreciated and calming to everyone. It is very important to remember to ask the family what they want you to do with this item when the time is over.

Q: I recently encountered my first Jehovah's Witness patient, a child who was dying from a simple bleeding condition. It was very painful to watch his parents repeatedly refusing a blood transfusion that could easily save the boy's life. Then I heard the physician trying to obtain a court order that would enable him to act as the child's guardian so he could administer the needed blood transfusion. What a relief, he was able to save the child's life. But I still do not fully understand why the parents were so angry. Will you kindly explain this, and why they were refusing a simple treatment that has saved millions of lives? —B.B., Kansas.

A: It is very hard and often very painful for care providers to have to watch the process of slow death, or to do nothing for a dying patient whom they think they can save. Many times, we tend to forget that there is a limit to our role and that we need to realize and accept this.

To help you understand why this young patient's parents were so resistant to the child being given a blood transfusion, let me first explain the significance of blood in the Jehovah's Witness faith. Jehovah's Witnesses believe blood is sacred, representing life. Because of the Bible's command to "keep abstaining from . . . blood," their religion prohibits the ingestion of blood and the transfusion of blood and/or blood products. Some artificial blood products may be permissible but never natural human blood or its byproducts.

Often, Jehovah's Witnesses who require medical or surgical treatment will request the use of nonblood alternatives. To be a culturally competent care provider means recognizing that adult patients have a right to make this choice. Therefore, obtaining the patient's clear written permission before performing any auto-transfusion procedure is the safest practice for both the provider and the receiver. Failure to do so constitutes violating the patient's bill of rights and can lead to litigation or legal actions.

However, under U.S. law, providing care to a Jehovah's Witness patient who is a minor (as in the case you describe) differs from caring for a Jehovah's Witness adult. For minors, the physician can obtain a court order allowing administration of blood or blood products against the parents' will if he or she knows the procedure can and will save the child's life. The reason behind the physician's action is to protect the minor's life until he/she becomes an adult and can make his/her own faith decision. Of course, when physicians take this action it is not surprising that care providers, especially nurses, will face angry parents.

In future, to resolve this issue easily and safely for everyone, it would be helpful for you to learn about the bloodless treatment alternatives that are available for Jehovah's Witness patients. If the facility where you work is unable to provide these alternatives, be aware of the health care centers in your area that are specialized and authorized to manage Jehovah's Witness patients. Contacting the Witnesses' Hospital Liaison Committee in your area to obtain more information on bloodless treatment options, patient transfers and/or consultation can also be very helpful. This service is available 24 hours a day, seven days a week.

Q: I had a dying Muslim patient. I tried to provide her with spiritual support but instead I made her upset. I told her, innocently, that I would call the priest for her. Her tears and facial expressions were alarming enough to send a message of pain. Will you please explain what went wrong? In the future, how can I provide appropriate assistance to Muslims patients who are dying?—Linda

A: Before answering your questions, I need to explain an Islamic concept/principal first. In Islam there is no religious figure, such as a priest or rabbi, through which one communicates with Allah (God) on one's deathbed. Muslims communicate directly with Allah anytime and anywhere as they wish. In other words, they don't need a human religious figure to act as a spiritual "middleman." Nor do they need to give confession to absolve their sins before they die.

Secondly, while it was culturally inappropriate in itself to offer to send a Catholic priest to comfort a Muslim patient, what really made this patient upset was probably that she perceived your action as a message that she was about to die. After death, Islam, like many other religions, requires conducting a prayer for the dead, asking for Allah's mercy and forgiveness before burial takes place. This prayer may be performed by an Imam—a respected member of the community who, through his memorizing of the Quran (Muslim holy book), leads prayers—or by a Shiekh, or Islamic Scholar, who is a knowledgeable person who spent most of his life studying Islam and usually earns a PhD degree in Islamic Shariah (or "Islamic Laws Jurisprudence"). Therefore, even if you had offered to call an Imam or Shiekh instead of a priest, the patient would probably still have been upset, because she would have interpreted this as meaning that her death was imminent.

In the future, the most culturally appropriate way to assist a dying Muslim patient is to offer them the Quran and to facilitate their prayers.

Critical Thinking

1. In relating to dying patients, why is it important that nurses be well versed in how different cultures and religions view dying and death?

2. What beliefs do Jehovah's Witnesses have regarding medical attention which differ significantly from other religions?

3. What is different regarding the Muslin religion and other religions' views on dying and death?

Editor's Note—Meet Minority Nurse's cultural competence expert: GIHAN ELGINDY, RN, MSN, an internationally recognized authority on cross-cultural issues in nursing. Her advice column is designed to answer your questions about incorporating cultural competence into your nursing practice and resolving cultural conflicts in today's diverse health care workplace. Do you need expert advice on how to provide culturally sensitive care to patients from a particular ethnic or religious background? Are you looking for ways to increase understanding and acceptance of cultural differences in your work environment? Our expert can help!

Send your Cultural Competence Q&A questions to pam.chwedyk@ alloyeducation.com.

Are They Hallucinations or Are They Real? The Spirituality of Deathbed and Near-Death Visions

L. STAFFORD BETTY, PhD

When I try to unpack the many meanings of the word "spirituality," I try not to forget that the word comes from "spirit," and that one of the main meanings of "spirit" is, as my dictionary puts it, "a supernatural being or essence." Thanatologists have long been aware that people very near death, especially if they have *not* been heavily sedated, frequently "see spirits." French historian Philippe Ariès reports that a thousand years ago throughout Western Europe, most slowly dying people saw such spirits—presumably because sedation was unknown (M. Morse, 1990, p. 60). Even today, with heavy sedation the rule rather than the exception, some hospice nurses report that seeing and communicating with spirits is a "prevalent theme" of the dying patients they provide care for (Callanan & Kelley, 1992, p. 83). Usually these spirits bring comfort and a sense of wonder, not only for the dying, but also for the family of the dying. To put it another way, they "spiritualize" death. They suggest to all concerned that this world is not the only one, but that a "spiritual" world awaits the deceased. What is the nature of these spirits and the world they apparently live in? Is the "romance of death" generated by them a false comfort, a useful fiction, or is there something real and sturdy about them? In this article we will look at the evidence on both sides of the question, then come to a tentative conclusion.

Typical Deathbed or Near-Death Visions

According to Callanan and Kelley, visions of the dying come in two types. The first, and more common, are sightings of spirits who come, for the most part, to greet and encourage those who are dying. Most spirits are recognized by the one dying as a dead relative or friend. These spirits may visit for minutes or even hours; they are not seen by those at the bedside of the dying person, but it is often obvious that the dying person is communicating with an unseen presence or presences. Dozens of such communications are recorded by Callanan and Kelley, of which the following is typical: "Martha described several visitors unseen by others. She knew most of them—her parents and sister, all of whom were dead—but couldn't identify a child who appeared with them" (Callanan & Kelley, pp. 87–88). Martha goes on to explain to her nurse, "They left a little while ago. They don't stay all the time; they just come and go. . . . sometimes we talk, but usually I just know that they're here. . . . I know that they love me, and that they'll be here with me when it's time" (p. 88).

The other type of vision is a transcendental glimpse of the place where the dying think they're going. "Their descriptions are brief—rarely exceeding a sentence or two—and not very specific, but usually glowing" (p. 99). At the end of Tolstoy's famous novella "The Death of Ivan Ilych," Ivan exclaims on his deathbed, "So that's what it is! What joy!" (1993, p. 63)—the last words he ever spoke. His words are typical of visions of this second kind. But since there is no way to ascertain whether this type of vision is veridical or hallucinatory, I won't give much attention to it. Suffice it to say that those who have such visions invariably report them as glimpses of a real world, not as chimeras.

So we will be concentrating on the visions that people close to death have of beings, not of places. Are these visions more than likely veridical? Are they sightings of real beings that any of us, properly equipped, could see, and who exist in their own right whether we see them or not? Or are they hallucinations? Are they as the word is commonly used, sensory perceptions that are unrelated to outside events—in other words, seeing or hearing things that aren't there?

I should add here that two types of people close to death have visions of deceased spirits: (1) those dying slowly, often of cancer, who see spirits at their bedside, and (2) those not necessarily dying who have a potentially fatal experience that culminates in a near-death experience (NDE). Those dying slowly are usually aware of their surroundings and can communicate simultaneously with both the living and the dead—as if they have one foot in this world and one in the next. Those who meet dead relatives or friends during NDEs are completely cut off from our world as they communicate with the deceased. Yet the descriptions of these spirits given by NDErs after their return from the "Other World" are the same as the descriptions given by the slowly dying. The spirits are usually recognizable, loving, and supportive. Sometimes they are described as "takeaway spirits" or "greeters."

The Argument for the Spirit Hypothesis

Social scientists usually have little patience with any theory that takes seriously the reality of beings on the "Other Side." Words used to describe them like "transcendental" or "spiritual" are often looked at with suspicion if not dismissed as nonsense. But there are excellent reasons for taking them seriously. I will list them under four headings.

1. First, persons near death usually insist that the phantasms they see are not hallucinations, but living spirits existing in their own right. This insistence is especially impressive when the dying person is an atheist or materialist who does not believe in life after death. "I'm an atheist. I don't believe in God or Heaven," a 25-year-old woman named Angela, and dying of melanoma, declared to her nurse (Callanan & Kelley, p. 89). Blind and partially paralyzed, she nevertheless had a vision, and it changed her outlook on death. "I don't believe in angels or God," she told her nurse, "but someone was here with me. Whoever it was loves me and is waiting for me. So it means I won't die alone" (p. 90).

Angela's claim is of course easy to dismiss. One can claim, not without reason, that Angela hallucinated a takeaway spirit to ease her despair in the face of eternal extinction. NDErs are typically just as adamant about the reality of the spirits they encounter while out of their body, and social scientists usually react to these claims in the same skeptical fashion. But the sheer volume of such claims by persons near death is impressive. And it is all the more impressive when put alongside similar claims made by other visionaries *not* near death. Conant's study of bereaved but otherwise healthy widows (1996), to take but one example, reveals the same insistence by some of the widows that the spirits who visited them were real. Conant reports that the "vividness of the experience amazed them. The comparison to hallucinations was voiced simultaneously five times and was always rejected. These were *not* hallucinations" (p. 186). Some of the widows "seemed to be amazed by the emotional power of the experience more than by its vividness because of the conviction they had been in contact with the spirit of the deceased [husband]" (p. 187). Not all the widows in the study were confident that the spirits of their

husband actually paid them a visit; most felt that their culture discouraged a "spiritual interpretation" of their visions, and several worried about "the connotation of craziness" (p. 188) that such an interpretation carried. But all agreed that the vision "feels real" (p. 194). And all, even the most skeptical, derived "reassurance that life after death was possible for the deceased . . . as well as for themselves when they would eventually die" (p. 192). I myself am impressed enough by all these visions, especially their feeling of "realness," to keep an open mind about their ontological status. Not so Conant herself. While acknowledging that such visions "served as a safe haven to help mend the trauma of loss, as an inner voice to lessen current social isolation, as an internal reworking of self to meet new realities, and as reassurance of the possibility of immortality" (p. 195), she describes them as "vivid hallucinations." The ontological status of the visions is never discussed. She appreciates that the visions are useful fictions and therefore salutary, but the possibility that they might be real apparently never occurred to her.

Conant's study is especially relevant to our study for two reasons. First, even though she is not studying visions of the dying or potentially dying, the visions of her collection of widows seem to be of the same quality. Though invisible to everyone else, they are convincingly real to the one having the vision, they are recognizable, and they usually convey a message of reassurance. Second, Conant is a cautious, thoroughgoing social scientist with, if anything, a bias against drawing transcendental conclusions based on her research. What she wanted to show was that visions of the deceased should be regarded as successful coping mechanisms, not as delusions that should be discouraged. Her interests run in a completely different direction from mine, yet I find her useful. When two minds so differently attuned find a common ground, there is often something important going on.

2. The second prong of the argument for the reality of spirits comes from a careful analysis of them. The spirits of persons who are identified by NDErs or by the slowly dying have one thing in common: They are almost always spirits of the deceased. You might ask yourself why all these hallucinations are so tidy. Everywhere else hallucinations are higgledy-piggledy. Aunt Adelaide alive on earth is just as likely to be hallucinated as Aunt Jill who died five years before. But these hallucinations, if that's what they are, have sorted themselves out. With uncanny regularity only the dead show up. Why should that be?

The materialist might answer that it would be *illogical* to hallucinate someone you thought was still alive. After all, a person can't be living on earth and living on the Other Side at the same time. If you had a vision of someone alive on this side of the veil, that would be *proof* you were hallucinating and would undercut the benefit you might derive from the hallucination. So the subconscious mind sorts out who's died and who hasn't. It keeps track. And when your time is up, it decks out a nice dead relative for you to hallucinate, a nice dead relative to take care of you when you finally die. Your fear of death vanishes. So the argument goes. But this argument is not as convincing as it might first appear. After all, how logical *are* hallucinations? Hallucinations are made of memory fragments, and those fragments are no more orderly as they come and go in the theater of the mind than the stuff of our daydreams. Zen masters compare the behavior of this mental detritus to a pack of drunken monkeys. And Aldous Huxley refers to them as "the bobbing scum of miscellaneous memories" and as "imbecilities—mere casual waste products of psycho-physiological activity" (1945, pp. 126–127). The materialist's line of reasoning is plausible up to a point, but it overlooks the almost random nature of hallucinations.

But let us grant for the sake of argument that it does have force. I think I can show that whatever force we grant it for the moment is not good enough in the face of the facts. Here is why.

Let us say I am very sick in my hospital bed and have a near-death experience. I see in my vision my grandpa, long dead, and my cousin Manny, whom I think to be very much alive. They present themselves as spirits, and I recognize them as such, but I am confused. For how can Manny be a spirit since he's alive in the flesh? I come out of my NDE, and I express this confusion to the loved ones gathered around me. But they know something I don't know. They know that Manny was killed in an automobile accident two days before. They didn't tell me because they thought it would upset me. There are quite a few cases like this in the literature, and one whole book, a classic, devoted to them (Barrett, 1926). More recently, Callanan and Kelley presented three cases like this in their book on the slowly dying (Chapter Seven), and the Guggenheims (1995) devote a whole chapter to them in their study of after-death communications (ADCs). Here is why I think these cases are so important. If I believe my dear Aunt Mary and Uncle Charlie and my five siblings and my wife and dozens of other relatives and friends, *including my cousin Manny,* are all alive, why should I hallucinate only my cousin Manny from among all these possibilities? Why should my hallucination be so well informed and so selective? It could be a coincidence, but there are too many cases like this for them all to be coincidences. There is always the possibility that I could have known telepathically that Manny, and only Manny from among those I just named, was dead. But if I had never had any powerful telepathic experiences before, isn't this explanation *ad hoc?* I think the best explanation for Manny's appearance alongside my grandpa in my vision is that the newly dead Manny *actually came* (in spirit), along with grandpa, to greet me during my NDE. He was not a hallucination after all. He was not a delusion. He should be taken at face value.

3. The third prong of the argument derives from the physiology of near-death experiences. Recent research by a team of Dutch doctors, led by van Lommel (van Lommel, van Wees, Meyers, & Elfferich, 2001), makes it clear that the typical features of the NDE, including

meetings with deceased relatives, occur while the electro-encephalogram (EEG) is flat-lined—in other words, when the brain is inactive and the whole body is "clinically dead." Van Lommel summarizes the findings:

> From these studies [involving 344 cardiac patients studied over an 8-year period] we know that . . . no electric activity of the cortex of the brain (flat EEG) must have been possible, but also the abolition of brain stem activity like the loss of the cornea reflex, fixed dilated pupils and the loss of the gag reflex is a clinical finding in those patients. However, patients with an NDE [18% of the total] can report a clear consciousness, in which cognitive functioning, emotion, sense of identity, and memory from early childhood was possible, as well as perception from a position out of and above their "dead" body. (van Lommel, no date)

Van Lommel elaborates further: Even though the EEG is flat, people

> experience their consciousness outside their body, with the possibility of perception out of and above their body, with identity, and with heightened awareness, attention, well-structured thought processes, memories and emotions. And they also can experience their consciousness in a dimension where past, present and future exist at the same moment, without time and space, and can be experienced as soon as attention has been directed to it (life review and preview), and even sometimes they come in contact with the "fields of consciousness" of deceased relatives. And later they can experience their conscious return into their body. (van Lommel, no date)

Van Lommel then asks the obvious question: "How could a clear consciousness outside one's body be experienced at the moment that the brain no longer functions during a period of clinical death with flat EEG?" (van Lommel et al., 2001).

What does all this mean for our thesis? It means that the typical elements of the NDE, including meetings with deceased relatives, are not hallucinations. Hallucinations are produced by an *active* brain, one whose wave pattern would be anything but flat. What, then, could account for the visions of deceased loved ones? It appears that the dying person or nearly dead person, free from her physical body for a few moments, enters a world, an ethereal world, close by but undetectable by the physical senses. She looks like a corpse to an outside observer, but she is having the experience of a lifetime—in another dimension. An experience of what? She says an experience of real beings, embodied beings, dead people she recognizes. Is there any good reason to keep our minds closed to this possibility, given the unintelligibility of the alternative?

4. The fourth and last prong of the argument is, like the one we've just looked at, exclusively concerned with the near-death experience, and not the visionary experiences of the slowly dying who do not have an

NDE. Glimpsing spirits of deceased relatives is a standard feature of the NDE, so anything that argues for the veridicality of the NDE *as a whole* gives support for our thesis.

There is quite a bit that does. I will organize it under three headings.

First, many reports of things seen by NDErs having an out-of-body experience (OBE) turn out to be veridical. There are hundreds of examples in the serious literature on NDEs. One woman saw a shoe sitting on an upper-story ledge of her hospital—a shoe invisible from the street or from her room—as she drifted out of the building during her NDE; the shoe, upon inspection, turned out to be exactly where she said it was. Another woman took a trip to see her sister and later reported what her sister was doing and wearing at the time—a report later verified by the surprised sister who wondered how she knew. A five-year-old child described in detail, and with impressive accuracy, what happened when her body was being resuscitated while she, out of her body, watched from near the ceiling of her hospital room. In fact it is common for NDErs to describe their resuscitations while they are clinically dead. Michael Sabom, an Atlanta cardiologist, conducted an experiment involving resuscitation accounts to see how accurate they were:

> Sabom asked twenty-five medically savvy patients to make educated guesses about what happens when a doctor tries to get the heart started again. He wanted to compare the knowledge of "medically smart" patients with the out-of-body experiences of medically unsophisticated patients.
>
> He found that twenty-three of the twenty-five in the control group made major mistakes in describing the resuscitation procedure. On the other hand, none of the near-death patients made mistakes in describing what went on in their own resuscitations. (M. Morse, 1990, p. 120)

It is difficult to account for the accuracy of NDE accounts if NDErs are hallucinating. Why should hallucinations be so accurate? Why should they yield far more accuracy than the accounts of imagined resuscitations provided by "medically savvy" patients relying on their memory?

Second, NDEs are often profoundly life-changing. Melvin Morse did an extensive "Transformations study" to quantify what every NDE researcher already knew: that people who have a deep, well-developed—or "core"—NDE are dramatically transformed by their experience. He reported "amazing results": "After we finished analyzing the data from the more than four hundred people who participated in the research project, we discovered that the near-death experience causes many long-term changes" (M. Morse, 1992, p. 60). He grouped them under four headings: decreased death anxiety, increase in psychic abilities, higher zest for living, and higher intelligence. In the exhaustive study referred to above, van Lommel and his cohorts reported that the "transformational processes after

an NDE were very similar" and encompassed "life-changing insight, heightened intuition, and disappearance of fear of death" (van Lommel et al., 2001, p. 3).

The question that is natural to ask at this point is, Can hallucinations transform the people who have them? D. Morse, a clinical psychologist and hard-nosed materialist until he had his own NDE, has this to say about hallucinations:

> Descriptions given of hallucinations are often hazy and contain distortions of reality, while NDE descriptions are usually normally ordered and lifelike. Hallucinations are often accompanied by anxiety feelings, while NDEs are generally calm and peaceful. Hallucinations afterwards rarely cause life-changing occurrences as do NDEs. (D. Morse, 2000, pp. 48–49)

NDErs, like the widows we surveyed above, typically insist on the "realness" of their experience and that it is this realness that gives them hope of seeing their loved ones again. This quality of "realness," and the transformative quality that derives from it, is verified by van Lommel. He found in follow-up studies that most of his patients who did not have an NDE (the control group) did not believe in an afterlife, whereas those who had one "strongly believed in an afterlife" (no date, p. 8) and showed "positive changes." Furthermore, these changes were more apparent at the eight-year follow-up than the two-year (p. 8). Something deeply and lastingly transformed this second group of people. Which is more likely: That a hallucination did this, or that an overwhelming slap in the face by something very real did it?

Third, near-death researchers, beginning with Moody (1975), have consistently identified the "core features" of the NDE, and claim that these features recur in individuals having very little in common other than their NDE. It appears that NDEs from cultures as different as Japan, India, sub-Saharan Africa, and the West all exhibit these core features. Now, it is known that hallucinations vary radically from person to person—so much so that it would be surprising if one person's hallucination was at all similar to his next-door neighbor's, not to mention someone's from a different culture. How can the similarity in this core experience be explained? If by hallucination, then obviously not by any ordinary hallucination.

Rather than go out on a limb and posit a universal hallucination that all humans carry seed-fashion deep in their brains, most NDE researchers suspect the commonality is explainable by a common environment, or world, that opens up to the NDEr. In other words, they all see much the same thing because the world that opens up to them is not infinitely variable, like hallucinations, but is simply the way it is. It is real, in other words; and reality, while it admits of considerable variation and can be interpreted in a variety of ways, is malleable only up to a point. Beyond that point, all NDErs experience very much the same thing—just as an Inuit and a Zulu, in spite of radically different cultures and geographies, would experience the one world that belongs to us all and be able to talk about it meaningfully to each other. The Zulu and the Inuit might have different feelings about the spirits they met in their respective NDEs, but they would at least be able to say they encountered beings, many whom they recognized, that did not belong to the world of the living.

So again we must choose: Is it more reasonable to explain away the core experience as hallucinatory, or as a reflection of something that is real and is encountered? The only skeptical theory that makes sense is the "seed theory" I mentioned above. It is not a preposterous explanation, but is it the more likely? We must each decide for ourselves. Given the other prongs of the argument presented here, however, it seems much more likely, at least up to this point, that the spirits we see during our NDEs or as we near death after a long illness are what they seem to be: real beings from the world we might be about to enter.

The Weakness in the Spirit Hypothesis

It would be dishonest of me to fail to point out the weak link in the spirit hypothesis I've been defending up to this point. Melvin Morse appreciates it fully and asks the question:

> But we shouldn't forget about the woman who saw Elvis in the light, should we? As one skeptic pointed out, "If these experiences are real and not just dreams, how can you explain Elvis?" Or Buddha? How can NDEs of children be explained where they see pet dogs, or elementary school teachers who are still alive? They show up in some NDEs too. How can they be explained? (M. Morse, 1992, p. 128)

The skeptic asks a good question, and the skeptic in me worries more than a little about the idiosyncratic features of some NDEs, especially as found in children. Morse presents a cornucopia of cases involving children, and quite a few play into the skeptic's hands as he dredges the literature for signs of hallucination. For example, take the NDE of a five-year-old who nearly drowned in a swimming pool. Now a scientist in his forties of distinguished reputation, "Tom" recalls passing down a long tunnel toward the Light. All seems quite normal for an NDE until he sees "God on a throne. People—maybe angels—were below looking up at the throne." He goes on: "I sat on the lap of God, and he told me that I had to go back. 'It's not your time,' he said. I wanted to stay but I came back" (M. Morse, 1990, p. 167). Suffice it to say that very few NDErs report seeing God sitting on a throne. In another case, eight-year-old Michelle had an NDE during a diabetic coma. In typical NDE fashion she felt herself float out of her body and watched the resuscitation effort, later describing it in accurate detail. Eventually she was allowed to make a decision to return or not to return to her body, a typical feature of the NDE. But Michelle expressed her will to return in a novel manner: "In front of me were two buttons, a red one and a green one. The people in white kept telling me to push the red button. But I knew I should push the green one because the red one would mean I wouldn't come back. I pushed the green one instead and woke up from the coma" (M. Morse, 1990, p. 39).

Is there really a red and a green button in a world beyond ours? Does God really sit on a throne and talk to little children in that world? Not a chance, I would say. "Then the NDErs must have been hallucinating these bizarre features of the NDE," says the skeptic, "and if these are hallucinations, then doesn't it stand to reason that the entire experience is a hallucination?"

I raised this question to Greyson, editor of the *Journal of Near-Death Studies,* and this was his reply:

> As for Melvin Morse's 8-year-old patient who pushed the green button to return from her coma, I also find it hard to believe that the button was "real." But then I also have difficulty taking as concretely "real" a lot of things described by NDErs, including, in SOME cases, encounters with deceased loved ones and religious figures. I do not think that these are hallucinations, however, or that the experiencers are lying or fabricating memories. What I think is happening is that they are interpreting ambiguous or hard-to-understand phenomena in terms that are familiar to them.
>
> Many NDErs tell us that what they experienced was ineffable—and THAT I believe wholeheartedly. I think that what happens after death is so far beyond our feeble understanding that there is no way for us to describe it accurately in words. Although experiencers may understand fully while they are "on the other side," once they return to the limitations of their physical brains, they have to unconsciously force-fit their memories of incomprehensible events into images they CAN understand. That's why we hear Christians talk about seeing Jesus or Mary, and we hear Hindus talking about yamatoots (messengers of Yama, the god of the dead), and we hear NDErs from "advanced" Western societies—but not NDErs from "primitive" societies—talk about tunnels. (One NDEr who was a truck driver told me about traveling through a chrome tailpipe, an image he could relate to.)
>
> Many NDErs talk about not wanting to return, and yet here they are, so they have to construct some reason to explain their return. Westerners often say that a deceased relative or religious figure told them it was not yet their time, or their work was not finished. That's an acceptable and believable reason for a time-conscious and achievement-oriented Westerner to return. On the other hand, it is common for Indians to say that they were told a mistake had been made, and that the yamatoots were supposed to have taken Ravi Singh the incense-maker, not Ravi Singh the baker. That kind of "bureaucratic bungling," I am told, is more believable in India, as it is typical of the way things often happen in their society. I suspect that an 8-year-old girl with limited understanding had to come up with a concrete image like pushing a green button to return. She did not hallucinate the button, but after the fact her mind came up with that interpretation of what really happened to her to effect her return. It was a misinterpretation rather than a hallucination.

Am I splitting hairs? I don't think so. A hallucination is a perception that occurs in the ABSENCE of any sensory stimulation. I think NDErs DO "see" SOMETHING that is "really" there—but it is so far beyond our understanding that they have to interpret it subsequently in terms of familiar images. It is more like an illusion than a hallucination. If at night you imagine out of thin air that there is a person in your room, that is a hallucination. But if, in the darkness, you misinterpret a hat-rack for a person in your room, that is an illusion, an imprecise interpretation of something that is really there rather than something that sprang up solely from your imagination. That's what I think a lot of NDE imagery is: imprecise interpretations of things that are comprehensible in the bright light of the NDE, but incomprehensible in the dim light of our physical brains. (Personal communication, January 10, 2005)

Greyson has given us a rich, plausible account of the idiosyncratic features of NDEs. But the skeptic might remain dubious. After all, if there really is a world beyond ours, it is hard to imagine what in it would be confused with a green and a red button. To deal with this challenge, I veer slightly away from Greyson's analysis. It seems more plausible to me that the subconscious imagination of the NDEr is *actively supplying material* for the experience; or, alternatively, that someone else over there is actively supplying it for the benefit of the NDEr. In other words, the mysterious world entered into by the NDEr is made more approachable and intelligible—more *friendly* is perhaps a better word—by his own imagination or someone else's (a spirit guide's?) interpretive or artistic power. Whatever be the case, on balance there are, in my judgment, far too many indicators that the NDE is an experience of another world that exists *in the main* independently of the experiencer, even though certain reported features of it might be explainable by a coloring of the experience or by faulty memory of exactly what happened. The claim that the *entire experience* is a hallucinated fictive world strikes me as incredible. Nevertheless, there is room, based on all the evidence at our disposal, for such a claim. It is not a claim with no basis.

A final clarification of my position is in order. I believe that visions of the dying or nearly-dying are a combination of real transcendental material and imaginative projection. For example, Julian of Norwich, very near death when she had her famous visions of the dying Christ, could not have seen Krishna or Vairocana Buddha: They would have had no meaning for her, and the Mind who assisted her in coloring the vision, or alternatively her own imagination, would not have allowed such a thing. Nor could a South American Indian shaman have glimpsed Christ while entranced. But their visions are not purely the stuff of imagination either: were there no transcendental "canvas" to project them onto, there would not have been any vision. As for glimpses of the dying, especially deceased relatives, these visions are much closer to the realities they seem to be. I don't believe they are so much projections outward from dying persons, as projections "toward" them from deceased relatives

who come to greet them. If the skeptic insists on reducing all transcendental phenomena to hallucination, we will not be able to agree on much. We *would* agree, however, that all these visions are, to some extent, cultural, personal, and historical. And we also would agree that most hallucinations in normal subjects (as when a moose charges a sleep-deprived sledder in the Arctic) are not grounded in a transcendental world. In contrast to the visions we have been studying, they exist only in the mind of the subject. They are truly hallucinations.

The Relevance of This Study to the Spirituality of Death

I agree with Lucy Bregman, in her article in this issue, that the word "spirituality" is a wonderful word in search of a meaning. As I tried to show in my opening paragraph, I think the word must be anchored in a transcendent world if it is to retain its distinctive meaning. Otherwise it can become a synonym for *mystique* or *romance*—as when we speak of the spirituality of motherhood or of a sunset or of golf. Each of these can provide wonderful experiences, but they are not what we have in mind when we speak of the *spirituality of death*. As Sherwin Nuland (1995) showed us in his award-winning book *How We Die,* death is not usually a time of wonderful experiences. It is frequently, however, a time of healing experiences, as when long estranged relatives or friends are coerced by death's finality into an act of mutual forgiveness. Perhaps it is not stretching too far the meaning of the word *spirituality* to apply it to such meaningful moments. But there is a time when the word is ideally applicable. That is when a person close to death glimpses a world he or she is about to enter—what we will call the spiritual world, a world where spirits reside, and where the dying will reside when he or she becomes a spirit.

My grandmother transmitted to her family something of the excitement of that world shortly before she died. A devout Christian, she became comatose, or apparently comatose, hours before her death at 94. None of us could reach her, even when whispering our love into her ear. But then my mother happened to whisper that she would soon be with Jesus. So suddenly that we were startled, her eyes opened and her face lit up in great excitement. Like Ivan Ilych, she died joyously. She had a foretaste of the eternal world, the world where spirits reside, and her spirit practically jumped out of her body. Hers was a spiritual experience in the truest sense of the word. The *spirituality of death* may mean many things, but Granny epitomized its meaning for all of us.

But I am not concerned with linguistics or etymology. What I have tried to show here is that books are available to get us ready for death. So are the dying. Callanan and Kelley tell the following story:

> Bobby [who was dying] had spoken clearly for the first time in three days.
>
> "He told us, 'I can see the light down the road and it's beautiful,'" Bill said.

This glimpse of the other place gives immeasurable comfort to many, and often is perceived as a final gift from the one who died.

"I've never been a religious person, but being there when Bobby died was a real spiritual experience," his sister said later. "I'll never be the same again."

Bill echoed her sentiments at the funeral. "Because Bobby's death was so peaceful, I'll never be as scared of death," he said. "He gave me a little preview of what lay beyond it for him, and, I hope, for me." (p. 102)

Whether dying persons are telling us of their glimpse of the next world or conversing with people we can't see, we should consider ourselves immensely blessed when it happens. If we don't make the mistake of assuming they are "confused," we are likely to feel some of the excitement they convey. For we are witnessing the momentary merging of two worlds that at all other times remain tightly compartmentalized and mutually inaccessible. That merging is what I mean by the spirituality of death

References

Barrett, W. (1926). *Death-bed visions*. London: Methuen.

Callanan, M., & Kelley, P. (1992). *Final gifts*. New York: Bantam.

Conant, R. (1996). Memories of the death and life of a spouse: The role of images and *sense of presence* in grief. In D. Klass, P. Silverman, & S. Nickman (Eds.), *Continuing bonds: New understandings of grief*. Washington, DC: Taylor & Francis.

Guggenheim, B., & Guggenheim, J. (1995). *Hello from heaven!* New York: Bantam.

Huxley, A. (1945). Distractions—I. In C. Isherwood (Ed.), *Vedanta for the western world*. Hollywood: Vedanta Press.

Moody, R. (1975). *Life after life*. New York: Bantam.

Morse, D. (2000). *Searching for eternity*. Memphis: Eagle Wing.

Morse, M. (1990). *Closer to the light*. New York: Ivy.

Morse, M. (1992). *Transformed by the light*. New York: Ivy.

Nuland, S. (1995). *How we die*. New York: Vintage.

Tolstoy, L. (1993). *The Kreutzer Sonata and other short stories*. New York: Dover.

van Lommel, P., van Wees, R., Meyers V., & Elfferich, I. (2001). Near-death experience in survivors of cardiac arrest: A prospective study in the Netherlands. *Lancet, 358*(9298). Retrieved from World Wide Web: . . ./get_xml.asp? booleanTerm=SO=The+Lancet+AND+SU+Near+Death+ Experiences&fuzzy Term

van Lommel, P. (no date). A reply to Shermer: Medical evidence for NDEs. Retrieved June 26, 2005 from the World Wide Web: www.skepticalinvestigations.org/whoswho/ vanLommel.htm.

Critical Thinking

1. After reading this article, what are your personal beliefs regarding deathbed and near-death visions?

2. What are the strengths/weaknesses of the spirit hypothesis?

3. What "evidence" can you present to support the idea that some individuals do indeed have deathbed and/or near-death visions?

A Spreading Appreciation for the Benefits of Hospice Care

Putting terminally ill patients at ease in their final months.

KERRY HANNON

In Robert and Beverly Stack's red-brick rambler in Orange, Va., the dining room has been transformed into a bedroom. It's furnished with a hospital bed and a dresser lined with medications and other supplies—all provided by Hospice of the Rapidan, a nonprofit agency based in Culpeper, Va., that cares for about 300 patients a year.

Robert, an 81-year-old World War II veteran and retired educator, has Alzheimer's disease. Diagnosed in 2000 and recently bedridden after breaking a hip, he's in declining health, and his daily care has become too demanding for his wife of 54 years to handle. "I can't do it all myself anymore," says 71-year-old Beverly. So with a referral from Robert's physician, she and her family made arrangements for hospice care at home.

Robert Stack is one of more than 1 million patients who began hospice care this year in the United States. Covered under Medicare, Medicaid, and most private insurance plans, hospice care is a swiftly growing healthcare field. About 1.4 million people received new or continuing hospice care last year, more than twice as many as did a decade ago, according to the National Hospice and Palliative Care Organization, the Alexandria, Va.-based industry group.

About 1.4 million Americans received new or continuing hospice care last year, more than twice as many as did a decade ago.

A shift toward the broader use of hospice by Alzheimer's patients has partly driven that growth. And new rules may make hospice care even more appealing. As demand has increased, so has the number of hospice programs nationwide. Today, there are more than 4,700 providers, up from about 3,300 five years ago, according to NHPCO. While the majority of providers are nonprofits, the for-profit sector is gathering steam, accounting for 47.1 percent of hospice agencies last year.

Generally speaking, hospice is intended for any person who has a terminal illness and a prognosis of six months or less to live. Depending on the needs of each patient, care can include pain management, medications, medical supplies and equipment, and assistance with the emotional, psychological, and spiritual aspects of dying. A hospice team usually consists of nurses, home health aides, social workers, bereavement counselors, and clergy, as well as a hospice physician and the patient's personal physician.

Hospice care is usually provided in the patient's home. It can also be made available at a special hospice residence designed with a homelike atmosphere, or in assisted living or skilled nursing facilities. The benefit for Medicare and Medicaid patients is remarkably generous. Medicare pays out $601 per patient per day for inpatient hospice care (and $789 per day for the typical patient who gets 24-hour home care), yet there are no copays, deductibles, or out-of-pocket expenses for the beneficiary. Private insurer hospice benefits offer a variety of hospice services, though they're typically not as generous, according to the Hospice Association of America. To get Medicare or private insurance to cover hospice care, a patient needs only a physician's referral.

Hurdles

Until recently, hospice care, which began as a community-based movement back in the 1960s, has been slow to gain a foothold. Perhaps the biggest hurdle, some say, has been doctors' reluctance to recommend it for their dying patients. Hospice is about caring, not curing, which is often a stumbling block for physicians. "They are focused on healing, and by referring someone to hospice care, they feel like something of a failure," says Michelle Hartman, a registered nurse and clinical director of Good Samaritan Hospice, a mission of Concordia Lutheran Ministries in Cabot, Pa. Patients and their families, too, can be resistant to the idea. "By accepting hospice, you are accepting that you are dying," says Kathy Clements, a nurse and executive director of Hospice of the Rapidan. "That's tough to think about."

As a result, referrals to hospice tend to come unnecessarily late in the game—though that's starting to change. The average time in hospice is currently just 20 days. "That makes it difficult for us to do our best work," says Hartman. "With four to six months, we can improve end-of-life care dramatically with pain management, music therapy, massage—and help family members deal with grief issues."

As demand for hospice care surges, Medicare has upped its scrutiny of the program's cost and quality. For the first time since Medicare began paying for hospice care 25 years ago, the Centers for Medicare and Medicaid Services, the federal health agency that administers Medicare, has new rules for providers. The new regulations, which ratchet up quality-of-care standards, go into effect in December. Hospice providers will be required to provide a closer accounting of the care they offer and show the agency they are improving in areas where they have been lacking. The rules also assure hospice patients a say in their treatment plans and the option to choose their own attending physician.

That's good news for patients. "It's a significant improvement and will bring better day-to-day management," says J. Donald Schumacher, NHPCO president and CEO. "The new regulations [ensure] a framework that will reduce disparities in care and ultimately help consumers pick a hospice provider." Initially, quality-of-care data will be available only to each hospice organization and Medicare, but eventually data are expected to be shared with the public, as the federal government has done with such data for nursing homes and hospitals and home health organizations.

The Bad News

But not all the changes are positive. In October, the agency that oversees Medicare also cut the average reimbursement hospices receive by more than 4 percent nationwide. The goal: to trim hospice expenditures by $2.2 billion over five years. Last year, Medicare spent about $10 billion on hospice care, up from nearly $3 billion in 2000.

Those cuts have hospice operators fuming. "I understand the need for Medicare to look seriously at total healthcare expenditures, and I understand the need to manage costs, but these cuts, if fully implemented, will mean that hospices will be forced to scale back care at the bedside or even shut their doors altogether," Schumacher says. Hospice executives argue that although the price tag for the benefit seems high, it pays for itself. In a study published last year in *Social Science and Medicine,* Duke University researchers found that hospice reduced Medicare costs by an average of $2,309 per hospice patient.

Other providers take a more sanguine view. "Hospice has to do its part to conserve Medicare dollars and should not be immune to the same kind of scrutiny done to business practices at hospitals and nursing homes," says Susan Levine, executive director of Hospice of the Valley, a Phoenix nonprofit founded in 1977 and one of the nation's oldest and largest hospices. "Although I do worry that small, rural hospices who never have enough money will suffer, I'm reluctant to believe that tightening the reimbursement will cause urban and suburban hospices to struggle to survive."

If Schumacher is right, however, the cuts are discouraging news for the mounting numbers of patients seeking hospice. As aging baby boomers face end-of-life situations for themselves

and their parents, the number of patients is likely to continue rising. Four out of 5 patients are 65 or older, and one third of all hospice patients are 85 or older, according to NHPCO data.

Cancer patients have traditionally been the primary group entering hospice care, followed by those in the final stages of heart disease. Yet demand is increasingly coming from dementia patients, including those with Alzheimer's disease, who now account for 10.2 percent of hospice admissions nationwide, up from 5.5 percent in 2000.

Alzheimer's patients' pressing need for hospice is due in large measure to the care-intensive later stages of the disease. Patients are often bedridden and unable to communicate or care for themselves. Nursing homes are often ill prepared to handle these patients, who may require multiple medications to ease pain, anxiety, agitation, and sleeplessness. Moreover, the patients can become aggressive if medication is not closely monitored and specially trained care taken in handling routine procedures such as bathing and feeding. As a result, a growing number of patients are turned away from nursing home facilities or removed from their existing one. With no place else to turn, frequently they wind up back under home care or in a hospice facility.

Dealing with Dementia

To handle the volume of patients with end-stage Alzheimer's and related conditions, some hospices have developed specialized programs for people with dementia. Hospice of the Valley, a Phoenix nonprofit founded in 1977, is one of the nation's oldest and largest hospices, and it initiated a special dementia program in 2003. The program's director, Maribeth Gallagher, says its core curriculum focuses on educating both professional caregivers, such as nurses and physicians, and spouses, friends, and volunteers on how to maximize a dementia patient's comfort and quality of life. The hospice currently serves 639 patients with a primary diagnosis of dementia, nearly three times the number of dementia patients it had when the program began.

Unfortunately, Gallagher says, too few hospices have specialized dementia programs, and too few dementia patients are referred to hospice in the first place. One reason is that the vagaries of the disease make it difficult to predict when death is near. Moreover, physicians, families, and caregivers often do not view Alzheimer's disease as a terminal illness because patients with the disease typically live for eight or nine years before dying of, say, an acute infection.

Beverly Stack, too, has trouble thinking of her husband's illness as terminal, but she is grateful that, at the doctor's urging, she made the call to the Hospice of Rapidan. "The nurses are giving me a lot of support," she says. "And that's what I need right now. They're here for him . . . and for me."

Critical Thinking

1. Who is qualified to be a patient in a hospice program?

2. What are some of the problems facing hospice programs in the United States today?

3. How is Medicare currently helping to finance hospice patients' treatments?

When Death Strikes without Warning

After years of neglect, a devastating effect of epilepsy, sudden death, is drawing new scrutiny.

JENNIFER COUZIN

The call came on a Thursday, 21 February 2002, while Jeanne Donalty sat at her desk at work. Her son Chris, a 21-year-old senior at a Florida college, had stopped breathing. His girlfriend found him on his bed, surrounded by the books he'd been studying and a summer job application. Paramedics were unable to revive him, and just like that, Chris Donalty was gone.

Chris Donalty had had epilepsy—he suffered his first seizure in school when he was 9 years old—but his mother at first saw no clear line connecting his death and the disease for which he was being treated. An autopsy found no visible cause of death, and it was shortly after that that Jeanne Donalty discovered a term she had never heard before: SUDEP.

Sudden unexpected death in epilepsy, SUDEP was first written up in *The Lancet* in 1868 by a British physician; he described the phenomenon as "sudden death in a fit." Neurologists today are familiar with SUDEP, which is thought to follow a seizure, and most specialists have lost patients in this way. "Four or five times a year, someone will not come to my clinic because they have a SUDEP death," says Mark Richardson, a neurologist at King's College London. Most victims, like Chris Donalty, are in their 20s or 30s.

SUDEP has been little studied and is rarely discussed in the medical and scientific communities. Families often learn of it only after a relative's death. In the United Kingdom, which is well ahead of the United States in tracking SUDEP, it's estimated that SUDEP strikes at least 500 people a year. It's thought to explain between 8% and 17% of deaths in people with epilepsy. Among those with frequent seizures, the number may be as high as 40%. This increased risk, recognized only recently, underscores that SUDEP is more likely to occur if seizures are more frequent or treatment is inadequate.

Chris Donalty was in that high-risk group: Despite taking his medications as prescribed, he suffered seizures regularly for 2 years before his death. But he never told his parents—because, they now believe, he did not want to lose his driver's license. "I don't know of any other disease that can be fatal where patients aren't aware of" that risk, says his mother.

Driven largely by grieving families, more doctors are discussing risk of SUDEP with patients, and research is picking up. A few studies are focusing on what happens to breathing and heart rhythm during seizures. In the U.K., researchers and advocates hope to set up a nationwide registry of SUDEP cases. The U.S. National Institutes of Health (NIH) will host several dozen specialists at its Bethesda, Maryland, campus this fall in a first-ever meeting on SUDEP. Still, the epilepsy community is divided on what to tell patients about the risk of sudden death—and exactly what should be done about it.

In from the Shadows

Epilepsy, characterized by recurrent seizures caused by abnormal electrical activity in the brain, has long carried a stigma. Some say this may explain why physicians swept SUDEP under the rug: They didn't want to magnify existing fears, especially because no way to prevent it is known. "There was a real concern that the main message should be, 'You can live a completely normal life with epilepsy,'" says Jane Hanna, who helped found the nonprofit Epilepsy Bereaved in Wantage, U.K., after her 27-year-old partner died of SUDEP shortly after he was diagnosed. Even textbooks on epilepsy omitted mention of SUDEP.

But this discretion carried drawbacks, burying historical knowledge of SUDEP cases and slowing clinical investigation, says Lina Nashef, a neurologist at King's College Hospital in London. Until the early 20th century, many people with epilepsy lived in asylums or other institutions, where staff recognized that patients sometimes died during or after seizures. But the collective memory of these deaths faded as antiepilepsy drugs became widely available and patients began living independently. Most who die of SUDEP now do so at home, unobserved.

Nashef began investigating SUDEP as a research project for a postgraduate degree in 1993, interviewing 26 families who had lost someone to sudden death. Although nearly all the deaths occurred without witnesses, Nashef was often told of signs, such as a bitten tongue, that occur after a seizure. The evidence in other cases was more circumstantial: One young man in his late teens, whose seizures were triggered by flickering light from television and computer screens, was found dead at a computer terminal in the library.

Nashef identified a handful of characteristics that the SUDEP victims shared. All but three were battling regular seizures, though sometimes not more than two or three a year. And all had suffered from a particular type, called generalized tonic-clonic or, colloquially, grand mal seizure. Such seizures, the kind most people associate with epilepsy, are accompanied by a loss of consciousness and violent jerking motions and affect large swaths of the brain.

What Goes Wrong?

Digging deeper into SUDEP, Nashef and others have focused on two life-sustaining functions: respiration and heartbeat. Most physicians now believe that SUDEP stems from arrested breathing, called apnea, or heartbeat, called asystole.

One broader question is whether apnea or asystole strike even during seizures that aren't fatal. Neurologists Maromi Nei and her mentor, Michael Sperling, both at Thomas Jefferson University in Philadelphia, provided an early clue in 2000 when they described electrocardiogram patterns from 43 people with epilepsy. Although none died of SUDEP, 17 of these patients had cardiac abnormalities during or right after seizures, including significant arrhythmias and, in one case, no heartbeat at all for 6 seconds.

More recently, Nei and her colleagues investigated hospital records from 21 people who later died, apparently of SUDEP, and compared their heart rhythms with those from the original study, to see whether the SUDEP cohort had some signs of susceptibility. The biggest difference, they reported in 2004, was not the prevalence of arrhythmias but "a greater degree of heart rate change," says Nei, with heart rate soaring by about 80 beats per minute during seizures that struck while they slept. Seizures tend to boost heart rate because they can provoke the autonomic nervous system, especially when the brain regions stimulated are those that trigger such "fight-or-flight" reactions. These data hinted that the phenomenon is exaggerated in those who later die of SUDEP.

"Four or five times a year, someone will not come to my clinic because they have a SUDEP death."

—Mark Richardson, King's College London

Now Nei is implanting devices under the left collarbone of 19 people with intractable epilepsy to gather data on their heart rhythm over a span of 14 months. Neurologist Paul Cooper of Hope Hospital near Manchester, U.K., is beginning a similar study with 200 people.

Both studies follow a related and troubling report in 2004 from *The Lancet*. There, a group of British researchers described cardiac data from 377 seizures in 20 patients gathered over 2 years. Four of the 20 had perilous stretches of asystole and later had pacemakers permanently implanted to jump-start their hearts if needed.

What might be behind this effect? Asystole isn't always dangerous, although it sounds alarming; it can happen even during some fainting spells. A normal heart starts beating again on its own—which leads clinicians to wonder whether the hearts of patients struck by SUDEP may harbor invisible defects. One possibility is that over time, repeated seizures can scar and damage the organ. Another is that a genetic defect may be causing both heart rhythm problems and epilepsy.

Earlier this year, Nashef, King's College geneticist Neeti Hindocha, and their colleagues intrigued epilepsy specialists with a report on a family with a rare form of inherited epilepsy, including two members who died from SUDEP. The researchers, after gathering DNA from the living, found that all 10 family members who had epilepsy also carried a previously undescribed mutation in a gene called *SCN1A,* which was responsible for their disease. A so-called ion channel gene, *SCN1A* helps control electrical signaling between cells. Similar genes have been linked to epilepsy and sudden cardiac death. The authors postulated that the SUDEP deaths in this family were also caused by *SCN1A,* which could have disrupted heart rhythm or brain-stem function in addition to triggering epilepsy. A group at Baylor College of Medicine in Houston, Texas, is now studying whether ion channel genes that can freeze the heart are also present in brain tissue.

If cardiac defects like these are behind SUDEP, "it might be something preventable," says Stephan Schuele, director of the Comprehensive Epilepsy Center at Northwestern Memorial Hospital in Chicago, Illinois. People with gene defects that cause sudden cardiac death, for example, receive pacemakers that can shock their hearts into beating again. Perhaps, doctors say, the same could be done for epilepsy—if they can determine who's at risk of SUDEP to begin with.

Missing Clues

But Schuele, who's looking for other causes of SUDEP, notes that despite a few reports pointing to genetics, "there is no direct evidence" that asystole is killing people with epilepsy. Schuele wonders if the body's way of stopping seizures in the brain could also be disturbing vital brainstem function in some patients. These mechanisms, which are just starting to be explored and involve surges of certain neurotransmitters, may go overboard and cause chaos in the autonomic nervous system, which governs heart rate and respiration.

The detective work is slow and arduous, in part because so few cases of SUDEP have come to light from epilepsy monitoring units in hospitals, where vital signs are recorded—perhaps, Schuele suggests, because health workers are loath to admit that a SUDEP death occurred on their watch. Last

August, neurologists Philippe Ryvlin of the Hospices Civils de Lyon in France and Torbjörn Tomson of the Karolinska Hospital in Stockholm, Sweden, began surveying 180 hospitals in Europe for information on SUDEP deaths or "near-misses" that required resuscitation. Two months ago, they extended their search worldwide, collecting cases from as far away as India and the United States. They expect to conclude their collection and analysis in about a year.

Just four cases have been published. The most detailed, in 1997 on a patient in Bristol, U.K., reported that that person's brain waves went flat before the pulse faded, perhaps causing a failure of the brain region that controls breathing. This suggests that heart failure could be a consequence, not a cause, of SUDEP. Still, "the mechanism of that brain-activated shutdown is very mysterious," says Ryvlin. "Nobody knows what it could be."

There are clues that respiration is key. By monitoring it in hospitalized epilepsy patients, Nashef found that episodes of apnea were common during seizures. And a mouse strain used for decades to test epilepsy drugs has the disconcerting habit of dying from respiratory failure after a severe seizure. That was "generally considered a nuisance," says Carl Faingold, a neuropharmacologist at Southern Illinois University in Springfield, until he and a handful of others realized the mice could be used to study SUDEP. At Boston College, biologist Thomas Seyfried found that putting the mice in an oxygen chamber during seizures prevented death in all of them.

Faingold considered whether the neurotransmitter serotonin, which functions in the brain's respiratory network, might play a role. He gave the mice the antidepressant Prozac, a serotonin booster, and found that though their seizures remained the same, they were at least 90% less likely to die afterward.

Faingold is disappointed that the mouse work has received little attention and no financial support from NIH—his SUDEP research is funded by an epilepsy advocacy group—and its relevance to humans has been questioned. Because no one can predict who will die of SUDEP or when, "if you don't have a way of investigating [SUDEP] in animals, you're very limited," he says.

Acknowledging the Unmentionable

Meanwhile, doctors face a more pressing question: what to tell their patients about SUDEP. "I admit, I am still trying to figure out the best way to do this," says Elizabeth Donner, a pediatric neurologist at the Hospital for Sick Children in Toronto, Canada. She has grown more willing to share the information, but still, "sometimes we worry in telling people about this phenomenon . . . we could actually make their lives worse." Already, one of the toughest aspects of epilepsy is its unpredictability. "When you add in a statement that some people die, and we don't know why and we can't predict it and we can't prevent it, that can be very scary."

U.K. national guidelines in 2004 recommended that physicians discuss SUDEP with everyone who has epilepsy. In reality, a survey of British neurologists published 2 years ago showed, "nobody told anybody anything," says Cooper. Cooper and some other physicians believe that the 30% or so of patients whose epilepsy does not respond to medication—or those reluctant to take it—ought to be told of SUDEP, because they are at a higher risk than people whose epilepsy is controlled. The latter group, he believes, does not need to know about SUDEP.

That perspective doesn't sit well with epilepsy advocates. "Anecdotally, we're aware of deaths every year in people with second or third seizures," says Hanna of Epilepsy Bereaved. "It does worry me a bit if there's going to be some basic clinical practice that just cuts the line with people who seem to have the most serious epilepsy."

Jeanne Donalty still struggles with her family's ignorance of SUDEP while Chris was alive. "I'm not insensitive to how hard this is for a physician," she says. If she had known of SUDEP then, "I would have been upset; . . . who wouldn't be? But I think you have the right to have all the knowledge about the disease that is out there, so that you can make your decisions based on that knowledge." When it comes to sharing information on SUDEP, says Donalty, "to me, it's easy. You tell everybody."

Critical Thinking

1. What is SUDEP? Do you know someone who has experienced SUDEP?

2. What does recent research suggest is the cause of SUDEP?

3. What are some of the problems involved in research on SUDEP?

UNIT 4
Suicide

Unit Selections

Learning Outcomes

After reading this unit, you should be able to:

- Discuss suicide risk assessment.
- Describe the effects of racial perceptions on suicide.
- Discuss how different racial groups might view behavior as suicidal or non-suicidal.
- Explain the effort to block Internet assistance in suicide.
- Discuss ethical and legal issues regarding the control of the Internet in suicide promotion.
- Explain why qualitative research is needed in suicidology.

Student Website

www.mhhe.com/cls

Internet References

Thanatolinks
   http://netsociology.tripod.com/thanalinks.htm
Yahoo: Society and Culture: Death and Dying
   http://dir.yahoo.com/Society_and_Culture/Death_and_Dying
UNICEF
   www.unicef.org/pon96/insuicid.htm
Suicide Awareness Voices of Education
   www.save.org
Light for Life Foundation
   www.yellowribbon.org
Centers for Disease Control and Prevention
   www.cdc.gov

Suicide Prevention Action Network
   www.spanusa.org
Canadian Association for Suicide Prevention
   www.suicideprevention.ca
San Francisco Suicide Prevention
   www.sfsuicide.org
Interactive Chat System: SuicideChat!
   www.4-lane.com/supportchat/pages/suicidechat.html
Euthanasia Research & Guidance Organization
   www.finalexit.org/index.html

The word *suicide,* meaning "self" and "to kill," was first used in English in 1651. Early societies sometimes forced certain members into committing suicide for ritual purposes and occasionally expected such of widows and slaves. There is also a strong inheritance from Hellenic and Roman times of rational suicide when disease, dishonor, or failures were considered unbearable. Attitudes toward suicide changed when St. Augustine laid down rules against it that became basic Christian doctrine for centuries.

In recent years, suicide has attracted increasing interest and scrutiny by sociologists, psychologists, and others in efforts to reduce its incidence. Suicide is a major concern in the United States today, and understanding suicide is important so that warning signs in others can be recognized. To what extent are nonfamily members responsible for the suicides of young adults when they do not intervene?

Just what constitutes suicide is not clear today. Risky behavior that leads to death may or may not be classified as suicide. We have differing attitudes toward suicide. Suicide rates are high in adolescents, the elderly, and males. A person with high vulnerability is an alcoholic, depressed male between the ages of 75 and 84. Suicidal persons often talk about the attempt before the act and display observable signs of potential suicide. Males are more likely to complete suicide than females because they use more lethal weapons such as guns.

For suicidal persons, the act is an easy solution to their problems—a permanent answer to an often temporary set of problems. The public push for suicide prevention can also be a method of resolving the grief caused by a child taking his or her own life, whether as an adolescent or an adult. The father of Ramon Sampedro (played by Javier Badem in the movie *The Sea Inside*) said this about his adult son's wanting to commit suicide because of a diving accident that left him a quadriplegic:

© Getty Images

"There is only one thing worse than having a child die on you. It's having him want to die." Certainly a suicide not only leaves a void for family members but typically leaves them feeling guilty and asking where they went wrong.

A relatively new topic regarding suicide has to do with the Internet. "Ethical, Legal, and Practical Issues in the Control and Regulation of Suicide Promotion and Assistance over the Internet" addresses this issue. Literally, there are cookbook approaches to suicide to be found by simply going on the Internet. There is currently a movement to regulate what can be posted on the Internet about suicide.

Additionally, suicide risk assessment, different racial perceptions of suicidal/non-suicidal behavior, the need for more qualitative research on suicide, and suicide prevention programs for the military will be presented.

Self-Harming Behavior and Suicidality: Suicide Risk Assessment

MARK J. GOLDBLATT, MD AND JOHN T. MALTSBERGER, MD

Case Report

Erica Severese is 40-year-old single woman with a long history of self-harming behaviors. In the past, she had cut and burnt herself many times on her arms and thighs. On this occasion, she has made a near-lethal suicide attempt by overdose and has been an inpatient in the psychiatric unit for 2 weeks. Since recovery from the effects of the overdose, she has not demonstrated the signs and symptoms of acute depression. She denies current suicidal ideation and is requesting discharge. However, Erica has also expressed persistent hopelessness to the nursing staff, who feel uneasy about the suicide risk if she were to be discharged. Her treatment team requests a suicide risk assessment from a colleague to assist in their evaluation and discharge planning.

What goes into such an assessment? What more can one learn beyond the patient's denial of suicidal thoughts? How might the consultant help her treatment in addition to adding an opinion about suicide risk?

Case Discussion

Mark Schechter, MD
  Chair, Department of Psychiatry,
  North Shore Medical Center,
  Instructor in Psychiatry, Harvard Medical
  School, Salem, MA

The suicide risk assessment includes a psychiatric history and clinical interview, assessment of mental status, and "collateral" information from other sources such as family, friends, and other clinicians. An often-overlooked aspect of this assessment is the clinician's effort to understand the subjective inner experience of the patient. This includes an appreciation of the patient's affective experience, as well as his or her beliefs, motivations, and fantasies regarding suicide. Understanding the potentially suicidal patient in this way makes the clinical interview essential both in assessing risk and also in enhancing the treatment alliance.

The Expression of Suicidal Thoughts

Ms. Severese currently denies thoughts of suicide. This is an important piece of data, but is not sufficient as an assessment of her risk for acting to kill herself. Although patients often communicate suicidal thoughts and intent, they do not always; when they do, it may be to others but not to the clinician (Fawcett, Clark, & Busch, 1993; Fawcett et al., 1990; Robins, 1981). In a chart review of 76 inpatient suicides, 78% had documented denial of suicidal thoughts just prior to the event (Busch, Fawcett, & Jacobs, 2003). Thus, observation of the patient's behavior and the use of collateral information from family, friends, and other clinicians are critical to the risk assessment.

Identification of Risk Factors

Risk factors for suicide are helpful in identifying patients who fall into high risk groups, but there is no set or number of risk factors that predict suicide risk in an individual patient (Goldstein, Black, Nasrallah, & Winokur, 1991; Pokorny, 1983). Ms. Severese made a near-lethal attempt just prior to admission, putting her in one of the highest risk groups for eventual completion of suicide (Rosen, 1976). This tells us to be vigilant, but does not help us to decide at what point the risk has decreased enough for us to move forward with discharge. In addition, if a patient has not made a prior suicide attempt, we cannot be reassured if there are other significant reasons for concern; approximately two thirds of completed suicides occur on the first attempt (Mann, Waternaux, Haas, & Malone, 1999).

Ms. Severese has a long-standing history of deliberate self-harm prior to her recent near-lethal suicide attempt. Such patients are often seen as having manipulative motives; that they have not made more potentially deadly attempts may be taken as an indication that they are at low risk of ever actually completing suicide, as implied by the commonly used term *suicide gesture*. However, patients with a history of low lethality self-harm—even in the absence of suicidal intent—are at increased risk of eventual suicide (Gunderson & Ridolfi, 2001). The clinician should be vigilant in looking for changes in the patient's affective state or psychosocial situation that might increase his or her risk of a higher lethality attempt.

High Risk Clinical Symptoms

Patients with affective disorders are at highest risk for suicide, particularly when they are in depressed or mixed states (Robins, 1981; Tondo et al., 1998; Tondo, Isacsson, & Baldessarini, 2003). Psychotic features (Roose, Glassman, Walsh, Wood-ring, & Vital-Herne, 1983) and concomitant substance abuse (Sher, 2006) increase the risk. Hopelessness, anxiety, and sleep disturbance are also major factors in the clinical risk assessment. The extent of a patient's hopelessness is more highly correlated with eventual suicide than is severity of depression (Beck, Brown, Berchick, Stewart, & Steer, 1990; Beck, Steer, Kovacs, & Garrison, 1985; Brown, Beck, Steer, & Grisham, 2000). Patients may continue to feel hopeless even after apparent clinical improvement (Young, Fogg, Scheftner, Fawcett, Akiskal, & Maser, 1996).

In prospective studies of patients with affective disorders, both panic attacks and "psychic" anxiety were strongly associated with increased short-term risk of suicide, within weeks to 1 year (Fawcett et al., 1990). It may often be anxiety that makes the experience of depression and hopelessness intolerable, adding a potentially lethal urgency to act (Fawcett et al., 1993). It is important to assess explicitly for anxiety, as it may be readily treatable, and some patients who are extremely anxious will not report this spontaneously.

Sleep disturbance may increase suicide risk for certain patients. Global insomnia has been identified a short-term risk factor for completed suicide (Fawcett et al., 1990). Subjective sleep disturbance was associated with completed suicide in a study of depressed elderly patients (Turvey et al., 2002). In other studies, both insomnia and severe nightmares were associated with suicidal thoughts (Bernet, Joiner, Cukrowicz, Schmidt, & Krakow, 2005; Tanskanen et al., 2001). In the clinical risk assessment the clinician should evaluate whether clinical symptoms have been found to increase the potential for suicide. Efforts to intervene clinically can often lead to improvement in these symptoms, and in this way lower the degree of acute risk.

The Patient's Subjective Experience

Escape from subjectively intolerable suffering has been widely described as one of the primary drivers of suicidal behavior (Linehan, 1993; Maltsberger, 1988; Orbach, Mikulincer, Giloba-Schechtman, & Sirota, 2003; Shneidman, 1992), and relief from such an unbearable mental state is the reason patients most commonly give for their suicide attempts (Michel, Valach, & Waeber, 1994). When affective intensity becomes unbearable, cognition narrows, the experience may feel interminable, and the capacity for self-soothing and problem solving may transiently be lost. Although these overwhelming affects may be temporarily relieved under certain circumstances, such as in the hospital or at the therapist's office, it does not generally indicate a longer term decrease in suicide risk following discharge. Ideally, this period of relative calmness may be used as an opportunity to work on coping strategies and develop a crisis plan so that the patient will be better prepared to deal with the next affective storm. The clinician's efforts to understand the distress from the patient's point of view enhances the treatment alliance, and provides an opportunity for collaborative intervention to cope with distress when it becomes most severe.

Beliefs, Motivations, and Fantasies

Patient's beliefs about suicide, and the rigidity of these beliefs, are important in risk assessment. The idea of suicide has different meanings for each individual. For example, patients may see suicide as a deserved punishment; a fantasized reunion with a lost other; a wish for retaliation; or the destruction of a hated aspect of the self, such as an identification with an abuser (Maltsberger & Buie, 1980). The risk for future suicide attempts is increased in patients who view suicide as an effective solution to their problems (Chiles, Strosahl, McMurtray, & Linehan, 1985). Patients who endorse positive beliefs about capacity to cope, concerns for family/children, fear of social disapproval, and moral/religious objections to suicide as "reasons for living" have been found to have less suicidal ideation, to make fewer suicide attempts, and to have less suicidal intent than those who do not (Linehan, Goodstein, Nielson, & Chiles, 1983; Malone et al., 2000; Strosahl, Chiles, & Linehan, 1992).

The clinical assessment of suicide risk involves a number of factors that include but go beyond the patient's statements about suicidally. These factors include attention to known risk factors for suicide, as identification of clinical symptoms have been found to contribute to suicide risk. Also critical is the clinician's effort to understand the patient's subjective experience of distress. This enhances the treatment alliance, and provides an opportunity for collaborative intervention and problem solving. With patients like Ms. Severese, for whom concern about the degree of suicide risk arouses anxiety in the clinical staff, consultation with a clinician who is not directly involved in the day-today care can be very helpful. The consultant may be able to provide a fresh perspective and to engage the patient in a way that can help to further the understanding of the patient's distress and risk of suicide.

Case Discussion

Timothy W. Lineberry, MD
  Psychiatry and Psychology,
  Mayo Clinic, Rochester, Minnesota

Suicide in the hospital is the second leading adverse health care event in the United States (Joint Commission, 2008), and suicide risk is highest immediately after discharge from the hospital (Goldacre, Seagroatt, & Hawton, 1993). Most patients admitted to psychiatric hospitals come in for heightened suicide risk or, like Ms. Severese, immediately after a suicide attempt. The length of admission is ordinarily very short. Only the most seriously ill patients are likely to remain longer than a week or two. Though the explicit question posed by Ms. Severese's treatment team is a request for a suicide risk assessment, implicitly the team is asking, "Is she safe to be discharged from the hospital?" This is a difficult but very common clinical problem.

Suicide Risk Assessment

A suicide risk assessment documents the clinician's thinking in evaluating a patient's risk for suicide. Routinely, we search for those factors that increase suicide risk and for those that are protective; we weigh suicidal intent and plan. We take a history and examine the patient's mental state to ascertain suicidal risk and to decide what treatment is needed (American Psychiatric Association, 2003). The Suicide Assessment and Five-Step Evaluation and Triage (Jacobs, 2007) provides a helpful framework to think about suicide risk assessment both for outpatients and inpatients, and is available as an online resource.

A suicide risk assessment arises from a thorough psychiatric evaluation. It must integrate three elements—the patient's subjective history, objective clinical observations including any testing, and collateral history from family and friends as well as from the outpatient treatment team. This evaluation is an ongoing process weighing subjective and objective data. It takes into account changes in symptoms and synthesizes new information obtained from all sources as hospitalization progresses. Differences in history and observations obtained by psychiatry and nursing staff should be discussed and reconciled. Suicide risk assessment begins at admission, continues through the hospitalization, and is especially important when considering therapeutic passes from the hospital. It is at the heart of deciding whether to discharge a patient from the hospital.

Ms. Severese's history is extremely brief, but suggests many questions about her previous clinical assessment and ongoing treatment needs. There are a number of risk factors placing her at higher risk for suicide, including a recent serious suicide attempt, inpatient psychiatric hospitalization, persistent hopelessness, possible diagnosis of borderline personality disorder, as well as several possible Axis I syndromes such as affective disorders, anxiety disorders, substance-use disorders, and psychotic disorders. Typical psychiatric inpatients will be diagnosed with an affective disorder and/or a substance-use disorder.

Protective Factors

While most research has focused on suicide risk factors, comparatively little is known about factors providing protection from suicide over the long term. Although the Joint Commission's National Patient Safety Goal on Suicide Risk Assessment requires documenting protective factors, there is minimal, if any, evidence regarding protective factors in acute assessment. It is important to keep this in mind and not overemphasize the power of clinician-perceived protective factors in the acute suicide assessment (Maltsberger, 1988). It is unclear what factors tie Ms. Severese to life; defining this with her is essential. At the Mayo Clinic, a brief patient self-report, the Suicide Status Form-II (SSF-II), is routinely included for psychiatric inpatients. The SSF-II specifically addresses both reasons for living and reasons for dying and provides a section allowing for open-ended patient responses (Jobes & Mann, 1999). In our practice, patients commonly describe family, hope for the future, and spiritual beliefs as the three most important reasons for living. This underscores the clinical need for family involvement, which is addressed in inpatient treatment.

What is the background of Ms. Severese's suicide attempt? What does it mean? We know of no previous suicide attempts. Is her suicidal ideation chronic or acute? Is there a family history of suicide? How deep and lasting are her relationships to others? Does she drink too much or abuse drugs? Are there legal or financial problems? What other precipitants may have triggered this crisis? Did the attempt occur in the context of intoxication, perceived abandonment, or trauma? Was it sudden, impulsive, or carefully planned?

We need collateral history to understand her suicidal crisis. The incongruity between her postattempt denial of suicidal ideation and the objective evaluation reflecting no apparent change is most important and calls for closest scrutiny. Her persistent hopelessness is a worrisome risk factor inconsistent with denial of suicide thinking (Beck, Brown, & Steer, 1989; Brown et al., 2000; Fawcett et al., 1990).

Suicide Inquiry

Ms. Severese denied any suicidal ideation following her dangerous suicide attempt. Clinicians, pressed by managed care exigencies, may overly emphasize the patient's current denial of suicidal ideation. To do so is perilous. Fawcett et al. (1990) showed that suicidal ideation may be only tangentially communicated to families. It is often denied when clinicians ask about it. Ms. Severese's denial of suicidal ideation is suspicious and should be seen in context of the collateral information and observation by the treatment team. Denial of suicidal ideation does not guarantee safety. Busch, Fawcett, and Jacobs (2003) studied 76 hospitalized patients who committed suicide in the hospital or immediately after discharge. Seventy-eight percent of their patients denied suicidal ideation at their last assessment. However, 79% were felt to have "severe or extreme anxiety and/or agitation." As part of Ms. Severese's evaluation, her levels of anxiety and agitation should be carefully assessed.

Level of Risk

It is clinically helpful to divide suicide risk into chronic and acute phases. Ms. Severese shows a number of risk factors pointing to higher chronic risk. These factors, which are nonmodifiable, include having made a medically serious suicide attempt and having been previously hospitalized. These details are now a part of her past history and are not changeable. Ms. Severese therefore remains at higher chronic risk than the general population.

Ms. Severese's acute risk pertains to her status while an inpatient and for the immediate weeks postdischarge. Acute risk assessment and management should aim to reduce risk by modifying those factors that can be changed. One would hope to build up hopefulness, quiet suicide brooding, and to treat die underlying Axis I and II disorders. Can her reasons for dying be reduced and her reasons for living be expanded? If anxiety and agitation are present, they require aggressive treatment. Have precipitating causes been identified, and can they be ameliorated? Resolving interpersonal conflicts and engaging her family in treatment are other ways to moderate risk factors.

Suicide risk assessment is an essential part of managing patients at risk for suicide and must be integrated into the treatment plan. However, performing it does not obviate the need to systematically address the following particulars in every case of inpatient hospitalization.

1. Identify access to firearms and ensure that access is restricted. Although over half of the suicides in the United States are by firearms, a recent survey of 205 Ohio adult psychiatrists revealed that only 27% routinely tried to identify patients who owned them. Almost half (45%) had "never thought

seriously" about discussing firearms safety with their patients (Price, Kimonos, Dake, Thompson, & Price, 2007).

2. Be sparing in the amount of medications dispensed in order to lower the risk of overdose.

3. Always try to obtain history from family and schedule a family session if possible.

4. Develop a suicidal crisis plan for the patient involving family and friends. This crisis plan should offer contingencies for responding in a crisis, restrict access to suicide means, prevent the use of alcohol and illicit drug use, and give telephone numbers to reach help during nights, holidays, and weekends.

5. Try to schedule patients for follow-up within 1 week of discharge and make sure that the outpatient treatment team knows about the treatment plan and anticipated problems. Close outpatient follow-up after discharge has the potential to decrease suicide risk, improve transition to outpatient care, and decrease readmission rates.

Suicide risk assessment is an essential part of clinical practice and organizes the ongoing treatment. It is never enough to accept at face value a patient's denial of suicidal ideation, plans, or intent. Although it is impossible to predict which patients may attempt suicide in the future, we can identify those most at risk and address common barriers to successful treatment (American Association of Suicidology, 2005). Providing good clinical assessment and treatment is most likely to reduce suicidal actions because protective factors alone are not guaranteed to eradicate future suicide attempts.

Editor's Note

The patient who is discussed in this article represents some of the difficulties regularly faced by clinicians dealing with suicidal patients, such as how to assess the real risks involved when a patient denies any plans to kill herself. The case consultants emphasize the importance of a thorough suicide risk assessment, and the importance of considering a broad overview of the patient's presentation. Protective factors, such as the patient's stated reasons for living, which are usually ties to loved ones or work, are not enough. Similarly, the patient's denial of current suicidal ideation does not necessarily mean that there is no further risk for suicide. The complexity of this evaluation and the tensions that it balances require knowledge, training, skill, and time. Short circuiting this process leads to unnecessary risk taking with potentially lethal consequences. Modern psychiatric inpatient stays put pressure on the clinician to discharge patients in a very short period of time, often prematurely. Consideration of the points raised by these consultants can help in this complicated assessment.

References

American Association of Suicidology. (2005). *AAS recommendations for inpatient and residential patients known to be at elevated risk for suicide.* Retrieved December 10, 2010, from www.suicidology.org/c/document_library/get_file?folderId=231&name=DLFE-106.pdf.

American Psychiatric Association. (2003). *American Psychiatric Association practice guideline for the treatment and assessment of suicidal behavior.* Retrieved December 10, 2010, from www.psychiatryonline.com/pracGuide/pracGuideTopic_14.aspx.

Beck, A. T., Brown, G, Berchick, R. J., Stewart, B. L., & Steer, R. A. (1990). Relationship between hopelessness and ultimate suicide: A replication with psychiatric outpatients. *American Journal of Psychiatry, 147,* 190–195.

Beck, A. T., Brown, G., & Steer, R. A. (1989). Prediction of eventual suicide in psychiatric inpatients by clinical ratings of hopelessness. *Journal of Consulting and Clinical Psychology, 57,* 309–310.

Beck, A. T., Steer, R. A., Kovacs, M., & Garrison, B. (1985). Hopelessness and eventual suicide: A longer prospective study of patients hospitalized with suicidal ideation. *American Journal of Psychiatry, 142,* 559–563.

Bernet, R. A., Joiner, T. E. Jr., Cukro-wicz, K. C., Schmidt, N. B., & Krakow, B. (2005). Suicidality and sleep disturbances. *Sleep, 28,* 1135–1141.

Brown, G. K., Beck, A. T., Steer, R. A., & Grisham, J. R. (2000). Risk factors for suicide in psychiatric outpatients: A 20-year prospective study. *Journal of Consulting and Clinical Psychology, 68,* 371–377.

Busch, K. A., Fawcett, J., & Jacobs, D. G. (2003). Clinical correlates of inpatient suicide. *Journal of Clinical Psychiatry, 64,* 14–19.

Chiles, J. A., Strosahl, K. D., McMurtray, L., & Linehan, M. M. (1985). Modeling effects of suicidal behavior. *Journal of Nervous and Mental Disease, 173,* 477–481.

Fawcett, J., Clark, D. C., & Busch, K. A. (1993). Assessing and treating the patient at risk for suicide. *Psychiatric Annals, 23,* 244–255.

Fawcett, J., Scheftner, W. A., Fogg, L., Clark, D. C., Young, M. A., Hedeker, D., et al. (1990). Time-related predictors of suicide in major affective disorder. *The American Journal of Psychiatry, 147,* 1189–1194.

Goldacre, M., Seagroatt, V., & Hawton, K. (1993). Suicide after discharge from psychiatric inpatient care. *The Lancet, 342,* 283–286.

Goldstein, R. B., Black, D. W., Nasrallah, A., & Winokur, G. (1991). The prediction of suicide. *Archives of General Psychiatry, 48,* 418–422.

Gunderson, J. C., & Ridolfi, M. E. (2001). Borderline personality disorder. Suicidality and self-mutilation. *Annals of the New York Academy of Science, 932,* 61–72, discussion 73–77.

Jacobs, D. G. (2007). SAFE-T pocket card. Screening for Mental Health, Inc. (SMH) and Suicide Prevention Resource Center (SPRC). Retrieved December 10, 2010, from http://www.stopasuicide.com/downloads/Sites/Docs/SAFE-T_One_Page_Final.pdf.

Jobes, D. A, & Mann, R. E. (1999). Reasons for living versus reasons for dying: Examining the internal debate of suicide. *Suicide and Life-Threatening Behavior, 29,* 97–104.

Joint Commission. (2008). *Sentinel event statistics as of September 30, 2010.* Retrieved December 10, 2010, from http://www.jointcommission.org/assets/1/18/Stats_with_all_fields_hidden30September2010_(2).pdf.

Linehan, M. M. (1993). *Cognitive-behavioral treatment of borderline personality disorder.* New York: Guilford.

Linehan, M. M., Goodstein, J. L., Nielson, S. L., & Chiles, J. A. (1983). Reasons for staying alive when you are thinking about killing yourself: The reasons for living inventory. *Journal of Consulting and Clinical Psychology, 51,* 276–286.

Malone, K. M., Oquendo, M. A., Haas, G. L., Ellis, S. P., Li, S., & Mann, J. J. (2000). Protective factors against suicidal acts in major depression: Reasons for living. *American Journal Psychiatry, 157,* 1084–1088.

Maltsberger, J. T. (1988). Suicide danger: Clinical estimation and decision. *Suicide and Life-Threatening Behavior, 18,* 47–54.

Maltsberger, J. T., & Bute, D. H. (1980). The devices of suicide: Revenge, riddance, and rebirth. *International Review of Psycho-Analysis, 7,* 61–72.

Mann, J. J., Waternaux, C., Haas, G., & Malone, K. M. (1999). Toward a clinical model of suicidal behavior in psychiatric patients. *American Journal of Psychiatry, 156,* 181–189.

Michel, K., Valach, L., & Waeber, V. (1994). Understanding deliberate self-harm: The patient's views. *Crisis, 15,* 172–178.

Orbach, I., Mikulincer, M., Giloba-Schechtman, E., & Sirota, P. (2003). Mental pain and its relationship to suicidality and life meaning. *Suicide and Life-Threatening Behavior, 33,* 231–241.

Pokorny, A. D. (1983). Prediction of suicide in psychiatric patients. *Archives of General Psychiatry, 40,* 249–257.

Price, J. H., Kimonos, A., Dake, J. A., Thompson, A. J., & Price, J. A. (2007). Psychiatrists' practices and perceptions regarding anticipatory guidance on firearms. *American Journal of Preventive Medicine, 33,* 370–373.

Robins, E. (1981). *The final months: A study of the lives of 134 persons who committed suicide.* New York: Oxford University Press.

Roose, S. P., Glassman, A. H., Walsh, T., Woodring, S., & Vital-Herne, J. (1983). Depression, delusions, and suicide. *American Journal of Psychiatry, 140,* 1159–1162.

Rosen, D. H. (1976). The serious suicide attempt: Five-year follow-up study of 886 patients. *Journal of the American Medical Association, 255,* 2105–2109.

Sher, L. (2006). Alcohol consumption and suicide. *QJM, 99,* 57–61.

Shneidman, E. (1992). What do suicides have in common? Summary of the psychological approach. In B. Bongor (Ed.), *Suicide: Guidelines for assessment, management, and treatment* (pp. 3–15). New York: Oxford University Press.

Strosahl, K., Chiles, J. A., & Linehan, M. M. (1992). Prediction of suicide intent in hospitalized parasuicides: Reasons for living, hopelessness, and depression. *Comprehensive Psychiatry, 33,* 366–373.

Tanskanen, A., Tuomilehto, J., Viina-maki, H., Vartiainen, E., Lehtonen, J., & Puska, P. (2001). Nightmares as a predictor of suicide. *Sleep, 24,* 844–847.

Tondo, L., Baldessarini, R. J., Hennen, J., Floris, G., Silvetti, F., & Tohen, M. (1998). Lithium treatment and risk of suicidal behavior in bipolar disorder patients. *Journal of Clinical Psychiatry, 59,* 405–414.

Tondo, L., Isacsson, G., & Baldessarini, R. J. (2003). Suicidal behavior in bipolar disorder: Risk and prevention. *CNS Dings, 17,* 491–511.

TURvey, C. L., Conwell, Y., Jones, M. P., Phillips, C., Simonsick, E., Pearson, J. L., et al. (2002). Risk factors for late-life suicide: A prospective, community-based study. *American Journal of Geriatric Psychiatry, 10,* 398–406.

Young, M. A., Fogg, L. F., Scheftner, W., Fawcett, J., Akiskal, H., & Maser, J. (1996). Stable trait components of hopelessness: baseline and sensitivity to depression. *Journal of Abnormal Clinical Psychology, 105,* 155–165.

Critical Thinking

1. What are some suicide risk assessments?

2. What is your opinion on how these assessments might work?

3. What experiences have you had with friends/acquaintances regarding self-harming behavior?

Effects of Race and Precipitating Event on Suicide Versus Nonsuicide Death Classification in a College Sample

Race group differences in suicide death classification in a sample of 109 Black and White university students were examined. Participants were randomly assigned to read three vignettes for which the vignette subjects' race (only) varied. The vignettes each described a circumstance (terminal illness, academic failure, or relationship difficulties) that preceded the vignette subject's ambiguously premature death. Participants were asked to describe "what happened." Black participants were significantly less likely than White participants to attribute a vignette target's death to suicide and also less likely to report that suicide is acceptable. Implications for future research and prevention efforts are discussed.

RHEEDA L. WALKER, PhD AND KELCI C. FLOWERS, BA

In the United States, suicide is the third leading cause of death among 15- to 24-year-old youth and young adults and accounts for 12.9% of all deaths in this age group (Centers for Disease Control and Prevention [CDC], 2005). Additionally, there are an estimated 825 nonfatal suicide attempts for each fatal attempt (Brickman & Mintz, 2003). Despite efforts to systematically address suicide and suicide attempts on college campuses (e.g., Furr, Westefield, McConnell, & Jenkins, 2001; Schotte & Clum, 1982; Westefeld & Furr, 1987; Westefeld, Whitchard, & Range, 1990; Westefeld et al., 2005), studies reveal that many students may not receive clinical intervention even when depression is accompanied by thoughts of suicide (Garlow et al., 2008). Inarguably, better methods are called for to address suicide vulnerability for those who are not in clinical care.

One public health approach to suicide prevention on college campuses and elsewhere is to increase mental health literacy specifically associated with suicide and attendant risk factors. Jorm and colleagues (Jorm, 2000; Jorm, Korten, Jacomb, et al., 1997; Jorm, Korten, Rodgers, et al., 1997) coined the term "mental health literacy" as an indicator of lay persons' knowledge and recognition of mental disorders, as well as their level of familiarity about help-seeking behaviors and prevention options. In the case of suicide, the assessment, decision making, and handling of relevant information is especially variable across ethnic groups. Persons who are members of underrepresented groups are more likely than European Americans to be "hidden ideators" who disclose suicidal thoughts less willingly (Morrison & Downey, 2000). Though there is little data

associated with stigmatized beliefs about suicide (cf. Walker, Lester, & Joe, 2006), there is some qualitative evidence that suicide might be considered a "white thing" by Black Americans (Early & Akers, 1993).[1] Such stereotyped beliefs may contribute to race group differences in disclosing suicide ideation and emerging plans including one's own ideation or plans and also those of others who may be vulnerable. Recognition, assessment, and appropriate responsiveness to suicide presentations require complex judgments that need not be further complicated by the addition of stereotypes. In the current study, we aim to test race group differences in suicide literacy by examining differences in how premature deaths are classified via vignette technique.

Previous research has indicated that individuals who identify with the Black community may be hesitant to disclose suicide vulnerability due to beliefs that suicide is a denial of Black culture and identity (Early & Akers, 1993). Early and Akers conducted one of the first studies to investigate lay suicide beliefs within the Black community. Following qualitative analysis, they describe beliefs that exist within the Black community because of the "Black struggle," and conclude that Black Americans are more resilient and, consequently, that suicide is more of a White American problem. Racialized suicide attitudes and beliefs potentially undermine universal suicide prevention campaigns aimed at increasing public awareness and education.

To our knowledge, only one published study to date has investigated race group differences in suicide beliefs and attributions. Walker et al. (2006) examined perceptions of suicide in a sample of African American and European American university students. Their findings revealed that African American participants were more likely than European Americans to report that God is responsible for life (vs. the individual or government) and less likely to indicate that suicide could be attributed to interpersonal problems or conflict (Walker et al., 2006). Though the study was cross-sectional by design, it provided some insight to group differences in how suicide might be conceptualized. The authors speculated that the differences might account for the seeming irony associated with Black suicide whereby chronic stress persists but that is unmatched by suicide fatalities. Despite this seeming resilience, suicide remains a leading cause of death for young African Americans.

Though only one known study has examined race group differences in suicide beliefs, several previous studies have considered sex and gendered differences in suicide attributions (e.g., Dahlen & Canetto, 2002). In one study, male college students were found to be more likely to agree with suicide decisions than females (Dahlen & Canetto, 2002). For female students, morally acceptable reasons for suicide included loneliness, loss of a parent, insecurities about attractiveness, and a partner cheating or leaving rather than financial or academic problems, physical illness, depression, hopelessness, and feelings of failure (McAndrew & Garrison, 2007). Certain suicide methods (e.g., shooting, hanging, etc.) have also been characterized as more masculine relative to others (McAndrew & Garrison, 2007). Research on lay beliefs of suicide across sex groups also has been conducted for international populations. Şahin, Şahin, and Tümer (1994) found that Turkish study participants assigned more causes of suicide to vignettes containing female characters than those with males. In sum, these studies provide some insight to group differences in attitudes and beliefs associated with suicide. These disparate beliefs may account, at least in part, for differences in fatal and nonfatal attempts.

Present Study

The goal of the present study was to test race group differences in suicide death classification in a sample of university students. Underlying assumptions associated with suicide are noteworthy because they potentially impact reporting of fatal and nonfatal suicide attempts and also help-seeking for vulnerable persons. The vignette technique is particularly appropriate to elicit potential attitudes toward suicide, a stigmatized and sometimes threatening subject matter. Finch (1987) noted that seemingly ambiguous circumstances permit the respondent to define the situation. The use of vignettes in the current study directs the participant to consider premature death and hypothesize likely causes of death. The explicit hypotheses for the study are: (1) participants will be more likely to classify the vignette subject's death as suicide if the subject is White than if the subject is Black across three conditions (academic failure, relationship difficulty, terminal illness); (2) Black participants will be less likely than White participants to classify the vignette subject's death as suicide across the same three conditions; and (3) participants' classification for cause of death will vary as a function of participant race and precipitating event.

Table 1 Demographic Variables by Participant Race

Variable	Black	White
Mean age (SD)	19.24 (3.99)	20.06 (2.09)
Female	64%	47.1%
Exposure to suicide attempt (self/other)	50.7%	73.5%
Exposure to suicide death	22.7%	61.8%

Method
Participants

The participants in this study were 111 college students enrolled in a moderately sized midwestern university. Participants ranged in age from 18 to 51 years ($M = 19.49$, $SD = 3.49$) and received academic credit for their participation. The ethnic composition of the sample was 67.6% Black ($n = 75$) and 30.6% White ($n = 34$) (see also Table 1). Two participants (1.8%) did not report race group membership; their study data were not included in statistical analyses. Socioeconomic status was assessed using the Hollingshead Four-Factor Index of social status (Hollingshead, 1975). The four factors taken into account in producing this index are education, occupation, sex, and marital status. Values on this scale range from 8 to 66, with higher numbers reflecting higher status. Hollingshead scores in the following sample ranged from 15 (*unskilled laborers, menial service workers*) to 63 (*major business and professional*) ($M = 50.2$, $SD = 12.82$).

Materials
Vignettes

To assess possible biases in suicide classification, participants were randomly assigned to read three short vignettes in which the vignette subject was Black or White. These vignettes were adapted from the Suicide Attitude Vignette Experience scale (SAVE; Stillion, McDowell, & Shamblin, 1984) which assessed the extent to which respondents sympathize and agree with suicidal actions. In the present study, SAVE situations were modified so that gender and cause of death would be presented ambiguously and also so explicitly identify race. This modification was accomplished by using a gender neutral name (i.e., "Pat, "Casey," or "Terry") as an identifier rather than personal pronouns ("he" or "she") that might affect suicide attitudes; also, the last sentence of the SAVE situation (e.g., "She attempts suicide") was replaced with a sentence at the beginning of the vignette stating that the subject "died in the last couple of days" (see Appendix). Each vignette describes a set of circumstances (terminal illness, academic failure, or relationship difficulties) that accompanies the vignette subject's death. After reading the vignettes, the participants were asked to respond to the open-ended question, "What do you think was (subject's) cause of death?"

Table 2   Death Classification by Precipitating Event and Vignette Character

Classification	Academic Failure "Casey"	Relationship "Pat"	Terminal Illness "Terry"
Suicide	69 (62.2%)	29 (26.1%)	30 (27.0%)
Psychological distress/mental illness	17 (15.3%)	16 (14.4%)	5 (4.5%)
Murder	0 (0%)	20 (18.0%)	0 (0%)
Physical illness	2 (1.8%)	8 (7.2%)	43 (38.7%)
Overdose	7 (6.3%)	2 (1.8%)	14 (12.6%)
Accident	3 (2.7%)	9 (8.1%)	5 (4.5%)
"I don't know"	2 (1.8%)	7 (6.3%)	1 (0.9%)
Ambiguous	11 (9.9%)	20 (18.0%)	13 (11.7%)

Suicide Acceptability. Participants' beliefs about the acceptability of suicide were assessed using three previously adopted items (Neeleman, Simon, & Lewis, 1998). The items prompted participants to indicate whether they believed suicide to be acceptable for women, for men, or for themselves. These items were scored on a 10-point Likert-type scale whereby a score of 1 was indicative that suicide is *never acceptable* and 10 is indicative that suicide is *always acceptable*. Several studies have demonstrated the reliability of this approach to assessing suicide acceptability in diverse samples that include African American/Black participants (e.g., Anglin, Gabriel, & Kaslow, 2005; Neeleman et al., 1998; Stack, 1998).

Suicide Exposure. To assess the participants' past exposure to suicide, two supplementary *yes/no* items were included in the questionnaire packet. These questions were: (1) Have you or anyone that you know ever attempted suicide?" and (2) Has anyone that you know ever died by suicide?"

Demographic Form. Each participant was asked to report age, sex, race, ethnicity, income, education, and employment status.

Procedure

The present study was granted institutional review board approval and conducted in groups of approximately 5–20 participants. Participants were informed that participation in the study could cease at any time and that referral to the university counseling center or psychology clinic for free services would be available if needed. Upon written consent, participants completed the initial study packet which included the demographics form and the three vignettes. Participants were randomly assigned to read vignettes for which the vignette subjects were either all White or the three vignette subjects were all Black. After returning the completed vignette packet to the study administrator, participants were administered the suicide acceptability items and suicide exposure items. None of the study participants discontinued participation, requested a referral for psychological services, or demonstrated imminent risk for danger.

All vignette classification responses for cause of death were transcribed to Microsoft Excel. Three independent undergraduate raters, blind to the vignettes and also to the overall nature of the study, developed a preliminary coding system for causes of death based on a sample of participant responses. In an iterative process led by the second author, the following final coding system was agreed upon in consensus: 1 = suicide, 2 = psychological distress or mental illness, 3 = murder or homicide, 4 = natural causes or physical illness, 5 = overdose,[2] 6 = accident, 7 = "I don't know" and 8 = ambiguous.[3] Each of the vignette responses was assigned a code. In the event of coding discrepancies, the three raters and graduate assistant discussed the discrepancy toward reaching consensus. For analytical purposes, a binary code was developed such that "1" was indicative of suicide and "0" was indicative of all other responses.

Results

Preliminary results revealed that the sample of White and Black participants together was most likely to classify the vignette character's death as suicide in the event of academic failure (62%) or relationship difficulties (26%; see Table 2). However, in the condition for which "Terry" died, 39% of respondents classified the death as physical illness; fewer respondents (27%) attributed the death to suicide. Of die 109 participants, 55 (50.5%) read vignettes for Black characters and 54 (49.5%) read vignettes for White characters.

Is There an Effect of Either Participant Race or Vignette Subject Race on Suicide Versus Nonsuicide Death Classification?

Our hypotheses associated with race and suicide classification were partially supported. To test the hypothesis that participants would be more likely to classify the vignette subject's death as suicide as a function of the vignette subject's race across the sum of three conditions (academic failure, relationship difficulties, terminal illness), we used the Mann-Whitney U-test for ordinal nonparametric data. The results revealed that there was no significant effect of vignette subject race for vignettes that included a White decedent compared to those that included a Black decedent ($z = -.578$, $p = .563$); see Figure 1 for distribution of deaths classified as suicide by vignette subject race. However, the Mann-Whitney U test revealed that

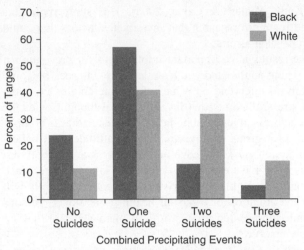

Figure 1 Percent of Black and White vignette targets' deaths classified as suicide across zero, one, two, and three conditions.

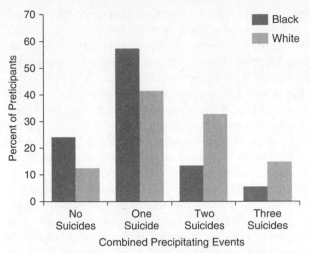

Figure 2 Percent of Black and White participants who classified one, two, three, or no condition as suicide.

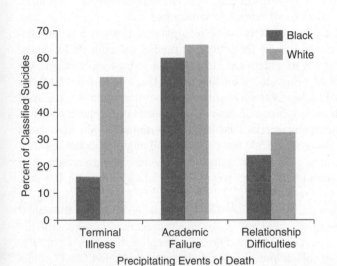

Figure 3 Suicide classification as a function of participant race per each precipitating event.

Black participants were significantly less likely than White participants to attribute a vignette subject's death to suicide ($z = -2.888$, $p = .004$); see Figure 2 for percent of participants by race who classified vignette subject's death as suicide.

Is There an Effect of Race on Suicide versus Nonsuicide Death Classification per Precipitating Event?

Chi-square analyses revealed that Black participants were significantly less likely to attribute the vignette subject's death to suicide when the nature of the precipitating event was terminal illness, $\chi^2 (1, n = 108) = 16.00$, $p = .000$ (Figure 3). However, there were no participant race group differences in death classification when the specific precipitating event was relationship difficulties, $\chi^2 (1, n = 108) = .84$, $p = .246$, or academic failure, $\chi^2 (1, n = 108) = .22$, $p = .402$. Consistent with previous analyses for vignette subject race effects, there were no differences in death classification as a function of vignette subject race and precipitating event.

Post hoc Analysis of Suicide Acceptability

Given previous reports that suicide has been characterized as an anomaly in Black culture, we examined responses to the acceptability of suicide in the current sample. Post hoc chi-square analyses supported previous claims that Black people may not find suicide to be acceptable. That is, White respondents in this sample were significantly, $F(1, 103) = 9.27$, $p = .003$, more likely to respond positively to the statement "suicide is acceptable for me" ($M = 1.42$, $SD = 1.30$) relative to Black respondents ($M = 1.07$, $SD = .64$). Interestingly, Black and White respondents did not differ in response to acceptability of suicide for men, $F(1, 103) = 1.29$, $p = .259$, with mean acceptability scores of 1.90 ($SD = 2.06$) and 1.85 ($SD = 1.48$), respectively. However, a nonsignificant trend was found for race group differences in suicide acceptability for women, $F(1, 103) = 3.17$, $p = .078$, whereby Black respondents ($M = 1.88$, $SD = 1.99$) found suicide to be more acceptable for women than did White respondents ($M = 1.70$, $SD = 1.16$). This pattern of results may be indicative of race group differences in actual suicide beliefs.

Discussion

Several studies and conceptual reports have indicated that Black Americans' suicide beliefs and attitudes differ from those of White Americans. In the present study, we attempted to experimentally test race group differences in classification (suicide vs. nonsuicide) of premature death via vignette analysis. We reasoned that (1) vignette subjects that were Black would be less likely classified as having had a suicide death than White vignette subjects; (2) Black respondents would be less likely than White respondents to classify a death as suicide; and that (3) within each precipitating event condition (academic failure, relationship difficulty, terminal illness), race group differences would affect how the death was classified. Our hypotheses were partially supported as suicide death classifications differed as a function of respondent race and also as a function of precipitating circumstance, though not as a function of the vignette subject's race. The finding that Black and White participants offered different assessments for identical stimuli is consistent with reports of racial differences in suicide-related phenomena. When the precipitating event was a terminal illness, there seemed to be far less ambiguity for Black participants who overwhelmingly indicated that the death was due to the illness (and not suicide). When the events preceding the death of a young adult is more dubious and there is no medical condition, young Black Americans may be as likely as young White adults to classify a death as suicide.

It is notable that more White than Black participants in the current study also reported having known someone who died by or attempted suicide. No known epidemiological reports to date have provided estimates of suicide exposure and how such exposure might affect subsequent suicide literacy. On the one hand, this exposure may have rendered White participants more sensitized to the possibility of a suicide-related death and thus more likely to have classified a death as suicide (regardless of terminal illness). On the other hand, if stereotypic beliefs affect reporting of suicidality in the Black population, the sample of participants in the current study may have been affected by underexposure to suicide. Analysis of 1999–2002 data from the Centers for Disease Control revealed that African American suicide deaths are significantly more likely to be misclassified by medical examiners as accidents relative to European American suicide deaths (Rockett, Samora, & Coben, 2006). While such mislabeling may not directly affect long-held stereotypes associated with who dies by suicide, racialized underreporting for this significant cause of life lost warrants future study.

The overall findings could have important implications for prevention planning. Since universal models of suicide prevention presume to implement widespread public education campaigns and school-based suicide awareness programming, internalized beliefs that differentially affect consumer receptivity and suicide literacy should be considered and evaluated. Since Black participants in this study were significantly less likely than their White counterparts to indicate that suicide is acceptable, we posit that this objection to suicide may have underscored classification of the suicide death. In all, the accumulation of possible factors (e.g., acceptability, racial bias, etc.) associated with death classification is cause for future investigation. Future studies should also test whether the current findings hold up in community samples and across groups that are more socioeconomically diverse.

Racial and cultural context is important for evaluating suicide literacy in that cultural patterns often influence the causes, method, prevalence, and reporting of suicide in a society. In Latin America and in Islamic nations, the problem of hidden and "non-confirmed" suicide has been systematically scrutinized in order to better suicide prevention efforts (Pritchard & Amanullah, 2007; Pritchard & Hean, 2008). In the United States, suicide attitudes and subsequent stigma in the Black community may contribute to underreporting of suicide, but are grossly understudied. It has been suggested that population-wide efforts may be necessary to meaningfully reduce suicide

rates (Knox, Yeates, & Caine, 2004). This study highlights the need for more research that investigates factors that could undermine such efforts.

These results have important implications for prevention if adults, young adults, and youth are less likely to seek help and less likely to intervene on behalf of a vulnerable other in the face of stressful events that invoke suicidal thoughts. Suicide must be addressed as a public health challenge that is complicated by race group differences. Suicide attitudes and beliefs undermine general knowledge and awareness across communities but may have especially deleterious effects in the Black community. Though some at-risk adolescents and adults will receive the attention of a mental health professional, persons from underrepresented groups in the United States are pervasively underserved.

Though this study provides interesting preliminary insights to race group differences in premature death classification, the results should be interpreted with some caution. The vignette-supported findings offered both advantages and disadvantages. The available findings demonstrated race group differences that could not otherwise be manipulated. However, the elicited beliefs do not confer actions or predict behavior. Individuals' responses to a fictional story are not indicative of one's own suicidal behavior or the likelihood that one would intervene should a suicide crisis evolve. Another limitation is associated with the intentions of the respondents and is an inherent artifact of suicide research. That is, some participants may have been unwilling to specify the death as a suicide per se though they considered "overdose" a means of suicide. However, only clear suicide classifications were designated as suicide for the purposes of this study.

In sum, we question whether actual responses to a suicidal person are consistent across racial and ethnic groups. Suicide awareness curricula and peer gatekeeping strategies potentially add to suicide prevention efforts when youth and young adults can be expected to identify at-risk peers and follow the necessary course of action. Some research has indicated that African Americans are chronically underserved by mental health systems due, at least in part, to youth's challenges in recognizing depression and anxiety among their peers and also ambivalence toward accepting mental health professionals as appropriate helpers (Molock et al., 2007). The current study provides some preliminary evidence for how group differences in suicide assessment and decision making might be integrated in future research.

Appendix

"Pat died in the last couple of days. Pat was a 22-year-old [White/Black] student who had been in a relationship for the past 3 years. The couple was in their senior year of college and had planned to be married after graduation. For the past 6 months they had been arguing frequently. A week before graduation, Pat broke off the relationship."

"Casey died in the last couple of days. Casey, a 24-year-old [White/Black] student wanted to be a lawyer for 4 years. Casey's grades had been failing during the last 6 months. Last week Casey got back a major exam that had a failing score. Casey would probably not be admitted to law school because of the low test score and failing grades."

"Terry died in the last couple of days. Terry was a 26-year-old [White/ Black] student who had been healthy and physically active. Six months ago, however, Terry was diagnosed with an incurable but nonfatal painful physical illness. Last week the pain increased to the point where the medication was no longer controlling it effectively."

Note. Each of the three vignette subjects was assigned a gender neutral name (cf. Rousseau & Anton, 1991).

Notes

1. The ethnic label "African American" and racial label "Black" are used interchangeably in this text to retain the level of identification observed in the cited research. For the purposes of this discussion, both labels represent persons of African descent living in the United States.

2. In cases for which the respondent indicated "accidental overdose," the coders agreed to declare the case as an "accident" rather than as an "overdose" given the respondents' choice of "accidental" as a qualifier.

3. All responses that included multiple causes of death (e.g., "Pat's cause of death was probably *suicide* or *chronic health issues* that led from the *stress* of the end of such a long relationship") were coded as "ambiguous."

References

Anglin, D. M., Gabriel, K.O.S., & Kaslow, N. J. (2005). Suicide acceptability and religious well-being: A comparative analysis of African American suicide attempters and non-attempters. *Journal of Psychology and Theology, 33,* 140–150.

Brickman, A. L., & Mintz, D. C. (2003). Datapoints: U.S. rates of self-inflicted injuries and suicide, 1992–1999. *Psychiatric Services, 54,* 168.

Centers for Disease Control and Prevention. (2005). *Web-based injury statistics query and reporting system (WISQARS)* [Online]. National Center for Injury Prevention and Control, CDC (producer). Retrieved February 11, 2009, from www.cdc.gov/injury/wisqars/index.html.

Dahlen, E. R., & Canetto, S. S. (2002). The role of gender and suicide precipitation in attitudes toward nonfatal suicidal behavior. *Death Studies, 25,* 99–116.

Early, K. E., & Akers, R. L. (1993). "It's a white thing": An exploration of beliefs about suicide in the African American community. *Deviant Behavior, 14,* 277–296.

Finch, J. (1987). The vignette technique in survey research. *Sociology, 21,* 105–114.

Furr, S. R., Westefield, J. S., McConnell, G. N., & Jenkins, J. M. (2001). Suicide and depression among college students: A decade later. *Professional Psychology, 32,* 97–100.

Garlow, S. J., Rosenberg, J., Moore, J. D., Haas, A. P., Koestxer, B., Hendin, H., et al. (2008). Depression, desperation, and suicidal ideation in college students: Results from the American Foundation for Suicide Prevention College Screening Project at Emory University. *Depression & Anxiety, 25,* 482–488.

Hollingshead, A. B. (1975). *Four factor index of social status.* Unpublished manuscript, Yale University, New Haven, CT.

Jorm, A. F. (2000). Public knowledge and beliefs about mental disorders. *British Journal of Psychiatry, 177,* 396–401.

Jorm, A. F., Korten, A. E., Jacomb, P. A., Christensen, H., Rodgers, B., & Pollitt, P. (1997) . "Mental health literacy": A survey of the public's ability to recognise mental disorders and their beliefs about the effectiveness of treatment. *The Medical Journal of Australia, 166,* 182–186.

Jorm, A. F., Korten, A. E., Rodgers, B., Pollitt, P., Jacomb, P. A., Christensen, H., et al. (1997). Beliefs systems of the general public concerning the appropriate treatments for mental illness. *Social Psychiatry and Psychiatric Epidemiology, 32,* 468–473.

Knox, K. L., Yeates, C, & Caine, E. D. (2004). If suicide is a public health problem, what are we doing to prevent it? *American Journal of Public Health, 94,* 37–45.

McAndrew, F. T., & Garrison, A. J. (2007). Beliefs about gender differences in methods and causes of suicide. *Achieves of Suicide Research, 11,* 1–9.

Molock, S. D., Barksdale, C., Matlin, S., Puri, R., Cammack, N., & Spann, M. (2007). Qualitative study of suicidality and help-seeking behaviors in African American adolescents. *American Journal of Community of Psychology, 40,* 52–63.

Morrison, L. L., & Downey, D. L. (2000). Racial differences in self-disclosure of suicidal ideation and reasons for living: Implications for training. *Cultural Diversity and Ethnic Minority Psychology, 6,* 374–386.

Neeleman, J., Simon, W., & Lewis, G. (1998) . Suicide acceptability in African- and White Americans: The role of religion. *Journal of Nervous and Mental Disease, 186,* 12–16.

Pritchard, C., & Amanullah, S. (2007). An analysis of suicide and undetermined dead is in 17 predominantly Islamic countries contrasted with the UK *Psychological Medicine, 37,* 421–430.

Pritchard, C., & Heax, S. (2008). Suicide undetermined deaths among youths and young adults in Latin America. *Crisis, 29,* 1–9.

Rockett, R. H., Samora, J. B., & Coben, J. H. (2006). The black-white suicide paradox: Possible effects of misclassification. *Social Science & Medicine, 63,* 2165–2175.

Rousseau, D. M., & Anton, R. J. (1991). Fairness and implied contract obligations in job terminations: The role of contributions, promises, and performance. *Journal of Organizational Behavior, 72,* 287–299/.

Şahin, N., Şahin, N. H., & Tümer, S. (1994). Stereotypes of suicide causes for three age/gender cohorts. *International Journal of Psychology, 29,* 213–232.

Schotte, D., & Glum, G. (1982). Suicide ideation in a college population: A test of a model. *Journal of Consulting & Clinical Psychology, 50,* 690–696.

Stack, S. (1998). The relationship between culture and suicide: An analysis of African Americans. *Transcultural Psychiatry, 35,* 253–269.

Stillion, J. M., McDowell, E. E., & Shamblin, J. B. (1984). The suicide attitude vignette experience: A method for measuring adolescent attitudes toward suicide. *Death Education, 8,* 65–79.

Walker, R. L., Lester, D., & Joe, S. (2006). Lay theories of suicide: An examination of culturally relevant suicide beliefs and attributions among African Americans and European Americans. *Journal of Black Psychology, 32,* 320–334.

Westefeld, J. S., & Furr, S. R. (1987). Suicide and depression among college students. *Professional Psychology: Research & Practice, 18,* 119— 123.

Westefeld, J. S., Homatfar, B., Spotts, J., Furr, S., Range, L., & Werth, J. L. (2005). Perceptions concerning college student suicide: Data from four universities. *Suicide and Life-Threatening Behavior, 35,* 640–644.

Westefeld, J. S., Whitchard, K. A., & Range, L. M. (1990). College and university student suicide: Trends and implications. *Counseling Psychologist, 3,* 464–476.

Critical Thinking

1. As a student of the social/behavioral sciences, how would you assess the methodology of this research endeavor?

2. Why do you think that the perception of black and white college students differed on suicide versus non-suicide behavior?

3. Might not a *quality of life* versus a *sanctity of life* philosophy contribute to different perceptions about suicide?

Ethical, Legal, and Practical Issues in the Control and Regulation of Suicide Promotion and Assistance over the Internet

Brian L. Mishara, PhD and David N. Weisstub, JD, LLD

There has been growing concern about the numerous reports of suicides following contact with websites that incite people to suicide and provide detailed information on suicide methods (Alao, Yolles, & Armenta, 1999; Australian IT, 2004; Baume, Cantor, & Rolfe, 1997; Becker & Schmidt, 2004; Dobson, 1999; Mehlum, 2000; Rajagopal, 2004; Reany 2004; Richard, Werth & Rogers, 2000; Thompson, 1999). The ethical, legal, and practical issues in the control and regulation of suicide promotion and assistance over the Internet are the focus of this article.

Media Reports

There are numerous reports in the media and scientific journals of suicides purportedly related to contact with Internet sites. Typical examples include the suicide that instigated the introduction of a bill in the Danish Parliament in February 2004 to ban websites that encourage and provide information about suicide. The son of a Danish journalist was apparently encouraged to end his life by a website which gave him information he used to kill himself. Two studies (Becker, El-Faddagh, & Schmidt, 2004; Becker, Mayer, Nagenborg, El-Faddagh, & Schmidt, 2004) that reported on a 17-year-old female suicide attempter concluded that websites may trigger suicidal behavior in predisposed adolescents. Several newspaper articles tell of distraught parents who blamed their child's suicide on Internet sites (Shepherd, 2004), and there was much media coverage of a 21-year-old man from Arizona who killed himself by overdose while chatting online with friends who egged him on.

Multiple suicides by people who meet on chat sites appear to be increasing. One much-publicized example concerned Louis Gillies from Glasgow who met Michael Gooden from East Sussex (England) in May 2002 on a suicide "newsgroup" (Innes,

2003). While on a cliff ready to jump, Gillies was talked out of killing himself by a friend on his cell phone, but Gooden refused to talk and jumped. Gillies was charged with aiding and abetting a suicide; he killed himself in April 2003 just before the trial was about to begin.

Meeting suicide companions online appears to be most prevalent in Japan (Japan, 2004) where, between February and early June 2003, at least 20 Japanese died in suicide pacts with companions they met on the Internet, many by strikingly similar carbon monoxide poisonings (Harding, 2004; "Seven Die in Suicide Pacts," 2004). It is believed that the first "wave" of Internet suicide pacts occurred in 2000 in South Korea when there were three cases. In March 2003, an Austrian teenager and a 40-year-old Italian who met on a suicide chat jointly committed suicide near Vienna ("Pair Planned Suicide," 2003). The man had also contacted two young Germans online, but police alerted their families before they could carry out their suicides.

Legal Provisions and Law Reform Projects

Many countries have laws prohibiting aiding and abetting suicide; however, we are not aware of any case where Internet activity has been pursued in a court of law for aiding or abetting suicide. That said, on February 13, 2005, Gerald Krein was arrested in Oregon for solicitation to commit murder after it was alleged that he used his Internet chat room to entice up to 31 lonely single women to kill themselves on Valentine's Day. The arrest followed a report to police by a woman in the chat room who said another participant talked about killing her two children before taking her own life (Booth, 2005).

So why have not current laws against aiding and abetting suicide been applied to Internet activities, given the compelling nature of specific case histories when people died by suicide in a manner communicated over the Internet and following a series of Internet contacts in which they were encouraged to kill themselves? It may be helpful to examine legal jurisprudence regarding standards for determining causality in such matters. When individuals are deemed to be responsible for having caused harm to another person, their actions are usually in close temporal and physical proximity to the victim's death. For example, a person who strikes another person who subsequently dies from the blow may be deemed responsible because that action had an immediate physical consequence for the victim. In addition, scientific and medical evidence must indicate according to reasonable probabilities that the action in question was causally related to the consequences (Bonger, 2002).

Scientific research on the influence of the media on suicides has concentrated on television and newspapers and their influence on population suicide rates. There are several excellent reviews of research in this area (e.g., Hawton & Williams, 2001; Pirkis & Warwick Blood, 2001; Stack, 2000, 2003, 2005). It is clear that news media depictions of deaths by suicide have a risk of increasing suicides among those who have contact with those media. Generally, the more the publicity, the higher the contagion effect (it has been reported that the suicide of Marilyn Monroe resulted in 197 additional suicides [Phillips, 1974]); however, there are no empirical data on changes in the risk of suicide that may be related to contacts with Internet sites. Nevertheless, it appears from numerous cases reported in the media that contact with Internet sites and with chat rooms preceded deaths by suicide and the methods used were precisely those described in the Internet contact. In sum, these case reports do not meet the requirements for scientific proof that Internet sites cause suicide, but they suggest that a relationship may exist.

Despite the compelling case reports, it can be argued that had the victims not contacted a specific suicide site, they may have still killed themselves. The suicide risk of people who contact suicide sites may have pre-dated their contact. In addition, if a person had not used a method found on a site, other methods are easily available.

Another challenge in determining a causal relationship is the difficulty in generalizing from epidemiological population statistics to individual cases. According to population statistics, it has been demonstrated that media publicity on suicide results in a small but significant increase in the number of people who die by suicide following the media reports. It is not possible, however, to generalize from these population data to determine if any one specific individual's death was facilitated by his or her having read a newspaper article or having watched a specific television program about suicide. The nature of epidemiological research is such that, given the great number of people at risk of committing suicide and the very small number who actually die by suicide, it is impossible to determine that one specific individual is likely to have died as a result of media exposure and that the death could have been avoided by non-exposure.

To date we do not have any epidemiological data on the relationship between contact with the Internet and suicides. All we have is a number of case histories in which there appears to be a link. It is dubious that one could make a good scientific or legal case for the causal relationship between Internet activities and suicide without conducting further research.

Self-Regulation

Even if one could prove that there is a risk associated with certain Internet sites, one must weigh that risk against possible dangers of compromising freedom of expression by attempting to control access to the site. In most countries, there is little or no control of Internet content because of constitutional guarantees of freedom of expression. EU decision number 276-1999, "The European Union Safer Internet Plan" (European Union, 1999), essentially proposes that Internet organizations and Internet service providers (ISPs) act responsibly to control what is available and limit or deny access to sites that are illegal or dangerous. Many countries, including Great Britain, Canada, the United States, and New-Zealand, attempt to control Internet content by self-regulation since guarantees of freedom of speech apparently preclude censorship or government control of access to sites. The use of self-regulation has been criticized for being ineffective, since those who produce the sites and distribute them are also being asked to censor them. It also has been criticized by persons who are concerned about the defence of freedom of expression, since there is no verification of which sites are blocked or censored and no explicit guidelines about what should be banned.

Filtering Techniques

An alternative to self-regulation is rating systems that use filtering techniques to block access to certain sites on personal computers. A primary issue is who actually rates the sites so that filter programs can identify sites to block. The World Wide Web Consortium (W3C) has developed the Platform for Internet Content Selection (PICS) standards in which creators of sites rate their own sites according to specific criteria. Yet ratings of sites, even if accurate, are useless if they are disregarded. Software used to filter sites by blocking access is only effective if they are used and they block target sites and do not block other permissible sites. For this reason, filtering software is mostly used by parents who attempt to control access to sites by minors; for example, sites depicting child pornography, violence, and racial hatred. But filters have limited intelligence to discriminate between desirable and undesirable sites. If filters block access to certain words or terms, for example "suicide" or "suicide methods," they may also block sites that provide helpful information in suicide prevention, such as the site of Befrienders International which offers help over the Internet to suicidal individuals (www.befrienders.org)

Blocking Access to Sites

A number of countries attempt to block access by all individuals to specific Internet content and sites, including Algeria, Bahrein, China, Germany, Iran, North Korea, Saudi Arabia, Singapore, South Korea, Sweden, United Arab Emirates, and Vietnam. For example, in Saudi Arabia all 30 of the ISPs go through a central node, and material and sites containing pornography, believed to cause religious offense, and information on bomb making are blocked. Germany requests that ISPs block media that is morally harmful to youth, including that which is "pornographic, depicts extreme violence, war mongering, racist, fascist or has anti-Semitic content." They have had success in blocking German sites with this material but have been less successful in blocking sites originating outside of Germany. Sweden has laws that require blocking of information instigating rebellion, racial agitation, child pornography, illegal description of violence, and material that infringes upon copyright laws.

In several countries, including the United States, Great Britain, and New Zealand, laws were passed to block certain Internet content but those laws were overturned by the courts because of constitutional guarantees of freedom of expression. Australia is the only country that currently has laws to specifically restrict sites that promote suicide or provide information on suicide methods.

Recent Modifications to the Australian Criminal Code

Public concern about the vulnerability of Australian youth recently gave rise to the enactment of amendments to the Australian Criminal Code making Internet activity intentionally relating directly or indirectly to the incitement of suicide a distinct crime (Commonwealth of Australia, 2004a). The Australian legislation also refers to the promotion of a particular method of committing suicide or providing instruction.

The parliamentary debate highlighted the vulnerability of young adults as a particular group based on both the level of Internet usage and their suicide rates (Commonwealth of Australia, 2004b, 2004c). It was argued that because of those factors there is a moral obligation on the part of society to provide protection. The legislators cited the failure of private ISPs to regulate themselves, thereby mandating government to do so. While acknowledging the division in public opinion, the Australian government argued that public protection trumped issues of liberty and freedom of expression.

There was strong vocal opposition, including from the Green Party. The critics said that the ambiguity of "intentionality" could give rise to unintended results and could render the law impossible to apply. The point was argued that given the volume of suicide items incorporated into daily activity on the Internet, it could be foreseen that ISPs could readily find themselves vulnerable to the legislation despite their efforts to control content, if an aggressive pattern of catchments would take place. It was submitted that attacking the causes of suicide, rather than operating with a wide net of surveillance and intervention, would be more likely to succeed in reducing the threat.

Other interventions addressed the foolhardiness of attempting to restrict information about matters such as suicide and voluntary euthanasia. The key issue, from the point of view of the opposition, was not the need to control Internet content, but the extent to which the government is prepared to devote resources to suicide prevention activities.

Ethical Presuppositions

There are several ethical considerations concerning the control of Internet content in order to prevent suicide. First and foremost is the ethical premise that suicide should be prevented (Mishara & Weisstub, 2005). Those who adopt a libertarian perspective might contend that people have the right to choose to end their life by suicide. Also, since suicide is not illegal in most countries, one could argue that suicidal people should have access to material they desire. If this libertarian position is adopted, it is not possible to justify controlling access to information encouraging suicide or providing information or advice on how to exercise the right to end one's life by suicide.

If one adopts a moralist ethical position that suicide must be prevented, and if controlling access to Internet sites can save lives, then controls must be instituted. If one holds a relativist position that some suicides are acceptable and others are not, one may morally justify some form of Internet control, although control of access for only some people is practically impossible. For example, a relativist who believes that terminally ill people should be allowed or have access to means to end their lives but people in good health who suffer from treatable psychiatric problems should not, would have a difficult time controlling access for some people and not others.

The Internet versus Other Mass Media

One of the questions concerning the ethics of controlling access to the Internet is the specificity of the Internet compared to other mass media. The Internet has been characterized as a "pull" technology, as opposed to the so-called push technologies including radio and television. Push technologies include television and radio; they provide access to the media without the user engaging in any specific and explicit attempt to find a specific media content. Television content is available in every home and because of its universal access, television has been regulated in most countries as to content. In contrast to the mass medias of television and radio, Internet users must actively seek out a specific content.

Also, anonymity of the provider can exist on the Internet and there is no ability to verify the authenticity of the information one finds on a website. No government agencies are ensuring that Web content is appropriate and accurate (unlike television and radio which are generally subject to government control). The Web can be extremely graphic in nature and individuals who display their suicidal intentions and behaviors on the Internet can expect possible exposure to thousands throughout the world, providing glorification of their suicidal acts.

The differences between "push" and "pull" technologies may be used to defend the Internet against control by claiming that the Internet is a private service that does not invade people's homes, and that specific content must be sought out by individuals actively searching through cyberspace. The down side, of course, is this same private nature provides for a level of anonymity of both the person contacting the site and the person providing information on a site, which may lead to an "anything goes" environment where there are no controls whatsoever about the authenticity and credibility of information transmitted or provided.

Different Internet Activities

Internet situations involving suicide vary. Some sites passively provide information, which encourage suicide in texts that suggest it is a good idea to end one's life. Other sites provide information on suicide methods, many including specific details about what medications to mix, how to hang oneself, and the strengths and weaknesses of alternative methods with respect to side effects and risks of failure. Yet still other sites involve the exchange of messages from "suicide encouragers" who interact with suicidal people, trying to stimulate them to proceed with their suicidal plans in chat rooms or in e-mail correspondence. "Suicide predators" seek out people who post messages suggesting they may be feeling suicidal but who are not explicitly asking for information or encouragement. These predators offer unsolicited incitation to suicide and may provide information about how to commit suicide without being asked. If one is considering some form of control of Internet activity, it is important to decide which of the above activities one would like to limit.

Vulnerable Populations

One of the major issues in control of the Internet in order to prevent suicides is the protection of minors and other vulnerable populations, such as persons with psychiatric disorders. The most successful attempts to control access over the Internet has involved child pornography sites and pornography aimed at minors, although these initiatives may be criticized for falling short of their goal of totally blocking access. Thus far, very little has been done to protect minors from suicide promotion sites.

In the area of the exposure of minors to extreme violence, research has shown beyond doubt that media exposure to violence is related to increased violent behavior (Bushman & Anderson, 2001); however, there has been little success in attempts to control violence on the Internet.

The Jurisdictional Factor

Even if one were able to resolve the legal and ethical issues, there are a number of practical considerations that make control of Internet suicide promotion activities extremely difficult (Geist, 2002; Smith, Bird, & Bird, 2002). The first is the issue of cross-border jurisdiction. Although countries may be able to control activities of Internet sites that originate within their borders, international jurisprudence makes it difficult to obtain jurisdiction over sites that originate outside the country. Jurisprudence generally distinguishes between passive Internet activity, such as simply operating a website which may be accessed from different countries, and active endeavors which involve sending information, interacting (for example, in a chat room), and doing business in a country. Furthermore, jurisprudence has favored limiting claims of harm to actual impact rather than claims of potential damage.

Two important cases underline the difficulties in cross-border jurisdiction issues. The first case, in Canada, *Braintech Inc. v. Kostivk* (1999), involved a libel complaint concerning a site in Canada. In denying jurisdiction, the judge found that there is a "need for better proof the defendant entered Texas than the mere possibility that someone in Texas may have reached to cyberspace to bring defamation material to a screen in Texas." The ability to access material from a site outside a jurisdiction was not sufficient to allow for jurisdiction in another area (Geist, 2002).

The "Calder test," based on the U.S. case of *Calder v. Jones* (1984) is often used to determine jurisdiction in Internet cases. This test requires that the defendant's intentional tortuous actions are: (1) expressly aimed at the forum state and (2) cause harm to the plaintiff in the forum state, of which the defendant knows is likely to be suffered. This test provides protection for Internet sites and activities which do not explicitly attempt to have an effect outside of their own jurisdiction or intentionally cause harm to an individual in another jurisdiction. Obviously, there is virtue in protecting individuals from being liable in every country in the world for actions, which may be perfectly legal in their own jurisdiction. Still, jurisdiction issues make attempts to control Internet activity extremely difficult.

Conclusion

There remains a great need for scientifically valid data on the extent that Internet sites contribute to the risk of suicide. Specifically, we need to determine if Internet activities increase suicide risk and, if so, which subpopulations are particularly vulnerable. Spectacular media reports of suicides following Internet contact and case reports of individuals who died by suicide using methods they found on the Internet or in pacts with people they met over the Internet, as impressive as they may seem, do not constitute scientific proof that Internet activities provoke suicides. One could try to build a case for the relationship between Internet activities and suicide using psychological autopsy methods. Qualitative assessments of the content of Internet contacts where seemingly vulnerable individuals appeared to be forcefully encouraged to kill themselves has high face validity; however, we need to develop more creative methodologies, perhaps inspired by the studies of the relationship between suicide reporting in other media and suicide rates. One of the greatest challenges is to determine if individuals who kill themselves after Internet contacts would have died by suicide if they did use the Internet.

It is also important to clarify the ethical basis upon which any form of suicide prevention activity is undertaken before applying one's beliefs to controlling Internet suicide promotion. Furthermore, any action to control Internet suicide promotion must consider the different forms of Internet activities, which range from passive posting of information on a website to interacting in a chat room or seeking out vulnerable individuals as an Internet predator.

Any attempt to control the Internet must be viewed along with the control and freedom of other media, unless special characteristics of the Internet are judged to lead to special laws or consideration. It can be argued that, unlike other media, the internet lacks quality control, and this may justify legislative intervention. Most keep in mind, however, that editors of newspapers, like Web masters, are free to publish what they please, even if it may incite suicides. If a journalist publishes a "dangerous" article, she may evoke the ire of readers and sales may decline (or increase due to the controversy). When a website or chat does something people do not like, users can simply not frequent that site. In this regard it is interesting to compare the Internet to published works. If one were to publish the philosopher David Hume's writings recommending suicide on an Australian Internet site, would this be banned? If so, would it be considered as more dangerous than publishing his book and selling it in a bookstore? Internet sites provide information on means to kill oneself in an often clear but informal manner; however, if the same information is available in medical textbooks, what would justify control of this information over the Internet while permitting the sale of medical textbooks and their availability in libraries?

The fact that the Internet allows for global access leads to complex jurisdiction issues and practical difficulties. Given the rapidly changing state of technologies which lead to the continued development of new ways to circumvent control, it may not be practically possible to ban sites, censor material, or limit access. Even if data to document that high risks of suicide are related to specific Internet activities were available, and even if a country decides to prevent access to suicide sites, the only way to ensure even a minimal level of success would be to install draconian censorship measures. Regardless, it is not certain that the controls would be effective. Therefore, alternatives to control and censorship should be considered, such as developing increased suicide prevention activities on the Internet to counterbalance Internet suicide promotion activities. Persons involved in suicide prevention should be encouraged to enter chat discussions to dissuade suicidal persons from killing themselves and encourage them to seek help. Finally, public education could be enhanced to facilitate ways and means to obtain help from the Internet in the interest of suicide prevention.

References

Alao, A. O., Yolles, J. C, & Armenta, W. (1999). Cybersuicide: The internet and suicide. *American Journal of Psychiatry, 156,* 1836–1837.

Australian IT. (2004). Crackdown on suicide chat rooms. Retrieved from http://australianit.news.com.au/wireless/story/0,8256,10340811,00.html

Baume, P., Cantor, C. H., & Rolfe, A (1997). Cybersuicide: The role of interactive suicide notes on the internet. *Crisis, 18,* 73–79.

Becker, K., & Schmidt, M. H. (2004). Letters to the editor: Internet chat rooms and suicide. *Journal of the American Academy of Child and Adolescent Psychiatry, 43,* 246.

Becker, K., El-Faddagh, M., & Schmidt, M. H. (2004). Cybersuizid over Werther-Effekt online: Suizidchatrooms und-foren im Internet. *Kindheit und Entwicklung, 13,* 14–25.

Becker, K., Mayer, M., Nagenborg, M., El-Faddagh, M., & Schmidt, M. H. (2004). Parasuicide online: Can suicide websites trigger suicidal behavior in predisposed adolescents? *Nordic Journal of Psychiatry, 58,* 111–114.

Bonger, B. (2002). *The suicidal patient: Clinical and legal standards of care* (2nd ed.). Washington, DC: American Psychological Association.

Booth, J. (2005, February 14). St-Valentine's Day mass suicide pact fears. *Times ONLINE.* Retrieved from www.timesonline.co.uk/article/0,,3-1484028,00.html

Braintech Inc. v. Kostivk, 171 D.L.R. (4+h) 46, British Columbia, Canada (1999).

Bushman, B. J., & Anderson, C. A. (2001). Media violence and the American public. *American Psychologist, 56,* 477–489.

Calder v. Jones, 465 U.S. 783 (1984).

Commonwealth of Australia. (2004a). Criminal Code Amendment. *Telecommunications Offences and Other Measures—Suicide Related Material Offences (Bill no. 2).*

Commonwealth of Australia. (2004b). *House of Representatives Official Hansard, no. 12.* (Wednesday, 4 August 2004, 30035–32038)

Commonwealth of Australia. (2004c). *House of Representatives Official Hansard, no. 12.* (Wednesday, 11 August 2004, 32473–32480)

Dobson, R. (1999). Internet sites may encourage suicide. *British Medical Journal, 319,* 337.

European Union. (1999). *The European union safer Internet plan.* Brussels: Author. (EU-Decision Number 276–1999)

Geist, M. (2002). *Internet law in Canada* (3rd ed.). Concord: Captus Press.

Harding, A. (2004, December 9). Japan's Internet "suicide clubs." *BBC News.* Retrieved from http://news.bbc.co.uk/go/pr/fr/2/hi/programmes/newsnight/4071805.stm

Hawton, K., & Williams, K. (2001). The connection between media and suicidal behaviour warrants serious attention. *Crisis, 22,* 137–140.

Innes, J. (2003, October 1). Coroner calls for police watch on web chat rooms. *The Scotsman.* Retrieved from http://news.scotsman.com/top ics.cfm?tid=746&id=1086122003>

Japon: Suicide collectif par Internet. (2004, November 13). *Le Devoir,* p. B6.

Mehlum, L. (2000). The Internet, suicide, and suicide prevention. *Crisis, 21,* 186–188.

Mishara, B. L., & Weisstub, D. N. (2005). Ethical issues in suicide research. *International Journal of Law and Psychiatry, 28,* 23–41.

Pair planned suicide online police. (2003, April 9). *New Report RE; Europe.* http://iafrica.com/news/worldnews/227377.htm

Phillips, D. P. (1974). The influence of suggestion on suicide: Substantive and theoretical implications of the Werther effect. *American Sociological Review, 39,* 340–354.

Pirkis, J., & Warwick Blood, R. (2001). Suicide and the media. *Crisis, 22,* 146–154.

Rajagopal, S. (2004). Suicide pacts and the Internet: Complete strangers may make cyberspace pacts. [electronic version]. *British Medical Journal, 329,* 1298–1299. Retrieved January 6, 2005, from www.bmj.com.

Reany, P. (2004, December 6). Internet pourrait encourager les suicides collectifs. *Le Devoir,* p. B6.

Richard, J., Werth, J. L., & Rogers, J. R. (2000). Rational and assisted suicidal communication on the internet: A case example and discussion of ethical and practice issues. *Ethics and Behavior, 10,* 215–238.

Seven die in suicide pacts, bringing death toll to 22. (2004, September 22). *New York Herald Tribune*, p. 3.

Shepherd, J. (2004, March 6). Suicide blamed on chatrooms. *Birmingham Post*. Retrieved from http://icbirmingham .icnetwork.co.uk/0100news/0100localnews/tm_objectid=14022 277%26method=full%26siteid=50002-name_page.html

Smith, G. H., BIRD, & BIRD. (2002). *Internet Law and Regulation* (3rd ed.). London, UK: Sweet & Maxwell.

Stack, S. (2000). Media impacts on suicide: A quantitative review of 293 findings. *Social Science Quarterly, 81,* 957–971.

Stack, S. (2003). Media coverage as a risk factor in suicide. *Journal of Epidemiology and Community Health, 57,* 238–240.

Stack, S. (2005). Suicide in the media: A quantitative review of studies based on nonfictional stories. *Suicide and Life-Threatening Behavior, 35,* 121–133.

Thompson, S. (1999). The Internet and its potential influence on suicide. *Psychiatric Bulletin, 23,* 449–451.

Critical Thinking

1. Should the Internet serve as a how-to-do-it source for individuals contemplating suicide?

2. What are some of the ethical issues involved in Internet suicide Web sites?

3. How might Internet Web sites serve in a positive way to counsel suicidal individuals to not take their own life?

BRIAN MISHARA is Director of the Centre for Research and Intervention on Suicide and Euthanasia, and Professor in the Department of Psychology at the University of Quebec at Montreal. **DAVID N. WEISSTUB** is Philippe Pinel Professor of Legal Psychiatry and Biomedical Ethics at the University of Montreal, Canada.

Address correspondence to Brian L. Mishara, PhD, CRISE/UQAM, C.P. 8888, Succ. Centre-Ville, Montreal (Quebec) Canada, H3C 3P8; E-mail: mishara.brian@uqam.ca.

Why We Need Qualitative Research in Suicidology

Using the differentiation between *explanations* and *understanding* from philosophy of science as the point of departure, a critical look at the current mainstream suicidological research was launched. An almost exclusive use of quantitative methodology focusing on *explanations* is demonstrated. This bias in scope and methodology has to a large extent taken the suicidological field into a dead-end of repetitious research. It is argued that an increased focus on *understanding* and thus extended use of qualitative methodology is essential in bringing the suicidological field forward.

HEIDI HJELMELAND, PHD, AND BIRTHE LOA KNIZEK, PHD

In this paper we discuss why it is necessary to increase the amount of qualitative research in suicidology. Firstly, we present the state of the art with regard to qualitative studies in suicidological journals. Secondly, we take a critical look at the present mainstream research in the field. Thirdly, we discuss how qualitative research is essential in bringing the suicidological field forward.

Qualitative Studies in Suicidological Journals, 2005–2007

Archives of Suicide Research published a special issue on "qualitative versus quantitative studies in suicidology" in 2002. There it was argued that we need both approaches in the field of suicidology (e.g., Goldney, 2002; Leenaars, 2002a). However, in the period 2005–2007, less than 3% of the studies (research articles) published in the three main international suicidological journals had used qualitative methods. In *Archives of Suicide Research* 1.9% (*n* = 2), in *Crisis* 6.6% (*n* = 4), and in *Suicide and Life-Threatening Behavior* 2.1% (*n* = 4) of the studies published had used a qualitative approach, most often in addition to a quantitative one.

In order to take a critical look at the present mainstream suicidological research, our point of departure is the division between *explanation* and *understanding* as it is described in philosophy of science (e.g., von Wright, 1971/2004).

Explanations Versus Understanding

Studies focussing on *explanations* most often use hypothesis-deductive or experimental methodology originating from the natural sciences (quantitative approaches). There are different kinds of explanations (e.g., causal, teleological), but causal explanations are most frequently used in suicidology. Although not always explicitly stated, researchers are often looking for underlying causes of suicidal behavior, normally in a linear cause-and-effect terminology. The frequent use of the concept "study *objects*" reflects a rather mechanistic view on human beings where the focus is on individual parts of the body within the framework of the biomedical illness model (von Uexküll & Wesiack, 1988). However, the adherence to causal models in psychology has been criticized by, for instance, Harré and Moghaddam (2003): "no doubt this orthodoxy arises in part from the assumption that 'real science' is about cause and effect relations, and the discovery of universal laws of 'what causes what.' But part of the explanation for the pervasiveness of this orthodoxy is also reductionism: the tendency to reduce explanations to the smallest units possible" (p. 2).

Studies concerned with *understanding* normally use qualitative approaches and focus on the meaning(s) suicidal behavior has for the individual (e.g., Fleischer, 2000). That is, such studies center on how individuals engaging in suicidal ideation and/or behavior interpret themselves, their actions, and their surroundings. Here hermeneutics, the theory of interpretation, is essential (Ricoeur, 1974). In many ways we are dealing with a double hermeneutics in that researchers are interpreting the subjects' interpretations of themselves (e.g., Smith & Osborn, 2003). A more humanistic way of looking at people is reflected by use of the concept "study *subjects?*" in qualitative studies (Mayring, 1990).

The concepts of *explanation* and *understanding* are interrelated in that causal explanations build on understanding and interpretation, and, to give a causal explanation might be the first step toward developing an understanding. Our point here is that these two approaches must be understood on their own terms and as interdependent. Most of today's mainstream suicidological research unilaterally focuses on explanations, very often in terms of a linear cause-effect-thinking (although the concept of cause is not always explicitly mentioned). In order to avoid repetitious research and bring the field forward, we need to focus more on understanding and thus increase the use of qualitative methodology.

Classification and Discussion of Today's Mainstream Research

A very coarse classification of the major part of the current suicidological research results in three groups of studies: (1) epidemiological research; (2) (neuro)biological research; and, (3) intervention studies (e.g., randomized controlled trials; RCT-studies). Very often the thinking behind all these three groups of studies is in terms of explanations and cause-effect relationships.

Epidemiological Studies

A very large number of epidemiological studies are published every year and most of them focus on risk factors for suicidal behavior in different groups or in different parts of the world. Although we have a lot of knowledge on risk factors for suicidal behavior, some of which are believed to be universal and some culture-specific (e.g., Vijayaku-mar, John, Pirkis, & Whiteford, 2005), we still know very little about *how* these risk factors are related to suicidal behavior. Studies of risk factors mainly use questionnaires or structured interview guides with predetermined and standardized questions. However, it is rarely taken into account that many of the questions asked can be answered differently by the same person at the same time if different contexts are related to them. Thus, we have no way of knowing whether the informants respond in an abstract way, or if they tie their answers to specific situations (Toomela, 2007).

(Neuro)biological Studies

The second major group consists of biological research, for instance, studies on hormones and neurotransmitters expected to be involved in suicidal behavior or in related mental disorders, as well as genetic studies and brain-imaging studies. A main challenge for (neuro)biological research is to show how the results can be utilized in suicide prevention. For instance, a genetic predisposition will depend on a lot of other factors to be activated, or not, seeing that suicidal behavior is a multifactorial phenomenon (Leenaars, 2002b). Research in neuroplasticity has demonstrated that there seems to be few limits to what the brain can do and develop into with different environmental stimulations (e.g., Doidge, 2007), and that biological patterns in the brain both can be created and changed by experience (Mogensen, 2007). Brain imaging can be utilized as a tool to estimate suicide risk in individuals (e.g., Mann, 2005), but this research raises a number of ethical questions in terms of how/ when/if such results can/should be utilized or not.

The (neuro)biological research focusing on the psychiatric disorders associated with suicide has not been able to demonstrate *how* mental disorders are related to suicidal behavior. The vast majority of people suffering from a mental disorder do not kill themselves. Moreover, the relation between mental disorders and suicidal behavior vary across cultures (e.g., Vijayakumar, 2005). Thus, it is obvious that suicidality is about something else, or at least something more, than mental disorders. We therefore need to look beyond mental disorders when we want to understand what suicidal behavior is all about. Charlton (2000) claimed that "the diagnosis tells you less than the symptoms about the best focus for therapeutic intervention" (p. 137). Hence, we need to investigate what these symptoms mean to the people displaying them. People are complicated, reflective beings and it is highly unlikely that we behave in a linear way. Still, we tend to deal with complexity by reducing or neutralizing aspects of it (Gilgen, 1995). However, in order to avoid such reductionism, psychiatry and neurobiology have to move away from the linear cause-effect thinking and instead adopt perspectives from modern physics; like, for instance, chaos theory (Tbomela, 2007). Chaotic systems analysis and epistemology are important in both biological and behavioral sciences (e.g., Krippner & Winkler, 1995) and thus also in suicidology.

RCT-Studies

RCT-studies are, at least in medical circles, recognized as the only valid approach to provide an evidence base for intervention (Chelmow, 2005). Furthermore, observational and other studies are often dismissed as useless in contributing to the evidence base (Chelmow, 2005; Smith & Pell, 2003). This was, however, elegantly refuted by Smith and Pell when they pointed out the lack of evidence for the usefulness of parachutes when jumping out of airplanes since this has not yet been demonstrated by RCT-studies. A major problem with RCT-studies is that they leave a great deal of the variance unexplained and "the nature of a relationship or a difference between groups cannot be understood unless all exceptions are understood" (Tbomela, 2007, p. 13). Exceptions to the "rule" must be understood, analyzed, and accounted for before we can get a complete understanding of the phenomenon under study. If an RCT-study shows a statistically significant difference between two different treatments, this result does not help us to understand *why* this intervention seems to be working very well in some of the individuals in the experimental group, fairly well in other persons, not at all in yet others, and may even be harmful to some, which sometimes happens in drug trials (Noller & Bibace, 2005).

Status of Today's Mainstream Suicidological Research

From the discussion above it is clear that most of the mainstream suicidological research has many weaknesses. Each of the three research approaches mentioned *explain* different parts of suicidal behavior, but none of them can provide a complete *understanding* of this phenomenon. We do, however, need epidemiological research so that we can follow the temporal and cultural trends of prevalence and risk factors. However, we need to improve the quality of this research by, for example, anchoring it within theoretical frameworks. We do need (neuro)biological research since suicidal behavior is a multifactorial phenomenon and this line of research contributes with pieces to the puzzle. Further, we do need RCT-studies to test if some interventions work better than others. However, if we are to come closer to an understanding of suicidal behavior, statistical probability prediction cannot be the endpoint of our research. Different psychological mechanisms can underlie the same "objective" score, and " 'objective scores'... may actually cover rich individual differences that can never be discovered unless studies explicitly go beyond numbers and start to ask questions whether there are different ways to reach the same 'objective' score or not" (Toomela, 2007, p. 11). Moreover, the same mean value can result from very different distributions of the data and therefore we have to look at individual scores in order to understand them. Facts isolated from the whole context or facts that describe the average group differences but not the exceptions are not sufficient to understand peoples' minds. The linear cause-and-effect thinking that focuses only on one or a few variables is too simplistic, too reductionist; it does not take the whole individual and his or her surroundings into consideration at the same time, which is necessary if we want to understand why that particular person at that particular time in his or her life is considering to or actually has carried out a suicidal act. A linear understanding of causality can actually contribute to the blurring of relationships that are essential for the individual if one is fixated on an organic cause of the suffering without seeing the context that is making the person suffer (Fernando, 2003; Toomela, 2007).

Moving the Suicidological Field Forward

Qualitative studies are often presented as a tool to generate hypotheses that then need to be verified by quantitative studies (e.g., Flick, 2007). However, if we want to understand the phenomenon we are studying, we need to follow up quantitative studies with qualitative ones (or just conduct qualitative studies in the first place). We do need to take the individual in his or her particular context into consideration since social behavior "is the collaborative construction of social reality and the mutual upholding of particular interpretations of the world" (Harré & Moghaddam, 2003, p. 3). A qualitative approach will thus allow us to look at relationships between important factors, which we would not be able to do in quantitative studies using standardized questions. When questions are standardized, the standard might not suit every individual; it might not elicit the important information from everyone. Qualitative studies can thus also help us to interpret and understand the relationships between variables used in quantitative studies (Flick, 2007).

Here hermeneutics comes to the fore (Ricoeur, 1974); however, a systematic hermeneutic analysis might result in several different interpretations of an informant's story. This is not in keeping with the natural science paradigm, where it is believed that there is one single truth to be found (Anderson, 1995). Within the paradigms of social sciences and humanities, on the other hand, there is no such thing as *the* truth (Lyotard, 1979; Rorty, 1991), especially not when mental phenomena are involved (Foucault, 1971). Human beings are not just mechanical machines that respond to stimuli; we are able to reflect about the world and our own actions. Thus, from a hermeneutic perspective there might be one truth for each individual since what is perceived as true depends on which perspective one is looking at a phenomenon from. According to Hafting (2005), an individual's experience cannot be true or false since it is genuine for the individual and cannot be tested or questioned by others. She also refers to Kvale, who says (our translation): "A patient always tells the truth, and it is the doctor's or psychologist's task to find out what he is telling the truth about" (in Hafting, 2005, p. 3440). An important part of hermeneutics is thus to substantiate our interpretations (Ricoeur, 1974), to demonstrate that the particular interpretation we end up with is plausible based on the data available. Interpretation can be done from many different theoretical perspectives. We are, for instance, working from a perspective where suicidal behavior is interpreted as communicative acts within the framework of communication theory (Hjelmeland et al., 2008; Hjelmeland, Knizek, & Nordvik, 2002; Knizek & Hjelmeland, 2007).

Not all qualitative approaches involve interpretation. Sometimes it might just be necessary or desirable to describe the informants' life world. Then we can use a phenomenological analysis (Giorgi & Giorgi, 2003). It has been shown, for instance, that phenomenological insights are important to the interpretation of brain imaging studies of dyslexia (Philpott, 1998; Rippon, 1998). Thus, this could also be relevant for brain imaging studies in suicidology. Fulford, Sallah, and Woodbridge (2007) argued that phenomenology is important within the mental health services since "phenomenology and related disciplines, as rigorous approaches to analysing experience supported by detailed theoretical frameworks, provide tools for more effective and inclusive ways of understanding differences not only between individuals but also between cultures in the way they experience the world" (p. 39).

Generalization

The standard objection toward qualitative research is that we cannot generalize the results from qualitative studies. Of course we cannot generalize statistically because we do not have any or just a few numbers, or we don't have representative samples, and so forth. However, there are other types of generalization; for instance, in theoretical generalization, we link the findings of our study with our own personal and professional experience as well as with what we find in the existing literature (Smith & Osborn, 2003). Or, in analytical generalization (Kvale, 1997), we look at to what degree a finding can be directive or instructive for what is going to happen in another situation. This is similar to what is done in the legal system or in clinical work. In analytical generalization, it is the users of the knowledge that are responsible for deciding what, if anything, of the results provided is applicable to their situation. The researchers' responsibility is thus to provide enough documentation to enable the users to generalize analytically based on the similarities and differences between the two situations. The validity of such generalization depends on how relevant the compared characteristics are, which again depends on detailed, compact, and rich descriptions of the case (Kvale, 1997).

Combining Qualitative and Quantitative Studies

A combination of quantitative and qualitative methods is perhaps the most fruitful approach. There are three possible outcomes of studies using quantitative and qualitative approaches in an integrated way: (1) the results are complementary and thus provide a fuller picture of how things are related to each other and how they contribute to suicidal ideation and/or behavior; (2) the results are convergent and thus contribute to validate each other; or, (3) the results are contradictory and then more research is needed (Flick, 2007). With the current almost complete dominance of quantitative studies, we argue that the field now also needs some pure qualitative studies.

Concluding Remarks

We need more studies focusing on understanding suicidal behavior. Human beings are not behaving in a linear fashion or disconnected from their context. Thus, we need to take both the complexity of the phenomenon as well as of human beings into account by employing a variety of methods and models. We have shown here that qualitative studies are few and far between in the main suicidological journals in spite of the *Archives of Suicide Research's* advocacy for more qualitative research (Leenaars, 2002a). Something Fernando (2003) has pointed out with regard to research on mental health in general might be relevant here: "Changing the culture of research so that it is bottom-up (i.e., starts with user views and needs identified by people who suffer mental health problems) is likely to threaten vested interests of the psychiatric establishment and so requires a political will to enforce" (p. 205). Thus, we challenge the editors of suicidology journals to encourage qualitative research, research that will help us to improve our understanding of suicidal behavior in different contexts.

References

Anderson, W. T. (1995). *The truth about the truth: De-confusing and re-constructing the post-modern world.* New York: G.P. Putnam's Sons.

Charlton, B. (2000). *Psychiatry and the human condition.* Abingdon, Oxon: Radcliffe Medical Press.

Chelmow, D. (2005). Evidence-based medicine: Quantitatively moving from the universal to the particular. In R. Bibace, J. D. Laird, K. L. Noller, & J. Valsiner (Eds.), *Science and medicine in dialogue: Thinking through particulars and universals* (pp. 139–158). Westport: Praeger.

Doidge, N. (2007). *The brain that changes itself.* Melbourne: Scribe.

Fernando, S. (2003). *Cultural diversity, mental health and psychiatry: The struggle against racism.* Hove: Brunner-Routledge.

Fleischer, E. (2000). *Den talende tavshed. Selvmord og selvmordsforsøg som talehandling* [The speaking silence: Suicide and suicide attempt as speech-act]. Odense: Odense Universitetsforlag.

Flick, U. (2007). *Managing quality in qualitative research.* London: Sage.

Foucault, M. (1971). *Sindssygdom og psyko-logi* [Madness and psychology]. København: Rhodos.

Fulford, K. W. M., Sallah, D., & Wood-bridge, K. (2007). Philosophical tools for cultural psychiatry. In K. Bhui & D. Bhugra (Eds.), *Culture and mental health: A comprehensive textbook* (pp. 37–46). London: Edward Arnold.

Gilgen, A. R. (1995). Prefatory comments. In F. D. Abraham & A. R. Gilgen (Eds.), *Chaos theory in psychology* (pp. XV–XVII). Westport: Praeger.

Giorgi, A., & Giorgi, B. (2003). Phenomenology. In J. A. Smith (Ed.), *Qualitative psychology: A practical guide to research methods* (pp. 25–50). London: Sage.

Goldney, R. D. (2002). Qualitative and quantitative approaches in suicidology: Commentary. *Archives of Suicide Research, 6,* 69–73.

Hafting, M. (2005). De individuelle historiene og den profesjonelle samtalen [The individual stories and the professional conversation]. *Tidsskrift for Den norske lægeforening, 125,* 3440–3441.

Harré, R., & Moghaddam, F. (2003). Introduction: The self and others in traditional psychology and in positioning theory. In R. Harré & F. Moghaddam (Eds.), *The self and others: Positioning individuals and groups in personal, political, and cultural contexts.* Westport: Praeger.

Hjelmeland, H., Knizek, B. L., Kiny-anda, E., Musisi, S., Nordvik, H., & Svarva, K. (2008). Suicidal behaviour as communication in a cultural context: A comparative study between Norway and Uganda, *Crisis, 29,* 137–144.

Hjelmeland, H., Knizek, B. L., & Nordvik, H. (2002). The communicative aspect of nonfatal suicidal behaviour—are there gender differences? *Crisis, 23,* 144–155.

Knizek, B. L., & Hjelmeland, H. (2007). A theoretical model for interpreting suicidal behaviour as communication. *Theory & Psychology, 17,* 697–720.

Krippner, S., & Winkler, M. (1995). Studying consciousness in the postmodern age. In W. T. Anderson (Ed.), *The truth about the truth: De-confusing and re-constructing the postmodern world* (pp. 161–169). New York: G.P. Putnam's Sons.

Kvale, S. (1997). *Interviews: An introduction to qualitative research interviewing.* London: Sage.

Leenaars, A. A. (2002a). The quantitative and qualitative in suicidological science: An editorial. *Archives of Suicide Research, 6,* 1–3.

Leenaars, A. A. (2002b). In defence of the idiographic approach: Studies of suicide notes and personal documents. *Archives of Suicide Research, 6,* 19–30.

Lyotard, J. F. (1979). *Viden og det postmoderne samfund* [Knowledge and the postmodern society]. Arhus: Sjakalen.

Mann, J. (2005). What does brain imaging tell us about the predisposition to suicidal behavior. *Crisis, 26,* 101–103.

Mayring, P. (1990). *Einführung in die qualitative Sozialforschung* [Introduction to qualitative social research]. München: Psychologie Verlags Union.

Mogensen, J. (2007, February). *Plasticity of the brain in relation to psychological traumas and their recovery.* Paper presented at the Traumatized Child International Conference: Symptoms, Consequences and Treatment in an International perspective, Copenhagen.

Noller, K. L., & Bibace, R. (2005). The centrality of die clinician: A view of medicine from the general to the particular. In R. Bibace, J. D. Laird, K. L. Noller, & J. Valsiner (Eds.), *Science and medicine in dialogue: Thinking through particulars and universals* (pp. 99–108). Westport: Praeger.

Philpott, M. J. (1998). A phenomenology of dyslexia: The lived-body ambiguity, and the breakdown of expression. *Philosophy, Psychiatry, and Psychology, 5,* 1–20.

Ricoeur, P. (1974). *Die Interpretation. Ein Versuch über Freud* [The interpretation: An attempt on Freud]. Frankfurt am Main: Suhrkamp.

Rippon, G. (1998). Commentary on "A phenomenology of dyslexia." *Philosophy, Psychiatry, and Psychology, 5,* 25–28.

Rorty, R. (1991). *Objectivity, relativism, and truth.* Cambridge: Cambridge University Press.

Smith, J. A, & Osborn, M. (2003). Interpretative phenomenological analysis. In J. A Smith (Ed.), *Qualitative research methods: A practical guide to research methods* (pp. 51–80). London: Sage.

Smith, G.C.S., & Pell, J. P. (2003). Parachute use to prevent death and major trauma related to gravitational challenge: Systematic review of randomised controlled trials. *British Medical Journal, 327,* 1459–1461.

Toomela, A. (2007). Culture of science: Strange history of the methodological thinking in psychology. *Integrative Psychological & Behavioral Science, 41,* 6–20.

Vijayakumar, L. (2005). Suicide and mental disorders in Asia. *International Review of Psychiatry, 17,* 109–114.

Vijayakumar, L., John, S., Pirkis, P., & Whiteford, H. (2005). Suicide in developing countries (2): Risk factors. *Crisis, 26,* 112–119.

von Uexküll, T., & Wesiack, W. (1988). *Theorie der human Medizin. Grundlagen ärtzlichen Denkens und Handelns* [Theory of human medicine: Foundations of medical thought action]. München: Urban & Schwarzenberg.

von Wright, G. H. (1971/2004). *Explanation and understanding.* Ithaca: Cornell University Press. (Original work published 1971)

Critical Thinking

1. How does qualitative research differ from quantitative research?

2. What is the difference in *explanations* versus *understanding* regarding suicide?

3. What are some of the types of research studies currently taking place regarding suicide?

A Search for Death: How the Internet Is Used as a Suicide Cookbook

RHEANA MURRAY

Literature Review

While reasons for suicides have long been analyzed, the Internet presents a comparatively unexamined influence. Recent news stories have begun to direct attention to the emergence of chat rooms, message boards and other resources on the web as a possible factor in the rise of suicide rates. As the Internet has become an increasingly vital technological development, some people have begun to worry about "suicide websites," a term that refers to websites that promote, encourage and/or offer methods to commit suicide.

Alao and colleagues (2006) address the role of the Internet on suicides in a manuscript composed of three parts. The first describes how the Internet can help users commit suicide; the second looks at cases in which this has happened; and the last explores how the Internet could be used to help suicidal users back to stable mental health. The authors include interesting and pertinent information about suicide websites, and they report that there are more than 100,000 of them that deal with suicide methods. Some sites do not allow entrance to anyone intending to persuade users to not commit suicide. Suicide notes, death certificates, color photographs of people committing suicide, messages supporting suicide or encouraging individuals to carry out planned suicides can all be found on these websites. Some of the websites are very graphic, even including "the best way to point a gun into the mouth for maximum effect," according to the journal article (Alao 490). The article "Cybersuicide: Review of the Role of the Internet on Suicide" also acknowledges that chat rooms, as well as websites, can provide information on suicide.

Few researchers have considered the idea that suicide websites might decrease suicides, but the second part of "Cybersuicide," though brief, insists that the Internet is also a potential source of help for suicidal people. Alao and colleagues refer to the possibility of online counseling, although they do not include evidence that proves its success (490).

Tam, Tang and Fernando (2007) also introduce the idea that the Internet may serve a double purpose when it comes to suicide, both harming and helping. They note that the Internet romanticizes suicide and that it "provides services and information ranging from general information to online orders of prescription drugs or other poisons that bypass government regulations and custom controls." This, the authors say, "bridges the gaps of locality and accessibility" (453). A suicidal person can use the Internet to learn methods to commit suicide. The person learns what a particular method calls for, be it chemicals, weapons, rope, drugs, etc. Then, inching closer to death, the person can use the Internet to *buy* the tools. CNN reporters Gutierrez and McCabe (2005) illustrate this process in the story of Suzy Gonzales, a 19 year-old college student from Florida, who killed herself by swallowing potassium cyanide. Through an online suicide message board, Gonzales learned how to pose as a jeweler to obtain the lethal cocktail.

While the article by Tam and colleagues makes the problem of suicide websites clear, it goes on to raise the interesting dilemma that the Internet could also help people escape their suicidal impulses. The authors provide little evidence, however, offering the idea as more of an opportunity than a reality. They mention self-help sites for suicidal persons and the potential for therapeutic chat rooms. Yet, once again, evidence of effectiveness is sparse.

Madelyn Gould, Patrick Jamieson and Daniel Romer (2003) researched suicide contagion from the news as well as fiction. Their research suggested a strong relationship between reports of suicide in the media and increased suicide rates. According to Gould (1271), "the magnitude of the increase in suicides following a suicide story is proportional to the amount, duration, and prominence of media coverage." Celebrities' suicides are 14.3 times more likely to result in a copycat effect than suicides of non-celebrities.

Gould and colleagues analyzed suicide stories from 1998 in the nine most widely circulated newspapers in the United States, tracking the number of suicide stories each paper published, the percentage of stories that were placed in the first nine pages, and the percentage of stories that referred to suicide in the headline. *The Los Angeles Times* reported the most suicides, 176, and *USA Today* reported the fewest, only 35. Interestingly, *USA Today* was the paper that most frequently placed the suicide article within the first nine pages, doing so 91.4% of the time, and *Newsday* did so the least. *The Washington Post* was the paper that referred to suicide in the headline most frequently, and *USA Today* did so the least. Gould and colleagues also included the most recently released recommendations for journalists covering suicides and the need for guidelines for fictional programming.

Studies by Katja Becker and colleagues (2004) further support Gould's report that suicides increase proportionally to the amount, duration and prominence of media coverage. They illustrate the Internet's influence on users, particularly adolescents. In a *Nord J Psychiatry* article, Becker and colleagues say suicide contagion is real and prevalent. Reasons include "inadvertent romanticizing of suicide or idealizing it as a heroic deed" (112).

Brian Mishara and David Weisstub (2007) discussed the ethical and legal implications of various ways to prevent using the Internet as an aid to committing suicide, considering self-regulation and blocking access to suicide websites. Viewpoints from a libertarian perspective and also from a moralist ethical position are analyzed. Mishara and Weisstub compare the Internet to other mass media in relation to censorship. Their research raises interesting questions and viewpoints without resolving qualms concerning Internet censorship.

In an article on "Internet Chat Rooms and Suicide" (2005), Becker and Schmidt discuss a 17 year-old female who visited suicide web forums to find suicide methods and a 15 year-old female who reported that "the Internet inspired her to commit suicide as a problem-solving strategy" (229). The article discusses the availability and ease associated with suicide websites, and how many portray suicide as a legitimate, even respectable solution to life's problems. "Ambivalence, an often-precarious balance between a chosen life and a chosen death, which is considered common to suicide attitude, may tip in the direction of death in response to suicide chat rooms," the article states (229). This warning makes for an adequate summary of the entire article.

Methods and Objectives

This paper aims to explain the existence of websites, newsgroups and online message boards that promote, condone, encourage and/or discuss suicide from a pro-suicide or pro-choice angle. Research involving human participants was conducted, and this project was approved by the Institutional Research Board (IRB) at the College of Charleston.

Interviews were conducted on two groups of participants: 1) people that use suicide websites and 2) creators and supporters of H.R. 940, a current bill aiming to make it illegal to help someone commit suicide via the Internet. To gather participants, I used a convenience sample. Participation was voluntary and communication occurred primarily through e-mail.

Group 1: My objective in interviewing people that use suicide websites, newsgroups and/or message boards was to understand the cause and objective of their participation, and how they are affected by the websites. The following questions were asked:

1. Why did you start using (website's name)?
2. Does (website's name) promote and/or encourage suicide and/ or suicidal tendencies?

3. Does (website's name) offer methods of committing suicide?
4. Are you aware of suicides connected with the Internet?
5. If so, do you feel regret upon hearing about suicides in the news?
6. Are you aware of suicides that have been linked to (website's name)?
7. Do you have any ethical issues with the website's content?
8. Are you concerned with the possibility that a law could force (website's name) to shut down?
9. How do you feel toward people who scorn (website's name)?

Each interview's significance lies within the responses, which serve as the primary research for this paper along with text drawn from suicide websites, newsgroups, and message boards. Results are qualitative and often based on case studies.

Group 2: My objective in interviewing creators of H.R. 940, also called "Suzy's Law," was to understand the origin of the bill and its components, so my readers will understand its intent. The following questions were asked of the bill's creators:

1. Explain the law.
2. When did the law come about?
3. How are you trying to get the law considered and passed?
4. Why did you create this law?
5. Are there similar laws that exist now?
6. How long do you think the Internet's influence on suicides has been a problem?
7. Do you think this law will be successful?
8. How does the law avoid impeding on free speech?

Findings

Following the established information revealed in the preceding literature review, I investigated suicide websites for my own research. I found several, and focused on three that appeared to be the most prevalent and frequented online spaces for suicidal people, the alt.suicide.holiday Usenet newsgroup (ASH), the alt.suicide.methods Usenet newsgroup (ASM) and alt.suicide .bus.stop, a channel in Internet Relay Chat (IRC) and known as ASBS.

None of these groups qualifies as a website, so the term "suicide website" loses its precision here, but the term is conventionally used to categorize ASH, ASM, ASBS. ASH, which has sustained many transformations and replacements since it was created in the 1950s, did begin as an actual website as opposed to a message board or chat room. Although the three groups are often called "sister sites," ASH is considered the original, and was first to appear. The creator of the original website, ash.xanthia.com, froze the site in 2002 and removed it in 2003 because, he wrote, "it represents a social space which no longer exists."

However, the popular Dutch journalist Karen Spaink offered to archive the ASH website materials on her own website, ash.spaink.net, which continues to provide an inactive copy of the former ASH site. Several sites have emerged to take the place of ASH, including ASM and ASBS, and a new site that uses the name ASH. This active version of ASH consists of message boards in which members post about life, depression and suicide-related topics. According to Google, the group has high activity, and "talk about why suicides increase at holidays" is the description. While sources, as well as the name itself, imply that the creation of ASH stemmed from intentions to brew discussion of suicides around holidays, it is no longer a topic of discussion, and certainly not the focal point of the boards it may once have been. As of April 3, 2008, ASH has 2459 subscribers.

ASM is also a Usenet newsgroup through Google, and was inspired by the infamous "Methods File," an extensive compilation of detailed suicide methods featured on the original ASH website. Members of ASM particularly discuss ways to commit suicide, saving less relevant discussion, such as the source of an individual's suicidal impulses, for the ASH newsgroup. However, members of one group are often members of the other, and conversations overlap. ASM also has high activity, according to Google, and is described as "discussions about how to do yourself in." As of April 3, 2008, ASM has 1994 subscribers.

ASBS, unlike ASH and ASM, is a channel in Internet Relay Chat (IRC) found at ashbusstop.org. The site offers live chat with other members, as opposed to message boards. ASBS provides more than the newsgroups, going far beyond interactive chatting and message boards. The website offers a plethora of information about suicide, a seemingly endless consideration of preparation and aftermath. There are pages that examine the purpose of living, offering pro-life and pro-death viewpoints, and information about euthanasia. The "Tying Loose Ends" page reminds people contemplating suicide to consider pets, bills, funeral plans and more. There are links to animal shelters, lists of funeral homes, as well as detailed instructions of how to close e-mail accounts and erase all ASH-related information from a personal computer, so that family members cannot discover the person's identity as an asher. The "How to Write a Suicide Note" page includes an introduction of suicide notes, with history and statistics, and detailed advice on how to write a note, whether the writer wants closure or revenge, to tell his or her story, or simply to provide an explanation. This page covers the five stages of receiving catastrophic news so that a note-writer can better understand the emotional state of his or her friends and family.

The "Methods" section of ASBS includes a page about the morality of publishing suicide websites, a page about how to compare different suicide methods, and features a Lethality-Time-Agony Method calculator (LTA). The calculator allows people to enter numbers in a space next to each factor— lethality, time and agony—to register the importance he or she assigns to that factor. The sum of the numbers must be 100. For example, if a suicidal person feels that lethality is the most important, but is not worried about experiencing agony, and mildly cares about the time the suicide takes, he or she might assign lethality 70 points, time 30 points, and agony 0 points. By typing these numbers in the calculator, and clicking the calculate button, a list of recommended suicide methods appears.

Table 1 Methods of Suicide from Ashbusstop.org

Method	Lethality (%)	Time (min)	Agony
Carbon Monoxide	71	21.5	18
Overdose Rx drugs	12.3	129	8.5
Overdose non-Rx drugs	6	456	22.5
Overdose illegal drugs	43.96	116.25	5.25
Household toxins	77.5	24	54.5
Cyanide	97	1.8	51.5
Gunshot of head	97	2.5	13
Gunshot of chest	89.5	7	21.7
Gunshot of abdomen	65	69	74
Shotgun to head	99	1.7	5.5
Shotgun to chest	96.4	1.4	16
Explosives	96.4	1.6	3.75
Electrocution	65.5	2.4	72
Set fire to self	76.5	57	95
Structure fire	73	52.5	91.5
Cut throat	51.5	15.5	86
Cut wrists/arms/legs	6	105	71
Stab of chest	58.5	96	76
Stab of abdomen	12.5	252	78
Auto crash	78.5	20.5	30
Jump from height	93.44	4.56	17.78
Hit by train	96.18	17.92	7.08
Hit by truck/auto	70	19	63
Hanging	89.5	7	25.5
Plastic bag over head	23	7	23
Drowning: ocean/lake	63	18.5	79
Drowning: bathtub	21.5	18.5	79
Drowning: pool	21.5	18.5	79

At the bottom of the page, a chart lists 28 suicide methods and their predicted lethality, the time each would take to complete, and a numeric measure of agony. See Table 1.

Upon entering ASH, ASM and ASBS, there is a warning that explains that the pages deal with serious topics intended for mature audiences. People visiting the ASH or ASM newsgroups are welcomed with an "Adult Content Warning" and must click an "I am at least 18 years old" button to proceed. ASBS instructs users to proceed only after reading a "Terms of Use" section and agreeing to not raise any complaints, verified by clicking the "I agree . . . let me in" button.

I interviewed ten people who use the ASH, ASM and ASBS groups. A convenience sample was used to select participants, and questions were asked and answered through direct e-mail to insure privacy. Users of any of these forums call themselves "ashers," since all three stem from the original ASH website. (From here on, I will refer to ASH, ASM and ASBS collectively as ASH to avoid redundancy.) Ashers use a set of terms that are unique to "ashspace," which they use as a term for these suicide forums. Other significant terms include "catch the bus" or "ctb," which both mean to commit suicide. Ashers tend to find ashspace by researching suicide or suicide methods on the Internet. Many say they were suicidal and ready to die. They began using ASH as a place to vent, to get input on their suicidal ideas and thoughts, and to feel less alone. Frequent responses to question 1, "Why did you start using ASH?" dealt with the isolation a suicidal person feels from the rest of the (non-suicidal) world.

According to an asher who uses the nickname Another-RubberDucky, "I feel like less of a freak," [by using ASH]. Another user, LSD, even referred to the cartoon X-Men, saying, "you know, the mutants were so criticized and left out." Like the outcast monsters, suicidal people feel alone in a world that scrutinizes and scorns them. By sharing her feelings with people in Ashland, LSD said she felt like less of an "alien."

While it was not a frequent explanation for using ASH, two ashers I interviewed said they came to ASH looking for someone to die with. User Joy Miller said, "I would like to find a partner, but there's not that many looking [on ASH]." LSD acknowledged that many people use the Internet to find partners to commit suicide, saying she was even involved in a suicide pact that went astray when the other person in the pact "turned out to be a freak with a suicide fetish that liked to watch people hang in the webcam."

More frequently, people use ASH as a place to talk to people with similar suicidal feelings. An asher who uses the name AndSheWas said, "ASH is not often a discussion about suicide. It's a diary of a spattering of people around the world who have been fortunate enough to find a place to vent their inner feelings. Everyone knows talking about your problems can help." Asher Lyllian Croft summed up the most popular reason people use ASH: "For me, it merely provides a place where I know someone is listening."

AnotherRubberDucky, who came to ASH after years of depression and skin disorders, thinks ASH's attractiveness to its users comes from its nonjudgmental atmosphere. She said:

> You'll find that if you talk suicide with a depressed person and you tell them that "it is not an option" or "[it is] a permanent solution to a temporary problem," well, this produces a sort of claustrophobic feeling in the patient. Making suicide in a way, more appealing and inevitable. As soon as you admit that suicide is an option, and that one is not crazy to consider it, the suicidal person can breathe again.

Question 2, "Does ASH promote and/or encourage suicide and or suicidal tendencies?" garnered a consistent response: that ASH is pro-choice, not pro-suicide, a viewpoint most participants seemed well-versed in defending. Being pro-choice translates to tolerance of, but not advocacy for, suicide. According to an asher named Maija, "suicide is neither to be encouraged or to be condemned; it's treated as a personal choice." LSD said, "It's not a 'yeah, go kill yourself' thing, but more of a 'we understand' thing."

Furthermore, half of the people interviewed said that ashers actually discourage young people from committing suicide. An asher named CTB said:

One ethical standard that tends to emanate throughout the group is that young people (teens and early twenties) are discouraged from suicide or for that matter even participating in the newsgroup. Many ashers will tell the youngsters to "leave us losers alone and get some life experience. Let your brain develop. If you feel the same way at age 25 then, 'welcome to ash, sorry you're here' (our standard greeting to a newcomer)."

Maija answered with a similar response and added, "The same thing goes for people who seem to have very hasty reasons for committing suicide, such as a breakup that happened just days before." Suicide is viewed as an option on ASH, but a last resort.

Some participants took their answers a step further, going as far as to say that ASH even helps its users to avoid suicide by serving as an outlet for frustration and depression. Another-RubberDucky said, "In truth, I have all the information that I need for my 'final exit' but I like the support that I get from the group. And this is support to continue living, not to kill myself."

Particular threads on the ASH message board support the answer that ASH prevents suicide, at least in some cases. In a 2004 thread entitled, "How does ASH impact suicidal ideation for you," ashers discussed whether ASH made them more or less suicidal. Many said that since joining ASH, their desire to commit suicide has decreased because they had found a place where suicide was accepted.

Even more straightforward is the thread from November 2005, "How ASH saved my life," posted by a former asher, jpatti. Jpatti explained that she had not used ASH in years and was no longer suicidal, but said "I'm posting because I'm pissed about the CNN thing." An article about Suzy Gonzales and her involvement in ASH had appeared on CNN.com two days before jpatti's thread. She explained how finding a community of suicidal people and being able to talk openly about suicide helped her out of suicidality. She further observed, "Those who claim to be opposed to suicide, under any circumstances, often have a sick way of expressing it—by attacking suicidal people. It's like coming upon a car accident and finding someone bleeding on the side of the road and *kicking* them as hard as you can because you're 'opposed' to car accidents."

Maija, an asher since 1999, is no longer suicidal, but still visits ASH. "It is always nice to discuss subjects that are taboo elsewhere, and in general to have in-depth conversations with very intelligent and thoughtful people," she said. "These, especially the latter, are the reasons why I still read ASH almost every day and occasionally post as well." Maija's loyalty to ASH wasn't unique; most of the ashers I interviewed seemed to rely heavily on ASH as an outlet or even as a hangout. On the message boards, dozens of new threads appear every day, and not all relate to suicide. Some are random questions or thoughts, or polls to get to know each other—signaling a desire for friendship. As asher AndSheWas said, "Ash is my lifeline."

Ashers' responses to my questions as well as the tone and language used in the message boards reveal a nonchalant and

111

accepting attitude toward suicide. Suicide isn't feared. It is discussed, dissected, awaited and anticipated. It's also something that can happen at any time. One interviewee, Robert Brown, ended an e-mail by politely adding that if I have any more questions, I should feel free to ask. Brown said he planned to kill himself that night, but that an old friend just called and made plans to stop by later that week to give him a tattoo. "So I should be here another week," he wrote. An argument could even be made that the language ashers use makes suicide less daunting and more natural. Saying "I'm going to catch the bus tonight" has a different manner than "I'm going to commit suicide tonight."

Several ashers admitted to knowing of suicides connected with ASH. Although few revealed names, Suzy Gonzales, an asher whose suicide was scrutinized by the media in 2003, was often mentioned. However, by searching the message boards, there are various memorial lists throughout the years. Ashers list names of fellow ashers who have committed suicide, and they discuss whether or not some missing ashers are dead or have simply stopped using ASH. In a post from March 31, 2008, an asher claimed to know of 26 confirmed suicides of ashers. Others simply listed the former usernames of friends they know to have committed suicide. Ashers expressed sadness over the loss of friends, but happiness for the dead. AnotherRubberDucky said, "Loss of life is always sad, but then again, so is intense suffering."

The Case of Suzy Gonzales and the Introduction of H.R. 940

In 2003, the daughter of Mike and Mary Gonzales committed suicide. Their daughter Suzy Gonzales was a frequent member to the ASH website, where she used the nickname Suzy California. Suzy consulted other ashers for advice on how to complete her suicide; she eventually chose to die by drinking a lethal cocktail of potassium cyanide. With the instruction she received through the online group, Suzy learned how to send her family and the police department delayed messages saying she had died, and how to pose as a jeweler to obtain her drug of choice. She ordered the cyanide along with other chemicals, so that the order appeared authentic, from a Massachusetts-based chemical company (Scheeres 2003). On March 23, 2003, she received the chemicals and, without missing a beat, she fed her kitten, rented a hotel room and lay down to die. "If you compared the information given on these sites and what Suzy did, you would see that she followed their recipes of deadly instructions," her parents said.

Mike and Mary Gonzales pursued their impulse to seek legal consequences for those aiding in their daughter's death. It wasn't that easy. "For two years," they said, "we asked law enforcement and legal firms to investigate what happened and they all told us that there were no relevant current laws to act upon."

Enter H.R. 940, a bill the Gonzales' helped develop to prevent stories like their own. The bill, also called "Suzy's Law," is backed by California congressman Wally Herger, and was introduced to the United States House of Representatives on February 8, 2007. According to Lindsay Bartlett, who assists in maintaining the H.R. 940 website, the bill "specifically makes it a crime to go on the Internet and tell someone who seems to be thinking of suicide, 'You should go through with it. Here's how to do it and where to get the materials.'"

To publicize the bill and garner support, Mike and Mary Gonzales have appeared on television shows including *Oprah, Dateline, Good Morning America* and various news programs, and granted interviews to several newspapers and magazines, among them the *San Francisco Chronicle, Cosmopolitan, Seventeen* and *Wired*. Across the country, radio stations have also told their story.

Since Suzy Gonzales' death, several threads on ASH have mentioned possible legal action from her parents and the bill they are pursuing. Most feel that their messages continue to be protected by the First Amendment. In relation to Suzy Gonzales, ashers seem to share the belief that her suicide was inevitable; the support she received from ASH was at most an advancing factor in her death, but in no way responsible. In response to a thread entitled, "Should we be banned," started on February 8, 2008, a user named Dan said:

> Suzy Gonzales' parents should realize SUZY is responsible for her own actions and her own suicide. Maybe she found information on how to obtain cyanide, but reading the archives a year ago, I remember that she was saying that she was so desperate as to resort to jumping, and even fantasizing about guillotines. She may have committed suicide regardless of ever finding ASH.

Mike and Mary Gonzales, Lindsay Bartlett, and Wally Herger, on the other hand, remain optimistic, although the bill is in the first step in the legislative process. "We have two years from date of introduction to get the bill voted on and out of the House to the Senate," Mike Gonzales said. From there, the Senate will discuss and debate the bill, and if the Senate chooses to pass the bill, it goes on to the President. "We'll keep revising it until it does become successful," Bartlett said, "We're in for the long haul!"

Conclusion

The Internet has not received nearly as much consideration as other suicide factors. While the literature review provided a great deal of relevant information about suicide and its components, this study has uncovered new information. While my data were qualitative and often based on case studies, the results are nonetheless significant. By exploring the content of suicide websites, newsgroups and message boards, and interviewing the people that use them, I have presented a fresh look into the connection between suicide and the Internet.

Previous research provided grounds for further investigation. My investigation unearthed the same graphic suicide paraphernalia Alao and colleagues (2006) discussed. Their article, "Cybersuicide: Review of the Role of the Internet on Suicide" went on to discuss how the Internet can be a potential source of help for suicidal people, a conclusion that other researchers and myself also reached. Alao and colleagues said that the Internet can be beneficial when suicidal people seek counseling online (490). Tam, Tang and Fernando (2007) called the Internet a "double-edged tool" in relation to suicide, explaining how the Internet could help suicidal people by providing online support groups, etc.

However, each instance of research merely illustrated the Internet's *potential* in serving as a source of help for suicidal people. None of the research thus far has offered compelling evidence that pro-suicide websites ironically help some people avoid suicide. In my research, responses to interviews provided evidence that suicide websites, or at least newsgroups such as ASH, can be beneficial to suicidal people and help them to not commit suicide. This is an unexamined perspective, but one that my research strongly supported.

Suicide has always yielded questions, but it is the high-speed development of the Internet and its effect on the age-old quandary of suicide, that calls for even more and newer research. The existence of suicide websites is verified and, as of now, the law does not interfere in their continuation. In an era in which search engines have replaced dictionaries and "Google it" has become a catchphrase, it is clear that suicide methods are only a click away. Websites, message boards, chat rooms and newsgroups can all harbor suicidal people, foster discussion about the best way to die, and reveal the means. Their effect, however, is not yet clear. It is far too soon to rule out the possibility that they might function to counteract suicidal impulses and hinder attempts.

References

Alao, Adekola, Maureen Soderberg, and Elyssa Pohl. "Cybersuicide: Review of the Role of the Internet on Suicide." *CyberPsychology & Behavior* 9.4 (2006): 489–93.

Becker, Katja, et al. "Parasuicide Online: Can Suicide Websites Trigger Suicidal Behaviour in Predisposed Adolesents?" *Nord J Psychology* 58.2 (2004): 111–14.

Becker, Katja, and Martin Schmidt. "When Kids Seek Help OnLine: Internet Chat Rooms and Suicide." *Reclaiming Children and Youth* 13.4 (2005): 229–30.

Gould, Madelyn, Patrick Jamieson, and Daniel Romer. "Media Contagion and Suicide Among the Young." *American Behavioral Scientist* 46.9 (2003): 1269–80.

Gutierrez, Thelma, and Kim McCabe. "Parents: Online Newsgroup Helped Daughter Commit Suicide." *CNN.* 10 Nov. 2005. 19 Feb. 2008 <www.cnn.com>.

Mishara, Brian, and David Weisstub. "Ethical, Legal, and Practical Issues in the Control and Regulation of Suicide Promotion and Assistance over the Internet." *Suicide and Life-Threatening Behavior* 37.1 (2007): 58–65.

Rhine, Clinton Ernest, et al. "Dimensions of Suicide: Perceptions of Lethality, Time and Agony." *Suicide and Life-Threatening Behavior* 25.3 (1995): 373–80.

Scheeres, Julia. "A Virtual Path to Suicide: Depressed Student Killed Herself With Help From Online Discussion Group." *San Francisco Chronicle* 8 June 2003. 27 Feb. 2008. <www.sfgate.com/cgi-bin/article.cgi?f=/c/a/2003/06/08/MN114902.DTL>.

Tam, J., W. S. Tang, D. J. S. Fernando. "The Internet and Suicide: A Double-Edged Tool." *European Journal of Internal Medicine* 18 (2007): 453–55.

Critical Thinking

1. Explain whether the Internet helps stem the tide of suicides in the United States.

2. Locate three Internet sites that advocate for and against suicide.

3. Can a website be liable for encouraging or "driving" one to commit suicide? If so, or not, explain why.

UNIT 5
Animals and Death

Unit Selections

Learning Outcomes

After reading this unit, you should be able to:

- Discuss pet attachment in the psychological health of individuals living alone.
- Explain something about the role of the veterinarian in euthanasia of companion animals.
- Describe some of the psychosocial variables related to the death of a pet.
- Discuss the void left within a family when a pet dies.
- Identify some of the common feelings when a pet dies.
- Point out benefits for an older person in having a pet.
- List ways that an individual can cope with the loss of a pet.

Student Website

www.mhhe.com/cls

Internet References

Association for Pet Loss and Bereavement (APLB)
www.aplb.org

In Memory of Pets
www.In-Memory-Of-Pets.Com

Lightning Strike Pet Loss Support
www.lightning-strike.com

Chance's Spot Pet Loss and Support Resources
www.chancesspot.org

Bereavement UK
www.bereavement.co.uk

College of Veterinary Medicine Pet Loss Support
www.vetmed.wsu.edu/PLHL

Pet Loss Support Page
www.pet-loss.net

Best Friend Services
www.bestfriendservices.com

In Memory of Pets Cemetery
www.in-memory-of-pets.com

Rainbows Bridge
www.rainbowsbridge.com

Angel Blue Mist
www.angelbluemist.com

Patsy Ann
www.patsyann.com

Four Paws in Heaven
www.fourpawsinheaven.com

My Cemetery
www.mycemetery.com

Tippie
www.tippie.com

Valor Rolls: Police Officers and Dogs Killed In Action
www.policek9.com/html/valor.html

Shaman
http://kimmurphy.net/shaman.html

Roadside America Pet Cemetery
www.roadsideamerica.com/pet

Gone to the Dog Star
www.gonetodogstar.com

Prince
www.catsdogs.com/prince.html

Odie
http://odiedog.com/

Bebe
www.bebemau.com

Justice for Junior
www.justiceforjunior.org

114

The first encounter that many children have with death is with that of an animal. It may be a pet or a dead bird or wild animal on the roadway. If that experience is indeed an animal, how do we as adults deal with the topic? The death of an animal presents a good opportunity for parents to help children learn their lessons of death by answering questions. If a family pet, the child may have had the pleasure of watching the animal grow from a small puppy, kitten, or guinea pig into a large dog, cat, or guinea pig. With non-human animals having shorter live spans than humans, children often observe a pet going through the life cycle, with the omega being death. Thus, a pet's death is a realistic orientation to death.

In this section of the anthology, we present articles on animals and death. How and when to "put down" one's animal is not an easy question to answer, thus one often relies heavily on the veterinarian's advice on this. An individual does not want to have the animal euthanized too soon and take away some of its life while it has some quality to it, yet at the same time one does not want to wait too long and let the animal suffer. Afterward, one may feel guilty if she or he felt that action occurred too soon or the same if it was too late. A not so win-win situation. "Good Mourning" touches on the role of the veterinarian in assisting with end-of-life concerns involving pets.

"When a Cherished Pet Dies" addresses the issue of the impact on the death of a pet on the elderly. Often an elderly person's best friend and companion may be her or his dog or cat or some other animal. When that animal dies, it can be devastating to the individual.

Our society is becoming more accepting of the significance of the death of a pet, as is evidenced by Hallmark sympathy cards

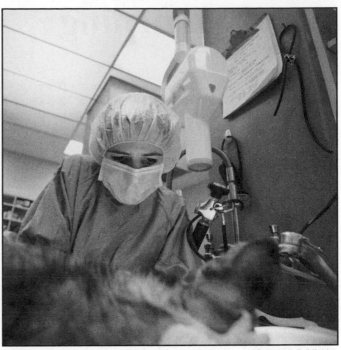

© Ingram Publishing

for when a pet dies and by veterinary clinics making available grief counselors for pet owners. The importance of attachment to a pet and the role played in the life of an individual, especially one living alone, and the psychosocial variables related to pet deaths are discussed in this section.

Good Mourning

For more than three decades, George Dickinson has been exploring the ways Americans handle death and end-of-life issues. So, we asked the 2009 Death Education Award recipient and acclaimed scholar to talk about one of his latest research interests—the issues surrounding the passing of a pet.

GEORGE DICKINSON

For many of us, a pet is a significant member of the family. We talk to pets and care for them as if they were our children. We tend to have a very human bond with our companion animals. Pets often live with us as many years as our children live at home before leaving for college or emancipation. Pets can make us feel needed, can relieve loneliness and can serve as friends and companions. Therefore, the death of a pet is a traumatic experience. As occurs with any other member of the family, that death leaves a huge void.

Our first childhood death experience typically is around the age of 8. And that first experience is often a pet. Recollections of this event are among our more vivid childhood memories. The death of a pet presents a good opportunity for a parent to explain death to a small child: The animal is immobile, not breathing, not eating or drinking because it is dead. This situation provides a setting for the parent to be a role model by being open with the child about what happened. If the parent cries, this lets the child know that crying is OK. It's helpful if the parent is involved in a burial, if earth burial is the chosen means of final body disposal.

Our children had guinea pigs. A guinea pig's lifespan is short, thus we had a lot of funerals for guinea pigs at our house. In our routine, I was the official grave digger; the children wrapped the animal in a cloth (shroud), placed it in the hole, covered it with dirt and then put a rock or something else over it to mark the spot in the backyard. As the ceremony progressed and the children related a memory of the pet, each of us felt tears rolling down our cheeks. Such parental participation showed my children that our companion animals had importance.

For adults, and especially the elderly, pets can be excellent companions. A dog, for example, typically wags its tail and genuinely seems happy to see its owner enter the house. The pet can help lessen a feeling of isolation and loneliness for a person living alone. The companion animal does not seem to get out of sorts about the stresses in life. A pet can be most relaxing for an individual stroking it and thus even contribute to better health for the individual. The loss of a beloved pet, therefore, can certainly be traumatic for the owner, who—no longer being needed by the companion animal—may feel a true sense of emptiness.

Unlike the person who loses a friend or relative and receives outpourings of sympathy and support, one who loses a pet is often ridiculed for overreacting or for being foolishly emotional. Such an unsympathetic response is called disenfranchised grief (grief not openly acknowledged, socially sanctioned or publicly shared). Today, however, the death of a pet is being recognized in many circles similarly to that of the death of a human—as evidenced by the recent development of Hallmark sympathy cards for owners of deceased pets. Grieving for a pet and for a human has many similarities: feeling preoccupied, experiencing guilt and mistaking shadows and sounds as being from the dead companion.

The death of a pet is experienced uniquely by veterinarians —especially when they are performing euthanasia, granting "merciful relief" from irreversible pain or an incurable malady. Though the states of Oregon and Washington now allow physician-assisted suicide, medical doctors are not allowed to practice euthanasia; and, for them, their role ends when the patient dies, as the follow-up functions are handled by medical staff, then the mortuary. Veterinarians, however, are often asked to dispose of the animal's body. Additionally, veterinarians have the added pressure of a client asking for advice as to whether or not to "put the pet to sleep" (*sleep,* an interesting euphemism for *death*), and if so, when. The owner of the companion animal does not wish to euthanize too quickly, yet does not want to wait beyond the time when death perhaps should have occurred. Thus, veterinarians give advice, themselves not knowing when is "just right" for the death. Such stress is somewhat limited to the veterinary medicine profession.

From the veterinarian's perspective, the most legitimate reasons for euthanizing a companion animal revolve around the animal's quality of life. The final decision, however, rests with the human guardian. Following a decision to euthanize, the owner often has a feeling of regret for having given permission for euthanasia, no matter the severity of the illness or the animal's incapacity.

Together with Paul and Karin Roof, I recently conducted an end-of-life survey of 463 veterinarians in the Southeast, and found that the average veterinarian practices euthanasia 7.53 times per month. The majority of companion animal owners opt to stay with the animal during the procedure, and two-thirds of owners leave the pet with the veterinary clinic for disposal. Those who leave the animal at the clinic more often choose cremation, while those who take the dead animal away typically bury the animal. It also found that veterinarians feel that more education on end-of-life issues is needed in veterinary school, though the more recent graduates feel more favorable toward their end-of-life education than earlier graduates. Currently, the 28 veterinary medicine schools in the United States average 15 hours on end-of-life issues within their curriculum. This is similar to U.S. baccalaureate nursing schools' 14 hours and U.S. medical schools' 12 hours on end-of-life issues.

Good, open communication by professionals is pivotal in any end-of-life discussion, be it involving a companion animal or a human. Whether the terminally ill family member is a human or a pet, the process of dying and the event of death are among the more stressful experiences humans have. We can be supportive of each other and remember that a death—pet or human—should not be reacted to as disenfranchised grief; rather, it should be socially sanctioned and publicly shared.

Much like those for humans, hospices for pets are evolving in the 21st century. Some of these hospice programs focus on teaching pet owners how to care for their terminally ill pets at home, yet others handle the pet at a free-standing hospice facility. If euthanasia isn't an option (the owner "simply cannot put Fido down"), hospice care might be the solution for a terminally ill companion animal. Palliative care within a hospice setting, where pain control is paramount, presents a peaceful way for an animal to die. And who wants to see anything/anyone die in pain when analgesics are a reasonable option? Is not quality of life better than quantity of life?

Pets—like family members—leave a tremendous void in our lives when they die. Life goes on, however, and we must cope with the loss. We should talk openly about our feelings. Grief shared is grief relieved. We don't "get over" the loss of a family member, pet or human, but we simply learn to live with the fact that that member will no longer be literally present. Through memories, however, the human or companion animal "lives on." Gone but not forgotten.

Critical Thinking

1. How did your family handle the death of your pets when you were a child?

2. What is your experience with veterinarians regarding their role in the death of one of your pets?

3. Should we have hospice facilities for pets, as we now have for humans?

George Dickinson is a professor of sociology.

When a Cherished Pet Dies

"After several months I am still so distraught over the death of my dog, Pixie, I can't even talk about her. I miss watching TV with her on my lap and I miss her companionship."

—Diane, 74 years old

Pets can be an important part of life, holding a special place in the heart. A pet can be a faithful companion, an integral part of one's home life and daily schedule. A pet can provide unconditional love that many people, particularly older adults, may get from no one else. When a special pet dies, this loss can have a significant impact on a person's health and well-being. Today, there is a growing public awareness about the anguish people can feel when a cherished pet dies, and more community resources are available to help those grieving a pet.

How Do Older People Benefit from Having a Pet?

Pets can provide their owners with a sense of purpose and fulfillment, companionship, affection, acceptance and friendship. Pets rely on their owners for food, water, exercise and medical care, which may give the owner a feeling of responsibility and of being needed. In return, pets often express contentment through their chirps, wags, licks or purrs. A pet may provide opportunities for physical contact, such as touching, hugging, cuddling, and can even be a sleep partner. Owners talk to, spend time with, and have fun with a pet. Through these interactions, a pet can become an integral part of everyday life. For many, a pet can hold the rank of "valued friend" or "close family member."

Caring for and providing a loving home to an animal can help an older person remain active and healthy. This active involvement with an animal can help lower blood pressure, decrease stress, reduce bone loss, lower cholesterol levels, and improve blood circulation. A pet may also provide an opportunity to meet and socialize with others, such as gathering with other pet owners in the park or conversing with the staff at the vet's office. Thus, a pet can help lessen or prevent feelings of isolation and loneliness.

How Might the Death of a Pet Affect Older People?

Losing a cherished pet means losing a significant relationship. Your pet loss can feel overwhelming, particularly if you are experiencing other losses, many of which are common to the aging process.

It is not unusual, for example, for older adults to have long-time friends, a spouse, and a pet die all within a short time of each other. Your pet may have been the one link left to your past, or perhaps was your loyal companion during an otherwise lonely time. Or you may have moved from your old neighborhood to a new environment, and your pet may have been a source of strength during the transition to your new home. For those coping with a chronic illness, your pet may have comforted you, by staying nearby or licking your hand. For others, your pet may have been trained to help you with daily activities. For example, just as a seeing-eye dog is specifically trained to help someone with vision impairment get around, your pet may have been trained to be able to move easily and fetch things in the house for you or alert others in case you needed help in an emergency.

The loss of your pet may change your outlook on your life. For example, you may lose a sense of purpose in your day if you experience feelings of emptiness or sadness when no longer having a dog to walk, a bird to talk to or a cat to brush. In addition, the loss of a beloved pet can remind you of your own vulnerability and mortality. This can lead to feelings of worry about getting another pet, wondering if the pet will become orphaned if you have a prolonged hospitalization or die.

What Are Common Feelings When a Pet Dies?

Grieving is a natural response to the loss of an attachment. It is normal to grieve a pet that has been a part of your life. There is no right or wrong way to express your feelings related to the loss of a beloved pet. Some people are outwardly emotional while others emote privately. Some will grieve for days or weeks while others may take months or even years to recover from the loss of a beloved animal friend. Your own reactions and feelings connected to this loss will likely depend on the nature of the relationship you had with your pet, how long the pet was part of your life, if the death was sudden or gradual, and the situation in which the pet died.

When a pet dies, it is not unusual for a person to experience a range of feelings. When the loss of a pet occurs under particularly stressful circumstances, the emotional response can be quite intense. For example, you may experience anger or helplessness if a precious pet needs to be given away because of financial limitations, ill health or because of a move to a new place that does not accept pets, like a nursing home or assisted living facility. You might experience anguish if faced with the difficult decision to euthanize a pet. Or, if your pet died from an accident, you may feel guilt if you believe you could have been more protective. Holiday and birthday celebrations may feel less joyful after the loss of a pet. After a pet dies, you might feel sad each year on the anniversary marking the date your pet came into your heart and home.

If your sadness or pain seems to grow over time, or you find the loss of your pet affecting your ability to get things done on a daily basis, it is probably time to seek professional counseling to help you cope with your continued grief.

Why Are Feelings about Losing a Pet Often Hidden?

You might feel upset and sad about the loss of your pet and find yourself hiding these feelings from others. You may believe it is inappropriate, silly or weak to be so concerned about an animal's death. Or you may have been raised believing that showing emotion is improper making it difficult for you to express personal feelings. If you feel embarrassed, ashamed, or uncomfortable about your emotional reaction to your pet's death, trying to ignore or disguise your grief is common.

In addition, sometimes otherwise well-meaning people may say careless things like, "You can always get another one." This might be true, yet this statement does not acknowledge the uniqueness of your pet and the special relationship you enjoyed. Feeling misunderstood, you might decide not to share the sadness you feel.

Our society does not always recognize the depth of feeling that can accompany the loss of a pet. Thus, many communities offer no way or only very limited ways to share the loss of a pet with others (e.g., rituals, ceremonies, or memorials). Without an organized opportunity to remember a pet, many people feel uncomfortable expressing grief.

Grieving the loss of a pet, while difficult, can be a healthy process. Holding back may leave you with a heavy heart for a prolonged period of time.

How Can I Cope with the Loss of My Pet?

It is common to feel sorrow with the loss of a pet. It is important to realize that things will get better over time. Here are some things you can do to cope with the loss of your pet:

Talk about your feelings for your pet with others who are compassionate, sensitive and understanding.

Remember your pet by creating a scrapbook about them, place a framed picture of them in a special place, or write a story or poem about them.

Participate in a support group, counseling session, Internet chat room or call a pet loss hotline. Your veterinarian or local Humane Society can recommend counselors or support groups that might help you.

Consider holding a memorial service, buying a burial site, or putting a stone marker in your garden or in a room in your house.

Make a memorial contribution in your pet's name to a favorite charity or to an animal rescue organization. Saying good-bye can give you an opportunity to express your feelings, reach some closure, and to think about the role of the pet in your life.

Volunteer with a charity or religious group that you are affiliated with to keep yourself busy and with other people. Animal shelters and animal organizations need people to walk, pet, and care for abandoned animals.

Increase your interaction with family, friends and social groups in your community.

Read books and magazines about pet loss and how to deal with your feelings of grief.

Critical Thinking

1. How do elderly individuals benefit from having a pet and how might they feel when the pet dies?

2. What are some ways to cope with the loss of a pet?

3. Why are feelings about losing a pet often hidden?

An Examination of the Potential Role of Pet Ownership, Human Social Support and Pet Attachment in the Psychological Health of Individuals Living Alone

NIKOLINA M. DUVALL ANTONACOPOULOS AND TIMOTHY A. PYCHYL

An area that is receiving considerable attention is the relationship between pet ownership and psychological health (Roberts et al. 1996; Headey 1999; Gilbey, McNicholas and Collis 2007; Wood et al. 2007). The potential psychological health benefits that pets may confer to individuals living in one-person households is of particular interest, given that worldwide there is a growing trend toward one-person households (Euromonitor International 2008). In Canada, for example, the percentage of one-person households has increased over time from 6% in 1941 to 27% in 2006 (Milan, Vézina and Wells 2007). One-person households accounted for 26% of American households in 2005, 28% of households in Western Europe in 2006, 22% of households in Eastern Europe in 2006, and 26% of households in Australasia in 2006 (US Census Bureau 2006; Euromonitor International 2008). It is expected that the number of one-person households will continue to increase in years to come at a faster rate than other types of households (Euromonitor International 2008).

The limited number of studies that have examined the impact of pet ownership on the psychological health of individuals living alone were cross-sectional in nature and only assessed psychological health through measures of mood and loneliness. For example, a study conducted in the general population in Switzerland found that people who lived alone with a cat were less likely to report being in a bad mood than people who lived alone without a cat (Turner, Rieger and Gytax 2003). Two other studies conducted in the United States using female subgroups of university students and seniors found that female pet owners who lived alone with a pet were less lonely than females who lived alone without a pet (Goldmeier 1986; Zasloff and Kidd 1994). However, a study conducted in Australia found no evidence that seniors who lived alone with a pet were less lonely than seniors who lived alone without a pet (Wells and Rodi 2000). In a final study, conducted with American university faculty who were classified as either Alone (unmarried and not living with children) or Not Alone (married and/or living with children), Staats, Sears and Pierfelice (2006) found that faculty who were unmarried and did not have children living with them were more likely than faculty who lived with either a spouse, children, or both to report that they owned a pet because it helped them in difficult times and that they would be lonely without it. Taken together, these studies suggest that, with the possible exception of seniors, pet ownership may be beneficial for the psychological health of individuals living alone.

Pets may assume an important psychological role in the lives of individuals who live alone, particularly in terms of the level of emotional attachment between the pet owner and their pet. A number of studies have found that pet owners who lived alone were more attached to their pet than individuals who lived with others (Holcomb, Williams and Richards 1985; Gilmer and Nicholson 1996; Poresky and Daniels 1998; Stammbach and Turner 1999). It is noteworthy that one study found that the relationship between attachment and living situation only held for dogs, not cats (Zasloff and Kidd 1994). When researchers examined the relationship between attachment and psychological health for pet owners as a whole, they found mixed results. Some researchers found that the more attached pet owners were to their pet, the better their psychological health (Ory and Goldberg 1983; Garrity et al. 1989; Budge et al. 1998), while other researchers did not find evidence that such a relationship exists (Miller and Lago 1989; Stallones et al. 1990; Zasloff and Kidd 1994; Raina et al. 1999). Possible explanations for the failure to find a relationship between attachment and psychological health may be due to the possible interactive effects of other factors such as sex, age, marital status, financial status, or personality with attachment levels. Another possible explanation is that psychological health varies depending on both attachment to pets and whether an individual lives alone or with other people. The one study that examined this possibility found that attachment to pets and living situation had interactive effects on psychological health, as assessed through a measure of positive mood (Turner, Rieger and Gytax 2003).

One way to understand the variation in attachment to pets may be to take into account co-variation in human social support. Three correlational studies, conducted in the general population, found that pet owners who lacked human social support were more attached to their pet (Johnson, Garrity and Stallones 1992; Stammbach and Turner 1999; Adamelli et al. 2005), while two other correlational studies did not reach the same conclusion (Cohen 2002; Marinelli et al. 2007). While these studies were not restricted to pet owners living alone, it is speculated that individuals living alone with low levels of human social support may be highly attached to their pet. If pet owners who live alone and lack human social support receive social support through their strong attachment to their pet, this may be beneficial for their psychological health. Two studies that examined whether psychological health varies according to levels of pet attachment and human social support provided mixed results. In the first study, Garrity et al. (1989) found that bereaved elderly pet owners who had two or less confidants and were strongly attached to their pet were less depressed compared with bereaved elderly pet owners who had two or fewer confidants and were weakly attached to their pet. However, among non-bereaved elderly, Garrity et al. (1989) found no evidence that pet attachment levels and human social support levels interacted to predict depression levels. In the second study, Budge et al. (1998) found no evidence that, among pet owners 21 to 79 years of age, psychological health depended on levels of pet attachment and human social support, which led them to suggest that this relationship may only hold for pet owners who are socially isolated. Unfortunately, neither of these studies examined whether pet attachment and social support had interactive effects on the psychological health of pet owners who lived alone.

Rationale for Present Study and Hypotheses

This study builds on previous work that examined the possible psychological health benefits of pet ownership for individuals living alone by considering the role of human social support and pet attachment. In the case of human social support, previous research comparing pet and non-petowners suggests that, for individuals in the general population who live alone and female students who live alone, pets provide psychological health benefits, such as reducing negative moods and loneliness levels (Zasloff and Kidd 1994; Turner, Rieger and Gytax 2003). However, the studies that examined the psychological health of individuals living alone with or without a pet (Goldmeier 1986; Zasloff and Kidd 1994; Wells and Rodi 2000; Turner, Rieger and Gytax 2003) did not explicitly examine the role of human social support. This is surprising given that, for individuals living alone, pet ownership (pet vs. no pet) and levels of human social support may both affect psychological health. In fact, we argue that, for individuals living alone, levels of human social support and pet ownership may interact to predict psychological health in terms of loneliness and depression levels.

In the case of pet attachment, there was no agreement in the existing literature as to whether high levels of attachment to pets were related to psychological health (Zasloff and Kidd 1994; Budge et al. 1998). However, this relation has not been examined among individuals in the general population who live alone. It may be that, for individuals living alone, the companionship provided

by their pet is advantageous for their psychological health by, for example, reducing their loneliness levels. Another limitation of previous studies is that researchers have not examined whether, among pet owners living alone, attachment levels to pets and levels of human social support have interactive effects on psychological health. Therefore, in this study we examined the possibility that attachment levels to pets and human social support levels interact to predict psychological health in terms of loneliness and depression levels.

The purpose of this study was to test the following hypotheses:

1. Individuals who live alone with a pet will have better psychological health (less lonely and depressed) compared with individuals who live alone without a pet.
2. Pet ownership (pet vs. no pet) and levels of human social support will have interactive effects on the psychological health (loneliness and depression) of individuals living alone.
3. Among pet owners living alone, there will be a positive relation between attachment to pets and psychological health (loneliness and depression).
4. Among pet owners living alone, attachment to pets and levels of human social support will have interactive effects on psychological health (loneliness and depression).

The four hypotheses were tested separately for dog and cat owners in order to determine whether, as expected, they were supported for both types of pet owners.

Methods

Participants

One hundred and thirty-two Canadian pet (dog and cat owners) and non-pet owners (defined as individuals who did not own a dog or cat) who were at least 18 years of age and living alone completed a 15 minute on-line survey of "factors affecting the well-being of individuals living alone." The sample consisted of 66 pet owners (40 dog owners and 26 cat owners) and 66 people who did not own a dog or a cat.

Materials

The survey package contained measures of participants' demographic characteristics (age, sex, education, income, whether they were a student and whether they were in a permanent relationship), social support, pet attachment, depression, loneliness, and open- and closed-ended questions about pet ownership.

Predictor Variables

Multidimensional Scale of Perceived Social Support (MSPSS): The 12-item social support scale developed by Zimet et al. (1988) was used to examine participants' overall levels of perceived social support. The scale ranges from 1 (very strongly disagree) to 7 (very strongly agree) and includes items such as "I can talk about my problems with my friends." Data were transformed using a square root transformation, to deal with moderate negative skew, and subsequently centered. According to Zimet et al. (1988), the scale is internally consistent, as assessed by Cronbach's alpha ($\alpha = 0.88$), and has adequate test-retest reliability after 2 to 3 months ($r = 0.85$).

Item analyses done in the present study revealed that Cronbach's alpha was 0.89. According to Zimet et al. (1988), the scale has moderate construct validity, as reflected by negative correlations between the MSPSS and the depression and anxiety subscales of the Hopkins Symptom Checklist. In the present study, total scores were divided by 12 to obtain mean item scores on the MSPSS.

Lexington Attachment to Pets Scale (LAPS): The 23-item LAPS developed by Johnson, Garrity and Stallones (1992) was used to assess participants' level of emotional attachment to their pet. The scale ranges from 0 (strongly disagree) to 3 (strongly agree) and includes items such as "Quite often, my feelings toward people are affected by the way they react to my pet." It should be noted that attachment scores were centered. According to Johnson, Garrity and Stallones, the LAPS has high internal consistency ($\alpha = 0.93$). In the present study, item analyses conducted to examine the homogeneity of the items revealed that Cronbach's alpha was 0.89. Evidence for the construct validity of the LAPS is provided by its correlations with respondent characteristics, such as gender, marital status, and whether or not children are present in the home; characteristics other researchers have found are associated with pet attachment (Kidd and Kidd 1989). In the present study, total scores were divided by 23 to obtain mean item scores on the LAPS.

Criterion Variables

Center for Epidemiologic Studies-Depression Scale (CES-D): The 20-item CES-D Scale by Radloff (1977) was used to examine how frequently participants experienced symptoms of depression during the past week. The scale ranges from 0 (rarely or none of the time [less than 1 day a week]) to 3 (most or all of the time [5–7 days a week]) and includes items such as "I had trouble keeping my mind on what I was doing." In order to deal with severe positive skew, the data were inversely transformed. The scale is internally consistent ($\alpha = 0.85$) and has modest test-retest correlations after 2 to 12 weeks; all but one test-retest correlation ranged between 0.45 to 0.70 (Radloff 1977). Item analyses in the present study revealed that Cronbach's alpha was 0.88. The CES-D Scale demonstrates concurrent validity, as reflected by its high correlation with the Beck Depression Inventory ($r = 0.86$) (Santor et al. 1995). In the present study, total scores were divided by 20 to obtain mean item scores on the CES-D.

UCLA Loneliness Scale (Version 3): The 20-item UCLA Loneliness Scale (Version 3) by Russell (1996) was used to assess participants' feelings of loneliness. The scale ranges from 1 (never) to 4 (always) and includes items such as "How often do you feel that you lack companionship?" Using data from studies involving college students, nurses, teachers, and the elderly, Russell demonstrated that the UCLA Loneliness Scale (Version 3) has high internal consistency, with coefficient alphas ranging from 0.89 to 0.94, and also demonstrated adequate test-retest reliability when it was re-administered after a one-year period to a sample consisting of elderly people ($r = 0.73$). In the current study, Cronbach's alpha was 0.92. With respect to the construct validity of the scale, Russell (1996) found that, as expected, the scale positively correlates with other loneliness scales, such as the NYU Loneliness Scale and the Differential Loneliness Scale, while it negatively correlates with measures of social support, such as the Social Provisions Scale. In addition, there were significant relations between the scale and measures of personality, mood, health, and well-being. In the present study, total scores were divided by 20 to obtain mean item scores on the UCLA.

Additional Questions

An open-ended question was included in which participants were asked "What benefits have you received from the dog(s) or cat(s) that you presently own? Begin with the most important benefit." In addition, a question was included in which pet owners were asked to rate the impact that their pet had had on their life on a 7-point scale ranging from 1 (strong negative impact) to 7 (strong positive impact).

Procedure

Participants completed the on-line survey using "Survey Monkey," a tool designed to create and customize on-line surveys, which ensures that participants' responses are anonymous and confidential (http://www.surveymonkey.com/). Participants were recruited from May to July, 2008 through snowball sampling by sending an e-mail with the survey link to family and friends, posters placed in various locations in the community (e.g., libraries, community centers and laundromats), information distributed in-person at local dog parks and pet stores, and links posted on various pet and non-pet related Internet websites. Prior to data collection, permission to conduct this survey was granted by the Carleton University Ethics Committee for Psychological Research.

Results

Demographic Characteristics of Pet Owners and Non-Owners

To examine whether pet owners and non-owners had similar demographic characteristics, chi-square and *t*-tests were conducted (Table 1). Participants in the two groups were compared with respect to their age, sex, education, income, whether they were a student and whether they were in a permanent relationship. With respect to education, participants were divided according to whether they had at least one university degree, given that researchers have found that as education levels increase, loneliness and depression levels decrease (Hanley-Dunn, Maxwell and Stanos 1985; Ross and Van Willigen 1997). Given that the average household income in 2005 for Canadians living in one-person households was $35,372 (Statistics Canada 2006), participants were classified as having an income of less than $40,000 or $40,000 or more.[1] In order to ensure that the sample did not include a disproportionate number of students, participants were asked to indicate whether they were a full-time university or college student. Finally, participants were asked whether they were in a permanent relationship, given that individuals in a permanent relationship have an additional source of social support, which may be beneficial for their psychological health. Comparisons revealed that the two groups did not differ significantly on any of the demographic variables.

Hierarchical regression procedures were used to test all hypotheses, with any demographic variables that were significantly correlated with the criterion variables (loneliness and depression) entered in the first step of the regression models, in order to reduce error variance in the criterion variables. We hypothesized that: 1) individuals who lived alone with a pet would have better psychological health (less lonely and depressed) than individuals who lived alone without a pet, and 2) pet ownership (dog or cat vs. no pet) and levels of human social support would have interactive effects on the psychological health (loneliness and depression) of individuals who live alone.

Table 1 Demographic Characteristics of Pet Owners and Non-owners ($n = 132$)

Demographic Variable	Pet Owners (n = 66)	Non-Owners (n = 66)
Age		
Mean (*SD*)	37.56 (14.45)	41.30 (14.36)
Range	22–68	22–78
Sex (%)[a]		
Male	32.3	21.2
Female	67.7	78.8
Education (%)		
< A University Degree	22.7	18.2
≥ One University Degree	77.3	81.8
Income (%)[b]		
< $40,000	36.4	21.9
≥ $40,000	63.6	78.1
Student (%)		
Yes	13.6	14.1
No	86.4	85.9
Permanent Relationship (%)[c]		
Yes	21.5	13.8
No	78.5	86.2

[a] One pet owner did not indicate their sex.
[b] Two non-owners did not indicate their income.
[c] One pet owner and one non-owner did not indicate whether they were in a permanent relationship.

Table 2 Summary of Hierarchical Regression Analysis for Variables Predicting the Loneliness Levels of Individuals Who Live alone with or without a Pet ($n = 130$)

Variable	F_{change}	df	R^2_{change}	β
Step 1				
Age	5.02*	128	0.04	0.19*
Step 2				
Age	48.86**	126	0.42	0.13
Pet Ownership (Pet Owner = 1)				−0.04
Social Support				−0.65**
Step 3				
Age	4.18*	125	0.02	0.14*
Pet Ownership (Pet Owner = 1)				−0.03
Social Support				−0.49**
Pet Ownership × Social Support				−0.21*

*$p < 0.05$; **$p < 0.001$

To begin, these hypotheses were examined with respect to loneliness levels. It should be noted that two dog owners who did not answer a sufficient number of items in the loneliness scale were excluded from these analyses. As may be seen from Table 2, age was a significant predictor of the loneliness levels of individuals living alone (β = 0.14, $p < 0.05$). Older participants who lived alone reported higher loneliness scores. The first hypothesis, that individuals living alone who owned a pet would be less lonely than people without a pet, was not supported (β = −0.03, $p > 0.05$). However, as expected, based on previous research conducted in the general population (Russell 1996; Mahon, Yarcheski and Yarcheski 1998), individuals with high levels of human social support were significantly less lonely than individuals with low levels of human social support (β = −0.49, $p < 0.001$). Furthermore, the second hypothesis, that among individuals living alone there would be an interaction between pet ownership and human social support, was also supported (β = −0.21, $p < 0.05$).

Table 3 Summary of Hierarchical Regression Analysis for Variables Predicting the Depression Levels of Individuals Who Live alone with or without a Pet ($n = 132$)

Variable	F_{change}	df	R^2_{change}	β
Step 1				
Pet Ownership (Pet Owner = 1)	8.18**	129	0.11	0.00
Social Support				−0.34**
Step 2				
Pet Ownership (Pet Owner = 1)	6.09*	128	0.04	−0.00
Social Support				−0.09
Pet Ownership × Social Support				−0.32*

*$p < 0.05$; **$p < 0.001$

In order to interpret the direction of the interactive effects between pet ownership and human social support, a median split analysis was conducted to divide participants into two groups, according to whether they had low or high levels of human social support. Simple effects revealed that, among individuals living alone with low levels of human social support, pet owners and non-owners did not differ significantly in their loneliness levels (2.37 vs. 2.31, $p > 0.05$). Similarly, among individuals living alone with high levels of human social support, pet owners and non-owners did not differ significantly in their loneliness levels (1.79 vs. 1.90, $p > 0.05$).

In order to test whether the first two hypotheses held for dog and cat owners, hierarchical regression analyses were conducted comparing, first, dog owners vs. non-owners and, second, cat owners vs. non-owners. In the hierarchical regression analysis including dog owners and non-owners, the first hypothesis, that dog owners who live alone would be less lonely than non-owners who live alone, was not supported (β = −0.08, $p > 0.05$). However, human social support was a significant predictor of the loneliness levels of individuals living alone (β = −0.51, $p < 0.001$). Furthermore, the second hypothesis, that among individuals living alone there would be an interaction between dog ownership and human social support, was supported (β = −0.25, $p < 0.05$). Simple effects revealed that among individuals living alone with low levels of human social support, the loneliness levels of dog owners and non-owners did not differ significantly (2.54 vs. 2.33, $p > 0.05$). However, among individuals living alone with high levels of human social support, dog owners were significantly less lonely than non-owners (1.62 vs. 1.91, $p < 0.01$). These findings are displayed in Figure 1.

When only cat owners and non-owners were included in a hierarchical regression analysis, age was a significant predictor of the loneliness levels of individuals living alone (β = 0.19, $p < 0.05$). The first hypothesis, that cat owners who live alone would be less lonely than non-owners, was not supported (β = 0.00, $p > 0.05$). As expected, human social support was a significant predictor of the loneliness levels of individuals living alone (β = −0.47, $p < 0.001$). However, the second hypothesis, that loneliness would be predicted by an interaction between cat ownership and human social support, was not supported (β = −0.01, $p > 0.05$).

The first two hypotheses were also examined with depression used as the criterion variable to assess psychological health. As may be seen from Table 3, the first hypothesis, that among individuals living alone people who owned a pet would be less

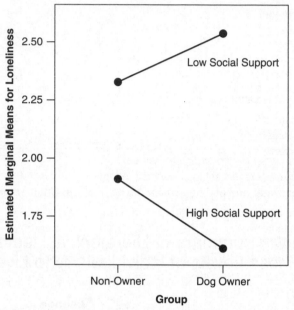

Figure 1 Mean loneliness scores for dog ownership by level of social support.

depressed than individuals without a pet, was not supported (β = −0.00, $p > 0.05$). Human social support also was not a significant predictor of the depression levels of individuals living alone (β = −0.09, $p > 0.05$), which is surprising given that previous research in the general population has found that higher levels of human social support are associated with lower levels of depression (Ross and Van Willigen 1997; Budge et al. 1998). However, the second hypothesis, that among individuals living alone there would be an interaction between pet ownership and human social support, was supported (β = −0.32, $p < 0.05$).

Simple effects revealed that among individuals living alone with low levels of human social support, the depression levels of pet owners and non-owners did not differ significantly (0.36 vs. 0.32, $p > 0.05$). Similarly, among individuals living alone with high levels of human social support, the depression levels of pet owners and non-owners did not differ significantly (0.23 vs. 0.28, $p > 0.05$).

Two hierarchical regression analyses were run separately, in order to examine whether these hypotheses held when, first, dog owners vs. non-owners were compared, and, second, when cat

Table 4 Summary of Hierarchical Regression Analysis for Variables Predicting the Loneliness Levels of Individuals Who Live alone with a Dog or Cat ($n = 63$)

Variable	F_{change}	df	R^2_{change}	β
Step 1				
Attachment	44.81**	58	0.61	0.01
Social Support				−0.78**
Step 2				
Attachment	1.88	57	0.01	0.02
Social Support				−0.74**
Attachment × Social Support				−0.12

* $p < 0.05$; ** $p < 0.001$

owners vs. non-owners were compared. In the hierarchical regression analysis related to dog ownership, the first hypothesis, that dog owners who live alone would be less depressed than non-owners who live alone, was not supported ($\beta = -0.04$, $p > 0.05$). Human social support also was not a significant predictor of the depression levels of people living alone ($\beta = -0.10$, $p > 0.05$). However, the second hypothesis, that among individuals living alone there would be an interaction between dog ownership and human social support, was supported ($\beta = -0.37$, $p < 0.01$). When simple effects were conducted, it was apparent that among individuals living alone with low levels of human social support, the depression levels of dog owners and non-owners did not differ significantly (0.39 vs. 0.32, $p > 0.05$). As well, among individuals living alone with high levels of human social support, the depression levels of dog owners and non-owners did not differ significantly (0.19 vs. 0.28, $p > 0.05$).

When only cat owners and non-owners were included in a hierarchical regression analysis, the first hypothesis, that cat owners living alone would be less depressed than non-owners, was not supported ($\beta = 0.04$, $p > 0.05$). Human social support also was not a significant predictor of the depression levels of individuals living alone ($\beta = -0.08$, $p > 0.05$). Finally, the second hypothesis, that among individuals living alone there would be an interaction between cat ownership and human social support, was not supported ($\beta = -0.09$, $p > 0.05$).

There were two further objectives in this study. We hypothesized that: 3) among pet owners living alone, there would be a positive relation between attachment to pets and psychological health (loneliness and depression), and 4) among pet owners living alone, attachment to pets and levels of human social support would have interactive effects on psychological health (loneliness and depression). Given that there were only 40 dog owners and 26 cat owners, these hypotheses were not tested for dog and cat owners separately. These hypotheses were first examined with loneliness as the criterion variable. In addition to excluding the two dog owners who did not answer a sufficient number of items in the loneliness scale, one additional case, which exerted too much influence on the regression model, was excluded from this analysis. In the first hierarchical regression model (Table 4), the third hypothesis, that pet owners who were highly attached to their pet would be less lonely than pet owners with low levels of attachment to their pet, was not supported ($\beta = 0.02$, $p > 0.05$). However, human social support was a significant predictor of the loneliness levels of pet owners living alone ($\beta = -0.74$, $p < 0.001$). The fourth

hypothesis, that among pet owners living alone there would be an interaction between attachment to pets and human social support, was not supported ($\beta = -0.12$, $p > 0.05$).

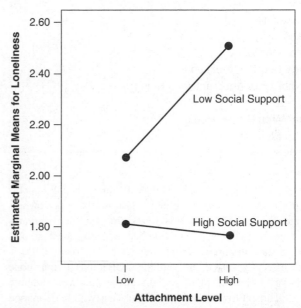

Figure 2. Mean loneliness scores for attachment to pets by level of social support.

Although the interaction between attachment to pets and human social support was not significant in the regression model, given the small sample size used for this analysis, we still examined the simple effects. When we interpreted the interaction by conducting simple effects, we found that among pet owners living alone with low levels of human social support, pet owners who were highly attached to their pet were significantly more lonely than pet owners with low levels of attachment to their pet (2.51 vs. 2.07, $p < 0.05$). However, among pet owners living alone with high levels of human social support, pet owners with high and low levels of attachment to their pet did not differ significantly in their loneliness levels (1.77 vs. 1.81, $p > 0.05$). These findings are displayed in Figure 2.

When depression was used as the criterion variable in a hierarchical regression analysis (Table 5), the third hypothesis, that pet owners who were highly attached to their pet would be less depressed than pet owners with low levels of attachment to their pet, was not

Table 5 Summary of Hierarchical Regression Analysis for Variables Predicting the Depression Levels of Individuals Who Live alone with a Dog or Cat ($n = 66$)

Variable	F_{change}	df	R^2_{change}	β
Step 1				
Attachment	11.87**	60	0.28	0.08
Social Support				−0.52**
Step 2				
Attachment	5.94*	59	0.07	0.05
Social Support				−0.48**
Attachment × Social Support				−0.26*

*$p < 0.05$; **$p < 0.001$

Table 6 Main Benefits of Dog and Cat Ownership

Main Benefits	Dog Owners ($n = 39$)	Cat Owners ($n = 25$)
Companionship	85%	68%
Physical Activity	59%	—
Love and Affection	41%	40%
Increased Social Interaction	33%	—
Responsibility for Another Living Being	31%	32%
Entertainment	21%	40%
Greeting When Return Home	8%	24%
A Comfort	—	8%

supported (β = 0.05, $p > 0.05$). However, human social support was a significant predictor of the depression levels of pet owners living alone (β = −0.48, $p < 0.001$). In addition, the fourth hypothesis, that there would be an interaction between attachment to pets and human social support, was supported (β = −0.26, $p < 0.05$).

Simple effects revealed that, among individuals living alone with low levels of human social support, pet owners who had high levels of attachment to their pet were significantly more depressed than pet owners who had low levels of attachment to their pet (0.43 vs. 0.27, $p < 0.01$). However, among individuals living alone with high levels of human social support, the depression levels of pet owners with high versus low levels of attachment to their pet did not differ significantly (0.19 vs. 0.28, $p > 0.05$). These findings are displayed in Figure 3.

Table 6 provides information about the main benefits of dog and cat ownership as reported by the participants. Both dog and cat owners identified companionship as the most important benefit. For dog owners, physical activity with the dog and love and affection were the next most important benefits, while for cat owners, love and affection and being responsible for another living being were the next most important benefits. In response to a question about the impact of pet ownership, the overwhelming majority of dog and cat owners, 84.2% of dog owners and 80% of cat owners, indicated that their pet had had a strong positive impact.

Discussion

The purpose of this research was to explore the impact of pet ownership on the psychological health of individuals living alone, in

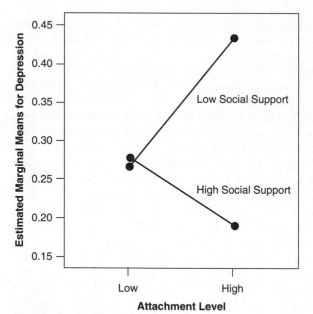

Figure 3. Mean depression scores for attachment to pets by level of social support.

terms of loneliness and depression levels. Contrary to expectations, pet owners and non-owners living alone did not have significantly different levels of loneliness or depression. This was particularly surprising given that the one other similar study conducted in the general population found that individuals who lived alone with a cat had better psychological health than individuals who lived alone without a cat (Turner, Rieger and Gytax 2003). However, this earlier study differed from the present study in that psychological health was assessed using a measure of mood, not specific measures of loneliness and depression. Despite these differences between the studies, our finding that there was not a direct relation between pet ownership and either loneliness or depression was unexpected, given that, in their responses to an open-ended question, both dog and cat owners indicated that the most important benefit of pet ownership was companionship. Furthermore, 82.5% of participants indicated that their pet had had a strong positive impact on their life. It should be noted that this high percentage may be the result of a demand characteristic. It is possible that, as a result of media reports on the benefits of pet ownership, the pet owners in the present study expected that owning a pet would be beneficial. However, although pets may be a source of companionship, the fact that pet owners living alone were not less lonely or depressed than individuals living alone without a pet raises the possibility that the benefits of pet ownership for dog and cat owners may only be apparent when other factors, such as levels of human social support, are considered.

When we examined the influence of human social support, results revealed that dog owners, but not cat owners, with high levels of human social support were significantly less lonely than non-owners with high levels of human social support. However, among individuals with low levels of human social support, there was no difference in the loneliness levels of dog and cat owners compared with non-owners. Furthermore, there were no differences in the depression levels of either dog or cat owners compared with non-owners, according to their level of human social support.

The findings regarding loneliness suggest that, among individuals living alone, dog ownership may be most beneficial for individuals who have sufficient human social support. While our findings only held for dog owners, the results are consistent with Wells and Rodi's (2000) qualitative findings for senior dog and cat owners, which led them to conclude that, "individuals who benefited most from pet ownership were likely to already be well-supported in their social relationships and not dependent on the pet for company or to boost self-esteem" (p. 147).

One possible explanation for the finding that dog owners with high levels of human social support were significantly less lonely than non-owners with high levels of human social support is provided by examining types of perceived social support. Schaefer, Coyne and Lazarus (1981) distinguish three types of social support: emotional support (meeting an individual's need for love), tangible support (practical assistance, such as buying groceries when an individual is ill) and informational support (helping to solve problems and provide guidance). While it is unlikely that a dog could provide either tangible or informational support, a dog could provide emotional support. Indeed, the third most frequently cited benefit of dog ownership in our study was love and affection, endorsed by 41% of the sample. Further evidence is provided by Stammbach and Turner (1999), who argued that companion animals are capable of providing emotional support to their owners, and Serpell (1986, p. 114) who stated that many pet owners feel that they can confide in their pet. Among individuals living alone with high levels of human social support, their dog may provide an additional source of emotional support that is not available to non-owners. However, among individuals with low levels of human social support, the emotional support provided by a dog may not be sufficient to compensate for insufficient human social support, which may explain why they do not differ from non-owners with low levels of human social support in terms of loneliness levels. A key question for future research is why this might be the case.

There are a number of possible explanations for the finding that dog ownership, but not cat ownership, was beneficial for the loneliness levels of individuals living alone with high levels of human social support. Dog owners differ from cat owners in that dog owners need to walk their dog. In fact, the second most commonly cited benefit of dog ownership, endorsed by 59% of the participants, was that dog owners received exercise walking their dog. Furthermore, given that researchers have found that increased levels of physical activity are associated with mental health benefits (US Department of Health and Human Services 1996; Gilmour 2007), it is probable that dog owners are receiving mental health benefits from their exercise. Researchers have also found that dogs act as social catalysts by increasing dog walkers' number of human–human social interactions (Messent 1983; McNicholas and Collis, 2000; Wells 2004), possibly because people are perceived as more likable when they are with their dog (Geries-Johnson and Kennedy 1995), and dogs provide a neutral topic for conversation and, therefore, act as social "ice-breakers" (Veevers 1985). In addition, McNicholas and Collis (2000) have suggested that these human–human interactions may increase people's social networks and subsequently confer health advantages to dog owners. Taken together, this research suggests that, among individuals living alone, dog owners may avoid becoming lonely through meeting people and making new friends, as a result of dog walking.

The exercise and social interaction benefits from dog walking provide a possible explanation for the fact that, among individuals living alone with high levels of human social support, dog owners, but not cat owners, had lower levels of loneliness than non-owners. However, it is less clear why, if dog owners with low levels of human social support also receive these benefits, they did not have lower levels of loneliness than non-owners with low levels of human social support. Given that past research has found that people with high levels of human social support are more likely to engage in leisure-time physical exercise (Steptoe et al. 1997), it may be that dog owners with high levels of human social support are more likely to have other people with whom they can walk their dog and, therefore, they may be more likely to walk their dog compared with dog owners with low levels of human social support.

Attachment to Pets and Well-Being

We also examined whether pet owners who were highly attached to their pet were less lonely and depressed than pet owners with low levels of attachment to their pet. The direct effect of attachment was not significant. Instead, we found an intriguing moderating effect of social support. Among pet owners living alone with low levels of human social support, those who were highly attached to their pet were significantly *more* lonely and depressed than pet owners with low levels of attachment to their pet. In contrast, among pet owners with high levels of social support, loneliness and depression levels did not vary according to level of attachment to the pet. It should be noted that, although we found that among individuals with low levels of human social support, pet owners who were highly attached to their pet were more lonely and depressed than pet owners who had low levels of attachment to their pet, there may be subgroups for whom this finding does not hold. For example, Garrity et al. (1989) found that among bereaved seniors with low levels of human social support, pet owners who were highly attached to their pet were less depressed than pet owners with low levels of attachment to their pet.

Another possible interpretation of these findings is that individuals who lack human social support and become highly attached to their pet may spend more time at home caring for their pet compared with individuals who are less attached to their pet. For example, individuals with high levels of attachment may feel a stronger obligation to rush home from work or leave a social event early to care for their pet. Support for this suggestion comes from Cohen's (2002) finding that a positive correlation exists between attachment to pets and the number of hours spent with the pet. Among individuals with low levels of human social support, if they choose to spend time with their pet rather than socializing with other people, they may begin to feel somewhat socially isolated. Furthermore, if these individuals decline social invitations in order to be with their pet, they may end up in a vicious cycle, whereby the number of social invitations extended to them decreases. Given the recent research that indicates that acting extraverted, being social, is beneficial for well-being, as reflected by increased levels of positive affect (e.g., McNiel and Fleeson 2006), social isolation in favor of pet companionship may undermine psychological well-being.

Limitations of the Research

Given that in 2006 only 23% of Canadians 25 to 64 years of age had a university degree (Statistics Canada 2008b), the education level of participants in our sample, 79.5% of whom had at least one university degree, was not representative of the Canadian population. Furthermore, given that Ross and Mirowsky (1989) found a positive correlation between level of education and human social support, differences in the social support levels of participants might have been greater had our sample not included such a high percentage of highly educated people. One possible explanation for the high percentage of educated participants is that our survey was only available on-line. According to results from the 2007 Canadian Internet Use Survey, people with higher levels of education are more likely to use the Internet (Statistics Canada 2008a). Another limitation of our study was that females accounted for 73.3% of the sample. In light of the small number of males in our study, it was not possible to examine our hypotheses separately for males and females. Flood's (2005) study, using national Australian survey data, emphasizes the need to examine gender differences, given that he found that males, but not females, who lived alone had less social support, fewer friendships and poorer psychological health compared with their counterparts who lived with other people.

The present study needs to be replicated using a larger sample in order to ensure that, given the small number of cat owners, loneliness levels and depression levels do not vary depending on cat ownership (cat vs. no cat) and human social support levels. In addition, given the small number of dog and cat owners in the sample, we did not have sufficient statistical power to examine whether the interaction between attachment and human social support held when dog and cat owners were examined separately. Zasloff and Kidd (1994) found that females living alone with a dog were more attached to their dog than females living with others; however, the opposite was true with respect to cat owners. This finding raises the possibility that it may be only dog, not cat,

owners who have poorer psychological health, if they have higher levels of attachment to their pet. Further support comes from the fact that, when we compared dog and cat owners' level of attachment, we found that dog owners living alone were significantly more attached to their dog compared with cat owners living alone ($p < 0.001$).

An additional limitation is that, in the present study, non-owners were defined as individuals who did not own a dog or cat. According to Leger Marketing, 10% of all Canadians owned a pet other than a dog or cat in 2002. In the present study, it is likely that some non-owners owned pets such as ferrets, rabbits, gerbils or fish. If owning a pet other than a dog or cat affected the loneliness and depression levels of non-owners who owned pets other than dogs and cats, it is possible that comparisons between pet and non-owners were weakened by the fact that non-owners included owners of pets other than dogs and cats.

A different type of limitation results from the loneliness measure used in the present study, as researchers have noted that the UCLA Loneliness Scale may not be sensitive to the ways in which companion animals affect pet owners' loneliness levels (Gilbey, McNicholas and Collis 2006, 2007). Many of the items in Russell's (1996) loneliness scale inquire solely about human relationships (e.g., "How often do you feel there are people you can turn to" and "How often do you feel part of a group of friends"). Therefore, there is a need for a new measure of loneliness that takes into consideration the impact of pet ownership.

Given the nature of our study, it was not possible to determine whether, among individuals living alone with high levels of human social support, dog owners were less lonely than non-owners before they acquired their dog or whether acquiring a dog reduced their loneliness levels. Similarly, among pet owners living alone with low levels of human social support, it was not possible to determine whether pet owners who were highly attached to their pet were more lonely and depressed before they acquired their pet, or whether after they acquired their pet and became highly attached to it they became more lonely and depressed. A longitudinal study is needed to address these questions.

Suggestions for Future Research

Future studies need to consider the possible role of anthropomorphism in the interaction between pet attachment and human social support. Duvall Antonacopoulos and Pychyl (2008) found that dog owners with low levels of human social support were more likely to humanize their dog. Furthermore, there was a negative relation between anthropomorphism and stress, which raises the possibility that increased levels of anthropomorphism, may lead to increased levels of stress. Given that Albert and Bulcroft (1988) found a positive correlation between attachment and anthropomorphism, future research needs to examine the possibility that the psychological health of individuals living alone varies depending on pet attachment, social support, and anthropomorphism levels. As well, researchers need to consider other factors, which may also affect the psychological health of individuals living alone. For example, personality differences may interact with pet ownership and levels of human social support to predict psychological health. Furthermore, among pet owners, factors such as the temperament of the pet and perceived levels of social support from the pet may also interact with attachment levels and human social support levels to predict psychological well-being.

Another area for future research is the potential impact of pet ownership on the physical health of individuals living alone. The limited number of studies to date that examined the interactive effects, which were explored in the present study, have primarily been conducted with seniors and did not specifically consider individuals living alone (Garrity et al. 1989; Siegel 1990; Raina et al. 1999; Wells and Rodi 2000). Therefore, future research needs to examine whether pet ownership and human social support levels have interactive effects on the physical health of individuals living alone and whether among pet owners living alone physical health varies depending on both attachment to pets and human social support levels.

Conclusions

Given the growing number of single person households (Euromonitor International 2008), it is important to understand the factors affecting the psychological health of individuals living alone. Our findings emphasize the complexity of the relationship between pet ownership and psychological health and suggest that pet ownership may not be beneficial for the psychological health of all individuals living alone. From this study, it is apparent that there is a need for longitudinal studies to explore the effect of pet ownership on the psychological health of individuals living alone, while considering the influence of additional factors such as human social support and attachment to pets.

Notes

1. Participants were divided at $40,000 rather than at $35,000 because in the survey participants were asked to choose from the following income categories: less than $20,000, $20,000–39,999, $40,000–59,999, $60,000–79,000, and $80,000 or more.

References

Adamelli, S., Marinelli, L., Normando, S. and Bono, G. 2005. Owner and cat features influence the quality of life of the cat. *Applied Animal Behaviour Science 94: 89–98.*

Albert, A. and Bulcroft, K. 1988. Pets, families, and the life course. *Journal of Marriage and the Family 50:* 543–552.

Budge, R. C., Spicer, J., Jones, B. and St. George, R. 1998. Health correlates of compatibility and attachment in human–companion animal relationships. *Society & Animals 6:* 219–234.

Cohen, S. P. 2002. Can pets function as family members? *Western Journal of Nursing Research 24:* 621–638.

Duvall Antonacopoulos, N. M. and Pychyl, T. A. 2008. An examination of the relations between social support, anthropomorphism and stress among dog owners. *Anthrozoös 21:* 139–152.

Euromonitor International. 2008. One person households: Opportunities for consumer good companies. <http://www. euromonitor.com/One_person_households_Opportunities_for_ consumer_goods_companies> Accessed on May 8, 2008.

Flood, M. 2005. Mapping loneliness in Australia. <https://www.tai.org. au/documents/downloads/DP76.pdf> Accessed on May 14, 2008.

Garrity, T. F., Stallones, L., Marx, M. B. and Johnson, T. P. 1989. Pet ownership and attachment as supportive factors in the health of the elderly. *Anthrozoös 3:* 35–44.

Geries-Johnson, B. and Kennedy, J. H. 1995. Influence of animals on perceived likability of people. *Perceptual and Motor Skills* 80: 432–434.

Gilbey, A., McNicholas, J. and Collis, G. M. 2006. Companion animal separation and loneliness. *Anthrozoös 19:* 257–264.

Gilbey, A., McNicholas, J. and Collis, G. M. 2007. A longitudinal test of the belief that companion animal ownership can help to reduce loneliness. *Anthrozoös 20:* 345–353.

Gilmer, N. and Nicholson, J. 1996. The role of the dog as a pet: A comparison between single, bi-person and multi-person households. In *Further Issues in Research in Companion Animal Studies,* 59, ed. J. Nicholson and A. Podberscek. Callander: The Society for Companion Animal Studies.

Gilmour, H. 2007. Physically active Canadians. *Health Reports 18:* 45–65.

Goldmeier, J. 1986. Pets or people: Another research note. *The Gerontologist 26:* 203–206.

Hanley-Dunn, P., Maxwell, S. E. and Santos, J. F. 1985. Interpretation of interpersonal interactions: The influence of loneliness. *Personality and Social Psychology 11:* 445–456.

Headey, B. 1999. Health benefits and health cost savings due to pets: Preliminary estimates from an Australian National Survey. *Social Indicators Research 47:* 233–243.

Holcomb, R., Williams, C. R. and Richards, P. S. 1985. The elements of attachment: Relationship maintenance and intimacy. *Journal of the Delta Society 2:* 28–33.

Johnson, T. P., Garrity, T. F. and Stallones, L. 1992. Psychometric evaluation of the Lexington Attachment to Pets Scale (LAPS). *Anthrozoös 5:* 160–175.

Kidd, A. H. and Kidd, R. M. 1989. Factors in adults' attitudes toward pets. *Psychological Reports* 65: 903–910.

Leger Marketing. 2002. Canadians and their pets. <www. legermarketing.com> Accessed on December 14, 2008.

Mahon, N. E., Yarcheski, A. and Yarcheski, T. J. 1998. Social support and positive health practices in young adults: Loneliness as a mediating variable. *Clinical Nursing Research 7:* 292–308.

Marinelli, L., Adamelli, S., Normando, S. and Bono, G. 2007. Quality of life of the pet dog: Influence of owner and dog's characteristics. *Applied Animal Behaviour Science 108:* 143–156.

McNicholas, J. and Collis, G. M. 2000. Dogs as catalysts for social interactions: Robustness of the effect. *British Journal of Psychology 91:* 61–70.

McNiel, J. M. and Fleeson, W. 2006. The causal effects of extraversion on positive affect and neuroticism on negative affect: Manipulating state extraversion and state neuroticism in an experimental approach. *Journal of Research in Personality 40:* 529–550.

Messent, P. R. 1983. Social facilitation of contact with other people by pet dogs. In *New Perspectives on Our Lives with Companion Animals,* 37–46, ed. A. H. Katcher and A. M. Beck. Philadelphia: University of Pennsylvania Press.

Milan, A., Vézina, M. and Wells, C. 2007. *Family Portrait: Continuity and Change in Canadian Families and Households in 2006* (Cat. No. 97-553-XIE). Ottawa: Statistics Canada.

Miller, M. and Lago, D. 1989. The well-being of older women: The importance of pet and human relations. *Anthrozoös 3:* 245–251.

Ory, M. G. and Goldberg, E. L. 1983. Pet possession and life satisfaction in elderly women. In *New Perspectives on Our Lives with Companion Animals,* 303–317, ed. A. H. Katcher and A. M. Beck. Philadelphia, PA: University of Pennsylvania Press.

Poresky, R. H. and Daniels, A. M. 1998. Demographics of pet presence and attachment. *Anthrozoös 11:* 236–241.

Radloff, L. S. 1977. The CES-D Scale: A self-report depression scale for research in the general population. *Applied Psychological Measurement 1:* 385–401.

Raina, P., Waltner-Toews, D., Bonnett, B., Woodward, C. and Abernathy, T. 1999. Influence of companion animals on the physical and psychological health of older people: An analysis of a one-year longitudinal study. Journal of the American Geriatrics Society 47: 323–330.

Roberts, C. A., McBride, E. A., Rosenvinge, H. P., Stevenage, S. V. and Bradshaw, J. W. S. 1996. The pleasure of a pet: The effect of pet ownership and social support on loneliness and depression in a population of elderly people living in their own homes. In *Further Issues in Research in Companion Animal Studies,* 64, ed. J. Nicholson and A. Podberscek. Callander: The Society for Companion Animal Studies.

Ross, C. E. and Mirowsky, J. 1989. Explaining the social patterns of depression: Control and problem solving—or support and talking? *Journal of Health and Social Behavior 30:* 206–219.

Ross, C. E. and Van Willigen, M. 1997. Education and subjective quality of life. *Journal of Health and Social Behavior 38:* 275–297.

Russell, D. W. 1996. UCLA Loneliness Scale (Version 3): Reliability, validity, and factor structure. *Journal of Personality Assessment 66:* 20–40.

Santor, D. A., Zuroff, D. C., Ramsay, J. O., Cervantes, P. and Palacios, J. 1995. Examining scale discriminability in the BDI and CES-D as a function of depressive severity. *Psychological Assessment 2:* 131–139.

Schaefer, C., Coyne, J. C. and Lazarus, S. 1981. The health-related functions of social support. *Journal of Behavioral Medicine 4:* 381–406.

Serpell, J. 1986. *In the Company of Animals: A Study of Human–Animal Relationships.* New York: Basil Blackwell.

Siegel, J. M. 1990. Stressful life events and use of physician services among the elderly: The moderating role of pet ownership. *Journal of Personality and Social Psychology 58:* 1081–1086.

Staats, S., Sears, K. and Pierfelice, L. 2006. Teachers' pets and why they have them: An investigation of the human animal bond. *Journal of Applied Social Psychology 36:* 1881–1891.

Stallones, L., Marx, M. B., Garrity, T. F. and Johnson, T. P. 1990. Pet ownership and attachment in relation to the health of US adults, 21 to 64 years of age. *Anthrozoös 4:* 100–112.

Stammbach, K. B. and Turner, D. C. 1999. Understanding the human–cat relationship: Human social support or attachment. *Anthrozoös 12:* 162–169.

Statistics Canada. 2006. *Income and Earnings, 2006 Census* (Cat. No. 97-563-XCB2006051). Ottawa: Statistics Canada.

Statistics Canada. 2008a. Canadian Internet use survey. <http://statcan.ca/Daily/English/080612/d080612b.htm> Accessed on June 24, 2008.

Statistics Canada. 2008b. *Educational Portrait of Canada, 2006 Census* (Catalogue No. 97-560-X). Ottawa: Statistics Canada.

Steptoe, A., Wardle, J., Fuller, R., Holte, A., Justo, J., Sanderman, R. and Wichstrøm, L. 1997. Leisure-time physical exercise: Prevalence, attitudinal correlates, and behavioral correlates among young Europeans from 21 countries. *Preventive Medicine 26:* 845–854.

Turner, D. C., Rieger, G. and Gytax, L. 2003. Spouses and cats and their effects on human mood. *Anthrozoös 16:* 213–228.

US Census Bureau. 2006. Families and living arrangements. <http://www.census.gov/Press-Release/www/releases/archives/families_households/006840.html> Accessed on April 25, 2008.

US Department of Health and Human Services. 1996. *Physical Activity and Health: A Report of the Surgeon General.* Atlanta: US Department of Health and Human Services, Centers for Disease Control and Prevention, National Center for Chronic Disease Prevention and Health Promotion.

Veevers, J. E. 1985. The social meaning of pets: Alternative roles for companion animals. In *Pets and the Family,* 10–30, ed. M. B. Sussman. New York: Haworth Press.

Wells, D. L. 2004. The facilitation of social interactions by domestic dogs. *Anthrozoös 17:* 340–353.

Wells, Y. and Rodi, H. 2000. Effects of pet ownership on the health and well-being of older people. *Australasian Journal on Ageing 19:* 143–148.

Wood, L. J., Giles-Corti, B., Bulsara, M. K. and Bosch, D. A. 2007. More than a furry companion: The ripple effect of companion animals on neighborhood interactions and sense of community. *Society & Animals 15:* 43–56.

Zasloff, R. L. and Kidd, A. H. 1994. Loneliness and pet ownership among single women. *Psychological Reports 75:* 747–752.

Zimet, G. D., Dahlem, N. W., Zimet, S. G. and Farley, G. K. 1988. The Multidimensional Scale of Perceived Social Support. *Journal of Personality Assessment 52:* 30–41.

Critical Thinking

1. What impact on the psychological health of an individual living alone can having a pet have?

2. Why does dog ownership, as opposed to cat ownership, seem to be more beneficial for the loneliness levels of individuals living alone?

3. Why did the study find no significant differences in loneliness and depression with pet owners who are highly attached to their pet versus those with low levels of attachment? Would not one expect the opposite to be true?

Veterinary Hospice

Ways to Nurture Our Pets at the End of Life

Amy Souza

Kramer, a black poodle/terrier mix with warm brown eyes, has silky black ears and a slightly tousled tuft of hair above his triangular face that makes him resemble his *Seinfeld* namesake. He has lived with Frank and Carol Miller for eight of his nine years, ever since the couple adopted him from a local shelter. To an outsider, Kramer appears healthy and vibrant, as a dog his age should. But the Millers see what a stranger cannot: slight stubble on his chin and thinning back hair caused by chemotherapy, and a slight thickening around the waist from taking prednisone.

Last September, during a routine dental cleaning, Kramer's vet discovered a mass on the dog's tongue. The news was dire. Though pathologists were unable to pinpoint exactly what type of tumor Kramer has, they know it's an aggressive immune-cell cancer. Because of the tumor's location, radiation was not an option, but vets estimated that with surgery and chemotherapy, Kramer could live for one more year. The Millers were told not to expect a cure.

Seven months and many treatments later, it's unclear whether their beloved pet will make it to another September. Whatever happens, the Millers are determined to do everything they can to keep Kramer healthy, happy and by their sides for as long as possible. So, they are taking his care into their own hands.

In a small room bordering the sitting area of their Maryland home, near a small refrigerator holding Kramer's medications, Carol maintains a calendar to keep track of Kramer's treatments. She has filled in each day of the month: "C" for chemo; "P" for prednisone; and "1," "2" or "3" for the particular homeopathic remedy he is to receive that day. The drugs keep Kramer's tumor in check, minimizing his discomfort and allowing him to eat.

The Millers haven't given it a name, but essentially what they're giving Kramer is hospice care.

What Is Veterinary Hospice?

Veterinary hospice has existed for more than a decade, but it is far from mainstream. That appears to be changing, however, as more and more practitioners begin to focus on end-of-life care and discover a huge demand for their services. It's not surprising: An increasing number of people with pets are willing to give subcutaneous fluids or learn how to inject pain medication, especially if it means a few more months, weeks or days with their pets.

Dr. Liz Palmer of Charlottesville, Virginia, opened a mobile end-of-life care practice a year and a half ago. Though she has never marketed her services, Palmer has an extensive client list. After a local newspaper published an article about her business, she received more phone calls than she could handle. Other hospice providers report similar experiences; when people read or hear about their services, they receive an influx of calls.

"There's a Catch-22 right now, and that is we don't have very many people who see themselves as providers in this area, and there are a lot of potential users of animal hospice who have no idea that it exists," says Dr. Amir Shanan, who has offered veterinary hospice for more than 10 years in his Chicago general practice. "Pet owners don't ask about hospice services, and veterinarians don't offer information because, they say, pet owners aren't asking about it."

Part of the reason is that neither general-practice vets nor the general public know exactly how to define pet hospice. The confusion stems, in part, from the term itself, because "hospice" also refers to a standard of care provided to dying humans. Pet hospice takes many forms, however: a couple like the Millers tending to their dying pet, veterinarians who travel to people's homes, or even a physical location where animals live out their final days. In the broadest sense, hospice is a philosophy of caring for a dying animal in a loving, appropriate manner, while also supporting the pet's family.

Many people agree that the best place for a pet to die is at home, surrounded by familiar sights and smells and the people who love them. Veterinarians focused on hospice or end-of-life care aim to make the time before death comfortable for animals by teaching people how to administer medications and fluids, and helping them decide when euthanasia is warranted.

During more than 25 years as a general practitioner, Palmer says she never had time to deal with end-of-life care properly. "I was so focused on treating disease, spay/neuter and primary care," she says. "When I was trying to figure out what I was doing [with this new business], I was trying to find a word for it. It's care in the end of life, but I also consider it ending life. I'm involved in the dying process."

During an initial visit, Palmer conducts a thorough exam, particularly to detect pain, but she believes it's equally important to assess an animal's environment. "I really pay attention to how much an animal has to struggle to get through daily life. I like to go to homes, to sit on the couch and observe. I like to see the obstacles a pet faces and give the owners the 'What are you going to do if . . .' scenarios," Palmer says. "I look at the quality of life of the owner, too. I don't want the relationship to be a frustrating burden. That's not good for the animal or the human."

Making Tough Choices

As animal guardians, we must make choices for our pets, but on the whole, the veterinary profession—while excellent at offering medically oriented solutions—is not well equipped to help people make end-of-life decisions. These decisions are fraught with emotions and bring up all sorts of practical, ethical and existential questions. What value do we place on life? Does that extend to animals as well as humans? What constitutes suffering? How do we know when euthanasia is warranted?

The Argus Institute at Colorado State University's veterinary teaching hospital has on-site counselors who are available around the clock to assist people facing difficult medical decisions about their pets. Dr. Jane Shaw directs the institute and teaches veterinary communication at the school. Students often ask her what to do if someone doesn't want to euthanize a pet.

"We ask questions of the client and can discover whatever barriers are there," Shaw says. "There's a subset of clients, mostly because of spiritual reasons, for whom euthanasia is not an option. For other people who desire a natural death for their pet, we walk them through what that death might look like. In many disease conditions, the death is not peaceful, and we have to have pretty frank conversations about that. Euthanasia is a controlled process and, done appropriately, is peaceful. Natural death is completely unknown, and that makes some vets uncomfortable. They're worried about the animal's welfare and the client's welfare."

In non-emergency cases, quality-of-life scales can help people evaluate their animals. One widely used scale, created by oncologist Dr. Alice Villalobos, asks people to rate their pet from 1 to 10 in six areas: hurt, hunger, hydration, happiness, mobility, and more good days than bad. "Every member of the family should do the scale separately, because there's always one person who has blinders on," Villalobos says.

Dr. Nancy Ruffing, a mobile hospice veterinarian in Pittsburgh, Pennsylvania, supplements Villalobos's scale with a handout containing her own words of wisdom about end-of-life decisions. "A lot of people don't want to make it a numerical decision," she says. Yet, assessing a pet's quality of life is crucial, and she considers it a big part of her job. "Owners have to have some type of a mental plan for what to do at the end of life, but you have to look at your pet critically when they're having a good day so you can recognize the subtle differences on a bad day," Ruffing says. "You really have to be in tune with your pet, and that starts at the beginning."

To End Life or Let Life End?

Gail Pope, founder of BrightHaven, a residential hospice on 10 acres in Santa Rosa, California, believes strongly in letting an animal's life play out to the very end. It's a stance she arrived at slowly. For many years, Pope worked at a conventional veterinary office and was schooled in conventional practices, including the idea that euthanasia constituted a normal end to an animal's life. She and her husband started BrightHaven in 1996 with the simple goal of caring for elderly and infirm animals.

When one of their resident cats, Mariah, began showing signs that she was about to die, Pope panicked. She was alone and couldn't leave the other animals, so she called a vet to come euthanize the cat—a notion that now makes Pope shake her head. "It's the old thought of 'She's dying, hurry up, let's kill her.' "

Her veterinarian promised to send someone out during the lunch hour, and in the meantime Pope phoned a friend and animal communicator who instructed her to carry Mariah outside to an oak tree and sit with her in her arms. "I was terrified. I didn't know what was going to happen," she says.

Pope remained agitated, but Mariah was calm. The cat died quietly in Pope's lap. She says, "My friend told me, 'Mother Nature designed this,' and that has stuck with me to this day." Over the next few years, as Pope moved toward administering alternative medicine, such as homeopathy, and feeding animals a natural diet, she saw amazing things happen. Animals came to BrightHaven to die, but more and more of them instead grew healthier and livelier. Now, she says, her cats routinely live into their 20s.

Though Pope is not opposed to euthanasia in cases when she feels it is absolutely warranted, her philosophy and practice are to allow for natural death with few to no drugs other than natural remedies. Euthanasia is often employed too quickly, she says, and in an effort to relieve suffering, people actually may be ending their animals' lives prematurely.

Pope's position is atypical in the pet hospice community but it is shared by some, including Kathryn Marocchino of Nikki Hospice Foundation for Pets in Vallejo, California. Marocchino thinks that in many instances, people would rather not euthanize an ill animal, but they're not presented with any other option, such as hospice care.

"There is intense debate in the community around what is hospice for animals," says Marocchino, who helped organize a pet hospice symposium in 2008. "Hospice to vets means, 'I will do everything to help you, but I have a quality of life scale, and when the dog reaches a certain number, it's time for euthanasia.'"

At the symposium, Marocchino says only two veterinarians in attendance had ever witnessed the natural death of an animal. This fact suggests to her that euthanasia is used too frequently and too readily by veterinarians. "They're not giving death a chance," Marocchino says. "Euthanasia should be a last resort."

The majority of people working in pet hospice, however, do believe that euthanasia is a necessary—and humane— tool. Some of them worry that the larger veterinary community, and the general public, will misinterpret the term "pet hospice," believing that death without euthanasia is a fundamental tenet.

"Hospice is not about replacement of euthanasia," says Dr. Robin Downing, owner of the Downing Center for Animal Pain Management in Windsor, Colorado. "In 23 years of practicing oncology, I have a fairly high conviction that the number of animals who die a natural death is few and far between. Most animals reach a point where they are actively in distress, and we have an obligation to let them leave while they still know who they are and who their family is. The only time a client has expressed regret to me is the regret that they waited too long."

The subject of death prompts strong feelings in most humans, and there are no easy answers for doctors or people with pets when confronting an animal's final days. As the veterinary hospice field grows, it is crucial that practitioners remain open to divergent opinions and values, says Shanan, who this year co-founded the International Association for Animal Hospice and Palliative Care. "We must humbly accept that the subjective experience of dying is a great mystery," Shanan says. "Also, we are acting as proxy for the wishes of a patient who is not of our species. It is very easy to err no matter what guiding principle we choose to follow."

Hoping for a Miracle

A few weeks ago during a walk at a nearby lake, Kramer became short of breath and had to be carried home. The Millers made an appointment with the vet, who x-rayed the dog's lungs to see if the cancer had spread there. (It hadn't.) Two days later at the same lake, Kramer acted like his old self, chasing geese twice his size.

"Animals don't know they're dying," Carol Miller says. "Toward the very end I think they might, but they don't get anxious about it all the time like we do. Sometimes when I'm upset, he looks up at me like, 'What's wrong? What can I do for you to make you feel better?'"

Above all, the Millers don't want Kramer to suffer. One form of chemo made him violently ill, and neither Frank nor Carol wants that to happen again. Their oncologists presented options for new treatments, and the Millers chose one that seems to be working.

"We are enjoying every precious day," Carol says. "Kramer's spirits are high." But if the drugs lose effectiveness and his cancer spreads, they've decided to stop chemotherapy and continue herbal treatments and prednisone until Kramer's body gives out or he indicates to them that it's time to go. They still hope for a miracle, but the Millers are practical and know they must plan. They've contacted a mobile veterinarian, who, when the time comes, will perform euthanasia in their home.

Critical Thinking

1. Does a veterinary hospice mean the same thing for all people? Explain.
2. Do you believe that euthanasia should be a part of a veterinary hospice's offerings? Why or why not?
3. In your opinion, do veterinary hospices represent a growing trend toward better end-of-life care for animals?

UNIT 6

Ethical Issues of Dying and Death

Unit Selections

Learning Outcomes

After reading this unit, you should be able to:

- Understand the difference between a durable power of attorney and a living will.

- Understand the importance of having a living will and the limitations of such legal documents.

- Understand the complexities of administering and the use of cannabis in a medical setting for the betterment of patients who are in end care.

- Gain an appreciation for the difficulty in determining issues relationship between extra-ordinary and ordinary measures of treating patients and withholding and withdrawing life support.

- Make distinctions between providing medical treatment for illness and providing end-of-life care.

- Realize that palliative care is a subspecialty of medicine.

- Understand that sometimes the best medical care is not providing cure but providing care, support, and comfort.

Student Website

www.mhhe.com/cls

Internet References

Moral Debates of Our Times
www.trinity.edu/~mkearl/death-5.html#eu

Biomedical Ethics and Issues of Euthanasia
http://pwa.acusd.edu/~hinman/euthanasia.html

Yahoo: Society and Culture: Death and Dying Euthanasia
http://dir.yahoo.com/Society_and_Culture/Death_and_Dying/Euthanasia

Deathnet
www.deathnet.com

Thanatolinks
http://netsociology.tripod.com/thanalinks.htm

Living Will (Advance Directive)
www.mindspring.com/~scottr/will.html

Euthanasia Research & Guidance Organization
www.finalexit.org/index.html

Euthanasia in the Netherlands
www.euthanasia.com/netherlands.html

The Choice in Dying
www.choices.org

Last Rights Organization
http://lastrights.info

Euthanasia and Christianity: Christian Views of Euthanasia and Suicide
www.religionfacts.com/euthanasia/christianity.htm

Not Dead Yet!
www.notdeadyet.org/pressrel.html

Patients Rights Council
www.patientsrightscouncil.org

United Network for Organ Sharing
www.unos.org

TransWeb
www.transweb.org

One of the concerns about dying and death that is pressing hard upon our consciences is the question of helping the dying to die sooner with the assistance of the physician. Public awareness of the horrors that can visit upon us by artificial means of ventilation and other support measures in a high-tech hospital setting has produced a literature that debates the issue of euthanasia—a "good death." As individuals think through their plans for care when dying, there is a steady increase in the demand for control of that care. The case of Terri Schiavo had brought national attention to the need for more clarity in end-of-life directives and the legitimacy of passive euthanasia. Another controversial issue is physician-assisted suicide. Is it the function of the doctor to assist patients in their dying—to actually kill them at their request? The highly publicized suicides in Michigan, along with the jury decisions that found Dr. Kevorkian innocent of murder, as well as the popularity of the book *Final Exit,* make these issues prominent national and international concerns. Legislative action has been taken in some states to permit this, and the issue is pending in a number of others. We are in a time of intense consideration by the courts, by the legislatures, and by the medical and nursing professions of the legality and the morality of providing the means by which a person can be given the means to die. Is this the role of healthcare providers? The pro and contra positions

© Royalty-Free/CORBIS

are presented in several of the unit's articles. Although the issue is difficult and personally challenging, as a nation we are in the position of being required to make difficult choices. There are no "right" answers; the questions pose dilemmas that require choice based upon moral, spiritual, and legal foundations.

What Living Wills Won't Do
The Limits of Autonomy

ERIC COHEN

In the aftermath of the Terri Schiavo case, it seems clear that most Americans are uncomfortable at the prospect of politicians' intervening in family decisions about life and death. This is not only understandable, but usually wise. Americans understand that eventually they will have to make medical decisions for loved ones, and that such decisions are wrenching. Most people have little faith that the state—or the courts—can make better judgments than they can. And they are usually right.

But it is precisely the complexity of these life-and-death decisions that sometimes makes state involvement inevitable. The state was involved in the Schiavo case long before Congress intervened, from the time Terri's parents went to court in Florida to challenge her husband's fitness as a guardian back in 1993. State judiciaries must decide when family members clash, or when doctors and families disagree, or when surrogates wish to override a loved one's living will. And state legislatures have a responsibility to set the parameters for judicial decisions in particular cases. They must decide the admissibility of casual conversations in determining a person's prior wishes, or the appropriate weight to give a person's desires (such as requests for assisted suicide) even when they are clearly expressed.

For decades, we have deluded ourselves into believing that living wills would solve our caregiving problems; that healthy individuals could provide advance instructions for what to do if they became incompetent; that such a system would ensure that no one is mistreated and that everyone defines the meaning of life for himself until the very end. But it is now clear that living wills have failed, both practically and morally.

In the March–April 2004 issue of the *Hastings Center Report,* Angela Fagerlin and Carl E. Schneider survey the social science data, and their conclusions are damning: Most people do not have living wills, despite a very active campaign to promote them; those who do usually provide vague and conflicting instructions; people's opinions often change from experience to experience; and people's

instructions are easily influenced by how a given scenario is described. These are not problems that any reform can fix. A person simply can't grasp in the present every medical and moral nuance of his own future case.

Most people do not have living wills, despite a very active campaign to promote them; those who do usually provide vague and conflicting instructions.

The dream of perfect autonomy—everyone speaking for himself, never deciding for another—should fade each time we change a parent's diaper, or visit a grandparent who does not recognize us, or sell an uncle's property to pay for the nursing home. After all, the only fully autonomous death—with every detail governed by individual will—is suicide. And suicide is hardly a basis for dealing more responsibly with the burdens of caregiving.

As the baby boomers age, we are entering a period when long-term dementia will often be the prelude to death, and when caregivers will regularly have to make decisions about how or whether to treat intervening illnesses like infections, heart trouble, or cancer. When should we accept that death has arrived, and when does stopping treatment entail a judgment that Alzheimer's patients are "better off dead"? What do we owe those who are cognitively disabled and totally dependent?

On these hard questions, the most vocal critics of Congress and "the religious right" in the Schiavo case have revealed the shallowness of their own thinking. Defending the "right to privacy" ignores the moral challenge of deciding how we should act in private, as both patients and caregivers. Asserting that "the state should stay out" of these decisions ignores the fact that some hard cases will always end up in court; that legislatures have a civic responsibility to pass the laws that courts apply; and that a decent society should set some minimum moral boundaries, such as laws against euthanasia and assisted suicide. And claiming that we should "defer to medical experts" ignores the potential conflict between the ideology of living wills and the ethic of medicine, since some people will leave instructions that no principled physician could execute.

In the end, the retreat to moral libertarianism and liberal proceduralism is inadequate. We need, instead, a moral philosophy, a political philosophy, and a medical philosophy that clarify our roles as caregivers, citizens, and doctors attending to those who cannot speak for themselves.

Any moral philosophy of care should begin with the premise that disability—even profound disability—is not grounds for seeking someone's death. But seeking death and accepting death when it arrives are very different matters. And while we should not seek death, neither should we see extending life at all costs as the supreme goal of care.

Imagine, for example, that a person with advanced Alzheimer's is diagnosed with cancer, and there is a burdensome treatment (like radiation) that might extend the person's remaining life from three months to six months. In this case, family members seem morally justified in rejecting the treatment, even knowing that an earlier death is the likely result. But they don't reject treatment *so that* the patient will die; they reject it so that the patient will not suffer excessively as death arrives. They choose minimum discomfort, not death. By contrast, if the same Alzheimer's patient gets an infection that is easily treated by antibiotics, it is hard to see any moral ground for withholding treatment. Holding back ordinary care is not the same as euthanasia, but it is still a choice that hastens death as its aim.

In reality, many dementia cases involve multiple illnesses, with uncertain prognoses, and a menu of treatment options. Often, there are various morally justifiable choices. Personal values do matter. But what is always needed is a moral framework that governs such private decisions, based on the belief that every life is equal, and no life should be treated as a burden to be relinquished, including one's own.

Given the infinite complexity of these clinical situations, the scope of the law should always be limited. What is legally permissible is not always morally right, but what is morally wrong should not always be outlawed. Nevertheless, it is foolish to ignore the extent to which the current legal framework shapes how people make private decisions, or to ignore the proper role of the state in setting certain minimum boundaries. Legally, no competent person should ever be forced to accept medical treatment in the present that he does not want. Legally, no one should have the right to commit suicide or procure assistance in doing

so, and no one should be killed or forced to die against his will or that of his guardians. And legally, guardians should not be forced to implement living wills that aim at death as their goal.

As for the courts that are called upon to settle certain cases, they will need some political guidance or governing principles to do so. For example, what if a tenured professor of bioethics, unable to bear the loss of his cognitive powers, leaves written instructions not to treat any infections if he ever suffers dementia? Decades later, now suffering from Alzheimer's, the former professor is mentally impaired but seemingly happy. He can't recognize his children, but he seems to enjoy the sunset. He's been physically healthy for years, but then gets a urinary tract infection. All his family members believe he should be treated.

Should the state intervene to prohibit antibiotics—to protect the incompetent person's "right to die"? Or should the state leave the family members alone, so they can do what they believe is in the best interests of the person the professor now is? If Andrew Sullivan and other critics are worried about "theocons" using the power of the state to undermine the right to self-determination, are they willing to use the power of the state to impose death when families choose life? Is this what their idea of "autonomy" really requires?

And this leads us, finally, to the ethics of medicine. We have already gone very far in turning medicine into a service industry and doctors into technicians who simply use their skills to do our bidding. The physicians who perform abortions when the life and health of the mother are not in danger, or the cosmetic surgeons who give breast implants to healthy women, or the doctors who prescribe growth hormone for kids of average height are not really practicing medicine; they are serving desires. Most doctors take their medical oath seriously, struggling daily and often heroically to provide for those entrusted to their care. But some have succumbed to various forms of utilitarianism, or simply believe that people with cognitive disabilities are already humanly dead. In cases like Terri Schiavo's—a disabled woman, not dead or dying, whose feeding was keeping her alive without imposing additional burdens—it is hard to see how any doctor could ethically remove a feeding tube. And if we are to respect medicine as a moral profession, no court should compel doctors of conscience to do so.

As America ages and dementia becomes a common phenomenon, the dilemmas that the Schiavo case thrust onto the nightly news will only become more urgent and more profound. As a society, we will need to navigate between two dangers: The first is the euthanasia solution, and the prospect of treating the old and vulnerable as burdens to be ignored, abandoned, or put to sleep at our convenience. The second is that the costs of long-term care will suffocate every other civic and cultural good—like educating the young, promoting the arts and sciences, and preserving a strong defense.

We will face imperfect options, as societies always do. In navigating the dangers, we will need to rely on more than the gospel of autonomy, and we will need to confront the failure of living wills and the ideology they rest upon: that deciding for others is always to be avoided. In reality, deciding for others is what many of us will be required to do as parents age or spouses decline, and we will do well to accept this burden with moral sobriety rather than pretending it does not exist.

Critical Thinking

1. Why do people need living wills?
2. Why did the Teri Schiavo case create issues raised by this article?
3. Why don't living wills solve the problem faced by patients in end-of-life care?

ERIC COHEN is editor of the *New Atlantis* and resident scholar at the Ethics and Public Policy Center.

From *The Weekly Standard,* by Eric Cohen, April 18, 2005, pp. 18–19. Copyright © 2005 by Weekly Standard. Reprinted by permission.

When Students Kill Themselves, Colleges May Get the Blame

ANN H. FRANKE

Experts estimate that more than a thousand students at American colleges and universities will commit suicide this year. After a death, the grieving family will pack up the victim's belongings and, within a matter of months, lose touch with the institution. A few families, however, will return with their lawyers to charge that the institution bears legal responsibility.

While the number of such lawsuits remains very small, they are growing in frequency. Five years ago college lawyers discussed among themselves perhaps one or two pending suicide cases at any given moment. Today the cases total about 10 nationwide, with the prospect that many more suicides could, over time, move into the courts. Although a study of student suicides committed between 1980 and 1990 at 12 large Midwestern universities, published in 1997, found that college students killed themselves at a lower rate than others of their same age in the general population, whenever a death does occur, the potential for institutional liability looms larger today than ever before.

Whose responsibility is it to put the pieces together? When and how should well-meaning people intervene?

These are awful lawsuits. They can exacerbate grief, guilt, and blame on all sides. The cases can drag on for years. The courts have, so far, provided little guidance on the legal tests for institutional responsibility. We have only a fairly small number of reported decisions (many court decisions are unpublished), and the outcomes of each of those cases have turned less on general legal principles than on close analyses of the facts.

The current wave of litigation will likely lead to some clarification. In the meantime, we might usefully look at the types of claims that the families typically assert. Evaluating previous allegations can help us re-examine campus policies and procedures with two goals in mind: preventing deaths and, should a suicide occur, preventing institutional liability.

The most common claims have been:

The institution put the student in harm's way. Take the example of when a college holds a student in custody for some reason. In 1992 a Michigan court held that a state university might bear some responsibility for the 1982 suicide of a student who hanged himself with his socks and belt while detained for about 35 minutes in a campus-security, short-term holding cell. The institution had in effect at the time a policy that no prisoner should be left unattended unless he (in the vocabulary of the era) was first searched and relieved of objects that might be used to harm himself or others. The message for today is that all institutions owe a heightened duty of suicide prevention to those who may be in their custody.

Custodial suicides are, fortunately, rare. More common is the allegation that the institution negligently created unreasonable access to the means of suicide. To understand that allegation, it is helpful to review the most common methods of student suicide. According to the study of Midwestern universities, those methods are hanging or asphyxiation, jumping, gas inhalation, chemical poisoning (including drugs and cyanide), firearms, and, to a lesser degree, vehicles, knives, and drowning. If cyanide from the chemistry lab or a gun from an unlocked cabinet in the public-safety office were used in the suicide death of a student, the family could seek to blame the institution.

For example, in the 1990s the mother of a college football player who committed suicide argued that the athletics department's carelessness in casually dispensing large quantities of prescription medications, including Darvocet and Tylenol #3, contributed to her son's death. The young man had died from a self-inflicted gunshot wound, yet the family argued that the drugs were a phase in his general deterioration, and the Arkansas Supreme Court found that argument plausible enough to send the case back to the trial court for further proceedings.

Take note. From a public-health perspective, as well as a legal one, it is prudent to keep under lock and key dangerous substances and objects that might appeal to students as a means of suicide. Colleges should lock their roofs, towers, and other high perches from which depressed students can jump.

Sometimes differentiating suicide from an accidental death can be tricky. A student's fatal alcohol or drug overdose, for

Some Suicide Warning Signs among Young Adults

Behaviors Requiring Immediate Response

- Indicating intent to harm themselves (talking, threatening)
- Seeking availability of or obtaining ropes, weapons, pills, or other ways to kill themselves
- Talking or writing about death, dying, or suicide

Associated Behaviors Requiring Evaluation

- Feeling hopeless
- Expressing rage or anger; seeking revenge
- Acting recklessly or impulsively or engaging in risky activities, seemingly without thinking
- Feeling trapped, like there's no way out, or nothing else will help
- Increasing alcohol or drug use or abuse
- Withdrawing from friends, school activities, community, and family
- Expressing anxiety, agitation, an inability to sleep, or sleeping all the time
- Exhibiting dramatic mood changes
- Expressing loss of interest or reason for living; no sense of purpose or meaning in life
- Acting "immaturely" and/or displaying disregard for others' safety, feelings, or property

Source: M. Silverman, "College Student Suicide Prevention," *College Health Spectrum* (March 2004).

themes of despair in a student's poetry. Whose responsibility is it to put these pieces together? When and how should well-meaning people intervene?

Many institutions conduct educational programs to raise campus awareness about suicide and increase the possibility that fellow students, residence-hall workers, and faculty members will help the student into treatment. Good online screening programs—available through organizations like the Jed Foundation and Screening for Mental Health—reach students directly, providing a rough evaluation of their own suicide risk and encouraging them to seek treatment. Although such programs are not legal necessities, they certainly can advance student well-being.

Some colleges have also created committees that meet weekly to evaluate the behavior of students who pose potential risks to themselves or others. A leading program at the University of Illinois at Urbana-Champaign enlists many people across the campus, including public-safety officers, residence-hall administrators, and faculty members, to report any signs that a student might be considering self-harm to a suicide-prevention task force. The task force has the authority to require students to attend four mandatory assessment sessions at the counseling center, sessions that have proved very effective in reducing students' suicidal thoughts and intentions.

Administrators sometimes worry that any program to increase student safety may also increase the institution's liability, should a problem fall through the cracks. College lawyers can help structure programs to minimize that possibility. For example, should an institution conduct a screening program and retain in its records, without following up, information that a specific student is at high risk of suicide, then the prospect of its liability for that student's suicide is greatly increased. To protect against that, a screening program could clearly state that it is voluntary and anonymous, and that the institution will not keep a record of the results or follow up with the student.

The institution failed to respond appropriately to warning signs. Family members could argue that the institution knew, or at least should have known, that the student was at high risk of suicide. With the clarity of hindsight, they will point to steps that the institution should have taken, including, most pointedly, notifying them about the problem.

Issues of how to notify parents about a student's potential for self-harm have confounded many administrators. Some campus mental-health providers argue strenuously that they enjoy a legally privileged and confidential relationship with their patients. (The specifics vary by state and by type of profession.) A dean of students may feel that the Family Educational Rights and Privacy Act, which restricts the information that colleges can release about students, inhibits her from picking up the phone. The student's consent can, of course, avert the impasse. Experienced student-affairs staff members and counselors can usually build sufficient trust with a disturbed student to persuade him to contact his family. But sometimes the student adamantly refuses.

Administrators should then begin a collaborative analysis of the situation. The element of collaboration spreads the burden of

example, might have arisen from ignorance or miscalculation, or it might have been an intentional act of self-harm. After such deaths, the families may point to lax enforcement of institutional policies against drug and alcohol abuse. Do the trash cans in the first-year dorms overflow with beer bottles every Monday morning? If so, whether they view the death as accidental or intentional, the grieving parents may allege that the institution recklessly contributed to the student's alcohol poisoning. An institution that fails to enforce its existing policies faces an uphill battle in court.

The institution failed to recognize suicide warning signs. Depression can impair an individual's ability to seek help, and fewer than 20 percent of students who seriously consider suicide have received either therapy or antidepressant medication. Campus mental-health professionals are often not on the front lines of these problems, as suicidal students frequently don't come to see them, leaving to others the task of catching the cues and enlisting assistance for such students. A residence-hall adviser may notice signs of a student's emotional deterioration. An English professor may become concerned by the dark the decision whether to notify the family beyond the shoulders of just one individual. As a substantive matter, both the therapist–patient privilege and FERPA contain exceptions for emergencies, and a risk of self-harm counts as an emergency. In fact, some prudent student-health and counseling centers disclose on their websites, in their brochures, and on their patient paperwork that in emergency situations they may contact others.

From a legal standpoint, the safest course is to notify the family of a genuinely suicidal student unless previously known indicators, like a history of child abuse, suggest that parental notification would be harmful. Sometimes it just comes down to picking your lawsuit. A student's suit for invasion of privacy is, by most any reckoning, preferable to a suit over a suicide. Be ready, however, for the unexpected. One college, after making the decision to contact the family of an international student, ran into the unanticipated difficulty that the overseas parents did not speak English.

Hospitalization can be another appropriate response to a suicidal student. One large private university had 18 student psychiatric hospitalizations during a five-week period at the beginning of a recent fall semester. A national provider of student health insurance reported a rate of psychiatric hospitalizations in 2002 of 3.4 per 1,000 students.

Such numbers reflect the important role that community resources play in responding to student mental-health needs. The counseling center at Northwestern University, for example, devotes considerable attention to coordinating care with the hospitals and community mental-health practitioners who may be treating a student. Hospitalization may be easier if a suitable facility is nearby and the student has health insurance, or if the state has a flexible involuntary-commitment law.

Whether or not a college plays an active part in hospitalizing the student, it may be that a suicidal student's mental health is too fragile for him or her to function on the campus. Involuntary medical withdrawal is a good option in such situations, and it is prudent to have rules in place establishing the standards and procedures for that withdrawal, as well as for the return of such students to the campus. Washington and Lee University, Cornell University, and the University of North Carolina at Greensboro are among the institutions with involuntary-medical-withdrawal protocols available on their websites.

Perhaps the most important message about a college's liability for student suicide is to know your personal and institutional limits as a helper. An institution can work to resolve some problems internally, but others are beyond its scope and call for the intervention of families and external resources. A counseling center struggling even to meet its nonemergency appointment load should not lead students and parents to think that it provides full emergency care. A faculty member can do more harm than good by providing, over an extended period, a shoulder for a depressed student to cry on rather than aiding the student in getting treatment. If the student is relying on the pro-fessor for general comfort, then that student may be disinclined to get the medical help that he or she really needs.

The institution mishandled the emergency response to a suicide attempt. If a young man reports that his girlfriend is locked in her dorm room sending instant messages saying farewell and announcing plans to end it all, will the institution respond swiftly and effectively? The best approach is to contact local emergency services or to respond immediately with trained campus public-safety officers or medical personnel. College personnel should not, in any event, leave the student alone.

Institutions should plan for such emergencies in advance and develop operating procedures, conducting drills of imaginary student-suicide scenarios and working through the communications and response issues that might involve student-affairs and counseling staff members, residence-hall personnel, and public-safety officers. During what may be the last moments of a student's life, the institution's emergency response needs to be credible and to follow established protocols.

Fewer than 20 percent of students who seriously consider suicide have received either therapy or antidepressant medication.

After a suicide, sensitive outreach to the family is crucial. Senior campus officials should attend the funeral and express condolences in writing. The college should involve the family in planning college-sponsored memorial services and other activities in the name of the student, as well as maintain contact over an extended period. Most families welcome the occasional phone call just to say "We're thinking of you." The student's birthday and the anniversary of the death will be especially hard for them, so a note or call on those occasions would be particularly appropriate. Caring outreach will not increase the risk of institutional liability, and demonstrations of genuine concern can help keep the family's grief from turning to rage at the institution.

Critical Thinking

1. Why do you think suicides occur on college campuses?
2. Do you think college-age suicides are more prevalent than in other age groups? Explain your answer.
3. Do colleges have responsibility and liability as regards suicides among their student body? If so, what are they?

ANN H. FRANKE is vice president for education and risk management at United Educators Insurance and a former counsel to the American Association of University Professors.

Cannabis Use in Long-Term Care: An Emerging Issue for Nurses

Conflicting laws at the state and federal levels put nurses in the middle.

ROXANNE NELSON

The use of cannabis as a medicinal agent is a hotly debated and contentious issue in the United States. Cannabis has been touted as a treatment for many conditions, including nausea and anorexia caused by chemotherapy, AIDS-related wasting, neuropathic pain, spasticity associated with multiple sclerosis, and glaucoma. Its use for medical purposes has enjoyed strong support among professional health care organizations and the public at large; 14 states and the District of Columbia now allow its use, although regulations and qualifications vary widely. (The advocacy group Americans for Safe Access dedicates a site to explaining those laws state by state: http://bit.ly/gs7hIw.)

Although the U.S. Department of Justice announced in 2009 that users and distributors of medical cannabis wouldn't be pursued as long as they followed state laws, the federal government has resisted any change to the drug's illegal status at the national level.

This isn't only an issue of state laws conflicting with federal law; even within states that permit medical cannabis, the rules about its use in the institutional setting may be hazy. These ill-defined regulations can put health care professionals in a precarious position. And because many nursing homes rely on federal or state funding, there are unanswered questions as to whether health care providers can legally provide or administer any form of medical cannabis to residents.

"There are issues of loss of licenses and certifications," said Allen St. Pierre, executive director of the National Organization for the Reform of Marijuana Laws, or NORML. "The idea of a Schedule I drug being used or tolerated at a facility that's licensed by a state or federal government is anathema."

But this isn't a new issue, and for NORML it began even before the advent of "medical cannabis proper," according to St. Pierre. In 1990, he said, NORML would take calls from organizations that provided homes away from home for families and patients dealing with painful diseases. In these cases, said St. Pierre, "we would have older teenagers, who, with their physician's recommendation, wanted to use cannabis on site."

The legal counsels or managers of such organizations were caught between wanting to provide the best possible health care for people at a very difficult time in their lives and trying not to jeopardize the operation for future clients, given that this was a clear violation of the law. St. Pierre contends that the conflict—between providing good health care and breaking the law—has wrapped itself around nearly every tier of the health care industry.

Federal vs. State Rules

Cannabis sativa is available in leaf form (known as marijuana, pot, weed, or reefer) or in various extracted forms (as hashish or oil) and can be taken in a variety of ways (smoked, ingested, or vaporized). It's best known as a recreational drug, although its medicinal properties have been documented for thousands of years. It was legally available in the United States until the beginning of the 20th century. In 1937 the first federal laws against cannabis use were passed. (For more on the history of cannabis in the United States, see "A Brief History of Medical Marijuana" in *Time:* http://bit.ly/3NFI7d.)

Cannabis is currently listed as a Schedule I drug, which means that the government doesn't recognize any medical value. Despite the federal laws, a growing number of states are liberalizing their laws and allowing patients varying degrees of access to cannabis. Although firm numbers remain somewhat elusive, it's believed that the percentage of older users is growing. If that's true, it would indicate that long-term care facilities will increasingly have to address the situation. (This year NORML plans to roll out the NORML Senior Alliance, which will offer information to older adults about the medical uses of cannabis.)

One of the main problems is that many state laws don't specifically address the use of cannabis in nursing homes and other institutions. For example, Alaska law doesn't require any facility monitored by its Department of Administration to accommodate cannabis users. In Montana, smoking is prohibited in all health care facilities, but cannabis may be used in other forms; individual facilities may set their own rules, including under what conditions and circumstances cannabis use would be permitted. Maine, on the other hand, permits nursing homes and inpatient hospice workers to act as registered caregivers for patients using medical cannabis.

Another pressing concern is that these facilities often receive federal funding, either directly through Medicare or indirectly through Medicaid. This places administrators in an awkward position, having to choose between complying with federal law (and maintaining funding) and permitting access to cannabis to residents who rely on it.

"We may only find out what will happen if a brave nursing home takes the risk and does the right thing for its patients," said Mary Lynn Mathre, MSN, RN, an addiction specialist and president of the nonprofit group Patients Out of Time. "Given the Obama administration's statement about not interfering with medical marijuana patients who are getting legal recommendations from their care provider, it seems very wrong to *not* allow nursing home patients to use it because the facility receives federal funding." She added that "it would be great to see nursing home administration organizations pass a formal resolution recognizing this potential problem and asking the federal government to allow patients the option to use this medicine as they would any other medicine."

Nursing's Stance on the Issue

Overall, nursing organizations, including the American Nurses Association and more than a dozen state nursing associations, support supervised access to medical cannabis. But if experts are correct, and the number of older adult cannabis users escalates in nursing homes and assisted living facilities, nurses may find themselves in a rather unusual situation. Aside from possibly violating federal drug laws, there are other issues to consider. Who dispenses the cannabis? What is the dosage? How will the facility obtain it?

California has been a pioneer in exploring the issue of medicinal cannabis use, having been the first state in the nation to pass an initiative that loosened its laws and allowed for medical usage.

"In California, we have laws that protect patients' rights," said Deborah Burger, RN, copresident of the California Nurses Association (National Nurses United), which supports the use of medical cannabis. "If patients have been prescribed the medication, they should get it. Nurses in those areas are bound by California law to advocate on behalf of the patient." And if California nurses have had problems with it, Burger hasn't heard about it. "I haven't heard that there were any issues with nursing homes refusing to allow patients to use it," she said.

Sometimes the "don't ask, don't tell" approach is the best option, according to Mathre. "I can tell you that many hospice nurses turn a blind eye to cannabis use in the home because they know it helps." She explained that during a legislative committee hearing on a medical cannabis bill in Wisconsin, a nurse who represented her hospice organization spoke in favor of the legislation and acknowledged the problem that nurses in this situation face. "They may be witnessing illegal activity, but they pretend not to see or know what's going on because, in their hearts, they know the patient benefits from the use of cannabis."

Critical Thinking

1. Why is cannabis great medicine?
2. How do state and local laws interfere with medical treatments involving cannabis?
3. Why are nursing home administrators in an awkward position when using medical cannabis in treating the elderly?

Ethics and Life's Ending
An Exchange

ROBERT D. ORR AND GILBERT MEILAENDER

eeding tubes make the news periodically, and controversies over their use or non-use seem unusually contentious. But feeding tubes are not high technology treatment; they are simple, small-bore catheters made of soft synthetic material. Nor are they new technology; feeding tubes were first used in 1793 by John Hunter to introduce jellies, eggs, sugar, milk, and wine into the stomachs of patients unable to swallow. Why does this old, low-tech treatment generate such controversy today? The important question is not whether a feeding tube *can* be used, but whether it *should* be used in a particular situation.

Too often in medicine we use a diagnostic or therapeutic intervention just because it is available. This thoughtless approach is sometimes called the technological imperative, i.e., the impulse to do everything we are trained to do, regardless of the burden or benefit. Kidney failure? Let's do dialysis. Respiratory failure? Let's use a ventilator. Unable to eat? Let's put in a feeding tube. By responding in this way, the physician ignores the maxim "the ability to act does not justify the action." Just because we know how to artificially breathe for a patient in respiratory failure doesn't mean that everyone who cannot breathe adequately must be put on a ventilator. Such a response also represents a failure to do the moral work of assessing whether the treatment is appropriate in a particular situation.

The moral debate about the use or non-use of feeding tubes hinges on three important considerations: the distinction between what in the past was called "ordinary" and "extraordinary" treatments; the important social symbolism of feeding; and a distinction between withholding and withdrawing treatments.

It was recognized many years ago that respirators, dialysis machines, and other high-tech modes of treatment are optional. They could be used or not used depending on the circumstances. However, it was commonly accepted in the past that feeding tubes are generally not optional. Part of the reasoning was that feeding tubes are readily available, simple to use, not very burdensome to the patient, and not very expensive. They were "ordinary treatment" and thus morally obligatory.

Ordinary [versus] Extraordinary

For over four hundred years, traditional moral theology distinguished between ordinary and extraordinary means of saving life. Ordinary means were those that were not too painful or burden-some for the patient, were not too expensive, and had a reasonable chance of working. These ordinary treatments were deemed morally obligatory. Those treatments that did involve undue burden were extraordinary and thus optional. This distinction was common knowledge in religious and secular circles, and this language and reasoning was commonly applied in Western society.

As medical treatments became more complicated, it was recognized that this distinction was sometimes not helpful. The problem was that the designation appeared to belong to the treatment itself, rather than to the situation. The respirator and dialysis machine were categorized as extraordinary while antibiotics and feeding tubes were classed as ordinary. But real-life situations were not that simple. Thus began a change in moral terminology first officially noted in the *Declaration on Euthanasia* published in 1980 by the Catholic Church's Sacred Congregation for the Doctrine of the Faith in 1980: "In the past, moralists replied that one is never obligated to use 'extraordinary' means. This reply, which as a principle still holds good, is perhaps less clear today, by reason of the imprecision of the term and the rapid progress made in the treatment of sickness. Thus some people prefer to speak of 'proportionate' and 'disproportionate' means."

This newer and clearer moral terminology of proportionality was used in secular ethical analysis as early as the 1983 President's Commission report, *Deciding to Forgo Life-Sustaining Technologies.* The "ordinary/extraordinary" language, however, continues to be seen in the medical literature and heard in the intensive care unit. Reasoning on the basis of proportionality requires us to weigh the burdens and the benefits of a particular treatment for a particular patient. Thus a respirator may be proportionate (and obligatory) for a young person with a severe but survivable chest injury, but it may be disproportionate (and thus optional) for another person who is dying of lung cancer. The same is true for (almost) all medical treatments, including feeding tubes. There are two treatments that always remain obligatory, as I shall explain below.

A second aspect of the discussion about the obligation to provide nutritional support, especially in secular discussions but also in religious debate, was the symbolism of food and water— feeding is caring; nutrition is nurture; food and water are not treatment, and therefore they are never optional. The reasoning commonly went as follows: we provide nutritional support for vulnerable infants because this is an important part of "tender loving care." Shouldn't we provide the same for vulnerable adults as well?

Certainly when a patient is temporarily unable to swallow and has the potential to recover, artificially administered fluids and nutrition are obligatory. Does that obligation change if the prognosis is poor?

This aspect of the debate continued through the 1970s and '80s. It appeared to be resolved by the U.S. Supreme Court in its 1990 decision in *Cruzan v. Director, Missouri Department of Health* when five of the nine Justices agreed that artificially administered fluids and nutrition are medical treatments and are thus optional. Since *Cruzan* medical and legal professions have developed a consensus that feeding tubes are not always obligatory. This debate is ongoing, however, and in some minds the symbolism of feeding remains a dominant feature.

Starvation

A parallel concern to the symbolism entailed in the use of fluids and nutrition is the commonly heard accusation, "But you will be starving him to death!" when discontinuation of a feeding tube is discussed. This is incorrect. Starvation is a slow process that results from lack of calories and takes several weeks or months. When artificially administered fluids and nutrition are not used in a person who is unable to swallow, that person dies from dehydration, not starvation, and death occurs in five to twelve days. Dehydration is very commonly the last physiologic stage of dying, no matter what the cause.

"But that is no comfort! Being dehydrated and thirsty is miserable." Yes and no. Being thirsty is miserable, but becoming dehydrated need not be. The only place in the body where thirst is perceived is the mouth. There is good empirical evidence that as long as a person's mouth is kept moist, that person is not uncomfortable, even if it is clear that his or her body is becoming progressively dehydrated.

I said earlier that there are two treatments that are never optional: these are good symptom control and human presence. Therefore, when a person is becoming dehydrated as he or she approaches death, it is obligatory to provide good mouth care, along with other means of demonstrating human caring and presence, such as touching, caressing, gentle massage, hair-brushing, talking, reading, and holding.

Withholding [versus] Withdrawing

A third feature of the debate over feeding tubes is the issue of withholding versus withdrawing therapy. Thirty years ago, it was common teaching in medicine that "it is better to withhold a treatment than to withdraw it." The thinking was that if you stop a ventilator or dialysis or a feeding tube, and the patient then dies from this lack of life support, you were the agent of death. Therefore, it would be ethically better not to start the treatment in the first place. Then, if the patient dies, death is attributable to the underlying disease and not to your withdrawal of life support.

Slowly, with help from philosophers, theologians, attorneys, and jurists, the medical profession came to accept that there is no moral or legal difference between withholding and withdrawing a treatment. In fact, it may be ethically better to withdraw life-sustaining treatment than it is to withhold it. If there is a treatment with a very small chance of helping the patient, it is better to give it a try. If it becomes clear after a few days or weeks that it is not helping, then you can withdraw the treatment without the original uncertainty that you might be quitting too soon, and now with the comfort that comes from knowing you are not the agent of death.

However, even if there is no professional, moral, or legal difference, it still may be psychologically more difficult to withdraw a treatment that you know is postponing a patient's death than it would have been not to start it in the first place. Turning down the dials on a ventilator with the expectation that the patient will not survive is more personally unsettling than is merely being present with a patient who is actively dying. Withdrawal of a feeding tube can be even more unsettling, especially if the professional involved has any moral reservations about the distinction between ordinary and extraordinary means, or about the symbolism of artificially administered fluids and nutrition.

Some develop this part of the debate with moral concern about intentionality. They contend that your intention in withdrawing the feeding tube is that the patient will die, and it is morally impermissible to cause death intentionally. In actuality, the intention in withdrawing any therapy that has been proven not to work is to stop postponing death artificially.

With these aspects of the debate more or less settled, where does that leave us in making decisions about the use or non-use of feeding tubes? The short-term use of a feeding tube for a patient who is unable to swallow adequate fluids and nutrition for a few days, because of severe illness or after surgery or trauma, may be lifesaving and is almost always uncontroversial. Such usage may even be morally obligatory when the goal of treatment is patient survival and a feeding tube is the best way to provide needed fluids and nutrition.

A feeding tube is sometimes requested by a loved one as a last-gasp effort to postpone death in a patient who is imminently dying and unable to swallow. This is almost always inappropriate. Good mouth care to maintain patient comfort and hygiene is obligatory, but in such cases maintenance of nutrition is no longer a reasonable goal of treatment. In fact, introduction of fluids may even lead to fluid overload that can cause patient discomfort as the body's systems are shutting down.

Long-Term Use

The situation that can generate ethical quandaries, front-page news, and conflicts in court is the long-term use of feeding tubes. And these situations are not as neatly segregated into proportionate or disproportionate usage.

Long-term use of a feeding tube remains ethically obligatory for a patient who is cognitively intact, can and wants to survive, but is permanently unable to swallow, an example being a patient who has been treated for malignancy of the throat or esophagus. Protracted use of a feeding tube is also morally required in most instances when it is uncertain whether a patient will regain awareness or recover the ability to swallow—for instance, immediately after a serious head injury or a disabling stroke.

Long-term use of a feeding tube becomes controversial in patients suffering from progressive deterioration of brain function (e.g., Alzheimer's dementia), or in patients with little or no likelihood of regaining awareness after illness or injury (e.g., the permanent vegetative state). Thus, the most perplexing feeding-tube questions involve patients who are unable to take in adequate fluids and nutrition by themselves but who have a condition that by itself will not soon lead to death. The reasoning is, the patient has no fatal condition; he or she can be kept alive with the simple use of tube feedings; therefore we are obligated to use a feeding tube to keep this person alive.

Alzheimer's dementia is the most common type of brain deterioration, afflicting five percent of individuals over sixty-five and perhaps as many as 50 percent of those over eighty-five. It is manifested by progressive cognitive impairment, followed by physical deterioration. This process generally takes several years, often a decade, and is ultimately fatal. In its final stages it almost always interferes with the patient's ability to swallow. Eventually the individual chokes on even pureed foods or liquids. Continued attempts at feeding by mouth very commonly result in aspiration of food or fluid into the airway, frequently leading to pneumonia. Aspiration pneumonia will sometimes respond to antibiotics, but other times it leads to death. Such respiratory infections are the most common final event in this progressive disease.

Feeding tubes have been commonly used in the later stages of Alzheimer's. The reasoning has been that this patient is not able to take in adequate fluids and nutrition and he is not imminently dying. Several assumptions then follow: a feeding tube will improve his comfort, will prevent aspiration pneumonia, and will ensure adequate nutrition which will in turn prevent skin breakdown and thus postpone his death. However, empirical evidence, published in the *Journal of the American Medical Association* in 1999, has shown each of these assumptions to be incorrect: using a feeding tube in a patient with dementia does not prevent these complications, nor does it prolong life.

In addition, there are several negative aspects to using a feeding tube in a person with advanced cognitive impairment. There are rare complications during insertion, some merely uncomfortable, some quite serious. Having a tube in one's nose is generally uncomfortable; even having one coiled up under a dressing on the abdominal wall can be annoying. Because the demented patient doesn't understand the intended purpose of the feeding tube, he or she may react by trying to remove it, requiring either repeated re-insertions or the use of hand restraints. In addition, using a feeding tube may deprive the patient of human presence and interaction: hanging a bag of nutritional fluid takes only a few seconds, as opposed to the extended time of human contact involved in feeding a cognitively impaired person.

End Stage Alzheimer's

There is a slowly developing consensus in medicine that feeding tubes are generally not appropriate for use in most patients nearing the end stage of Alzheimer's disease. This belief can be supported from a moral standpoint in terms of proportionality. And yet feeding tubes are still rather commonly used. A recently published review of all U.S. nursing home patients with cognitive impairment found that an average of 34 percent were being fed with feeding tubes (though there were large state-to-state varia-

tions, from nine percent in Maine, New Hampshire, and Vermont to 64 percent in Washington, D.C.).

The cases we read about in the newspaper—in which families are divided and court battles fought—most often involve patients in a permanent vegetative state (PVS). This is a condition of permanent unawareness most often caused by severe head injury or by the brain being deprived of oxygen for several minutes. Such deprivation may be the result of successful cardiopulmonary resuscitation of a patient whose breathing or circulation had stopped from a cardiac arrest, near-drowning, strangulation, etc. In a PVS patient, the heart, lungs, kidneys, and other organs continue to function; given good nursing care and artificially administered fluids and nutrition, a person can live in this permanent vegetative state for many years.

A person in a PVS may still have reflexes from the spinal cord (grasping, withdrawal from pain) or the brain stem (breathing, regulation of blood pressure), including the demonstration of sleep-wake cycles. He may "sleep" for several hours, then "awaken" for a while; the eyes are open and wander about, but do not fix on or follow objects. The person in a PVS is "awake, but unaware" because the areas of the upper brain that allow a person to perceive his or her environment and to act voluntarily are no longer functioning.

Uncertainty

Some of the clinical controversy about nutritional support for persons in a PVS is due to uncertainty. After a head injury or resuscitation from a cardiac arrest, it may be several weeks or months before a patient can rightly be declared to be in a PVS—months during which the provision of nutritional support via feeding tubes is often very appropriate. Loved ones usually remain optimistic, hoping for improvement, praying for full recovery. The length of time from brain damage to declaration of a PVS can extend, depending on the cause of the brain injury, from one month to twelve months. And just to muddy the waters even further, there are rare instances of delayed improvement after many months or even a few years, so that the previously unaware patient regains some ability to perceive his or her environment, and may even be able to say a few words. These individuals are now in a "minimally conscious state." More than minimal delayed improvement is exceedingly rare. (Treatment decisions for persons in a minimally conscious state are perhaps even more controversial than are those for PVS patients, but that discussion must wait for another time.)

The greatest ethical dilemma surrounding the use or non-use of nutritional support for persons in a PVS arises from the fact that they are not clearly dying. With good nursing care and nutrition, individuals in this condition have survived for up to thirty-five years. Those who advocate continued nutritional support argue thus: this person is alive and not actively or imminently dying; it is possible to keep him alive with minimal effort; this human life is sacred; therefore we are obligated to continue to give artificially administered fluids and nutrition.

It is hard to disagree with the various steps in this line of reasoning. (Some utilitarians do disagree, however, claiming that a patient in a PVS is "already dead" or is a "non-person." Those who believe in the sanctity of life must continue to denounce this line of thought.) Let us stipulate the following: the person in a PVS is alive; he can be kept alive for a long time; his life is sacred. But does the obligation to maintain that severely compromised human life necessarily follow from these premises?

Let's first address the issue of whether he is dying. One could maintain that his physical condition is such that he will die soon but for the artificial provision of fluids and nutrition. Thus the permanent vegetative state could be construed to be lethal in and of itself. However, that fatal outcome is not inevitable since the saving treatment is simple. How does this differ from the imperative to provide nourishment for a newborn who would die without the provision of fluids and nutrition? There are two differences. Most newborns are able to take in nutrition if it is placed in or near their mouths. PVS patients can't swallow, so the nutrition must be delivered further down the gastrointestinal tract. As for sick or premature infants, they have a great potential for improvement, growth, and development. The PVS patient has no such potential.

Kidney Failure

Rather than a newborn, a better analogy for this aspect of the discussion would be a person with kidney failure. The kidney failure itself is life-threatening, but it is fairly easily corrected by dialysis three times a week. If the person has another condition that renders him unaware of his surroundings, or a condition that makes life a continuous difficult struggle, most would agree that the person is ethically permitted to stop the dialysis even if that means he will not survive. The ultimate cause of death was treatable, so that death could have been postponed, possibly for years. However, other mitigating circumstances may make the dialysis disproportionate, and so one should be allowed to discontinue this death-postponing treatment in a person who is not imminently dying.

Someone coming from a mechanistic perspective can easily and comfortably decide that a person in a PVS with no potential for recovery has no inherent value and is even an emotional drain on loved ones and a financial drain on society. But what about a person of faith? Does the sanctity of life, a basic tenet of Christianity, Judaism, and Islam, dictate that life must always be preserved if it is humanly possible to do so? Our moral intuitions tell us the answer is no.

It might be possible to postpone the death of a patient from end-stage heart failure by doing one more resuscitation. It might be possible to postpone the death of someone with end-stage liver disease by doing a liver transplant. It might be possible to postpone the death of someone with painful cancer with a few more blood transfusions or another round of chemotherapy. But these therapies are often not used—because the burden is disproportionate to the benefit. Thus the timing of death is often a matter of choice. In fact, it is commonly accepted that the timing of 80 percent of deaths that occur in a hospital is chosen.

Believers do not like to use the words "choice" and "death" in the same sentence. Doing so recalls acrimonious contests about the "right to life" versus the "right to choose" that are the pivotal point in debates about abortion, assisted suicide, and euthana-

sia. And certainly belief in the sanctity of human life obligates believers to forgo some choices. But does this belief preclude all choices? No: life is full of difficult choices. This is true for believers and nonbelievers alike. Believers may have more guidance about what choices to make and perhaps some limits on options, but we still are faced with many choices—such as choices about the use or non-use of feeding tubes.

When engaging in moral debate on matters of faith, it is important not to focus exclusively on one tenet of faith to the exclusion of others. In debating the use of feeding tubes—or of any mode of treatment for that matter—one must not ignore the concepts of finitude and stewardship by focusing only on the sanctity of life.

If belief in the sanctity of human life translated automatically into an obligation to preserve each human life at all costs, we would not have to debate proportionate and disproportionate treatments. We would simply be obligated to use all treatments available until they failed to work. However, because of the Fall, human life is finite. All of us will die. Since that is inevitable, God expects us to care wisely for our own bodies and for those of our loved ones, and also for our resources. Healthcare professionals similarly must be wise stewards of their skills and services.

Taking into consideration the scriptural principle of stewardship and the tradition of proportionate treatment, I conclude that there must be some degree of discretion in the use or non-use of feeding tubes. There are clearly situations where a feeding tube must be used. There are other situations where a feeding tube would be morally wrong. But there are many situations where the use of a feeding tube should be optional. And this means that one individual of faith might choose to use a tube when another might choose not to use it.

Personal Values

Because of the patient's personal values, someone might choose to continue artificially administered fluids and nutrition for a loved one in a permanent vegetative state for many years. Another might choose to continue for one year and then to withdraw it if there was no sign of awareness. Still another might choose to stop after three months or one month.

What might those discretionary personal values include? Such things, among others, as an assessment of how to deal with uncertainty, concern about emotional burden on loved ones, and cost of care. Though beliefs in the sanctity of human life and in the obligation to care for vulnerable individuals are not optional for persons of faith, an assessment of whether or not to use a given technology requires human wisdom and thus entails some discretion.

Gilbert Meilaender

There is much to agree with in Robert D. Orr's measured discussion of the moral issues surrounding the use of feeding tubes, there are a few things that seem to me doubtful or in need of clarification, and then there is one major issue that requires greater precision.

Accepted Claims

It may be useful to note first some claims of Dr. Orr that few would dispute.

- Feeding tubes are a rather low-tech form of care.
- Our ability to do something does not mean that we should do it.
- Any distinction between "ordinary" and "extraordinary" care (if we wish to use that language) cannot simply be a feature of treatments but must be understood as patient-relative. What is ordinary treatment for one patient may be extraordinary for another, and what is ordinary treatment for a patient at one point in his life may become extraordinary at another point when his illness has progressed to a new stage.
- There is no crucial moral difference between withholding or withdrawing a treatment. (Dr. Orr actually writes that there is "no moral or legal difference" between these. The issue of legality is, I suspect, sometimes more complicated, but I take him to be correct insofar as a strictly moral judgment is involved.)
- There are circumstances, some noted by Dr. Orr, in which the use of feeding tubes seems clearly required and is relatively uncontroversial.
- Patients in a persistent vegetative state are not dying patients. (I don't quite know how to combine this with Dr. Orr's statement a few paragraphs later that the permanent vegetative state "could be construed to be lethal in and of itself." In general, I don't think his article ever really achieves clarity and precision on this question, and it will turn out to be a crucial question below.)
- A commitment to the sanctity of human life does not require that we always do everything possible to keep a person alive.

There are also places where Dr. Orr's discussion seems to me to be doubtful or, at least, underdeveloped. Among these are the following:

- The idea that the terms "proportionate" and "disproportionate" are more precise than the (admittedly unsatisfactory) language of "ordinary" and "extraordinary" is, at best, doubtful. On what scale one "weighs" benefits and burdens is a question almost impossible to answer. Even more doubtful is whether we can "weigh" them for someone else. My own view is that when we make these decisions for ourselves, we are not in fact "weighing" anything. We are deciding what sort of person we will be and what sort of life will be ours. We are making not a *discovery* but a *decision.* And if that is true, then it is obvious that we have not discovered anything that could necessarily be transferred and applied to the life of a different patient. In general, the language of "weighing" sounds good, but it is almost impossible to give it any precise meaning.
- No *moral* question was resolved by the Supreme Court's *Cruzan* decision. It established certain legal boundaries, but it did no more than that.

- I suspect that—despite the growing consensus, which Dr. Orr correctly describes—he is too quick to assume that the "symbolism" issue can be dispensed with, and too quick to assume that feeding tubes are "treatment" rather than standard nursing care. A consensus may be mistaken, after all. It is hard to see why such services as turning a patient regularly and giving alcohol rubs are standard nursing care while feeding is not. To take an example from a different realm of life, soldiers are combatants, but the people who grow the food which soldiers eat are not combatants (even though the soldiers could not continue to fight without nourishment). The reason is simple: they make not what soldiers need to fight but what they need, as we all do, in order merely to live. Likewise, we might want to think twice before endorsing the view that relatively low-tech means of providing nourishment are treatment rather than standard nursing care.

Intention

- Dr. Orr's discussion of the role of "intention" in moral analysis is, putting it charitably, imprecise. Obviously, if a treatment has been shown not to work, in withdrawing it we do not intend or aim at the patient's death. We aim at caring for that person as best we can, which hardly includes providing treatment that is useless. But the crucial questions will turn on instances in which the treatment is not pointless. If we stop treatment in such cases, it is harder to deny that our aim is that the patient should die.
- Dr. Orr's seeming willingness to allow the state of a patient's cognitive capacities to carry weight—or even be determinative—in treatment decisions is troubling. Obviously, certain kinds of higher brain capacities are characteristics that distinguish human beings from other species; however, one need not have or be exercising those capacities in order to be a living human being. Allowing the cognitive ability of a patient to determine whether he or she is treated will inevitably lead to judgments about the comparative worth of human lives.

If Dr. Orr is correct in arguing that the use of feeding tubes in end-stage Alzheimer's patients is of no help to those patients and may sometimes be burdensome to them, we would have no moral reason to provide them with tube feeding. This judgment, however, has nothing at all to do with "proportionality." It has to do, simply, with the two criteria we ought to use in making treatment decisions—usefulness and burdensomeness. If a treatment is useless or excessively burdensome, it may rightly be refused.

This brings us to the most difficult issue, which clearly troubles Dr. Orr himself, and which is surely puzzling for all of us; the patient in a persistent vegetative state. We cannot usefully discuss this difficult case, however, without first getting clear more generally on the morality of withholding or withdrawing treatment. As I noted above, on this issue the language of proportionality is unlikely to be of much use for serious moral reflection.

Morality of Treatment

At least for Christians—though, in truth, also much more generally for our civilization's received medical tradition—we begin with what is forbidden. We should never aim at the death of a sick or dying person. (Hence, euthanasia, however good the motive, is forbidden.) Still, there are times when treatment may rightly be withheld or withdrawn, *even though* the patient may then die more quickly than would otherwise have been the case. How can that be? How can it be that, as a result of our decision, the patient dies more quickly, yet we do not aim at his death? This is quite possible—and permissible—so long as we aim to dispense with the treatment, not the life. No one need live in a way that seeks to ensure the longest possible life. (Were that a moral requirement, think of all the careers that would have to be prohibited.) There may be many circumstances in which we foresee that decisions we make may shorten our life, but we do not suppose that in so deciding we are aiming at death or formulating a plan of action that deliberately embraces death as a good. So in medical treatment decisions the question we need to answer is this: Under what circumstances may we rightly refuse a life-prolonging treatment without supposing that, in making this decision, we are doing the forbidden deed of choosing or aiming at death?

The answer of our medical-moral tradition has been the following: we may refuse treatments that are either *useless* or *excessively burdensome*. In doing so, we choose not death, but one among several possible lives open to us. We do not choose to die, but, rather, how to live, even if while dying, even if a shorter life than some other lives that are still available for our choosing. What we take aim at then, what we refuse, is not life but treatment—treatment that is either useless for a particular patient or excessively burdensome for that patient. Especially for patients who are irretrievably into the dying process, almost all treatments will have become useless. In refusing them, one is not choosing death but choosing life without a now useless form of treatment. But even for patients who are not near death, who might live for a considerably longer time, excessively burdensome treatments may also be refused. Here again, one takes aim at the burdensome treatment, not at life. One person may choose a life that is longer but carries with it considerable burden of treatment. Another may choose a life that is shorter but carries with it less burden of treatment. Each, however, chooses life. Neither aims at death.

Rejecting Treatments

It is essential to emphasize that these criteria refer to treatments, not to lives. We may rightly reject a treatment that is useless. But if I decide not to treat because I think a person's life is useless, then I am taking aim not at the treatment but at the life. Rather than asking, "What if anything can I do that will benefit the life this patient has?" I am asking, "Is it a benefit to have such a life?" If the latter is my question, and if I decide not to treat, it should be clear that it is the life at which I take aim. Likewise, we may reject a treatment on grounds of excessive burden. But if I decide

not to treat because it seems a burden just to have the life this person has, then I am taking aim not at the burdensome treatment but at the life. Hence, in deciding whether it is appropriate and permissible to withhold or withdraw treatment—whether, even if life is thereby shortened, we are aiming only at the treatment and not at the life—we have to ask ourselves whether the treatment under consideration is, for this patient, either useless or excessively burdensome.

Against that background, we can consider the use of feeding tubes for patients in a persistent vegetative state. (I set aside here the point I noted above—that we might want to regard feeding simply as standard nursing care rather than as medical treatment. Now we are asking whether, even on the grounds that govern treatment decisions, we have good moral reason not to feed patients in a persistent vegetative state.)

Is the treatment useless? Not, let us be clear, is the life a useless one to have, but is the treatment useless? As Dr. Orr notes—quite rightly, I think—patients "can live in this permanent vegetative state for many years." So feeding may preserve for years the life of this living human being. Are we certain we want to call that useless? We are, of course, tempted to say that, in deciding not to feed, we are simply withdrawing treatment and letting these patients die. Yes, as Dr. Orr also notes, these patients "are not clearly dying." And, despite the sloppy way we sometimes talk about these matters, you cannot "let die" a person who is not dying. It is hard, therefore, to make the case for treatment withdrawal in these cases on the ground of uselessness. We may use those words, but it is more likely that our target is a (supposed) useless life and not a useless treatment. And if that is our aim, we had better rethink it promptly.

Is the treatment excessively burdensome? Alas, if these patients could experience the feeding as a burden, they would not be diagnosed as being in a persistent vegetative state. We may wonder, of course, whether having such a life is itself a burden, but, again, if that is our reasoning, it will be clear that we take aim not at a burdensome treatment but at a (presumed) burdensome life. And, once more, if that is our aim, we had better rethink it promptly.

Choosing Life

Hence, although these are troubling cases, Dr. Orr has not given us good or sufficient arguments to make the case for withdrawing feeding tubes from patients in a persistent vegetative state. I have not suggested that we have an obligation always and at any cost to preserve life. I have simply avoided all comparative judgments of the worth of human lives and have turned aside from any decisions which, when analyzed carefully, look as if they take aim not at a dispensable treatment but at a life. "Choosing life" does not mean doing whatever is needed to stay alive as long as possible. But choosing life clearly means never aiming at another's death—even if only by withholding treatment. I am not persuaded that Dr. Orr has fully grasped or delineated what it means to choose life in the difficult circumstances he discusses.

Critical Thinking

1. Why are each of these a problem: the distinction between extraordinary and ordinary treatments? the social symbolism of feeding? and the distinction between withholding and withdrawing of treatments?
2. Why do real-life situations complicate the distinction between extraordinary and ordinary treatments?

3. What does the author argue are never optional treatments for the dying?

MR. ORR is the Director of Ethics and a professor of family medicine at the University of Vermont College of Medicine. MR. MEILAENDER is a member of the President's Council on Bioethics. From "Ethics & Life's Ending: An Exchange," by Robert D. Orr and Gilbert Meilaender, *First Things*, August/September 2004, pages 31–38.

I Was a Doctor Accustomed to Death, but Not His

Working in nursing homes taught me about old age—but I was unprepared for my grandfather's last days.

MARC AGRONIN

I currently live and work in Miami as a doctor for old people—the very profession so derided in my early years of training. To be more specific, I am the psychiatrist at the Miami Jewish Health Systems, the site of one of the largest nursing homes in the United States. Although people sometimes call my place of work "God's waiting room," they miss a much bigger picture.

True, the average age of my patients is about 90 years old, meaning that I see a lot of people close to 100. The 80-year-olds who come to see me are like teenagers on my scale of things, and the 70-year-olds—babies! And true, my job is to tend to all of the maladies and infirmities of aging that I learned about in my medical and psychiatric training. But as I have learned from countless older individuals, the true scales of aging are not one-sided; the problems of aging must be weighed against the promises. In my work as a geriatric psychiatrist I have learned that aging equals vitality, wisdom, creativity, spirit, and, ultimately, hope. And for an increasing number of aged individuals, these vital forces are growing by the day.

In the spring of 1997 my beloved grandfather passed away. A week before his death, I stood vigil at his bedside while he flickered between confusion and insensibility. The once-brilliant mind of this retired doctor was soaked in a pool of morphine, and most rational thinking had already drowned. He insisted on wearing a large pair of sunglasses in the darkened room. He cursed and growled when I held his arms as he staggered into the bathroom.

I am not certain that he even recognized me on that final visit, as by then his lifelong persona had largely separated from the person. Nevertheless, his voice came to me as I watched him lying in bed, breathing slowly: "Notice the abnormal rate and pitch of the breath sounds," I imagined him saying; "they are quiet at first but become increasingly labored until they stop for a moment—called apnea—and then the pattern repeats. This is known as Cheyne-Stokes respiration, and it is often seen just prior to death." I pictured the seriousness of my grandfather's face as he taught me to observe the ebb and flow of the respirations and then quizzed me to make certain that I had absorbed the lesson. The distinctive cadence of his voice alternated between curt instructions and impatient pauses, waiting for my answer. He had a way of repetitively flipping his outstretched hand at the wrist as he spoke, one finger extending out like Michelangelo's God, as if to say, "It can be this way, or that, but you must choose one!"

The practice of medicine was his life, and he had taught me with both an earnestness and a severity about caring for patients. My grandfather had experienced the urgency of his work while serving as a field surgeon in the U.S. Army Air Corps stationed on Okinawa during World War II. This sensibility was reinforced after the war in his fifty years as a general practitioner in the small industrial town of Kaukauna, Wisconsin. In both circumstances the survival of a patient depended on his own wit and hands; there were few colleagues or other resources to help out.

My grandfather had an instinctive sense of independence, no doubt fashioned in his childhood. He was born in 1914 and grew up in a small town in Ukraine near Kiev, alone with his mother and grandmother after his father left for America. He survived the poverty and deprivation of rural Russia during World War I and recalled hiding in haystacks or in the forest to escape from the murderous pogroms of the Cossacks. At the age of twelve he came to America in the steerage of a transatlantic steamer, landing at Ellis Island with other similarly huddled masses. My grandfather remembered seeing the gleaming torch of the Statue of Liberty as the ship glided into New York harbor. He remembered the sweet, precious taste of an orange that he ate, for the first time, while on board. His subsequent journey in America slowly took him west along the rail-lines; he lived with relatives in New York, Chicago, Madison, and, finally, Appleton, Wisconsin.

Before becoming a doctor, my grandfather was, in succession, a milkman, a boxer, and a scientist. His appearance lent itself to each job, as he had the quick, thin legs of a deliveryman; the box-shaped, muscular trunk of a pugilist; and the round, balding, and bespectacled face of an intellectual. Photographs of him from youth to old age always show a dapper man, whether dressed in uniform, scrubs, or coat and tie. In 1938 he married my grandmother, and they stayed together for life. She was the consummate doctor's wife, who raised their three children, managed the books, and kept the home quiet, kosher, and revolving smoothly around his frenetic schedule. As a doctor my grandfather worried incessantly about his patients, but he hid it behind his obsessive work habits and sometimes-gruff demeanor. By the early 1970s probably half of Kaukauna's residents were either current or former patients, a good many of them having been birthed into his hands. Neighbors, strangers, and family alike all made visits to his modest-sized, spartan clinic, where he was renowned as a diagnostician. There weren't many secrets in our large extended family living throughout Wisconsin, but whatever they were, he knew and kept them hidden as a good doctor should.

Until the year before his death, aging had been a relatively benign process for my grandfather. He practiced medicine and surgery until the age of eighty and then retired not because he felt any desire to but because it just seemed logical. When he became ill, however, aging caught up to him quite quickly. In the summer of 1996 he was diagnosed with an aggressive form of prostate cancer. Suddenly, he needed me for support and advice, and we spoke nearly every day about how to manage some of his physical discomfort. Of course, as a newly minted psychiatrist I was of little value to his medical management, and I left that up to my uncle, who had taken over his practice. But our conversations were not really about my grandfather's pain; they were, it seemed to me, cover for dealing with aging and death.

As the de facto family historian I also knew that I had to record his life stories, and so at Thanksgiving we sat down on the porch of my grandparents' house for a taped interview. The life review was almost too painful for him, however, and he broke down crying at several points. I had never seen him cry before, let alone show sadness, but I persisted with the camera, knowing that time was short. In my work with older individuals it is always painful to witness the crumbling of their composure in the face of loss and grief, but I can steel my own emotions because I rarely know what the person was once like. But such was not the case with my grandfather, and I vacillated between denial and despair. As I was saying my good-byes and leaving my grandparents' home at the end of the weekend, he pulled me aside and stated rather perfunctorily that this was probably the last time I would see him. His words were sterile and clinical—a doctor's way of parting with a patient. But I knew that this was his best effort at saying good-bye. A doctor myself, I brushed off his words in the same manner I might use leaving the clinic at day's end—"No, Grandpa; I'll see you soon. Call me tomorrow."

I reflected on these moments as I sat at his bedside that spring and tried to contain my emotions. He was not only my grandfather, but also my mentor, my inspiration, and, from my earliest childhood days, my own doctor. But now his life of eighty-three years was drawing to a close, and I was standing witness at the point where aging meets death. Shortly after my grandparents passed away, I compressed much of my grief into an odd fantasy that in the afterlife they had moved down to Miami Beach and were experiencing eternal bliss together, with endless sunny beaches and Early Bird specials. Florida, I imagined, was actually some form of Shangri-La where all of our deceased elderly could be found happily wandering around if we just looked hard enough.

No other period of life has such a feared and mysterious ending. Childhood ends with the budding of puberty and the new challenges of adolescence. Adolescence passes away in the excitement of pulsating hormones, shedding its awkward, uncertain skin in the journey into young adulthood. The subsequent stages of adulthood bring undiscovered treasures of love, children, work, and spirit. Even in the face of failure or lost opportunities, there is always hope for something new. But aging seems to bring this process to a halt. The horizon is unknown except for the single fact that a true ending will come . . .

Critical Thinking

1. What is "God's waiting room"?

2. If the doctor's conversations were not really about his grandfather's pain and treatment; what were they really about?

3. Comment on the following quote: "Even in the face of failure or lost opportunities, there is always hope for something new."

MARC AGRONIN, M.D., a graduate of Harvard U niversity and Yale Medical School, is a board-certified geriatric psychiatrist. He is the author of "How We Age: A Doctor's Journey into the Heart of Growing Old."

UNIT 7
Funerals

Unit Selections

Learning Outcomes

After reading this unit, you should be able to:

- Know the needs of the bereaved.

- Understand the social function of the funeral.

- Assist and support children when they attend funerals.

- Understand different religious responses and social needs related to the funeral.

- Compare Jewish, Hindu, Buddhist, Christian, and Muslim beliefs and practices regarding death.

- How is planning and producing a funeral an important part of grief work?

- Understand how physical objects connected with the dead can facilitate therapeutic grieving.

Student Website

www.mhhe.com/cls

Internet References

Personal Impacts of Death
www.trinity.edu/~mkearl/death-6.html#funerals

Willed Body Program
www.utsouthwestern.edu/utsw/home/pcpp/willedbody

Mortuary Science
www.alamo.edu/sac/mortuary/mortuarylinks.htm

Funerals: A Consumer Guide
www.ftc.gov/bcp/edu/pubs/consumer/products/pro19.shtm

Funeral Net
www.funeral.net/info/notices.html

The Internet Cremation Society
www.cremation.org

Cremation Consultant Guidebook
www.funeralplan.com/funeralplan/cremation/options.html

National Academy of Mortuary Science
www.drkloss.com

Alcor
www.alcor.org

CyroCare
www.cyrocare.org

Funerals and Ripoffs
www.funerals-ripoffs.org

The Making of a Classic
www.monitor.net/monitor/decca/death.html

The End of Life: Exploring Death in America
www.npr.org/programs/death/index.html

Forensic Entomology
www.forensic-entomology.com

Hospice: A Guide to Grief Bereavement, Mourning, and Grief
www.hospicenet.org/html/grief_guide.html

Growth House
www.growthhouse.org

Directory of Grief, Loss and Bereavement: Support Groups
www.dmoz.org/Health/Mental_Health/
Grief,_Loss_and_Bereavement/Support_Groups

Bereaved Families of Ontario
www.bereavedfamilies.net

Death Notices
www.legacy.com/NS

Burial Insurance
www.burialinsurance.org

Decisions relating to the disposition of the body after death often involve feelings of ambivalence—on one hand, attachments to the deceased might cause one to be reluctant to dispose of the body; on the other hand, practical considerations make the disposal of the body necessary. Funerals or memorial services provide methods for disposing of a dead body, remembering the deceased, and helping survivors accept the reality of death. They are also public rites of passage that assist the bereaved in returning to routine patterns of social interaction. In contemporary America, 79 percent of deaths involve earth burial and 21 percent involve cremation. These public behaviors, along with the private process of grieving, comprise the two components of the bereavement process.

This unit on the contemporary American funeral begins with a general article on the nature and functions of public bereavement behavior by Michael Leming and George Dickinson. Leming and Dickinson provide an overview of the present practice of funeralization in American society, including traditional and alternative funeral arrangements. They also discuss the functions of funerals relative to the sociological, psychological, and theological needs of adults and children.

© Marmaduke St. John/Alamy

The remaining articles in this section reflect upon the many alternative ways in which funerals, rituals, and final dispositions for the deceased may be constructed.

The Contemporary American Funeral

MICHAEL R. LEMING AND GEORGE E. DICKINSON

Paul Irion (1956) described the following needs of the bereaved: reality, expression of grief, social support, and meaningful context for the death. For Irion, the funeral is an experience of significant personal value insofar as it meets the religious, social, and psychological needs of the mourners. Each of these must be met for bereaved individuals to return to everyday living and, in the process, resolve their grief.

The psychological focus of the funeral is based on the fact that grief is an emotion. Edgar Jackson (1963) indicated that grief is the other side of the coin of love. He contends that if a person has never loved the deceased—never had an emotional investment of some type and degree—he or she will not grieve upon death. As discussed in the opening pages of Chapter 2, evidence of this can easily be demonstrated by the number of deaths that we see, hear, or read about daily that do not have an impact on us unless we have some kind of emotional involvement with those deceased persons. We can read of 78 deaths in a plane crash and not grieve over any of them unless we personally knew the individuals killed. Exceptions to the preceding might include the death of a celebrity or other public figure, when people experience a sense of grief even though there has never been any personal contact.

In his original work on the symptomatology of grief, Erich Lindemann (1944) stressed this concept of grief and its importance as a step in the resolution of grief. He defined how the emotion of grief must support the reality and finality of death. As long as the finality of death is avoided, Lindemann believes, grief resolution is impeded. For this reason, he strongly recommended that the bereaved persons view the dead. When the living confront the dead, all of the intellectualization and avoidance techniques break down. When we can say, "He or she is dead, I am alone, and from this day forward my life will be forever different," we have broken through the devices of denial and avoidance and have accepted the reality of death. It is only at this point that we can begin to withdraw the emotional capital that we have invested in the deceased and seek to create new relationships with the living.

On the other hand, viewing the corpse can be very traumatic for some. Most people are not accustomed to seeing a cold body and a significant other stretched out with eyes closed. Indeed, for some this scene may remain in their memories for a lifetime. Thus, they remember the cold corpse, not the warm, responsive person. Whether or not to view the body is not a cut-and-dried decision. Many factors should be taken into account when this decision is made.

Grief resolution is especially important for family members, but others are affected also—the neighbors, the business community in some instances, the religious community in most instances, the health-care community, and the circle of friends and associates (many of whom may be unknown to the family). All of these groups will grieve to some extent over the death of their relationship with the deceased. Thus, many people are affected by the death. These affected persons will seek not only a means of expressing their grief over the death, but also a network of support to help cope with their grief.

Sociologically, the funeral is a social event that brings the chief mourners and the members of society into a confrontation with death. The funeral becomes a vehicle to bring persons of all walks of life and degrees of relationship to the deceased together for expression and support. For this reason in our contemporary culture the funeral becomes an occasion to which no one is invited but all may come. This was not always the case, and some cultures make the funeral ceremony an "invitation only" experience. It is perhaps for this reason that private funerals (restricted to the family or a special list of persons) have all but disappeared in our culture. (The possible exception to this statement is a funeral for a celebrity—in which participation by the public may be limited to media coverage.)

At a time when emotions are strong, it is important that human interaction and social support become high priorities. A funeral can provide this atmosphere. To grieve alone can be devastating because it becomes necessary for that lone person to absorb all of the feelings into himself or herself. It has often been said that "joy shared is joy increased;" surely grief shared is grief diminished. People need each other at times when they have intense emotional experiences.

A funeral is in essence a one-time kind of "support group" to undergird and support those grieving persons. A funeral provides a conducive social environment for mourning. We may go to the funeral home either to visit with the bereaved family or to work through our own grief. Most of us have had the experience of finding it difficult to discuss a death with a member of the family. We seek the proper atmosphere, time, and place. It is during the funeral, the wake, the shivah, or the visitation with the bereaved family that we have the opportunity to express our condolences and sympathy comfortably.

Anger and guilt are often deeply felt at the time of death and will surface in words and actions. They are permitted within the funeral atmosphere as honest and candid expressions of grief, whereas at other times they might bring criticism and reprimand. The funeral atmosphere says in essence, "You are okay, I am okay; we have some strong feelings, and now is the time to express and share them for the benefit of all." Silence, talking, feeling, touching, and all means of sharing can be expressed without the fear of their being inappropriate.

Another function of the funeral is to provide a theological or philosophical perspective to facilitate grieving and to provide a context of meaning in which to place one of life's most significant experiences. For the majority of Americans, the funeral is a religious rite or ceremony (Pine, 1971). Those grievers who do not possess a religious creed or orientation will define or express death in the context of the values that the deceased and the grievers find important. Theologically or philosophically, the funeral functions as an attempt to bring meaning to the death and life of the deceased individual. For the religiously oriented person, the belief system will perhaps bring an understanding of the afterlife. Others may see only the end of biological life and the beginning of symbolic immortality created by the effects of one's life on the lives of others. The funeral should be planned to give meaning to whichever value context is significant for the bereaved.

"Why?" is one of the most often asked questions upon the moment of death or upon being told that someone we know has died. Though the funeral cannot provide the final answer to this question, it can place death within a context of meaning that is significant to those who mourn. If it is religious in context, the theology, creed, and articles of faith confessed by the mourners will give them comfort and assurance as to the meaning of death. Others who have developed a personally meaningful philosophy of life and death will seek to place the death in that philosophical context.

Cultural expectations typically require that we dispose of the dead with ceremony and dignity. The funeral can also ascribe importance to the remains of the dead. In keeping with the specialization found in most aspects of American life (e.g., the rise of professions), the funeral industry is doing for Americans that necessary task they no longer choose to do for themselves.

The Needs of Children and Their Attendance at Funerals

For children, as well as for their elders, the funeral ceremony can be an experience of value and significance. At a very early age, children are interested in any type of family reunion, party, or celebration. To be excluded from the funeral may create questions and doubts in the minds of children as to why they are not permitted to be a part of an important family activity.

Another question to be considered when denying the child an opportunity to participate in postdeath activities is what goes through the child's mind when such participation is denied. Children deal with other difficult situations in life, and when denied this opportunity, many will fantasize. Research suggests that these fantasies may be negative, destructive, and at times more traumatic than the situation from which the children are excluded.

Children also should not be excluded from activities prior to the funeral service. They should be permitted to attend the visitation, wake, or shivah. (In some situations it would be wise to permit children to confront the deceased prior to the public visitation.) It is obvious that children should not be forced into this type of confrontation, but, by the same token, children who are curious and desire to be involved should not be denied the opportunity.

Children will react at their own emotional levels, and the questions that they ask will usually be asked at their level of comprehension. Two important rules to follow: Never lie to the child, and do not over answer the child's question.

At the time of the funeral, parents have two concerns about their child's behavior at funerals. The first concern is that the child will have difficulty observing the grief of others—particularly if the child has never seen an adult loved one cry. The second concern is that parents themselves become confused when the child's emotional reactions may be different than their own. If the child is told of a death and responds by saying, "Oh, can I go out and play?" the parents may interpret this as denial or as a suppressed negative reaction to the death. Such a reaction can increase emotional concern by the parents. However, if the child's response is viewed as only a first reaction, and if the child is provided with loving, caring, and supportive attention, the child will ordinarily progress into an emotional resolution of the death.

The final reasons for involving children in postdeath activities are related to the strength and support that children give other grievers. They often provide positive evidence of the fact that life goes on. In other instances, because they have been an important part of the life of the deceased, their presence is symbolic testimony to the immortality of the deceased. Furthermore, it is not at all unusual for children to change the atmosphere surrounding bereavement from one of depression and sadness to one of laughter, verbalization, and celebration. Many times children do this by their normal behavior, without any understanding of the kind of contribution being made.

Critical Thinking

1. What are the three basic needs of the bereaved according to Paul Iron?

2. Explain the following quote by Edgar Jackson: "Grief is the other side of the coin of love."

3. How can one help children when they attend funerals?

How Different Religions Pay Their Final Respects

From mummies to cremation to drive-up wakes, funeral rituals reflect religious traditions going back thousands of years as well as up-to-the-minute fads.

WILLIAM J. WHALEN

Most people in the United States identify themselves as Protestants; thus, most funerals follow a similar form. Family and friends gather at the funeral home to console one another and pay their last respects. The next day a minister conducts the funeral service at the church or mortuary; typically the service includes hymns, prayers, a eulogy, and readings from the Bible. In 85 percent of the cases today, the body is buried after a short grave-side ceremony. Otherwise the body is cremated or donated to a medical school.

But what could be called the standard U.S. funeral turns out to be the funeral of choice for only a minority of the rest of the human race. Other people, even other Christians, bury their dead with more elaborate and, to outsiders, even exotic rites.

How your survivors will dispose of your body will in all likelihood be determined by the religious faith you practiced during your life because funeral customs reflect the theological beliefs of a particular faith community.

For example, the Parsi people of India neither bury nor cremate their dead. Parsis, most of whom live in or near Bombay, follow the ancient religion of Zoroastrianism. Outside Bombay, Parsis erected seven Towers of Silence in which they perform their burial rites. When someone dies, six bearers dressed in white bring the corpse to one of the towers. The Towers of Silence have no roofs; within an hour, waiting vultures pick the body clean. A few days later the bearers return and cast the remaining bones into a pit. Parsis believe that their method of disposal avoids contaminating the soil, the water, and the air.

Out of the Ashes

The Parsis' millions of Hindu neighbors choose cremation as their usual burial practice. Hindus believe that as long as the physical body exists, the essence of the person will remain nearby; cremation allows the essence, or soul, of the person to continue its journey into another incarnation.

Hindus wash the body of the deceased and clothe it in a shroud decorated with flowers. They carry the body to a funeral pyre, where the nearest male relative lights the fire and walks around the burning body three times while reciting verses from Hindu sacred writings. Three days later someone collects and temporarily buries the ashes.

On the tenth day after the cremation, relatives deposit the ashes in the Ganges or some other sacred river. The funeral ceremony, called the *Shraddha,* is then held within 31 days of the cremation. Usually the deceased's son recites the prayers and the invocation of ancestors; that is one reason why every Hindu wants at least one son.

Prior to British rule in India, the practice of suttee was also common. Suttee is the act of a Hindu widow willingly being cremated on her husband's funeral pyre. Suttee was outlawed by the British in 1829, but occasionally widows still throw themselves into the flames.

Like the Hindus, the world's Buddhists, who live primarily in China, Japan, Sri Lanka, Myanmar, Vietnam, and Cambodia, usually choose cremation for disposing of a corpse. They believe cremation was favored by Buddha. A religious teacher may pray or recite mantras at the bedside of the dying person. These actions are believed to exert a wholesome effect on the next rebirth. Buddhists generally believe that the essence of a person remains in an intermediate state for no more than 49 days between death and rebirth.

While Hindus and Buddhists prescribe cremation, the world's 900 million Muslims forbid cremation. According to the Qu'ran, Muhammad taught that only Allah will use fire to punish the wicked.

If a Muslim is near death, someone is called in to read verses from the Qu'ran. After death, the body is ceremonially washed, clothed in three pieces of white cloth, and placed in a simple wooden coffin. Unless required by law, Muslims will not allow embalming. The body must be buried as soon as possible after death—usually within 24 hours. After a funeral service at a mosque or at the grave side, the body is removed from the coffin and buried with the head of the deceased turned toward Mecca. In some Muslim countries the women engage in loud wailing and lamentations during the burial.

Some Islamic grave sites are quite elaborate. The Mogul emperor Shah Jahan built the world-famous Taj Mahal as a mausoleum for his wife and himself. The Taj Mahal, which is one of the finest examples of Islamic architecture, was finished in 1654. It took 20,000 workers about 22 years to complete the project.

The Baha'i faith, which originated in Persia in the nineteenth century as an outgrowth of the Shi'ite branch of Islam, also forbids cremation and embalming and requires that the body not be transported more than an hour's journey from the place of death. Because Bahaism has no ordained clergy, the funeral may be conducted by any member of the family or the local assembly. All present at the funeral must stand during the recitation of the Prayer for the Dead composed by Baha'u'llah. Several million Baha'is live in Iran, India, the Middle East, and Africa; and an estimated 100,000 Baha'is live in the United States.

In Judaism, the faith of some 18 million people, the Old Testament only hints at belief in an afterlife; but later Jewish thought embraced beliefs in heaven, hell, resurrection, and final judgment. In general, Orthodox Jews accept the concept of a resurrection of the soul and the body while Conservative and Reform Jews prefer to speak only of the immortality of the soul.

Orthodox Judaism prescribes some of the most detailed funeral rites of any religion. As death approaches, family and friends must attend the dying person at all times. When death finally arrives, a son or the nearest relative closes the eyes and mouth of the deceased and binds the lower jaw before rigor mortis sets in. Relatives place the body on the floor and cover it with a sheet; they place a lighted candle near the head.

Judaism in its traditional form forbids embalming except where required by law. After a ritual washing, the body is covered with a white shroud and placed in a wooden coffin. At the funeral, mourners symbolize their grief by tearing a portion of an outer garment or wearing a torn black ribbon. The Orthodox discourage flowers and ostentation at the funeral.

The Jewish funeral service includes a reading of prayers and psalms, a eulogy, and the recitation of the Kaddish prayer for the dead in an Aramaic dialect. Like other Semitic people, Jews forbid cremation. Orthodox Jews observe a primary mourning period of seven days; Reform Jews reduce this period to three days. During the secondary yearlong mourning period, the Kaddish prayer is recited at every service in the synagogue.

Dearly Beloved

Christianity, the world's largest religion, carries over Judaism's respect for the body and firmly acknowledges resurrection, judgment, and eternal reward or punishment.

These Christian beliefs permeate the liturgy of a Catholic funeral. Older Catholics remember the typical funeral of the 1940s and '50s: the recitation of the rosary at the wake, the black vestments, the Latin prayers. They probably recall the *"Dies Irae,"* a thirteenth-century dirge and standard musical piece at Catholic funerals prior to the liturgical changes of the Second Vatican Council in the 1960s.

Nowadays, those attending a Catholic wake may still say the rosary, but often there is a scripture service instead. The priest's vestments are likely to be white or violet rather than black. Prayers tend to emphasize the hope of resurrection rather than the terrors of the final judgment.

As death approaches, the dying person or the family may request the sacrament of the Anointing of the Sick. Once called Last Rites or Extreme Unction, this sacrament is no longer restricted to those in imminent danger of death; it is regularly administered to the sick and the elderly as an instrument of healing as well as a preparation for death.

Sacred Remains

The Catholic Church raises no objections to embalming, flowers, or an open casket at a wake. At one time Catholics who wished to have a church funeral could not request cremation. In 1886 the Holy Office in Rome declared that "to introduce the practice (of cremation) into Christian society was un-Christian and Masonic in motivation." Today Catholics may choose the option of cremation over burial "unless," according to canon law, "it has been chosen for reasons that are contrary to Christian teaching."

The church used to deny an ecclesiastical burial to suicides, those killed in duels, Freemasons, and members of the ladies' auxiliaries of Masonic lodges. Today the church refuses burial only to "notorious apostates, heretics, and schismatics" and to "sinners whose funerals in church would scandalize the faithful." Catholics who join Masonic lodges no longer incur excommunication, although they still may not receive Communion.

The church has also softened its position on denying funeral rites to suicides. Modern pastoral practice is based on the understanding that anyone finding life so unbearable as to end it voluntarily probably was acting with a greatly diminished free will.

For Roman Catholics, the Mass is the principal celebration of the Christian funeral; and mourners are invited to receive the Eucharist. Most Protestant denominations, except for some Lutherans and Episcopalians, do not incorporate a communion service into their funeral liturgies. The Catholic ritual employs candles, holy water, and incense but does not allow non-Christian symbols, such as national flags or lodge emblems, to rest on or near the coffin during the funeral. In many parishes the pastor encourages the family members to participate where appropriate as eucharistic ministers, lectors, and singers. In the absence of a priest, a deacon can conduct the funeral service but cannot preside at a Mass of Christian burial.

The revised funeral liturgy of the Catholic Church is meant to stress God's faithfulness to people rather than God's wrath toward sinners. The Catholic Church declares that certain men and women who have lived lives of such heroic virtue that they are indeed in heaven are to be known as saints. The church also teaches that hell is a reality but has never declared that anyone, even Judas, has actually been condemned to eternal punishment.

Unlike Protestant churches, Catholicism also teaches the existence of a temporary state of purification, known as purgatory, for those destined for heaven but not yet totally free from the effects of sin and selfishness. At one time some theologians suggested that unbaptized babies spent eternity in a place of natural happiness known as limbo, but this was never church doctrine and is taught by few theologians today.

At the committal service at the grave site, the priest blesses the grave and leads the mourners in the Our Father and other prayers for the repose of the soul of the departed and the comfort of the survivors. Catholics are usually buried in Catholic cemeteries or in separate sections of other cemeteries.

Dressed for the Occasion

The funeral rite in the Church of Jesus Christ of Latter-day Saints, which is the fastest growing church in the United States, resembles the standard Protestant funeral in some ways; but one significant difference is in the attire of the deceased. Devout Mormons receive the garments of the holy priesthood during their endowment ceremonies when they are teens. These sacred undergarments are to be worn day and night throughout a Mormon's life. When a Mormon dies, his or her body is then attired in these garments in the casket. At one time Mormon sacred garments resembled long johns, but they now have short sleeves and are cut off at the knees. The garments are embroidered with symbols on the right and left breasts, the navel, and the right knee, which remind the wearer of the oaths taken in the secret temple rites.

Mormons who reached their endowments are also clothed in their temple garb at death. For the men, this includes white pants, white shirt, tie, belt, socks, slippers, and an apron. Just before the casket is closed for the last time, a fellow Mormon puts a white temple cap on the corpse. If the deceased is a woman, a high priest puts a temple veil over her face; Mormons believe the veil will remain there until her husband calls her from the grave to resurrection. Mormons forbid cremation.

Freemasons conduct their own funeral rites for a deceased brother, and they insist that their ceremony be the last one before burial or cremation. Thus, a separate religious ceremony often precedes the Masonic rites. Lodge members will bury a fellow Mason only if he is a member in good standing and he or his family has requested the service.

All the pallbearers at the Masonic services must be Masons, and each wears a white apron, white gloves, a black band around his left arm, and a sprig of evergreen or acacia in his left lapel. The corpse is clothed in a white apron and other lodge regalia.

Masonry accepts the idea of the immortality of the soul but makes no reference to the Christian understanding of the resurrection of the soul and the body. The Masonic service speaks of the soul's translation from this life to that "perfect, glorious, and celestial lodge above" presided over by the Grand Architect of the Universe.

In Memoriam

Other small religious groups have much less elaborate and formalized funeral services. Christian Scientists, for example, have no set funeral rite because their founder, Mary Baker Eddy, denied the reality of death. The family of a deceased Christian Scientist often invites a Christian Science reader to present a brief service at the funeral home.

Unitarian-Universalists enroll many members who would identify themselves as agnostics or atheists. Therefore, in a typical Unitarian-Universalist funeral service, the minister and loved ones say little about any afterlife but extol the virtues and good works of the deceased.

Salvation Army officers are buried in their military uniforms, and a Salvationist blows taps at the grave side. In contrast, the Church of Christ, which allows no instrumental music during Sunday worship, allows no organs, pianos, or other musical instruments at its funerals.

The great variety of funeral customs through the ages and around the world would be hard to catalog. The Egyptians mummified the bodies of royalty and erected pyramids as colossal monuments. Viking kings were set adrift on blazing boats. The Soviets mummified the body of Lenin, and his tomb and corpse have become major icons in the U.S.S.R.

In a funeral home in California, a drive-up window is provided for mourners so that they can view the remains and sign the book without leaving their cars. In Japan, where land is scarce, one enterprising cemetery owner offers a time-share plan whereby corpses are displaced after brief burial to make room for the next occupant. Complying with the wishes of the deceased, one U.S. undertaker once dressed a corpse in pajamas and positioned it under the blankets in a bedroom for viewing.

The reverence and rituals surrounding the disposal of the body reflect religious traditions going back thousands of years as well as up-to-the-minute fads. All of the elements of the burial—the preparation of the body, the garments or shroud, the prayers, the method of disposal, the place and time of burial—become sacred acts by which a particular community of believers bids at least a temporary farewell to one of its own.

Critical Thinking

1. What is the connection between one's religious faith and how one's body is disposed of?

2. From a Hindu perspective, why is cremation necessary?

3. How are Jews and Muslims similar in how they treat the body before final dispostion?

From *U.S. Catholic*, September 1990, pp. 29–35. Copyright © 1990 by Claretian Publications. Reprinted by permission.

Building My Father's Coffin

My dad spent his life writing books. His final, impractical request gave us a story like no other.

This is an excerpt from John Manchester's upcoming memoir. It appeared on his Open Salon blog.

JOHN MANCHESTER

In his last years my father, the writer William Manchester, told me, "When I die. I want you children to build my coffin." He'd gotten the idea sometime in the '70s, when a Wesleyan chemistry professor died, and his sons, following a Catalan custom, spent the night before the funeral building his coffin in their basement. My dad explained, "It will give you and your sisters a focus for your grief."

I nodded and held my tongue. It was pointless to explain what he already knew: My sisters had never done any carpentry, and my own modest skills had diminished since I'd become afflicted by carpal tunnel syndrome.

It was a focus, all right, not for grief but for worry. How were we going to build it? In the last spring of his life, as he declined, I prayed he would just forget about it.

But the morning after he died I found a list of instructions on his desk. No. 5: "My body is to be placed in a plain pine box. I would like my children to make the box."

Fuck. We really had to build it.

Down at the funeral home, I explained to the director how we planned to build the coffin. I felt awkward asking, but there were questions only he could answer. What were the interior measurements needed to accommodate the body? He told me, and I wrote them down. What about securing the lid? He would screw it onto the box. Good. As we spoke, I remembered my father telling me how funeral homes make their money selling fancy coffins, and wondered why this guy wasn't trying to sell me one. But then he told me about one homemade coffin he'd encountered. "The family made it years ahead of time, and by the time the person died, it had warped." He gave me a look: *You don't want to know the details.* There was his sales pitch, and I was tempted to go with it.

I had also heard a story about a funeral where the homemade coffin disintegrated as the pallbearers carried it, and the body fell out. My worst fear. That's what made me determined that ours would be the sturdiest, most reliable casket since Napoleon's seven-layered sarcophagus beneath the Invalides in Paris.

How were we going to build it? I called my older son, Shawn, who was an engineering major. He was already far more competent with his hands than my father, sisters and me combined. Home for the weekend from college, he devised a plan for the box. I vetted it with a friend of mine, a master cabinetmaker. It seemed up to snuff, but we still didn't have tools.

I called my sister, who was living in Florida. She was busy working and would have to scramble just to get to the funeral. So she'd join us in the coffin-building only in spirit.

I called my other sister, who was in Connecticut for the summer, and discussed the coffin. She explained that her mother-in-law's partner, David, would be happy to help us. "He's a professional. He teaches carpentry. He has a fully equipped workshop in his garage."

David invited us down to his place in Connecticut the following Saturday. It was only a two-hour drive from our house in Massachusetts. By the time we got off the phone, I felt relieved: We had Shawn's plan, good tools, and David to help us.

My wife, Judy, and I pulled into the driveway. David and Shawn stood in front of the garage around a couple of sawhorses with some boards on top.

Judy said, "Thank God they've already started."

I agreed.

It was one of those perfect days, the kind that comes only once or twice a year in New England. I smiled, remembering my father telling me, "One of the crucial things in my writing is my use of irony." He would have enjoyed the irony of this task on this day. It was in striking contrast to what I'd pictured all those years—us building the coffin in my father's gloomy basement storeroom.

For years I had a vision of me and my sisters making the coffin on top of our sad, warped Ping-Pong table, up to our waists in the tens of thousands of pages of his papers that filled the room.

161

I heard the bang of a hammer, looked over at Shawn and David around the sawhorse, and remembered why I was here. David looked at my worried face, rubbed his hands together, and gave me a smile that said, "This is going to be fun." His only question was how to do it.

He looked at Shawn's plan, nodded his head, then handed it back and said diplomatically, "Let's make it up as we go along." He looked down at the boards on the sawhorse, frowning, then turned and looked at the side of the garage, pointing: "It's a door." He added, "I know how to make a door."

He thought another moment, then nodded. "The sides and top are also doors." Following the measurements given by the funeral director, he cut the assembly to size. We had the first door. The rest was easy: four more doors for the sides and one for the top, and we'd be done.

I lost myself in the rhythm of making it. When we were done screwing the sides to the bottom, I asked, "Are you sure it's strong enough?" David picked up a length of strapping and said, "I think it's fine, but just for you we'll box all the edges with this." When that was done even I was pretty confident that it would hold my father, and the strapping lent it a kind of elegance.

After lunch David looked at the box and shook his head. "It's going to be hard to carry, hard to keep hold of, with us crowded in three to a side." I saw us pallbearers at the funeral dropping it and gave David a look. He said, "We'll make rails." We went to the hardware store and got two 1-inch dowels and lag bolts.

By this point we were both starting to feel pride in our work. David said, "Let's stain it."

I said, "No, it's supposed to be a plain pine box. Besides, if we leave it bare, people at the funeral will realize we built it." He nodded.

My sister, who had watched from the porch, put in a symbolic screw.

We stood around it, admiring its simple elegance. Still, I had to ask David, "Are you sure it's strong enough?"

He said, "Only one way to find out—take it for a test drive."

Judy bravely volunteered. We lifted it to the ground and she climbed in. Someone said, "Maybe we should put the lid on."

She said, "No, this is fine." We hauled her around the yard. The neighbors, out working in their yards, put down their clippers and rakes and gawked. Why not? How often did they, or anyone else for that matter, get an opportunity to watch their neighbors building a coffin on a sunny Saturday?

As we carried her, Judy laughed along with the rest of us. What else to do? Later I asked her, "How did it feel?"

"It scared the hell out of me."

We finished our tour of the lawn and let her out. The coffin was rock solid. We congratulated ourselves: "Look at that thing!" "It only took five hours!" I thanked Shawn and David.

As Judy and I pulled out of the driveway, I gave the coffin a last look and felt the excitement of the day dissolve. Sometime later that evening the funeral director would discreetly steal it away, then place my father's body in it. The next time we would see it would be at the funeral.

He would not be buried in it. His instructions stated that following the funeral, he would be cremated. It felt weird to have gone to all that trouble, just to have the coffin burned up a few days later. But its purpose was never practical. My father was a storyteller at heart, and this made a good one. It even had poetic potential: something about all those trees sacrificed to make all his books offering up a few boards for his last story.

Critical Thinking

1. Why would a father ask his children to build his coffin?
2. What is the function of becoming involved in funeral planning and implantation?
3. Explain the following quote: "It will give you and your sisters a focus for your grief."

JOHN MANCHESTER'S music has been heard worldwide for the last 25 years on TV, radio and the Internet. You can also hear it on his MySpace page and at Manchester Music Library.

Dealing with the Dead

JENNIFER EGAN

In 1980, when my mother co-owned an art gallery in San Francisco, she and her assistant were robbed at gunpoint by two jittery escaped convicts, who mistook the gallery for a cash business and openly discussed shooting them when the cash failed to materialize. The ordeal ended without serious harm (thanks to the miraculous arrival of a delivery man, who frightened the convicts away), but my mother never again wanted to wear the skirt she'd had on that day: a long black wraparound with a geometric pattern of magenta flowers and thick green stems. I appropriated the skirt, cut it short, took it with me to college, and wore it through my twenties. I never forgot its awful history; on the contrary, that history sharpened my pleasure in wearing it. The very act of tying the skirt around my waist felt restorative—as if, by paving over my mother's horrific experience with ordinary life, I were repairing an imbalance.

I was near the end of my twenties before I lost someone I was close to: my mother's mother, whose three-tiered necklace of small fake pearls I inherited. I wore that necklace constantly, even after it became clear that I would destroy it unless I put it aside. I had the same impulse when my father died, six years later, and, five years after that, my stepfather. From my father's closet, I borrowed a navy-blue wool V-neck, from my stepfather's a gray-and-burgundy argyle sweater. For years, on any given winter day I wore one of those two sweaters, partly for the obvious reason—wearing the garment of a person I loved was like being wrapped in a protective force field. But what drove me was also a kind of defiance. When the clock stops on a life, all things emanating from it become precious, finite, and cordoned off for preservation. Each aspect of the dead person is removed from the flux of the everyday, which, of course, is where we miss him most. The quarantine around death makes it feel unlucky and wrong—a freakish incursion—and the dead, thus quarantined, come to seem more dead than they already are. Those sweaters did more than remind me of their original owners; the sheer ordinariness of working in them, spilling on them, taking them off at the end of the day, and tossing them on the floor helped to diffuse that dour hush. Borrowing from the dead is a way of keeping them engaged in life's daily transactions—in other words, alive.

When my father-in-law, whom I adored, died a year and a half ago, I began with almost unseemly speed to lobby my mother-in-law for one of his sweaters. She gave me a few to choose from, two of which I kept: a scratchy green sweater that's too warm for everyday wear, and a vest, ginger-colored and wonderfully roomy, just as my stepfather's argyle sweater was for years, until I accidentally put it in the dryer and it shrank to fit me exactly. I'd forgotten, in the years since my father and stepfather died, what it was like to first wear their clothing. Starting fresh with my father-in-law's vest brought it back: the garment smelled so much like him—coffee, pepper, burning wood—that when I held it under my children's noses and asked, "Who does this smell like?" they both cried, startled, "Grandpa!"

After a few weeks, the vest went from smelling like Grandpa to smelling like me, until the latter fact was so pronounced that I had it dry-cleaned, at which point it became, in some sense, mine. But always on loan, to such an extent that I think Joe's vest each time I pull it from my closet, and I find the notion so heartening that I recently marvelled to my husband at his reluctance to avail himself of this obvious way to feel connected with—surrounded by—his father, whom I know he misses. "There are more sweaters!" I exhorted him. "I only took two." My husband paused a moment before replying, disconcerted, "What can I say? I don't have the impulse to wear them. I think about him constantly, but it's not bound up in physical things."

Of course, a loan from someone dead is—like any loan—temporary. It can't be renewed, and, eventually, the physical object begins to wear down. My grandmother's necklace broke on an East Village corner; the cheap plastic pearls went flying into the street. I gathered up as many as I could and sealed them in an envelope, which I've since lost track of. My father's and stepfather's sweaters are beginning to look threadbare, despite multiple repairs. This reminds me of how long it's been since I saw their owners. I find it ever harder to remember how it felt to be in a room with either of those men, but I know how their sweaters feel against my skin. I plan to wear them until they unravel into shreds.

Critical Thinking

1. How can wearing something associated with the dead facilitate grieving?

2. Explain the following quotation: "Of course, a loan from someone dead is—like any loan—temporary."

3. Explain the following quotation: "My father's and stepfather's sweaters are beginning to look threadbare, despite multiple repairs. This reminds me of how long it's been since I saw their owners. I find it ever harder to remember how it felt to be in a room with either of those men, but I know how their sweaters feel against my skin. I plan to wear them until they unravel into shreds."

Source: New Yorker; 10/11/2010, Vol. 86 Issue 31, p68–68.

UNIT 8

Bereavement

Unit Selections

Learning Outcomes

After reading this unit, you should be able to:

- Understand normal feelings and behaviors related to the grieving process.
- Understand the concept of disenfranchised grief and how grieving can become disenfranchised.
- Become a critical reader of research related to the grieving process.
- Understand how changes in the social environment will have effects on the bereavement process.
- Understand the limitation of stages in describing "normal" grieving.
- Understand high-risk factors that can predispose an individual to complicated grieving.
- Understand ways in which one can unburden parents who have lost a child.
- Understand ways in which one can assist children who are experiencing trauma in grieving.

Student Website

www.mhhe.com/cls

Internet References

After Death Communication Research Foundation
www.adcrf.org
Thanatolinks
http://netsociology.tripod.com/thanalinks.htm
Hospice: A Guide to Grief Bereavement, Mourning, and Grief
www.hospicenet.org/html/grief_guide.html
Growth House
www.growthhouse.org
Grief in a Family Context
www.indiana.edu/~famlygrf/sitemap.html
Directory of Grief, Loss and Bereavement: Support Groups
www.dmoz.org/Health/Mental_Health/Grief,_Loss_and_Bereavement/
Support_Groups
Bereaved Families of Ontario
www.bereavedfamilies.net
Grief Net
http://rivendell.org
Child Bereavement Charity
www.childbereavement.org.uk/home_page
Core Principles for Helping Grieving Children
www2.cfalls.org/hs_pdf/core_principles_for_helping_grieving_children.pdf

The Compassionate Friends
www.compassionatefriends.org/resources/links.aspx
American Academy of Child & Adolescent Psychiatry
http://aacap.org/page.ww?name=Children+and+Grief&section=Facts+for+Families
Children with AIDS Project
www.aidskids.org
Rites of Passage: Our Fathers Die
www.menweb.org/daddie.htm
Motherloss
www.freewebs.com/motherloss/front.htm
Widow Net
www.widownet.org
Web Healing
www.webhealing.com
Dearly Departed
http://dearlydprtd.com
In Memory of Pets
www.In-Memory-Of-Pets.Com
Burial Insurance
www.burialinsurance.org

In American society many act as if the process of bereavement is completed with the culmination of public mourning related to the funeral or memorial service and the final disposition of the dead. For those in the process of grieving, the end of public mourning only serves to make the bereavement process a more individualized, subjective, and private experience. Private mourning of loss for most people, while more intense at its beginning, continues throughout their lifetime. The nature and intensity of this experience is influenced by the relationship of the mourner to the deceased, the age of the mourner, and the social context in which bereavement takes place.

This unit on bereavement begins with two general articles on the bereavement process. The first article, by Michael Leming and George Dickinson, describes and discusses the active coping strategies related to the bereavement process and the four tasks of bereavement. The second and third articles by Kenneth Doka provide an alternative perspective on the understanding of the bereavement process. The next two articles discuss much of the misinformation most people assume about grieving. The final articles are focused upon bereavement and coping strategies employed by a special population of grievers.

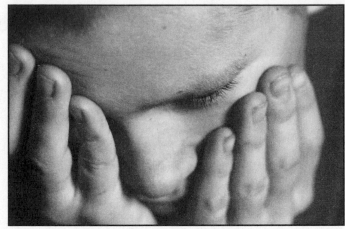

© Ingram Publishing

The Grieving Process

MICHAEL R. LEMING AND GEORGE E. DICKINSON

Grief is a very powerful emotion that is often triggered or stimulated by death. Thomas Attig makes an important distinction between grief and the grieving process. Although grief is an emotion that engenders feelings of helplessness and passivity, the process of grieving is a more complex coping process that presents challenges and opportunities for the griever and requires energy to be invested, tasks to be undertaken, and choices to be made (Attig, 1991).

Most people believe that grieving is a diseaselike and debilitating process that renders the individual passive and helpless. According to Attig (1991, p. 389):

> It is misleading and dangerous to mistake grief for the whole of the experience of the bereaved. It is misleading because the experience is far more complex, entailing diverse emotional, physical, intellectual, spiritual, and social impacts. It is dangerous because it is precisely this aspect of the experience of the bereaved that is potentially the most frustrating and debilitating.

Death ascribes to the griever a passive social position in the bereavement role. Grief is an emotion over which the individual has no control. However, understanding that grieving is an active coping process can restore to the griever a sense of autonomy in which the process is permeated with choice and there are many areas over which the griever does have some control.

Coping with Grief

The grieving process, like the dying process, is essentially a series of behaviors and attitudes related to coping with the stressful situation of a change in the status of a relationship. Many individuals have attempted to understand coping with dying as a series of universal, mutually exclusive, and linear stages. Not all people, however, will progress through the stages in the same manner.

Seven behaviors and feelings that are part of the coping process are identified by Robert Kavanaugh (1972): shock and denial, disorganization, volatile emotions, guilt, loss and loneliness, relief, and reestablishment. It is not difficult to see similarities between these behaviors and Kübler-Ross's five stages (denial, anger, bargaining, depression, and acceptance) of the dying process. According to Kavanaugh (1972, p. 23), "these seven stages do not subscribe to the logic of the head as much as to the irrational tugs of the heart—the logic of need and permission."

Shock and Denial

Even when a significant other is expected to die, at the time of death there is often a sense in which the death is not real. For most of us our first response is, "No, this can't be true." With time, our experience of shock diminishes, but we find new ways to deny the reality of death.

Some believe that denial is dysfunctional behavior for those in bereavement. However, denial not only is a common experience among the newly bereaved but also serves positive functions in the process of adaptation. The main function of denial is to provide the bereaved with a "temporary safe place" from the ugly realities of a social world that offers only loneliness and pain.

With time, the meaning of loss tends to expand, and it may be impossible for one to deal with all of the social meanings of death at once. For example, if a man's wife dies, not only does he lose his spouse, but also his best friend, his sexual partner, the mother of his children, a source of income, and so on. Denial can protect an individual from some of the magnitude of this social loss, which may be unbearable at times. With denial, one can work through different aspects of loss over time.

Disorganization

Disorganization is the stage in the bereavement process in which one may feel totally out of touch with the reality of everyday life. Some go through the 2- to 3-day time period just before the funeral as if on "automatic pilot" or "in a daze." Nothing normal "makes sense," and they may feel that life has no inherent meaning. For some, death is perceived as preferable to life, which appears to be devoid of meaning.

This emotional response is also a normal experience for the newly bereaved. Confusion is normal for those whose social world has been disorganized through death. When Michael Leming's father died, his mother lost not only all of those things that one loses with a death of a spouse, but also her caregiving role—a social role and master status that had defined her identity in the 5 years that her husband lived with cancer. It is only natural to experience confusion and social disorganization when one's social identity has been destroyed.

Volatile Reactions

Whenever one's identity and social order face the possibility of destruction, there is a natural tendency to feel angry, frustrated, helpless, and/or hurt. The volatile reactions of terror, hatred, resentment, and jealousy are often experienced as emotional manifestations of these feelings. Grieving humans are sometimes more successful at masking their feelings in socially acceptable behaviors than other animals, whose instincts cause them to go into a fit of rage when their order is threatened by external forces. However apparently dissimilar, the internal emotional experience is similar.

In working with bereaved persons over the past 20 years, Michael Lemming has observed that the following become objects of volatile grief reactions: God, medical personnel, funeral directors, other family members, in-laws, friends who have not experienced death in their families, and/or even the person who has died. Mild-mannered individuals may become raging and resentful persons when grieving. Some of these people have experienced physical symptoms such as migraine headaches, ulcers, neuropathy, and colitis as a result of living with these intense emotions.

The expression of anger seems more natural for men than expressing other feelings (Golden, 2000). Expressing anger requires taking a stand. This is quite different from the mechanics of sadness, where an open and vulnerable stance is more common. Men may find their grief through anger. Rage may suddenly become tears, as deep feelings trigger other deep feelings. This process is reversed with women, notes Golden. Many times a woman will be in tears, crying and crying, and state that she is angry.

As noted earlier, a person's anger during grief can range from being angry with the person who died to being angry with God, and all points in between. Golden's mentor, Father William Wendt, shared the story of his visits with a widow and his working with her on her grief. He noticed that many times when he arrived she was driving her car up and down the driveway. One day he asked her what she was doing. She proceeded to tell him that she had a ritual she used in dealing with her grief. She would come home, go to the living room, and get her recently deceased husband's ashes out of the urn on the mantle. She would take a very small amount and place them on the driveway. She then said, "It helps me to run over the son of a bitch every day." He concluded the story by saying, "Now that is good grief." It was "good" grief because it was this woman's way of connecting to and expressing the anger component of her grief.

Guilt

Guilt is similar to the emotional reactions discussed earlier. Guilt is anger and resentment turned in on oneself and often results in self-deprecation and depression. It typically manifests itself in statements like "If only I had . . . ," "I should have . . . ," "I could have done it differently . . . ," and "Maybe I did the wrong thing." Guilt is a normal part of the bereavement process.

From a sociological perspective, guilt can become a social mechanism to resolve the **dissonance** that people feel when unable to explain why someone else's loved one has died. Rather than view death as something that can happen at any time to anyone, people can **blame the victim** of bereavement and believe that the victim of bereavement was in some way responsible for the death—"If the individual had been a better parent, the child might not have been hit by the car," or "If I had been married to that person, I might also have committed suicide," or "No wonder that individual died of a heart attack, the spouse's cooking would give anyone high cholesterol." Therefore, bereaved persons are sometimes encouraged to feel guilt because they are subtly sanctioned by others' reactions.

Loss and Loneliness

Feelings of loss and loneliness creep in as denial subsides. The full experience of the loss does not hit all at once. It becomes more evident as bereaved individuals resume a social life without their loved one. They realize how much they needed and depended upon their significant other. Social situations in which we expected them always to be present seem different now that they are gone. Holiday celebrations are also diminished by their absence. In fact, for some, most of life takes on a "something's missing" feeling. This feeling was captured in the 1960s love song "End of the World."

> Why does the world go on turning?
>
> Why must the sea rush to shore?
>
> Don't they know it's the end of the world
>
> Cause you don't love me anymore?

Loss and loneliness are often transformed into depression and sadness, fed by feelings of self-pity. According to Kavanaugh (1972, p. 118), this effect is magnified by the fact that the dead loved one grows out of focus in memory—"an elf becomes a giant, a sinner becomes a saint because the grieving heart needs giants and saints to fill an expanding void." Even a formerly undesirable spouse, such as an alcoholic, is missed in a way that few can understand unless their own hearts are involved. This is a time in the grieving process when anybody is better than nobody, and being alone only adds to the curse of loss and loneliness (Kavanaugh, 1972).

Those who try to escape this experience will either turn to denial in an attempt to reject their feelings of loss or try to find surrogates—new friends at a bar, a quick remarriage, or a new pet. This escape can never be permanent, however, because loss and loneliness are a necessary part of the bereavement experience. According to Kavanaugh (1972, p. 119), the "ultimate goal in conquering loneliness" is to build a new independence or to find a new and equally viable relationship.

Relief

The experience of relief in the midst of the bereavement process may seem odd for some and add to their feelings of guilt. Michael Leming observed a friend's relief 6 months after her husband died. This older friend was the wife of a minister, and her whole life before he died was his ministry. With time, as she built a new world of social involvements and relationships of which he was not a part, she discovered a new independent person in herself whom she perceived was a better person than she had ever before been.

Relief can give rise to feelings of guilt. However, according to Kavanaugh (1972, p. 121): "The feeling of relief does not imply any criticism for the love we lost. Instead, it is a reflection of our need for ever deeper love, our quest for someone or something always better, our search for the infinite, that best and perfect love religious people name as God."

Reestablishment

As one moves toward reestablishment of a life without the deceased, it is obvious that the process involves extensive adjustment and time, especially if the relationship was meaningful. It is likely that one may have feelings of loneliness, guilt, and disorganization at the same time and that just when one may experience a sense of relief, something will happen to trigger a denial of the death.

What facilitates bereavement and adjustment is fully experiencing each of these feelings as normal and realizing that it is hope (holding the grieving person together in fantasy at first) that will provide the promise of a new life filled with order, purpose, and meaning.

Reestablishment occurs gradually, and often we realize it has been achieved long after it has occurred. In some ways it is similar to Dorothy's realization at the end of *The Wizard of Oz*—she had always possessed the magic that could return her to Kansas. And, like Dorothy, we have to experience our loss before we really appreciate the joy of investing our lives again in new relationships.

Four Tasks of Mourning

In 1982 J. William Worden published *Grief Counseling and Grief Therapy*, which summarized the research conclusions of a National Institutes of Health study called the Omega Project (occasionally referred to as the Harvard Bereavement Study). Two of the more significant findings of this research, displaying the active nature of the grieving process, are that mourning is necessary for all persons who have experienced a loss through death and that four tasks of mourning must be accomplished before mourning can be completed and reestablishment can take place.

According to Worden (1982), unfinished grief tasks can impair further growth and development of the individual. Furthermore, the necessity of these tasks suggests that those in bereavement must attend to "grief work" because successful grief resolution is not automatic, as Kavanaugh's (1972) stages might imply. Each bereaved person must accomplish four necessary tasks: (1) accept the reality of the loss, (2) experience the pain of grief, (3) adjust to an environment in which the deceased person is missing, and (4) withdraw emotional energy and reinvest it in another relationship (Worden, 1982).

Accept the Reality of the Loss

Especially in situations when death is unexpected and/or the deceased lived far away, it is difficult to conceptualize the reality of the loss. The first task of mourning is to overcome the natural denial response and realize that the person is dead and will not return.

Bereaved persons can facilitate the actualization of death in many ways. The traditional ways are to view the body, attend the funeral and committal services, and visit the place of final disposition. The following is a partial list of additional activities that can assist in making death real for grieving persons.

1. View the body at the place of death before preparation by the funeral director.
2. Talk about the deceased person and the circumstances surrounding the death.
3. View photographs and personal effects of the deceased person.
4. Distribute the possessions of the deceased person among relatives and friends.

Experience the Pain of Grief

Part of coming to grips with the reality of death is experiencing the emotional and physical pain caused by the loss. Many people in the denial stage of grieving attempt to avoid pain by choosing to reject the emotions and feelings that they are experiencing. As discussed by Erich Lindemann (1944), some do this by avoiding places and circumstances that remind them of the deceased. Michael Leming knows one widow who quit playing golf and quit eating at a particular restaurant because these were activities that she had enjoyed with her husband. Another widow found it extremely painful to be with her dead husband's twin, even though he and her sister-in-law were her most supportive friends.

Worden (1982, pp. 13–14) cites the following case study to illustrate the performance of this task of mourning:

One young woman minimized her loss by believing her brother was out of his dark place and into a better place after his suicide. This might not have been true, but it kept her from feeling her intense anger at him for leaving her. In treatment, when she first allowed herself to feel anger, she said, "I'm angry with his behavior and not him!" Finally she was able to acknowledge this anger directly.

The problem with the avoidance strategy is that people cannot escape the pain associated with mourning. According to Bowlby (cited by Worden, 1982, p. 14), "Sooner or later, some of those who avoid all conscious grieving, break down—usually with some form of depression." Tears can afford cleansing for wounds created by loss, and fully experiencing the pain ultimately provides wonderful relief to those who suffer while eliminating long-term chronic grief.

Assume New Social Roles

The third task, practical in nature, requires the griever to take on some of the social roles performed by the deceased person or to find others who will. According to Worden (1982), to abort this task is to become helpless by refusing to develop the skills necessary in daily living and by ultimately withdrawing from life.

An acquaintance of Michael Leming's refused to adjust to the social environment in which she found herself after the death of her husband. He was her business partner, as well as her best and only friend. After 30 years of marriage, they had no children, and she had no close relatives. She had never learned to drive a car. Her entire social world had been controlled by her former husband. Three weeks after his funeral she went into the basement and committed suicide.

The alternative to withdrawing is assuming new social roles by taking on additional responsibilities. Extended families who always gathered at Grandma's house for Thanksgiving will be tempted to have a number of small Thanksgiving dinners at different places after her death. The members of this family may believe that "no one can take Grandma's place." Although this may be true, members of the extended family will grieve better if someone else is willing to do Grandma's work, enabling the entire family to come together for Thanksgiving. Not to do so will cause double pain—the family will not gather, and Grandma will still be missed.

Reinvest in New Relationships

The final task of mourning is a difficult one for many because they feel disloyal or unfaithful in withdrawing emotional energy from their dead loved one. One of Michael Leming's family members once said that she could never love another man after her husband died. His twice-widowed aunt responded, "I once felt like that, but I now consider myself to be fortunate to have been married to two of the best men in the world."

Other people find themselves unable to reinvest in new relationships because they are unwilling to experience again the pain caused by loss. The quotation from John Brantner at the beginning of this chapter provides perspective on this problem:

"Only people who avoid love can avoid grief. The point is to learn from it and remain vulnerable to love."

However, those who are able to withdraw emotional energy and reinvest it in other relationships find the possibility of a newly established social life. Kavanaugh (1972, pp. 122–123) depicts this situation well with the following description:

At this point fantasies fade into constructive efforts to reach out and build anew. The phone is answered more quickly, the door as well, and meetings seem important, invitations are treasured and any social gathering becomes an opportunity rather than a curse. Mementos of the past are put away for occasional family gatherings. New clothes and new places promise dreams instead of only fears. Old friends are important for encouragement and permission to rebuild one's life. New friends can offer realistic opportunities for coming out from under the grieving mantle. With newly acquired friends, one is not a widow, widower, or survivor—just a person. Life begins again at the point of new friendships. All the rest is of yesterday, buried, unimportant to the now and tomorrow.

Critical Thinking

1. Describe the seven behaviors and feelings that are part of coping with grief and loss.

2. What are the four tasks of mourning and how can the loss of closure relative to these tasks lead to impaired grieving?

3. How can relief and reinvestment in new relationships be important in normal grieving?

Disenfranchised Grief

KENNETH J. DOKA

Introduction

Ever since the publication of Lindemann's classic article, "Symptomatology and Management of Acute Grief," the literature on the nature of grief and bereavement has been growing. In the few decades following this seminal study, there have been comprehensive studies of grief reactions, detailed descriptions of atypical manifestations of grief, theoretical and clinical treatments of grief reactions, and considerable research considering the myriad variables that affect grief. But most of this literature has concentrated on grief reactions in socially recognized and sanctioned roles: those of the parent, spouse, or child.

There are circumstances, however, in which a person experiences a sense of loss but does not have a socially recognized right, role, or capacity to grieve. In these cases, the grief is disenfranchised. The person suffers a loss but has little or no opportunity to mourn publicly.

Up until now, there has been little research touching directly on the phenomenon of disenfranchised grief. In her comprehensive review of grief reactions, Raphael notes the phenomenon:

> There may be other dyadic partnership relationships in adult life that show patterns similar to the conjugal ones, among them, the young couple intensely, even secretly, in love; the defacto relationships; the extramarital relationship; and the homosexual couple. . . . Less intimate partnerships of close friends, working mates, and business associates, may have similar patterns of grief and mourning.

Focusing on the issues, reactions, and problems in particular populations, a number of studies have noted special difficulties that these populations have in grieving. For example, Kelly and Kimmel, in studies of aging homosexuals, have discussed the unique problems of grief in such relationships. Similarly, studies of the reactions of significant others of AIDS victims have considered bereavement. Other studies have considered the special problems of unacknowledged grief in prenatal death, [the death of] ex-spouses, therapists' reactions to a client's suicide, and pet loss. Finally, studies of families of Alzheimer's victims and mentally retarded adults also have noted distinct difficulties of these populations in encountering varied losses which are often unrecognized by others.

Others have tried to draw parallels between related unacknowledged losses. For example, in a personal account, Horn compared her loss of a heterosexual lover with a friend's loss of a homosexual partner. Doka discussed the particular problems of loss in nontraditional relationships, such as extramarital affairs, homosexual relationships, and cohabiting couples.

This article attempts to integrate the literature on such losses in order to explore the phenomenon of disenfranchised grief. It will consider both the nature of disenfranchised grief and its central paradoxical problem: the very nature of this type of grief exacerbates the problems of grief, but the usual sources of support may not be available or helpful.

The Nature of Disenfranchised Grief

Disenfranchised grief can be defined as the grief that persons experience when they incur a loss that is not or cannot be openly acknowledged, publicly mourned, or socially supported. The concept of disenfranchised grief recognizes that societies have sets of norms—in effect, "grieving rules"—that attempt to specify who, when, where, how, how long, and for whom people should grieve. These grieving rules may be codified in personnel policies. For example, a worker may be allowed a week off for the death of a spouse or child, three days for the loss of a parent or sibling. Such policies reflect the fact that each society defines who has a legitimate right to grieve, and these definitions of right correspond to relationships, primarily familial, that are socially recognized and sanctioned. In any given society these grieving rules may not correspond to the nature of attachments, the sense of loss, or the feelings of survivors. Hence the grief of these survivors is disenfranchised. In our society, this may occur for three reasons.

1. The Relationship Is Not Recognized

In our society, most attention is placed on kin-based relationships and roles. Grief may be disenfranchised in those situations in which the relationship between the bereaved and deceased is not based on recognizable kin ties. Here the closeness of other non-kin relationships may simply not be understood or appreciated. For example, Folta and Deck noted, "While all of these studies tell us that grief is a normal phenomenon, the intensity of which corresponds to the closeness of the relationship, they fail to take this (i.e., friendship) into account. The underlying assumption is that closeness of relationship exists only among spouses and/or immediate kin." The roles of lovers, friends, neighbors, foster parents, colleagues, in-laws, stepparents and stepchildren, caregivers, counselors, co-workers, and roommates (for example, in nursing homes) may be long-lasting and intensely interactive, but even though these relationships are recognized, mourners may not have full opportunity to publicly grieve a loss. At most, they might be expected to support and assist family members.

Then there are relationships that may not be publicly recognized or socially sanctioned. For example, nontraditional relationships, such as extramarital affairs, cohabitation, and homosexual relationships have tenuous public acceptance and limited legal standing, and they face negative sanctions within the larger community. Those involved in such relationships are touched by grief when the relationship is terminated by the death of the partner, but others in their world, such as children, may also experience grief that cannot be acknowledged or socially supported.

Even those whose relationships existed primarily in the past may experience grief. Ex-spouses, past lovers, or former friends may have limited contact, or they may not even engage in interaction in the present. Yet the death of that significant other can still cause a grief reaction because it brings finality to that earlier loss, ending any remaining contact or fantasy of reconciliation or reinvolvement. And again these grief feelings may be shared by others in their world such as parents and children. They too may mourn the loss of "what once was" and "what might have been." For example, in one case a twelve-year-old child of an unwed mother, never even acknowledged or seen by the father, still mourned the death of his father since it ended any possibility of a future liaison. But though loss is experienced, society as a whole may not perceive that the loss of a past relationship could or should cause any reaction.

2. The Loss Is Not Recognized

In other cases, the loss itself is not socially defined as significant. Perinatal deaths lead to strong grief reactions, yet research indicates that many significant others still perceive the loss to be relatively minor. Abortions too can constitute a serious loss, but the abortion can take place without the knowledge or sanctions of others, or even the recognition that a loss has occurred. It may very well be that the very ideologies of the abortion controversy can put the bereaved in a difficult position. Many who affirm a loss may not sanction the

act of abortion, while some who sanction the act may minimize any sense of loss. Similarly, we are just becoming aware of the sense of loss that people experience in giving children up for adoption or foster care, and we have yet to be aware of the grief-related implications of surrogate motherhood.

Another loss that may not be perceived as significant is the loss of a pet. Nevertheless, the research shows strong ties between pets and humans, and profound reactions to loss.

Then there are cases in which the reality of the loss itself is not socially validated. Thanatologists have long recognized that significant losses can occur even when the object of the loss remains physically alive. Sudnow for example, discusses "social death," in which the person is alive but is treated as if dead. Examples may include those who are institutionalized or comatose. Similarly, "psychological death" has been defined as conditions in which the person lacks a consciousness of existence, such as someone who is "brain dead." One can also speak of "psychosocial death" in which the persona of someone has changed so significantly, through mental illness, organic brain syndromes, or even significant personal transformation (such as through addiction, conversion, and so forth), that significant others perceive the person as he or she previously existed as dead. In all of these cases, spouses and others may experience a profound sense of loss, but that loss cannot be publicly acknowledged for the person is still biologically alive.

3. The Griever Is Not Recognized

Finally, there are situations in which the characteristics of the bereaved in effect disenfranchise their grief. Here the person is not socially defined as capable of grief; therefore, there is little or no social recognition of his or her sense of loss or need to mourn. Despite evidence to the contrary, both the very old and the very young are typically perceived by others as having little comprehension of or reaction to the death of a significant other. Often, then, both young children and aged adults are excluded from both discussions and rituals.

Similarly, mentally disabled persons may also be disenfranchised in grief. Although studies affirm that the mentally retarded are able to understand the concept of death and, in fact, experience grief, these reactions may not be perceived by others. Because the person is retarded or otherwise mentally disabled, others in the family may ignore his or her need to grieve. Here a teacher of the mentally disabled describes two illustrative incidences:

> In the first situation, Susie was 17 years old and away at summer camp when her father died. The family felt she wouldn't understand and that it would be better for her not to come home for the funeral. In the other situation, Francine was with her mother when she got sick. The mother was taken away by ambulance. Nobody answered her questions or told her what happened. "After all," they responded, "she's retarded."

The Special Problems of Disenfranchised Grief

Though each of the types of grief mentioned earlier may create particular difficulties and different reactions, one can legitimately speak of the special problem shared in disenfranchised grief.

The problem of disenfranchised grief can be expressed in a paradox. The very nature of disenfranchised grief creates additional problems for grief, while removing or minimizing sources of support.

Disenfranchising grief may exacerbate the problem of bereavement in a number of ways. First, the situations mentioned tend to intensify emotional reactions. Many emotions are associated with normal grief. Bereaved persons frequently experience feelings of anger, guilt, sadness and depression, loneliness, hopelessness, and numbness. These emotional reactions can be complicated when grief is disenfranchised. Although each of the situations described is in its own way unique, the literature uniformly reports how each of these disenfranchising circumstances can intensify feelings of anger, guilt, or powerlessness.

Second, both ambivalent relationships and concurrent crises have been identified in the literature as conditions that complicate grief. These conditions can often exist in many types of disenfranchised grief. For example, studies have indicated the ambivalence that can exist in cases of abortion, among ex-spouses, significant others in nontraditional roles, and among families of Alzheimer's disease victims. Similarly, the literature documents the many kinds of concurrent crises that can trouble the disenfranchised griever. For example, in cases of cohabiting couples, either heterosexual or homosexual, studies have often found that survivors experience legal and financial problems regarding inheritance, ownership, credit, or leases. Likewise, the death of a parent may leave a mentally disabled person not only bereaved but also bereft of a viable support system.

Although grief is complicated, many of the factors that facilitate mourning are not present. The bereaved may be excluded from an active role in caring for the dying. Funeral rituals, normally helpful in resolving grief, may not help here. In some cases the bereaved may be excluded from attendance. In other cases they may have no role in planning those rituals or in deciding whether even to have them. Or in cases of divorce, separation, or psychosocial death, rituals may be lacking altogether.

In addition, the very nature of the disenfranchised grief precludes social support. Often there is no recognized role in which mourners can assert the right to mourn and thus receive such support. Grief may have to remain private. Though they may have experienced an intense loss, they may not be given time off from work, have the opportunity to verbalize the loss, or receive the expressions of sympathy and support characteristic in a death. Even traditional sources of solace, such as religion, are unavailable to those whose relationships (for example, extramarital, cohabiting, homosexual, divorced) or acts (such as abortion) are condemned within that tradition.

Naturally, there are many variables that will affect both the intensity of the reaction and the availability of support. All the variables—interpersonal, psychological, social, physiological—that normally influence grief will have an impact here as well. And while there are problems common to cases of disenfranchised grief, each relationship has to be individually considered in light of the unique combinations of factors that may facilitate or impair grief resolution.

Implications

Despite the shortage of research on and attention given to the issue of disenfranchised grief, it remains a significant issue. Millions of Americans are involved in losses in which grief is effectively disenfranchised. For example, there are more than 1 million couples presently cohabiting. There are estimates that 3 percent of males and 2–3 percent of females are exclusively homosexual, with similar percentages having mixed homosexual and heterosexual encounters. There are about a million abortions a year; even though many of the women involved may not experience grief reactions, some are clearly "at risk."

Disenfranchised grief is also a growing issue. There are higher percentages of divorced people in the cohorts now aging. The AIDS crisis means that more homosexuals will experience losses in significant relationships. Even as the disease spreads within the population of intravenous drug users, it is likely to create a new class of both potential victims and disenfranchised grievers among the victims' informal liaisons and nontraditional relationships. And as Americans continue to live longer, more will suffer from severe forms of chronic brain dysfunctions. As the developmentally disabled live longer, they too will experience the grief of parental and sibling loss. In short, the proportion of disenfranchised grievers in the general population will rise rapidly in the future.

It is likely that bereavement counselors will have increased exposure to cases of disenfranchised grief. In fact, the very nature of disenfranchised grief and the unavailability of informal support make it likely that those who experience such losses will seek formal supports. Thus there is a pressing need for research that will describe the particular and unique reactions of each of the different types of losses; compare reactions and problems associated with these losses; describe the important variables affecting disenfranchised grief reactions; assess possible interventions; and discover the atypical grief reactions, such as masked or delayed grief, that might be manifested in such cases. Also needed is education sensitizing students to the many kinds of relationships and subsequent losses that people can experience and affirming that where there is loss there is grief.

Critical Thinking

1. What is the meaning of disenfranchised grief?
2. How can grief be enfranchised?
3. Why does Dr. Doka believe that the proportion of disenfranchised grievers in the general population will rapidly increase in the future?

KEN DOKA, PhD, is a professor of gerontology at the College of New Rochelle in New York. He became interested in the study of death and dying quite inadvertently. Scheduled to do a practicum in a facility that housed juvenile delinquents, he discovered that his supervisor had changed the assignment. Instead, Doka found himself counseling dying children and their families at Sloan-Kettering, a major cancer hospital in New York.

This experience became the basis of two graduate theses, one in sociology entitled "The Social Organization of Terminal Care in Two Pediatric Hospitals," and the other in religious studies entitled "Pastoral Counseling to Dying Children and Their Families." (Both were later published.) His doctoral program pursued another longstanding interest: the sociology of aging. In 1983, Dr. Doka accepted his present position at the College of New Rochelle where he specializes in thanatology and gerontology.

Active in the Association for Death Education and Counseling since its beginnings, Dr. Doka was elected its president in 1993. In addition to articles in scholarly journals, he is the author of *Death and Spirituality* (with John Morgan, 1993), *Living with Life-Threatening Illness* (1993) and *Disenfranchised Grief: Recognizing Hidden Sorrow* (1989), from which the following selection is excerpted. His work on disenfranchised grief began in the classroom when a graduate student commented, "If you think widows have it rough, you ought to see what happens when your ex-spouse dies."

Challenging the Paradigm: New Understandings of Grief

Kenneth J. Doka, Ph.D.

Introduction

In 1989, Wortman and Silver published a controversial yet influential article entitled "The Myths of Coping With Loss," in which they identified five "myths" that were widely accepted by professionals treating bereavement:

- Depression and distress are inevitable in grief.
- Distress is necessary, and its absence is problematic.
- Survivors must "work through" a loss.
- Survivors can expect to recover from a loss.
- Survivors can reach a state of resolution.

The research, in Wortman and Silver's evaluation, did not support the widespread acceptance of these propositions.

Wortman and Silver's article crystallized a challenge to what might be called the *grief work hypothesis*. This hypothesis was really a conceptual belief that one must work through powerful feelings in order to detach from the deceased, reinvest in life, and recover from and resolve the loss. Originally derived from Freud's seminal 1917 article "Mourning and Melancholia," (Freud, 1957) the concept is pervasive in self-help books. Staudacher (1991), for example, expresses this notion:

> Simply put, *there is only one way to grieve* [emphasis in original]. That way is to go through the core of grief. Only by experiencing the necessary emotional effects of your loved one's death is it possible for you to eventually resolve the loss. (p. 3)

Although the grief work hypothesis was evident in much work in the field, especially in trade and self-help literature, it was not universally accepted. In the professional literature, the hypothesis was continually challenged in one way or another and coexisted with other ideas and approaches. In many ways, Wortman and Silver had over-simplified some very subtle and nuanced approaches to

the understanding of grief and loss, but their article had great heuristic value, bringing forth many modifications and challenges to these early and popular understandings of grief.

The past 15 years have seen an increasing number of challenges to the early paradigms. In this chapter, I will describe five significant ways in which earlier understandings or paradigms of grief have been challenged. I will also discuss three current challenges to the field and two others that are likely to occur in the not-too-distant future.

Five New Understandings of Grief

1. Extending the Definition of Grief

One of the basic questions in the field relates to the definition of grief. Is grief a reaction to the death of a significant person, or can it be more broadly understood as a reaction to loss? Freud's illustration of grief in "Mourning and Melancholia" is a bride left standing at the altar. Most contemporary work emphasizes grief as a reaction to death. Yet confusion over the issue still remains. The major death-related professional organization founded in the United States (though international in membership) was called the Association for Death Education and Counseling (ADEC). The Australian counterpart is called NALAG, the National Association for Loss and Grief. Yet, it remains unclear if the differences between these organizations, in terms of focus or mission, are, in fact, significant.

However, recent work has begun to emphasize grief as a more widespread reaction to loss. Some of this loss is certainly related to dying or death. For example, there has been long-standing recognition that people grieve *secondary losses;* that is, losses that follow a primary loss and engender additional grief. For example, a parent who has experienced the death of a child may mourn not only the loss of the child but also the absence of the child's friends, who were often present in the home. Rando's (1986, 2000) work on anticipatory mourning further develops the idea that losses other than death can generate grief. The original concept of anticipatory grief was that at the onset of a life-limiting disease, a person anticipated a future death and mourned that expected loss. Rando considerably expanded the concept to include anticipatory mourning, which she defined as a response to all the losses encountered—past, present, and future—in the course of an illness. For example, both patient and family may mourn the progressive disabilities and role losses that accompany the disease, as well as the loss of dreams, such as for an idyllic retirement, that now seem unlikely to be fulfilled. Rando's sensitivity to the myriad forms of loss is illustrated in *The Treatment of Complicated Mourning* (1993), in which she discusses tangible losses, such as an object that is stolen or a fire that destroys one's home, and intangible or symbolic losses, such as a divorce.

My work on disenfranchised grief (Doka, 1989, 2002) also addresses the wide range of losses that engender grief, stressing that the very lack of recognition of the grief experienced in such losses complicates grief. Some of these losses involved deaths that were unacknowledged by others—such as the deaths of former spouses, lovers, friends, and even animal companions. The work also emphasized the effects of other types of losses—such as incarceration, divorce, or infertility—that can generate significant grief. The concept of disenfranchised grief emphasizes that every society has "grieving rules" that determine a socially conferred "right to grieve." Generally, for example, these rules give family members the right to grieve the deaths of other family members. But in many situations—including non-death-related losses—a person might experience a significant loss but be deprived of the opportunity to publicly acknowledge the loss, openly mourn, and receive social support. This is disenfranchised grieving.

Harvey (1998) also notes the pervasiveness of loss and suggests the need for a larger psychology of loss that would complement and move beyond the study of dying and death. This shift is a critical one, as it allows the application of the study of grief to areas such as divorce and job loss, and allows the study to draw from the considerable literature around stress, coping, and adaptation (i.e., seeing grief as a type of stress reaction and mourning as a form of coping or adaptation).

However, the danger exists that grief will be trivialized. If every loss evokes "grief," the word becomes less important and signifies little. The antidote is to support research that clarifies the grief reactions and outcomes in a wide array of losses, allowing comparisons between grief reactions and outcomes from a death with those from other losses.

2. The Application of New Models

Most of the early models of grief were drawn from the work of Kubler-Ross (1969) and emphasized that people were likely to experience grief by going through a series of predictable reactions, or stages. Kubler-Ross originally studied the ways adults with life-threatening illness coped with impending death, but her work quickly was applied to the process of grief, in which a person was expected to experience a relatively linear movement through denial, bargaining, anger, and depression to reach a state of acceptance. This understanding of grief has become widespread.

Despite the popular embrace of these stages, most of the newer models have avoided the language and assumptions of stage theories. Worden (1982) broke new ground in his book *Grief Counseling and Grief Therapy* by conceptualizing mourning as a series of four tasks:

1. To accept the reality of the loss
2. To work through the pain of grief
3. To adjust to an environment where the deceased is missing.
4. To withdraw emotional energy and invest it in another relationship (In the second and third editions (1991, 2002), this task was revised to read "To emotionally relocate the deceased and move on with life," a modification that is discussed later in this chapter.)

While Worden's tasks clearly identified grief and mourning with death, they represented a significant paradigm shift from the predominant stage theories. Worden's task model was not linear; people worked on whatever issues arose in the process of mourning. The model stressed individuality (different survivors completed the tasks differently) and autonomy (survivors could choose when they were ready to tackle any task).

I recognized the value of Worden's approach and suggested a fifth task: to rebuild spiritual systems challenged by the loss (Doka, 1993). This task recognizes that some losses challenge personal spiritual belief systems, causing individuals to question and possibly redefine their faith.

After Worden, other models appeared. Rando (1993), for example, proposed the "R" processes of mourning: recognizing the loss; reacting to the separation; recollecting and reexperiencing the deceased and the relationship; relinquishing the old attachments to the deceased and the old assumptive world; readjusting to move adaptively into the new world without forgetting the old; and reinvesting. Stroebe and Schut (1999) offered a dual-process model, suggesting that successful coping in bereavement means oscillating between loss-oriented and restoration-oriented processes.

Both these models, along with Worden's task model, reaffirmed that mourning was more than simply a series of affective responses to loss. In addition, the new models asserted that mourning involved not only a response to the loss of another but also an effort to manage life in a world altered by significant loss.

All these new models offer value to counselors in assisting bereaved persons. Stage models suggested a limited role for counselors: interpreting the reactions of bereaved persons and helping them move through the stages. The newer models allow a more significant role, in which the counselor helps the bereaved person understand what factors are complicating the completion of certain tasks or processes and develops interventions that can help the person adapt to loss.

The models also have implications for group programs. One way to evaluate a program is to determine the underlying model. Programs based on newer models should do more than simply allow participants to express affect. They should reflect the variety of tasks and processes that are part of the experience of grief and mourning.

3. Beyond Affect

While research from Lindemann (1944) on has emphasized that grief is manifested in many ways—including cognitive, physical, emotional, behavioral, and spiritual reactions—much attention has been placed on affect, to the exclusion of other responses. This focus reflects a general Western preoccupation with affect in counseling and therapy (see Sue & Sue, 1999). A number of writers have stressed reactions to loss other than affect; two will serve as examples.

Neimeyer (2001) emphasizes that the reconstruction of meaning is a critical issue—if not *the* critical issue—in grief, adding strong cognitive and spiritual components to the study of grief. Neimeyer's "narrative" approach to therapy helps people "reweave" the narrative of their lives, which has been torn apart by significant loss.

Martin and Doka (2000) suggest a continuum of grieving styles ranging from the intuitive to the instrumental. Intuitive grievers experience, express, and adapt to grief in strongly affective ways. Instrumental grievers, on the other hand, are likely to experience muted affective reactions. Their experience is more likely to be cognitive and behavioral, and they will favor such strategies for expression and adaptation to loss. Martin and Doka's work

strongly challenges the notion that expressing feelings is the most effective way to adapt to loss. The work began as an attempt to understand the grieving patterns of males; the authors now see these patterns as related to, but not determined by, gender.

Other researchers have strongly challenged the idea that expression of feelings and emotions in grief should be encouraged and that a lack of open affect suggests difficulty. In his social-functioning approach, Bonanno (2004) suggests that adaptation to loss is facilitated when grief-related distress is minimized and positive affect is accentuated. Similarly, Nolen-Hoeksema, McBride, and Larson (1997) suggest that excessive rumination might not be helpful and, in fact, is associated with poor outcomes. The excessive processing of loss can exacerbate distress. Resilient individuals minimize rumination by distraction—shifting their attention in a positive direction. However, Nolen-Hoeksema and her associates also found that deliberate avoidance and suppression of grief were maladaptive.

These insights have important implications for grief counselors, grief groups, and grief curricula. The ideas reflected in the newer models reaffirm that grief is more than emotion. They suggest that leaders should try to move their groups beyond shared anguish to discussions of effective ways to cope with grief and should encourage the recognition of positive memories and experiences, even within a state of grief. These concepts reaffirm the individuality of the grief experience and discourage dogmatic, one-size-fits-all strategies.

4. Beyond Coping

Early work in the field tended to emphasize the difficulty of coping with loss and focused on restoring a sense of equilibrium while slowly and painfully withdrawing emotional energy from the deceased. The perception of the survivor was primarily passive, besieged to cope with changes out of his or her control.

This concept was strongly challenged in the work of Catherine Sanders (1989). In her phase model of grief, Sanders suggested that the process of grieving involves a series of phases, and most people follow a common sequence. The first phase is *shock,* as the person begins to feel the impact of the death. In each phase, Sanders related the psychological, cognitive, and physical sequelae of grief. For example, in the shock phase, physical symptoms may include weeping, tremors, and loss of appetite. Bereaved persons may experience psychological distancing, egocentric phenomena, or preoccupation with thoughts of the deceased. Cognitive manifestations at this phase may include disbelief, restlessness, and a heightened state of alarm or a sense of unreality or helplessness. In each of the phases, Sanders recognized both the individuality and the multiplicity of grief reactions—a significant advance over the stage theory (Kubler-Ross, 1969).

The second phase, Sanders said, is *awareness of loss*. Here the funeral rituals are over and support has ebbed. Until now, shock and support have acted as a buffer. Now, as the shock recedes and family and friends withdraw, the primary grievers experience the full force of their loss. This is a period of high emotional and cognitive arousal; separation anxiety is intense and stress is prolonged. Grief is both raw and deeply painful. The bereaved person becomes exhausted and needs to withdraw from others to conserve limited energy.

Sanders proposed *conservation-withdrawal* as the third phase of bereavement. This is a long (possibly endless) phase of grief. The grieving person seems to be functioning, and pain is more chronic than acute. But the person feels physically weak and helpless—going through the motions rather than actively living life. Bereaved persons in this phase often express a belief that they are in state of hibernation, a sort of holding pattern as they struggle to adapt to the loss.

Sanders said that in the first and second phases, people are motivated largely by unconscious or biological factors. In this phase, she suggested that people have three choices. In the face of extreme physical and psychological stress, some may consciously or unconsciously seek their own death rather than live without the person who died. Others may assume that the necessary major life adjustments require more strength and power than they possess. They may choose the status quo, living the rest of their lives in a diminished state of chronic grief. Still others may decide to move forward and adjust to their loss.

According to Sanders, bereaved persons who choose to move forward often experience a fourth phase: *healing/the turning point*. In her research, many persons could point to a moment when they consciously decided that their lives needed to change. In one vignette, a widow recalled hearing her young granddaughter ask her mother, "Why does Grandma always cry?" The widow resolved then and there that she would not be remembered as "the grandma who always cried." In this phase, people reconstruct their identities and lives, and enjoy restored physical health, increased energy, and psychological vigor.

Finally, those who experience the turning point move to a fifth phase that Sanders called *renewal*. While they still experience occasional bad days and episodic moments of grief, they experience a new level of functioning characterized by enhanced self-awareness, increased levels of energy, personal revitalization, and the renewal of social ties. At this phase, the bereaved person has learned to live without the physical presence of the loved one, while retaining an internal sense of the deceased person's presence. Sanders noted that in this phase, people could often process and even enjoy memories of the deceased without the high emotional arousal experienced earlier in the grieving process.

Later, Sanders began to develop the notion of a sixth phase: *fulfillment*. In this phase, the grieving person can look back on his or her own life in a way that integrates the loss into the fabric of that life. While the loss was neither expected nor welcomed, the person can no longer imagine what life would be like without the loss (Doka, 2006).

Sanders was one of the first theorists to affirm that people had choices in the mourning process. Her writing emphasized that bereaved persons were active participants in the mourning process rather than passive copers with little control. Her renewal phase presaged such trends in contemporary bereavement theory as grief as a transformative experience (Neimeyer, 2001; Prend, 1997; Schneider, 1994), in which loss can lead to significant personal growth as the bereaved person struggles to adapt to life without the deceased. These concepts are supported in the research of Calhoun and Tedeschi (2004), which emphasizes the human capacity for reliance and notes that loss may trigger growth and change.

This work emphasizes that the point of therapy is not to "recover" from the loss. Rather, it suggests therapists can pose a larger question: "How will this loss change you?" The question implies an active response. Grieving persons are not passive: While they might have no choice about grief, they do have choices about what they will do with their loss.

5. Continuing Bonds

The Freudian notion that the work of grief is to detach from the deceased and reinvest in other relationships has been strongly challenged. In 1987, Attig compared "letting go" in grief to letting go of an adult child. By that Attig meant that even though there may be less physical presence, the connective bonds and sense of presence remain strong. Synthesizing other work, I suggested in the *Encyclopedia of Death* (Doka, 1984) that rather than emotionally withdraw, survivors might find ways to creatively retain their attachments to the loss object. Using his own research, Worden (1991) revised the wording of his fourth task from the Freudian concept of withdrawing emotional energy from the deceased to relocating the deceased, emphasizing that the bond between the deceased and the survivor continues, albeit in a different form.

In other work, LaGrand (1999) described a connection he labeled "extraordinary experiences," in which bereaved persons recounted dreams, sense experiences, and other phenomena after the death of someone they loved. Often these experiences were therapeutic—reaffirming a bond and offering comfort. Such experiences are so common that I suggest counselors routinely ask bereaved persons about them—they may be comforted by the experiences but reluctant to bring them up.

The challenge to the idea of withdrawal received its fullest treatment in the groundbreaking book *Continuing Bonds: New Understandings of Grief,* edited by Klass, Silverman, and Nickman (1996). The editors emphasize that throughout history and across cultures, bereaved persons have maintained bonds with their deceased. The research in this book deeply challenges the idea that emotional withdrawal is essential or even desirable.

Counselors should assure clients that the goal of grief therapy is not to abolish memories of the deceased. The amelioration of grief means that over time the intensity of the grief experience lessens and the bereaved person functions as well as (or perhaps even better than) before the loss, although surges of grief may occur even years later, brought on by significant transitions or other experiences. The point is that relationships continue even beyond death, and the grief process has no final end point.

However, not all bonds with the deceased are helpful. Some persons may retain connections to a loved one who has died that impair relationships with others or adaptation to the loss. Recent research described by Stroebe (2006) suggests that bonds may be supportive for some persons but maladaptive for others. The therapeutic challenge is to recognize that not all attachments are positive.

Current Challenges

These new understandings have received considerable attention and widespread acceptance. Three current challenges may further modify the way we understand grief.

1. Increasing Diversity: The Challenge of Culture

The United States and many other nations are becoming increasingly racially and ethnically diverse. Much of the research has been based on white, middle-class samples, so it may not be possible to generalize our understanding of grief. A more diverse society will cause us to rethink basic questions. For example, what does loss actually mean? Different societies, with different patterns of attachment and different expectations about life and death, may respond to a loss quite differently. What, for example, is the impact of a child's death in a society with high levels of infant and child mortality?

A more diverse society may challenge what we believe we know about grief. Different cultures may have distinct ways of describing the experience of grief, as well as their own modes of expressing grief and adapting to loss. It

may be that the only thing all cultures share is that each one responds and adapts to loss. We may be able to learn from other cultures—their rituals and methods of expression and adaptation may teach us effective strategies and offer insights on different approaches to dealing with loss.

The issue of diversity also has programmatic implications for hospices and bereavement programs. How sensitive are the programs to ethnic and cultural differences? Are there significant differences in participation or withdrawal from grief programs or bereavement groups? Do other programs reflect sensitivity to diversity? Do "interfaith services" truly reflect religious and cultural diversity? As Islam and other nonwestern faiths grow in the United States and many other western nations, is this growth reflected in the religious affiliations of chaplains and the nature of spiritual care? Are resources on grief—such as books or brochures—available in all the languages spoken in our communities?

Social class is another aspect of diversity, and strategies and programs need to acknowledge the differences. Are fees for services based on a sliding scale? Social class also encompasses differences in life style. For example, for many lower income families, photographs are a luxury. A common activity in children's groups involves creating photographic montages and picture boxes. Such exercises may isolate lower income children or expend a precious and not easily replaced resource.

Sexual orientation is yet another source of diversity. How inclusive are groups and materials? Are bereavement groups solely for widows and widowers or also for partners? Would bereaved unmarried partners—either gay or straight—be comfortable in the grief groups offered, or is it clear that the groups are meant to serve heterosexual widowed spouses?

Sue and Sue (2003) remind us that counseling is a culture itself, with its own distinct values. How well do these values match the values and approaches of the cultures being served?

2. The Challenge of Research and Evidence-Based Practice

As Neimeyer (2000) notes, little research has been done on the actual methods of grief counseling and grief therapy. In the past, we simply assumed that these methods worked. Grief counseling requires the integration of theory, practice, and research. Interventions need to be theoretically grounded and empirically assessed. Evidence-based practice is becoming the standard.

This standard has implications for practitioners, including the need for constant evaluation of grief programs. How can we be sure that the programs we offer are effective? On what evidence do we base programs?

More integration is needed between clinical practice and research. This integration is facilitated when researchers and theoreticians explore the practice applications of their work and when clinicians take an empirical approach to therapy—constantly assessing how well their therapy is helping the client adapt to loss. Research on the link between theory and practice will likely cause us to reassess and reevaluate the concepts and models that underlie the study of grief.

3. The Challenge of Technology

The challenge to research and evaluate is especially clear with regard to the many resources offered through the Internet. Online resources include grief information, grief groups, chat rooms, counseling, and opportunities for memorialization. Yet there has been little evaluation of these resources and little study of their efficacy.

The Internet may offer support for bereaved persons, but it may itself be a source of grief. The exponential increase in cyberspace relationships raises questions for the study of attachment and loss. If close relationships can form online, will these people constitute a future class of disenfranchised grievers? Will these relationships raise new questions regarding the processes of death notification?

On the Horizon

Two additional issues are likely to affect future understanding of grief. The first one is the move to add a "grief" category to the forthcoming *DSM-V.* One of the proposals before the American Psychiatric Association is on *complicated grief* (formerly called *traumatic grief*). Jacobs and Prigerson and others (see Jacobs & Prigerson, 2000; Prigerson & Maciejewski, 2006) suggest that certain symptoms evident early in the process of grieving predict problematic outcomes, and they recommend early intervention. For years, the field has eschewed a medical model of grief and avoided using terms like "symptoms." Grief, it is argued, is a normal part of the life cycle, not an illness. These proposals challenge that notion, asserting that at least some experiences of grief show evidence of psychiatric illness. The proposals are a sign of increasing recognition that there is a need for correction, that the emphasis on the normalcy of loss and grief has led to the neglect of problematic variants. Receptiveness to these proposals is probably also fueled by the growth of managed care in the United States and the need to have a clear grief-related diagnostic code. Regardless of the motivation, adding a diagnostic category for grief will constitute a paradigm shift.

The second issue is the demographic change as the baby boomers age. Many of them are experiencing the loss of their parents; in a few decades, they will face their own deaths. Also, each generation develops unique forms of attachment; many boomers have developed extremely close attachments to their children, so their deaths may create different problems for their offspring than in previous generations. This is a generation that has challenged and changed every institution it has experienced in its collective journey through the life cycle. Boomers demand choices in programs and avoid programs that ignore individual differences. They tend to trust individuals rather than institutions. They want to be active participants in programs rather than passive recipients. The baby boomers will surely change the ways we encounter loss, death, and grief.

Over the past 15 years, our understanding of grief has experienced major modifications. Changes and challenges are likely to continue to affect how we think about and respond to loss. As a popular Baby Boom song, Dylan's *"The World it Is a Changin"* put it "the wheel is still in spin."

References

Attig, T. (1987). Grief, love and separation. In C. Corr and R. Pacholski (Eds.), *Death: Completion and discovery.* Lakewood, OH: Association for Death Education and Counseling.

Bonnano, G. (2004). Loss, trauma and human resilience: Have we underestimated the human capacity to thrive after extremely aversive events? *American Psychologist, 59,* 20–28.

Calhoun, L. G., & Tedeschi, R. G. (2004). The foundations of posttraumatic growth: New considerations. *Psychological Inquiry, 15,* 93–102.

Doka, K. J. (1984). Grief. In R. Kastenbaum and B. Kastenbaum (Eds.), *Encyclopedia of death.* Phoenix, AZ: Oryx Press.

Doka, K. J. (1989). *Disenfranchised grief: Recognizing hidden sorrow.* Lexington, MA: Lexington Press.

Doka, K. J. (1993). The spiritual crises of bereavement. In K. J. Doka (with J. Morgan) (Ed.), *Death and spirituality* (pp. 185–195). Amityville, NY: Baywood Publishing Co.

Doka, K. J. (2002). *Disenfranchised grief: New directions, challenges, and strategies for practice.* Champaign, IL: Research Press.

Doka, K. (2006). Fulfillment as Sanders' sixth phase of bereavement: The unfinished work of Catherine Sanders. *Omega: The Journal of Death and Dying, 52,* 141–149.

Freud, S. (1957). Mourning and melancholia. London: Hogarth.

Harvey, J. (1998). *Perspectives on loss: A sourcebook.* Philadelphia: Brunner/Mazel.

Jacobs, S., & Prigerson, H. (2000). Psychotherapy of traumatic grief: A review of evidence for psychotherapeutic treatments. *Death Studies, 21,* 471–498.

Klass, D., Silverman, P., & Nickman, S. (Eds.). (1996). *Continuing bonds: New understandings of grief.* Washington, DC: Taylor & Frances.

Kubler-Ross, E. (1969). *On Death and Dying.* New York: Macmillan.

LaGrand, L. (1999). *Messages and miracles: Extraordinary experiences of the bereaved.* St. Paul, MN: Llewellyn Publications.

Lindemann, E. (1944). Symptomatology and management of acute grief. *American Journal of Psychiatry, 101,* 141–148.

Martin, T., & Doka, K. J. (2000). *Men don't cry, women do: Transcending gender stereotypes of grief.* Philadelphia: Brunner/Mazel.

Neimeyer, R. A. (2000). Grief therapy and research as essential tensions: Prescriptions for a progressive partnership. *Death Studies, 24,* 603–610.

Neimeyer, R. A. (2001). *Meaning reconstruction and the meaning of loss.* Washington, DC: American Psychological Association.

Nolen-Hoeksema, S., McBride, A., & Larson, J. (1997) Rumination and psychological distress among bereaved partners. *Journal of Personality and Social Psychology, 72,* 855–862.

Prend, A. (1997). *Transcending loss.* New York: Berkley Books.

Prigerson, H., & Maciejewski, P. (2006). A call for sound empirical testing and evaluation for complicated grief proposed for *DSM-V. Omega, The Journal of Death and Dying, 52,* 9–20.

Rando, T. A. (1986). *Loss and anticipatory grief.* Lexington, MA: Lexington Books.

Rando, T. A. (1993). *The treatment of complicated mourning.* Champaign, IL: Research Press.

Rando, T. A. (2000). *Clinical dimensions of anticipatory mourning: Theory and practice in working with the dying, their loved ones, and their caregivers.* Champaign, IL: Research Press.

Sanders, C. (1989). *Grief: The mourning after – Dealing with adult bereavement.* New York: Wiley.

Staudacher, C. (1991). *Men and grief.* Oakland, CA: New Harbinger Publications.

Stroebe, M., & Schut, H. (1999). The dual process model of coping with bereavement: Rationale and description. *Death Studies, 23,* 197–224.

Stroebe, M. (2006, April). *Continuing bonds in bereavement: Toward theoretical understanding.* Keynote presentation to the Association of Death Education and Counseling, Albuquerque, NM.

Sue, D.W., & Sue, D. (2003). *Counseling the culturally diverse: Theory and practice.* New York: John Wiley and Sons.

Worden, J. W. (1982, 1991, 2002). *Grief counseling and grief therapy: A handbook for the mental health practitioner* (eds.1–3). New York: Springer.

Wortman, C., & Silver, R. C. (1989). The myths of coping with loss. *Journal of Clinical Counseling, 57,* 349–357.

Critical Thinking

1. According to Dr. Doka, what are the five significant ways in which earlier understandings or paradigms of grief have been challenged?

2. Describe the three current challenges that may further modify the way we understand grief.

3. How will demographic changes change the way in which Americans grieve?

Enhancing the Concept of Disenfranchised Grief

Doka (1989a, p. 4) defined disenfranchised grief as "the grief that persons experience when they incur a loss that is not or cannot be openly acknowledged, publicly mourned, or socially supported." He suggested that disenfranchisement can apply to unrecognized relationships, losses, or grievers, as well as to certain types of deaths.

This article contends that disenfranchisement in bereavement may have a potentially broader scope than has been hitherto recognized. That claim is defended by exploring further the implications of disenfranchisement and by suggesting ways in which certain understandings or misunderstandings of the dynamic qualities of grief, mourning, and their outcomes may be open to disenfranchisement or may participate in disenfranchisement.

The aims of this argument are to enhance the concept of disenfranchised grief in itself and to deepen appreciation of the full range of all that is or can be experienced in bereavement.

CHARLES A. CORR, PhD

I n 1989 Doka (1989a) first proposed the concept of "disenfranchised grief." His suggestion had an immediate appeal to many and the concept of disenfranchised grief has since been widely accepted by practitioners, educators, and researchers in the field of death, dying, and bereavement. In particular, it has been applied in ways that seek to elucidate and validate the experiences of a broad range of bereaved persons.

In his initial proposal, Doka described the concept of disenfranchised grief, identified those aspects of the grief experience that he understood to have been subject to disenfranchisement, provided examples of many ways in which disenfranchisement has occurred, and indicated why attention should be paid to the concept of disenfranchised grief. This article seeks to enhance understanding of the concept of disenfranchised grief and by so doing to deepen appreciation of the full range of all that is or can be experienced in bereavement. The present analysis begins with a review of Doka's original description of the concept of disenfranchised grief. Thereafter, the inquiry is guided by two primary questions: 1) What exactly is meant by the disenfranchisement of grief?; and 2) What is or can be disenfranchised in grief? Responding to these questions may help to enrich understanding of Doka's seminal concept in particular, and of bereavement in general. On that basis, it may also be possible for helpers to identify better ways in which to assist grievers of all types, especially those whose experiences have been disenfranchised.

Disenfranchised Grief: The Original Concept

In his original work, Doka (1989a, p. 4) defined "disenfranchised grief" as "the grief that persons experience when they incur a loss that is not or cannot be openly acknowledged, publicly mourned, or socially supported." In addition, he suggested that grief can be disenfranchised in three primary ways: 1) the relationship is not recognized; 2) the loss is not recognized; or 3) the griever is not recognized. Some comments on each of these three types of disenfranchisement may help to clarify Doka's original proposal.

Disenfranchised Relationships

Why don't you just stop crying and grieving for that person who died. He wasn't even close to you.

I just don't see why you should be so upset over the death of your ex-husband. He was a bum, you hated him, and you got rid of him years ago. Why cry over his being gone for good?

With respect to a *relationship* that is disenfranchised, Folta and Deck (1976, p. 235) have noted that "the underlying assumption is that the 'closeness of relationship' exists only among spouses and/or immediate kin." Unsuspected, past, or secret relationships may simply not be publicly recognized or socially sanctioned. Disenfranchised relationships can include associations which are well-accepted in theory but not appreciated in practice or in particular instances, such as those between friends, colleagues, in-laws, ex-spouses, or former lovers. Disenfranchised relationships may also include nontraditional liaisons such as those involving extra-marital affairs and homosexual relationships. In referring to these as instances of disenfranchised grief, the implication is that such relationships have often been or may be deemed by society to be an insufficient or inappropriate foundation for grief.

Disenfranchised Losses

Why do you keep on moaning over your miscarriage? It wasn't really a baby yet. And you already have four children. You could even have more if you want to.

Stop crying over that dead cat! He was just an animal. I bet that cat wouldn't have been upset if you had been the one to die. If you stop crying. I'll buy you a new kitten.

In the case of a *loss* which is disenfranchised, the focus of the disenfranchisement appears to arise from a failure or unwillingness on the part of society to recognize that certain types of events do involve real losses. For example, until quite recently and perhaps still today in many segments of society, perinatal deaths, losses associated with elective abortion, or losses of body parts have been disenfranchised. Similarly, the death of a pet is often unappreciated by those outside the relationship. And society is only beginning to learn about grief which occurs when dementia blots out an individual's personality in such a way or to such a degree that significant others perceive the person to be psychosocially dead, even though biological life continues. As one husband said of his spouse with advanced Alzheimer's disease, "I am medically separated from my wife—even though she is still alive and we are not divorced." To say that loss arising from a "medical separation" of this type is disenfranchised is to note that society does not acknowledge it to be sufficient to justify grief—or at least not sufficient to justify grief of the type that society associates with a physical death.

Disenfranchised Grievers

I don't know why that old guy in Room 203 keeps moaning and whimpering about the death of his loud-mouthed daughter who used to visit him every week.

With his poor memory and other mental problems, he hardly even knew when his daughter came to visit anyway.

I told Johnnie he should grow up, be a man, and stop whining about his grandfather's death. He's too young to really remember much about his grandfather or even to understand what death really means.

In the case of a disenfranchised *griever,* disenfranchisement mainly has to do with certain individuals to whom the socially-recognized status of griever is not attached. For example, it is often asserted or at least suggested that young children, the very old, and those who are mentally disabled are either incapable of grief or are individuals who do not have a need to grieve. In

this case, disenfranchisement applies not to a relationship or to a loss, but to the individual survivor whose status as a leading actor or protagonist in the human drama of bereavement is not recognized or appreciated.

Disenfranchising Deaths

That teenager who killed himself must not have had all his marbles. His family is probably all screwed up, too. Don't be sorry for them. Just stay away from them.

It's just too bad that actor died of AIDS. God punished him for having all that sex. And now his boyfriends will probably wind up with all his money. They sure don't need us to feel sorry for them.

In his original concept, Doka (1989a) added that some types of deaths in themselves may be "disenfranchising." He offered as examples deaths involving suicide or AIDS. The point seems to have been that our society is repelled or turns away from certain types of death, mainly because their complexities are not well understood or because they are associated with a high degree of social stigma. As a result, the character of the death seems to disenfranchise what otherwise might have been expected to follow in its aftermath. But not all societies at all points in time would or have disenfranchised deaths associated with suicide or AIDS. In other words, what is disenfranchised in one social context may not be disenfranchised in another social context. This clearly recalls Doka's fundamental point that disenfranchised grief is always founded on a specific society's attitudes and values.

Why Pay Attention to Disenfranchised Grief?

The purpose of drawing attention to the meaning of disenfranchised grief and to the ways in which it can be implemented can be seen in Doka's (1989a, p. 7) observation that, "The very nature of disenfranchised grief creates additional problems of grief, while removing or minimizing sources of support." Additional problems arise that go beyond the usual difficulties in grief because disenfranchised grief typically involves intensified emotional reactions (for example, anger, guilt, or powerlessness), ambivalent relationships (as in some cases of abortion or some associations between ex-spouses), and concurrent crises (such as those involving legal and financial problems). In circumstances of disenfranchised grief there is an absence of customary sources of support because society's attitudes make unavailable factors that usually facilitate mourning (for instance, the existence of funeral rituals or possibilities for helping to take part in such rituals) and opportunities to obtain assistance from others (for example, by speaking about the loss, receiving expressions of sympathy, taking time off from work, or finding solace within a religious tradition).

Clearly, issues associated with disenfranchised grief deserve attention. They indicate that social outlooks often embody a judgmental element (whether explicitly articulated or not) and the short-term concerns of the group when dealing with some bereaved persons. That is, societies which disenfranchise grief appear to act on specific values or principles at the expense of an overarching interest in the welfare of all of their members. In these ways, disenfranchised grief can be seen to be an important phenomenon. It is also a phenomenon that is lived out in different ways in different societies, easily observed by those who pay attention to social practices, and hurtful to individual members of society if not to society itself. For all of these reasons, it is worth exploring further what is meant by saying that some grief is disenfranchised and what is or can be disenfranchised in grief.

What Is Meant by Saying That Some Grief Is Disenfranchised?

As has been noted, grief always occurs within a particular social or cultural context. The concept of disenfranchised grief recognizes that in various spoken and unspoken ways social and cultural communities may deny recognition, legitimation, or support to the grief experienced by individuals, families, and small groups.

It is important to recognize that the grief under discussion here is not merely silent, unnoticed, or forgotten. Any griever may keep silent about or decide not to reveal to the larger society the fact of his or her grief, or some of its specific aspects. Failing to disclose or communicate to others what one is experiencing in grief does not of itself mean that such grief is or would be disenfranchised. Society might be fully prepared to recognize, legitimize, and support grief that an individual, for whatever reason, holds in privacy and does not share.

Further, even when an individual is willing to share his or her grief, some grief experiences may still go unnoticed or be forgotten by society. Thus, Gyulay (1975) wrote of grandparents following the death of a grandchild as "forgotten grievers." She meant that all too often attention associated with the death of a child is focused on the child's parents or siblings to the exclusion of grandparents. In fact, however, bereaved grandparents often find themselves grieving both the death of their grandchild and the loss experienced by an adult who is simultaneously their own child (or son/daughter-in-law) and the child's parent (Hamilton, 1978). Typically, when this two-fold grief of grandparents is brought to the attention of members of society, it is not disenfranchised but acknowledged and respected.

In short, the concept of disenfranchised grief goes beyond the situation of mere unawareness of grief to suggest a more or less active process of disavowal, renunciation, and rejection. Not surprisingly, the word "disenfranchise" takes its origin from the term "enfranchise," which has two basic historical meanings: 1) "To admit to freedom, set free (a slave or serf)"; and 2) "To admit to municipal or political privileges" (*Oxford English Dictionary*, 1989, Vol. 5, p. 246). In the most familiar sense of this term, to enfranchise is to set an individual free from his or her prior condition by admitting that person to the electoral franchise or granting permission to vote for representatives in a government. Disenfranchisement applies to those who are

not accorded a social franchise extended by society to individuals who are admitted to full participation in the community.

A more contemporary meaning of enfranchisement is to be granted a franchise or license to offer for sale locally some national or international product or service. For example, one might purchase or be awarded a franchise to sell a certain brand of fast food or automobile, or to advertise one's local motel as a member of a national chain of motels. Often one has to earn or somehow pay for the use of a franchise, and there may also be obligations to uphold certain service standards or to deliver a product of a certain type in a certain way. When the use of a franchise has not been earned or implemented properly, it may come into dispute or even be withdrawn by those in authority. In all of these examples, it is the permission to behave in a certain way (to vote, to act as a franchisee or agent of a franchise holder) that is central to both enfranchisement and disenfranchisement.

In the case of bereavement, enfranchisement applies in particular to those who are recognized by society as grievers. These are individuals who are free to acknowledge their losses openly, mourn those losses publicly, and receive support from others—at least within that society's accepted limits. Disenfranchised grief goes beyond the boundaries of what is regarded as socially accepted grief. It is therefore denied the legitimacy and freedom that comes with social sanction and approval (Doka, 1989b; Pine et al., 1990).

What Is or Can Be Disenfranchised in Grief?
Bereavement

Doka is clearly correct in recognizing that disenfranchisement can apply to relationships, losses, and grievers. These are, in fact, the three key *structural elements* that define the meaning of the term "bereavement." Thus, what Doka has really defined is "disenfranchised bereavement." For that reason, it may help to begin our exploration of how disenfranchisement applies to grief by reminding ourselves of how we understand the root concept of bereavement.

The word "bereavement" is widely understood to designate the objective situation of one who has experienced a significant loss. If there were no significant person or object to which an individual was attached, there would be no bereavement. For example, when a parent threatens to take away from a child a much-disliked serving of spinach as a "punishment" for the child's refusal to clean his or her plate at dinner, the child is not likely to experience a loss or to grieve. Further, if the object were a significant one to the child, but the child perceived (as a result of previous parental behavior patterns) that the threatened loss would not come about in fact, again there would be no bereavement or grief. Finally, if there were no individual to grieve a loss—as when someone threatens to or actually does take away a significant object, but the threat and the loss are not effectively communicated to the individual to whom they would presumably have been directed—again there is no bereavement or grief. A griever is effectively absent when the threat is merely an empty gesture made in his or her absence or when, for some other reason, there is no awareness or experience of a significant loss—as during the period between the death of a loved one in a far-off land and the communication of that fact to the survivor.

In short, the noun "bereavement" and the adjective "bereaved" only apply to situations and individuals in which there exists an experience such that one believes oneself to have been deprived of some important person or object. Both "bereavement" and "bereaved" (there is no present participial form, "bereaving," in standard English today) are words that derive from a verb not often used today in colloquial English. That word is "reave"; it means "to despoil, rob, or forcibly deprive" (*Oxford English Dictionary*, 1989, Vol. 13, p. 295). In short, a bereaved person is one who has been deprived, robbed, plundered, or stripped of something. This indicates that the stolen person or object was a valued one, and suggests that the deprivation has harmed or done violence to the bereaved person. In our society, all too many bereaved persons can testify that dismissal or minimization of the importance of their losses are familiar components of the experience of survivors, with or without added burdens arising from disenfranchisement.

We could explore further each of the central elements identified by Doka in describing his concept of disenfranchised grief. Such an exploration might produce: 1) a rich and varied portrait of the many types of *relationships* in which humans participate, including those fundamental relationships called "attachments" which serve to satisfy the basic needs of human beings; 2) a panorama of *losses* which may affect relationships involving human beings—some permanent, others temporary, some final, others reversible; and/or 3) a list of many different types of *grievers*. If we did this, it would become apparent (among other things) that loss by death is but one category of loss, and that certain types or modes of death are more likely to be disenfranchised than others. And we might also learn that while disenfranchising the bereaved involves costs of different types for individuals and societies themselves, enfranchising the disenfranchised might also involve costs of other types (Davidowitz & Myrick, 1984; Kamerman, 1993).

All of the above are ways to enrich appreciation of the concept of disenfranchised grief. Most involve simply accepting the conceptual scheme as it was originally proposed by Doka and applying it to specific types of relationships, losses, and grievers. Applications of this type have been prominent in written reports and conference presentations in recent years (e.g., Becker, 1997; Kaczmarek & Backlund, 1991; Schwebach & Thornton, 1992; Thornton, Robertson, & Mlecko, 1991; Zupanick, 1994).

In this article, it seems more useful to try to enhance or enlarge the concept of disenfranchised grief by examining it critically in relationship to the *dynamic components* of the bereavement experience, especially as it is related to grief, mourning, and their outcomes.

Grief

Stop feeling that way! You'll be better off if you just pack up all those bad feelings and throw them away with the garbage.

In reactions to being "reaved" or to perceiving themselves as having been "reaved," those who have suffered that experience typically react to what has happened to them. In normal circumstances, one would be surprised if they did not do so. Failure to react would seem to imply that the lost person or object was actually not much prized by the bereaved individual, that the survivor is unaware of his or her loss, or that other factors intervene. "Grief" is the reaction to loss. The term arises from the grave or heavy weight that presses on persons who are burdened by loss (*Oxford English Dictionary,* 1989, Vol. 6, pp. 834–835).

Reactions to loss are disenfranchised when they—in whole or in part; in themselves or in their expression—are not recognized, legitimated, or supported by society. How many times have grieving persons been told: "Don't feel that way"; "Try not to think those thoughts"; "Don't say those things (about God, or the doctor, or the person who caused the death)"; "You shouldn't act like that just because someone you loved died." Sometimes any reaction is judged to be inappropriate; in other circumstances, some reactions are accepted while others are rejected. In some cases, it is the existence of the reaction that is disenfranchised; in other examples, it is only the expression of the reaction that meets with disapproval. Through what amounts to a kind of "oppressive toleration" society often presses a griever to hold private his or her grief reaction in order not to trouble or disturb others by bringing it out into the open or expressing it in certain ways. The effect of any or all of these practices is to disenfranchise either some aspects of the grief or some modes in which they are manifested.

Grief as Emotions?

I can understand why you're feeling upset about your mother's death. You can be sad if you want to. But you've got to start eating again and getting a good night's sleep.

My co-worker used to be a such a great guy. But ever since his younger sister died, he comes to work and sometimes it's like he's wandering around in a fog and not concentrating on the job. I told him today that he needs to pull himself together and get focused on his work again.

My friend was always such a cheery person at the Senior Citizen's Center. But ever since her grandchild died, she keeps asking all those difficult questions about why God let such a bad thing happen to an innocent child. I told her that it was OK to be sad, but she just had to accept God's will and stop questioning it.

In each of these examples, feelings of grief are legitimized but other aspects of the grief reaction are disenfranchised. One might also argue that something very much like this form of disenfranchisement can be found in much of the professional literature on bereavement. For example, quite often grief is described or defined as "the emotional reaction to loss." On its face, a definition of this type is at once both obvious and inadequate. Clearly, bereaved persons may or do react emotionally to loss; equally so, they may not or do not merely react emotionally to loss. Careless, unintentional, or deliberate restriction of the meaning of grief to its emotional components is an unrecognized form of disenfranchisement of the full grief experience.

In this connection, Elias (1991) reminded readers that, "Broadly speaking, emotions have three components, a somatic, a behavioral and a feeling component" (p. 177). As a result, "the term *emotion,* even in professional discussions, is used with two different meanings. It is used in a wider and in a narrower sense at the same time. In the wider sense the term *emotion* is applied to a reaction pattern which involves the whole organism in its somatic, its feeling and its behavioral aspects. . . . In its narrower sense the term *emotion* refers to the feeling component of the syndrome only" (Elias, 1991, p. 119).

The importance of feelings in the overall grief reaction to loss is undeniable. Equally undeniable is the importance of other aspects of the grief reaction. These include somatic or physical sensations and behaviors or behavioral disturbances, as Elias has indicated, as well as matters involving cognitive, social, and spiritual functioning. Establishing a comprehensive list of all of these aspects of the grief reaction to loss is not of primary importance here. What is central is the recognition that human beings may and indeed are likely to react to important losses in their lives with their whole selves, not just with some narrowly defined aspect of their humanity. Failure to describe grief in a holistic way dismisses and devalues its richness and breadth.

Grief as Symptoms?

As a psychiatrist and her son-in-law, I tried to talk to your mother about your father's death. She refused and got upset after I told her that her unwillingness to discuss with me her reactions to the death was a classic symptom of pathological grief. She said she had talked to her sister and just didn't want to talk to you or me or her other children about it.

Sadness and crying are two of the main symptoms of grief. Whenever we identify them, we should refer the individual for therapy.

Another form of depicting or categorizing grief in a limiting and negative way involves the use of the language of *symptoms* to designate both complicated and uncomplicated grief. In principal, grief is a natural and healthy reaction to loss. There can be unhealthy reactions to loss. One of these would be a failure to react in any way to the loss of a significant person or object in our lives. However, most grief reactions are not complicated or unhealthy. They are appropriate reactions to the loss one has experienced. In cases of uncomplicated grief—which constitute the vast majority of all bereavement experiences—we ought to speak of signs, or manifestations, or expressions of grief. And we ought to avoid the term "symptoms" in relationship to grief, unless we consciously intend to use the language of illness to indicate some form of aberrant or unhealthy reaction to loss. When we use the language of symptoms to describe all expressions of grief, we have pathologized grief and invalidated or disenfranchised its fundamental soundness as the human reaction to loss.

Mourning

OK, we've had our grief ever since Kerri died. Now that the funeral is over, that's it. There's nothing more we can do and nothing more we need to do. So, let's just put all this behind us and forget it.

Many aspects of what is called grief in bereavement are essentially reactive. They seek to push away the hurt of the loss with denial, or turn back upon it with anger, or reply to its implacability with sadness. Much of this is like a defensive reflex. But there is more to most bereavement experiences than this. The other central element in a healthy bereavement experience is in the effort to find some way to live with the loss, with our grief reactions to that loss, and with the new challenges that are associated with the loss. As Weisman (1984, p. 36) observed, coping "is positive in approach; defending is negative." In brief, coping identifies the efforts that we make to manage perceived stressors in our lives (Lazarus & Folkman, 1984). In the vocabulary of bereavement, this is "mourning"—the attempt to manage or learn to live with one's bereavement. Through mourning grievers endeavor to incorporate their losses and grief into healthy ongoing living.

If we fail to distinguish between grief and mourning in appropriate ways, we run the risk of ignoring the differences between reacting and coping, between seeking to defend or push away our loss and grief, and attempting to embrace those experiences and incorporate them into our lives. This is another form of disenfranchisement insofar as it blurs distinctions between two central aspects of bereavement, misconceives what is involved in mourning an important loss, and refuses to acknowledge and support both grief and mourning.

At the simplest level, the efforts that one makes to cope with loss and grief in mourning are frequently not understood for what they are and thus are not valued by society. For example, a griever will be told not to go over the details of the accident again and again, as if such filling in of the stark outlines of a death is not an essential part of the process of *realization* or making real in one's internal, psychic world what is already real in the external, objective world (Parkes, 1996). Another familiar way of disenfranchising mourning occurs when a bereaved person is advised that the proper way to manage a loss is simply to "put it behind you" or "get beyond it." This assumes that one can simply hop over a stressful event in life, ignore the unwelcome interruption, and go on living without being affected by what has happened. Sometimes, bereaved survivors are even counseled to "forget" the deceased person as if he or she had not been a significant part of their lives. None of these are appropriate elements in constructive mourning.

Note that mourning is a present-tense, participial word. As such, it indicates action or activities of the type expressed by verbs. In the language of nouns, this is "grief work" (a phrase first coined by Lindemann in 1944). Lindemann understood "grief work" in a specific way, but the central point is that the grief work at the heart of mourning is an active, effortful attempt to manage what bereavement has brought into one's life (Attig, 1991, 1996).

Moreover, since the consequences of bereavement typically include both primary and secondary losses, as well as grief and new challenges, there is much to cope with in the whole of one's mourning. Indeed, contrasting loss and grief with the new challenges of bereavement could be said to require an oscillation between "loss-oriented" and "restoration-oriented" processes in mourning (Stroebe & Schut, 1995).

In other words, in his or her mourning a bereaved person is faced with the tasks of integrating into his or her life three major elements: 1) the primary and secondary losses that he or she has experienced, 2) the grief reactions provoked by those losses; and 3) the new challenges involved in living without the deceased person. For example, if my spouse should die I would be obliged to mourn or try to learn to live in healthy ways with her loss (the fact that she has been taken away from me constituting my primary loss), with the secondary losses associated with her death (e.g., being deprived of her company or being without her guidance in some practical matters), with my grief reactions to those losses (e.g., my anger over what has been done to me or my sadness at the apparent barrenness of the life that is now left to me), and with my new situation in life (e.g., after years of marriage I may be unclear how to function as a newfound single person). If any aspect of my losses, grief, or new challenges is disenfranchised, then my efforts to mourn or cope with those aspects of my bereavement will also be disenfranchised.

Mourning: Interpersonal and Intrapersonal Dimensions

Because each human being is both a particular individual and a social creature or a member of a community, mourning has two complementary forms or aspects. It is both an outward, public, or *interpersonal* process—the overt, visible, and characteristically shared public efforts to cope with or manage loss and associated grief reactions—and an internal, private, or *intrapersonal* process—an individual's inward struggles to cope with or manage loss and the grief reactions to that loss. Each of these dimensions of mourning deserves recognition and respect. Much of what has already been noted here about mourning applies to its intrapersonal dimensions, but disenfranchisement is also frequently associated with the interpersonal aspects of mourning.

Interpersonal Dimensions of Mourning

Don't keep on talking about how he died. It's not going to make any difference or bring him back. Nobody wants to be around you when you keep going on about it.

What's the point of having a funeral, anyhow? Couldn't they just bury their child privately and leave us out of it? I don't want to get dragged into it.

Many people in contemporary society are unwilling to take part in the public or *interpersonal* rituals of mourning. Some of this has to do with a certain weakness or shallowness in many interpersonal relationships in contemporary society and a loosening of the bonds that formerly bound together families, neighbors, church groups, and other small communities. But it also

appears to be linked to a discomfort with public ritual and open expression of strong feelings. Good funeral and memorial rituals are essentially designed to assist human beings in their need to engage in three post-death tasks: 1) to dispose of dead bodies appropriately; 2) to make real the implications of death; and 3) to work toward social reintegration and healthful ongoing living (Corr, Nabe, & Corr, 1994). Without indicating how these tasks will otherwise be met, many act as if society and individuals should do away with all public expressions of mourning. Young people in our society frequently state that when they die no one should be sad and that money that would otherwise be spent for a funeral should only be used for a party. Thoughts like this disenfranchise full appreciation of grief and the needs of individuals to mourn their losses within communities of fellow grievers.

This disenfranchisement of the interpersonal dimensions of mourning is not typical of all individuals in our society and is unacceptable to many ethnic or religious groups. Similarly, it does not apply to rituals following the deaths of public figures (e.g., a president) or very prominent persons (e.g., certain celebrities). In these instances, as well as in the very formal rituals of the armed forces which mandate specific conduct and ceremonial practice in a context of death and bereavement, or the informal but growing practice of members of sports teams wearing black bands on their uniforms or dedicating a game to the memory of someone who has died, the interpersonal needs of a community cry out for expression and guidance in public mourning practices.

In fact, formal or informal rituals—which are a prominent example of the interpersonal dimension of mourning—have been created by human beings as a means of helping to bring order into their lives in times of disorder and social disruption. Thus, Margaret Mead (1973, pp. 89–90) wrote: "I know of no people for whom the fact of death is not critical, and who have no ritual by which to deal with it." Bereavement rituals are intended precisely to give social recognition, legitimation, and support in times of loss and grief. Specific rituals may fall out of favor and no longer serve these purposes for the society as a whole or for some of its members. But to assume that such rituals can simply be abandoned without replacement, that society can satisfactorily conduct its affairs and serve its members without any ritual whatsoever in times of death, is to misconceive the needs of human beings and expose the dangers involved in disenfranchising mourning. As Staples (1994, p. 255) suggested, "The rituals of grief and burial bear the dead away. Cheat those rituals and you risk keeping the dead with you always in forms that you mightn't like. Choose carefully the funerals you miss."

Intrapersonal Dimensions of Mourning

I was proud of her at the funeral. She was so brave and she never cried. But now she's always crying and sometimes she just seems to be preoccupied with her inner feelings. I think she's just chewing on her grief like some kind of undigested food and simply won't let go of it. Last week, I told her that there were times when we all understood it was appropriate to grieve. But she's got to get over it and she just can't keep on gnawing at it when she thinks she's alone.

Why does she keep going back to the cemetary on the anniversary of her husband's death? That's morbid for her to keep on stirring up those feelings over and over again. She doesn't talk much to anyone else about it, but I think she needs to get on with her life without this behavior.

Some authors (e.g., *Oxford English Dictionary,* 1989, Vol. 10, pp. 19–20) seem to restrict the use of the term "mourning" to the expression of sorrow or grief, especially those expressions involving ceremony or ritual. For example, there is a traditional language that uses phrases like "wearing mourning" to refer to dressing in certain ways (e.g., in black or dark-colored garments) as a public expression of one's status as a bereaved person. Despite its historical justification, limiting the term mourning in this way leaves us without a term for the *intrapersonal* processes of coping with loss and grief.

Other authors (e.g., Wolfelt, 1996) maintain and emphasize the distinction between the intrapersonal and interpersonal dimensions of bereavement by using the term "grieving" for the former and reserving the term "mourning" for the latter. Again, there is justification for some linguistic distinction between intrapersonal and interpersonal aspects of coping with loss and grief. But the central point for our purposes is that this last distinction is a linguistic effort to fill out what is involved in both the intrapersonal and interpersonal realms when bereaved persons strive to cope with loss and grief. In this way, linguistic distinctions between intrapersonal and interpersonal aspects of mourning work to expand or enhance what is involved in coping with loss and grief, not to restrict or disenfranchise selected aspects of that coping.

Mourning: Outcomes

It's been almost three weeks and she's still not finished with her grieving. I told her she had to forget him and get on with her new life.

We invited John to come on a blind date with us and Mary's cousin, but he refused. Mary told him that he's got to stop wallowing in tears. He needs to get over his first wife and start looking around for someone new. Six months is long enough to mourn.

A final arena for possible disenfranchisement in bereavement relates to assumptions about the *outcomes* of mourning. This has been touched on above. If mourning is a process of coping with loss and grief, we can rightly ask: What are the results which it strives to achieve? Many would say "recovery," "completion," or "resolution." Each of these terms appears to imply a fixed endpoint for mourning, a final closure after which there is no more grieving and mourning. "Recovery," is perhaps the least satisfactory of the three terms, because it also seems to suggest that grief is a bad situation like a disease or a wound from which one must rescue or reclaim oneself (Osterweis, Solomon, & Green, 1984; Rando, 1993). Recovery is often implied in metaphors of "healing" from grief; talking in this

way may otherwise be quite helpful, but it tends to suggest a time at which one will be done with healing and after which one will apparently be back to one's former self essentially unchanged by the bereavement experience.

It has been argued earlier that it is not desirable to use symptom language to interpret grief and to impose disease models upon healthy experiences in bereavement. To that we can add here that there are no fixed endpoints in mourning. One can never simply go back to a pre-bereavement mode of living after a significant loss. In fact, there is ample evidence, for many at least, that mourning continues in some form for the remainder of one's life. Interpretations to the contrary disenfranchise processes related to loss and grief which take place after the assumed endpoint or completion of mourning. They also disenfranchise the life-changing power of significant losses and the ongoing need to continue to cope with loss, grief, and new challenges in life. The misconception that grief and mourning should be over in a short time or at some predefined point is what leads to the familiar experience of many bereaved persons that over time their grief appears to become disenfranchised (Lundberg, Thornton, & Robertson, 1987).

There are, in fact, different outcomes experienced by different individuals who are bereaved. That is not surprising. Individuals who live their lives in different ways may be expected to cope with loss and grief in different ways, and to come to different results in their coping work. Research by Martinson and her colleagues (McClowry, Davies, May, Kulenkamp, & Martinson, 1987) studied bereaved parents and other family members (mainly siblings) seven to nine years after the death of a child. Results suggested that different individuals and different families dealt with the "empty space" in their lives in different ways. Some worked diligently to "get over it," that is, to put the loss behind them and go on with their lives. Others sought to "fill the space" by turning their focus toward what they perceived as some constructive direction. This type of effort to find some positive meaning in an otherwise horrible event might be illustrated by those bereaved after automobile accidents associated with the use of alcoholic beverages who throw themselves into campaigns to prevent intoxicated drivers from driving motor vehicles or to take such drivers off the road when they have been identified. A third outcome identified in this research was that of "keeping the connection." This appeared in bereaved persons who struggled to maintain a place in their lives for the deceased individual, vividly illustrated by the mother who insists that she has two sons, despite her full awareness that one of them has died (e.g., Wagner, 1994).

The important point in this research is not to argue for one or the other of these three outcomes in mourning, or even to suggest that they are the only possible outcomes. The point is that mourning is a process of acknowledging the reality of a death, experiencing the grief associated with that loss, learning to live without the deceased, and restructuring one's relationship to the deceased in order that that relationship can continue to be honored even while the survivor goes on living in a healthy and productive way (Worden, 1991). This process can be carried out in different ways and it can be expected to have somewhat different results for different individuals. As one astute psychologist observed, it is not the time that one has to use but the use that one makes of the time that one has that makes all the difference in bereavement, grief, and mourning (S. J. Fleming, personal communication, 9/28/95).

Three widows in my own experience acted out their mourning in different ways. One removed her wedding ring after the death of her husband. She said, "I am no longer married to him." Another kept her wedding ring on the third finger of her left hand. She said, "We are still connected." A third removed her husband's wedding ring before his body was buried and had it refashioned along with her own wedding ring into a new ring which she wore on her right hand. She said, "I now have a new relationship with my deceased husband."

These and other possible variations identify alternative courses in bereavement and mourning. In each case, metaphors of healing or resolution are partly correct insofar as the survivor has found a constructive way in which to go forward with his or her life. The intensity of the bereaved person's grief may have abated, but many continue to experience grief and reoccurrences of mourning in some degree, in some forms, and at some times. Grief may no longer consume them as it seemed to do immediately after their loss. They have "gotten through" some difficult times in bereavement, but they are not simply "over" their grief. In fact, many bereaved persons report that their grief and mourning never completely end.

Outsiders must take care not to invalidate or disenfranchise the ongoing grief and mourning of the bereaved, as well as their healthy connectedness to the deceased, by speaking too facilely of closure and completion (Klass, Silverman, & Nickman, 1996; Silverman, Nickman, & Worden, 1992). Such language may speak not primarily about bereavement but about the time at which a helper judges that his or her role as a counselor or therapist is no longer required. Thus, when a bereaved child decides to leave one of the support groups at The Dougy Center in Portland, Oregon (because, as was once said, "he or she now has better things to do with his or her time"), he or she is given a drawstring pouch containing several small stones (Corr and the Staff of The Dougy Center, 1991). Most of the stones in the pouch are polished and thus serve to symbolize what the child has achieved in coping with loss and grief; at least one is left in a rough state to represent the unfinished work that always remains in bereavement.

Conclusion

What have we learned from this reflection on the concept of disenfranchised grief? First, it is a concept with immediate appeal. It resonates with the experiences of many bereaved persons and of many clinicians and scholars who have sought to understand experiences of bereavement or tried to be of assistance to bereaved persons. Second, disenfranchisement involves more than merely overlooking or forgetting to take note of certain types of bereavement and grief. It is more active than that in its nature and more determined in its messages, even if they are often conveyed in subtle and unspoken ways. Whatever is disenfranchised in grief is not free to experience or to express itself. It is prohibited, tied down, not sanctioned, and not supported by society.

Third, as Doka (1989a) originally pointed out, disenfranchisement can apply to any or all of the key structural elements in bereavement—relationships, losses, and grievers—as well as to certain forms of death. However, as this article has made clear, disenfranchisement can also be associated with the full range of the various reactions to loss (grief) and their expression, the processes of coping with or striving to manage loss, grief, and the new challenges which they entail (mourning), both the intrapersonal and the interpersonal dimensions of those processes, and various ways of living out their implications. In the aftermath of a death, the possible scope of disenfranchisement is not confined merely to the structural elements of bereavement or to grief understood in a kind of global way; it can extend to every aspect or dimension of the experience of bereavement and be applied to all of the dynamics of grief and mourning.

Enhancing our understanding of the concept of disenfranchised grief can contribute to improved appreciation of its breadth and depth. This same effort also provides an added way of drawing out some of the implications of the underlying concepts of bereavement, grief, and mourning. Further, attention to the enhanced concept of disenfranchised grief reminds helpers of the sensitivities they need to keep in mind in order not to devalue or rule out of bounds important aspects of the experiences of bereaved persons.

A caring society ought not incorporate within its death system—either formally or informally—thoughts, attitudes, behaviors, or values that communicate to bereaved persons inappropriate or unjustified messages such as: "Your relationship with the deceased person did not count in our eyes"; "Your loss was not really a significant one"; "You are not a person who should be grieving this loss;" "We do not recognize some aspects of your grief" or "Your grief is not acceptable to us in some ways;" "Your grief is in itself a symptom of psychic disorder or lack of mental health;" "Your mourning has lasted too long"; "You are mourning in ways that are publicly or socially unacceptable;" "You should not continue to mourn inside yourself in these ways"; or "Your mourning should be finished and over with by now."

Rather than the perspectives described in the previous paragraph, a caring society ought to respect the complexities and the individuality of each bereavement experience. While remaining sensitive to the deficits and excesses that define complicated mourning in a relatively small percentage of bereavement experiences (Rando, 1993), a caring society and its members ought to appreciate that healthy grief honors cherished relationships and that constructive mourning is essential for those who are striving to live in productive and meaningful ways in the aftermath of loss. Consider how different our society would be if it listened to and acted on comments such as the following from Frank (1991), who wrote: "Professionals talk too much about adjustment. I want to emphasize mourning as affirmation. . . . To grieve well is to value what you have lost. When you value even the feeling of loss, you value life itself, and you begin to live again" (pp. 40–41).

References

Attig, T. (1991). The importance of conceiving of grief as an active process. *Death Studies, 15,* 385–393.

Attig, T. (1996). *How we grieve: Relearning the world.* New York: Oxford University Press.

Becker, S. M. (1997, 26 June). *Disenfranchised grief and the experience of loss after environmental accidents.* Paper presented at the meeting of the Association for Death Education and Counseling and the 5th International Conference on Grief and Bereavement in Contemporary Society, Washington, DC.

Corr, C. A., and the Staff of The Dougy Center. (1991). Support for grieving children: The Dougy Center and the hospice philosophy. *The American Journal of Hospice and Palliative Care, 8*(4), 23–27.

Corr, C. A., Nabe, C. M., & Corr, D. M. (1994). A task-based approach for understanding and evaluating funeral practices. *Thanatos, 19*(2), 10–15.

Davidowitz, M., & Myrick, R. D. (1984). Responding to the bereaved: An analysis of "helping" statements. *Death Education, 8,* 1–10.

Doka, K. J. (1989a). Disenfranchised grief. In K. J. Doka (Ed.), *Disenfranchised grief: Recognizing hidden sorrow* (pp. 3–11). Lexington, MA: Lexington Books.

Doka, K. J. (Ed.) (1989b). *Disenfranchised grief: Recognizing hidden sorrow.* Lexington, MA: Lexington Books.

Elias, N. (1991). On human beings and their emotions: A process-sociological essay. In M. Featherstone, M. Hepworth, & B. S. Turner (Eds.), *The body: Social process and cultural theory* (pp. 103–125). London: Sage.

Folta, J. R., & Deck, E. S. (1976). Grief, the funeral, and the friend. In V. R. Pine, A. H. Kutscher, D. Peretz, R. C. Slater, R. DeBellis, R. J. Volk, & D. J. Cherico (Eds.), *Acute grief and the funeral* (pp. 231–240). Springfield, IL: Charles C. Thomas.

Frank, A. W. (1991). *At the will of the body: Reflections on illness.* Boston: Houghton Mifflin.

Gyulay, J. E. (1975). The forgotten grievers. *American Journal of Nursing, 75,* 1476–1479.

Hamilton, J. (1978). Grandparents as grievers. In O. J. Z. Sahler (Ed.), *The child and death* (pp. 219–225). St. Louis, MO: C. V. Mosby.

Kaczmarek, M. G., & Backlund, B. A. (1991). Disenfranchised grief: The loss of an adolescent romantic relationship. *Adolescence, 26,* 253–259.

Kamerman, J. (1993). Latent functions of enfranchising the disenfranchised griever. *Death Studies, 17,* 281–287.

Klass, D., Silverman, P. R., & Nickman, S. L. (Eds.) (1996). *Continuing bonds: New understanding of grief.* Washington, DC: Taylor & Francis.

Lazarus, R. S., & Folkman, S. (1984). *Stress, appraisal, and coping.* New York: Springer.

Lindemann, E. (1944). Symptomatology and management of acute grief. *American Journal of Psychiatry, 101,* 141–148.

Lundberg, K. J., Thornton, G., & Robertson, D. U. (1987). Personal and social rejection of the bereaved. In C. A. Corr & R. A. Pacholski (Eds.), *Death: Completion and discovery* (pp. 61–70). Lakewood, OH: Association for Death Education and Counseling.

McClowry, S. G., Davies, E. B., May, K. A., Kulenkamp, E. J., & Martinson, I. M. (1987). The empty space phenomenon: The process of grief in the bereaved family. *Death Studies, 11,* 361–374.

Mead, M. (1973). Ritual and social crisis. In J. D. Shaughnessy (Ed.), *The roots of ritual* (pp. 87–101). Grand Rapids, MI: Eerdmans.

Osterweis, M., Solomon, F., & Green, M. (Eds.) (1984). *Bereavement: Reactions, consequences, and care.* Washington, DC: National Academy Press.

The Oxford English Dictionary (1989). J. A. Simpson & E. S. C. Weiner (Eds.). 2nd ed.; 20 vols; Oxford: Clarendon Press.

Parkes, C. M. (1996). *Bereavement: Studies of grief in adult life* (3rd ed.). New York: Routledge.

Pine, V. R., Margolis, O. S., Doka, K., Kutscher, A. H., Schaefer, D. J., Siegel, M-E., & Cherico, D. J. (Eds.) (1990). *Unrecognized and unsanctioned grief: The nature and counseling of unacknowledged loss.* Springfield, IL: Charles C Thomas.

Rando, T. A. (1993). *Treatment of complicated mourning.* Champaign, IL: Research Press.

Schwebach, I., & Thornton, G. (1992, 6 March). *Disenfranchised grief in mentally retarded and mentally ill populations.* Paper presented at the meeting of the Association for Death Education and Counseling, Boston.

Silverman, P. R., Nickman, S., & Worden, J. W. (1992). Detachment revisited: The child's reconstruction of a dead parent. *American Journal of Orthopsychiatry, 62,* 494–503.

Staples, B. (1994). *Parallel time: Growing up in black and white.* New York: Pantheon.

Stroebe, M. S., & Schut, H. (1995, June 29). *The dual process model of coping with loss.* Paper presented at the meeting of the International Work Group on Death, Dying, and Bereavement, Oxford, England.

Thornton, G., Robertson, D. U., & Mlecko, M. L. (1991). Disenfranchised grief and evaluations of social support by college students. *Death Studies, 15,* 355–362.

Wagner, S. (1994). *The Andrew poems.* Lubbock, TX: Texas Tech University Press.

Weisman, A. D. (1984). *The coping capacity: On the nature of being mortal.* New York: Human Sciences Press.

Wolfelt, A. D. (1996). *Healing the bereaved child: Grief gardening, growth through grief and other touchstones for caregivers.* Fort Collins, CO: Companion Press.

Worden, J. W. (1991). *Grief counseling and grief therapy: A handbook for the mental health practitioner* (2nd ed.). New York: Springer.

Zupanick, C. E. (1994). Adult children of dysfunctional families: Treatment from a disenfranchised grief perspective. *Death Studies, 18,* 183–195.

Critical Thinking

1. Describe disenfranchised grief.
2. Explain the two dimensions of mourning.
3. How should we approach, or what should we say to a person who is morning?

We've Been Misled about How to Grieve

Why it may be wise to skip the months of journalling and group talk we've been taught we need.

Nicholas Köhler

Many years ago, Nancy Moules, a pediatric oncology nurse who specializes in grief, got a call from a family member of one of her clients, a woman in her late 20s whose six-year-old daughter had died of leukemia a month or so earlier. The relative told Moules the woman was carrying an urn full of her daughter's ashes everywhere she went; that if you met her for lunch she'd get a table for three; that, in a nutshell, the family was concerned about how she was coping. Sure enough, when Moules later met the client for lunch, they ate with the ashes at the table. "So, are you wondering why I invited you out?" Moules asked. "Oh no, I know," the woman said. "Somebody phoned you, they're worried about me. They think I'm crazy." Moules probed further: "Do *you* think it's crazy?" she asked. "No," said the woman. "F—k them. This is the last human, physical connection that I have to her and I'll put her down when I'm ready to put her down."

For Moules, who now lectures on grief as a nursing prof at the University of Calgary, the young mother's story helps illustrate the sometimes paradoxical relationship many of us have with the emotions accompanying a loved one's death. "There's all these cultural expectations of grief that are contradictory," she says. "One is, 'Get over it, you should be over it by now!' And the other is, 'What's wrong with you that you aren't continuing to feel it? Didn't you love the person?' And we turn all those judgments inward."

Many of these expectations have, over the past four decades, been set by Elisabeth Kübler-Ross, a Swiss-born psychiatrist who used her interviews with a handful of dying patients in Chicago in the mid-'60s as the basis for a theory of grief that quickly gripped the world's imagination and never let go. *On Death and Dying*, her milestone 1969 book, proposed that a person confronting his or her own death passes through five stages—denial,

anger, bargaining, depression and, finally, acceptance. The analysis was backed by no solid research—indeed, as Ruth Davis Konigsberg's new book *The Truth About Grief: The Myth of Its Five Stages and the New Science of Loss* notes, scientific studies around grief remain surprisingly scant even now, and Kübler-Ross hit upon her stages only after getting a book deal and at the end of a bout of writer's block. In an era in which the old customs of black armbands and crepe no longer applied, Kübler-Ross became widely embraced as a grief guru—no matter that her research had always been limited to the dying. Soon an industry had grown up around the funeral business that found it convenient to guide the bereaved through her stages.

"Grief culture" has stigmatized the common response of resilience, branding it "cold"

Published the year after her death in 2004 and co-written with David Kessler, Kübler-Ross's *On Grief and Grieving* stamped her imprimatur onto a field that she'd largely come to define anyway (better that she remain associated with that than, say, her later interest in contacting the dead via seance). She still does, though academics now pooh-pooh her work: Konigsberg refers to a 2008 Hospice Association of Ontario report that identifies Kübler-Ross as the most recommended resource for bereavement support in that province. Her stages now colour the way we discuss everything from divorce to coming out of the closet to beating addiction.

Yet in *The Truth About Grief*—the title is tongue-in-cheek, as one-size-fits-all models like Kübler-Ross's actually prove incomplete—Konigsberg, a journalist who has worked as an editor at *New York* and *Glamour* magazines, argues stage theory has promoted a view of grief as long and debilitating, when recent research actually suggests people usually accept a loved one's death quickly, experience a few months of pining for the deceased, and are over it all in as little as six to 12 months—a natural evaporation of sadness. Kübler-Ross's stages interrupt that process by casting grief as a "journey" we must "work" through, a notion that heralded a whole industry of "death services" and created standards of grief all of us feel we must now labour to meet. All this served to shift the emphasis away from the deceased and toward those left behind, whose important work it now was to overcome loss. The old mourning rites may be gone, Konigsberg writes, "but they have been replaced by conventions for grief, which are more restrictive in that they dictate not what a person wears or does in public but his or her inner emotional state."

For all that grief work, studies show people who undergo bereavement counselling emerge from grief no more quickly than people who don't—except in the lengthiest cases, where the death of an intimate has likely exposed underlying depression (a condition now often called "complicated grief"). Konigsberg marshals more research suggesting Kübler-Ross's stages don't accurately describe what we typically experience after a death, and argues that adherence to the model does more harm than good in that the doctrine "has actually lengthened the expected duration of grief and made us more judgmental of those who stray from the designated path."

Beamsville, Ont., resident Sandy McBay, whose husband of 35 years, Rick, died suddenly in December of an aortic dissection—"Just in case, I love you," he told her as they awaited the ambulance—found herself as blindsided as anyone despite two decades of work in palliative care and bereavement support. In leading therapy sessions, McBay often encounters a tacit faith in Kübler-Ross. "A lot of people expect they're going to grieve that way," she says. "They are pleasantly surprised, some of them at least, to realize—'Okay, just because I'm not doing it the way I've heard it's supposed to be done doesn't mean I'm doing it wrong.'" Rather than anger or depression, many instead report feelings of yearning. McBay, whose husband was a teacher and choir director, is no different. "I was there when he died, so I know he's not coming back," she says. "But when I am home and looking around and seeing the life that we created together—I look at my 1.3-acre property and go, 'What am I going to do?' Just—him simply not being there."

What to do with such feelings? In fact, the long, agonizing ordeal Kübler-Ross and her disciples have long steeled us for isn't the norm. Here Konigsberg outlines research led by George Bonanno, a psychology prof at Columbia University's Teachers College, that "tracked elderly people whose spouses died of natural causes, and the single largest group—about 45 per cent—showed no signs of shock, despair, anxiety, or intrusive thoughts six months after their loss," Konigsberg writes. "A much smaller group—only about 15 per cent—were still having problems at 18 months." Such numbers belie popular notions that widows and widowers find the second year worse than the first. While Konigsberg takes care not to pathologize those who suffer prolonged turmoil, she argues that what she calls the "grief culture" has stigmatized the more common response of resilience and strength by branding it "cold," even "pathological." Actually, she says, "You probably already have what you need to get through this on your own. If after six months or a year you find you're still having trouble, you should probably seek professional help."

Before that threshold, though, it may be wise to skip the months of disclosure, journaling and group talk that the bereavement services sector, channelling Kübler-Ross, says we need lest our grief fester. ("Telling your story often and in detail is primal to the grieving process," Kübler-Ross tell us. "Grief must be witnessed to be healed.") All that vocalizing may be just the trouble. Reminiscent of the critiques around critical-incident stress debriefing, an intense talk therapy aimed at preventing post-traumatic stress disorder, some studies now say grief can be aggravated by chit-chat. Konigsberg cites another Bonanno study that found bereaved people who did not communicate their "negative emotions" had fewer health complaints than those who did, opening up the tantalizing possibility that tamping down bad feelings "might actually have a protective function."

Not everyone agrees with all this. Mel Borins, a Toronto family physician who lectures doctors on grief, calls complicated grief "underestimated and I think quite common—more than 15 percent of people get left with unfinished business." And assuming one does tie up those emotional loose ends, what exactly does it feel like to dispense with grief and yet go on remembering the dead? It's a question Konigsberg's book isn't designed to answer, though Kübler-Ross's insistence on "acceptance" cries out for quibbling. Indeed, it's that punishing commitment to recovery that Moules, the Calgary nursing prof, most often sees in those she counsels. "Many people come and say, 'I must be doing this grieving thing wrong, because I still feel something,'" she says, adding: "You will feel that loss for the rest of your life. It won't be as consuming, it won't be as absolutely devastating, as unfathomable as it was. But you never get over it." She recalls the young mother who carted around her daughter's ashes. Several weeks after that lunch, Moules got a call from the woman inviting her to her daughter's inurnment. Finally she was ready to lay the ashes down. But never her daughter.

"Many people say, 'I must be doing this grieving thing wrong, because I still feel something'"

—Nancy Moules

Critical Thinking

1. Why do people who avail themselves of grief counseling emerge no more quickly than those who don't?

2. Explain the following quotation: "You probably already have what you need to get through this on your own. If after six months or a year you find you're still having trouble, you should probably seek professional help."

3. Why did a Bonanno study conclude that bereaved people who did not communicate their "negative emotions" had fewer health complaints than those who did?

The Increasing Prevalence of Complicated Mourning

The Onslaught Is Just Beginning

In this article, complicated mourning is operationalized in relation to the six "R" processes of mourning and its seven high-risk factors are identified. The main thesis is that the prevalence of complicated mourning is increasing today due to a number of contemporary sociocultural and technological trends which have influenced 1) today's types of death; 2) the characteristics of personal relationships severed by today's deaths; and 3) the personality and resources of today's mourner. Additionally, specific problems in both the mental health profession and the field of thanatology further escalate complicated mourning by preventing or interfering with requisite treatment. Thus, complicated mourning is on the rise at the precise time when caregivers are unprepared and limited in their abilities to respond. New treatment policies and models are mandated as a consequence.

THERESE A. RANDO, PHD

In the 1990s, the mental health profession (a term herein broadly used to encompass any caregiver whose work places him/her in the position of ministering to the mental health needs of another) and the thanatological community are at a crucial crossroads. Current sociocultural and technological trends in American society are directly increasing the prevalence of complicated mourning at the precise point in time at which the mental health profession is particularly both unprepared and limited in its abilities to respond to the needs created. Thanatology has a pivotal role to play in identifying this crisis, delineating the problems to be addressed, and advocating for the development of new policies, models, approaches, and treatments appropriate to today's grim realities. Failure of either profession to recognize these realities is bound to result not only in inadequate care for those who require it, but to place our society at greater risk for the serious sequelae known to emanate from untreated complicated mourning.[1]

After a brief review of complicated mourning, this article will: 1) identify the high-risk factors for complicated mourning; 2) delineate the sociocultural and technological trends exacerbating these factors, which in turn increase the prevalence of complicated mourning; 3) indicate the problems inherent in the mental health profession that interfere with proper response to complicated mourning and to its escalation; and 4) point out the pitfalls for addressing complicated

mourning that reside in the field of thanatology today. The focus on this article is restricted to raising awareness of the problem and discussing its determinants.

Complicated Mourning

Historically, there have been three main difficulties in defining complicated mourning. The first stems from the imprecise and inconsistent terminology employed. The very same grief and mourning phenomena have been described at various times and by various authors as "pathological," "neurotic," "maladaptive," "unresolved," "abnormal," "dysfunctional," or "deviant," just to name some of the designations used. Communication has been hampered by a lack of semantic agreement and consensual validation. This author's preference is for the term "complicated mourning." Such a term suggests that mourning is a series of processes which in some way have become complicated, with the implication being that what has become complicated can be uncomplicated. It avoids the pejorative tone of many of the other terms. Additionally, there is no insinuation of pathology in the mourner. Heretofore, complications typically have been construed to arise from the deficits of the person experiencing the bereavement. The term "complicated" avoids the assumption that the complications necessarily stem from the mourner him or herself. This is quite crucial because it is now well-documented that there are some circumstances of death and some postdeath variables that in and of themselves complicate mourning regardless of the premorbid psychological health of the mourner.

A second difficulty stems from the lack of objective criteria for what constitutes complicated mourning. Unlike the analogous medical situation in which the determination of pathology is more readily discerned and defined (e.g., the diagnosis of a broken bone usually can be easily agreed upon by several physicians following viewing of an x-ray), the phenomena in mourning tend not to be so concrete or unarguable. For instance, a woman hearing her deceased husband's voice in some circumstances is quite appropriate, whereas in others it reflects gross pathology.

The third and related difficulty is found because mourning is so highly idiosyncratic. It is determined by a constellation of thirty-three sets of factors circumscribing the loss and its circumstances, the mourner, and the social support received. No determination of abnormality technically ever can be made without taking into consideration the sets of factors known to influence any response to loss.[2] What may be an appropriate response in one circumstance for an individual mourner may be a highly pathological response for a different mourner in other circumstances. For this reason, it appears most helpful to look at complications in the mourning processes themselves rather than at particular symptomatology.

With this as a premise, complicated mourning can be said to be present when, taking into consideration the amount of time since the death, there is a compromise, distortion, or failure of one or more of the six "R" processes of mourning.[1] The six "R" processes of mourning necessary for healthy accommodation of any loss are:

1. Recognize the loss
   - Acknowledge the death
   - Understand the death
2. React to the separation
   3. Experience the pain
   4. Feel, identify, accept, and give some form of expression to all the psychological reactions to the loss
   5. Identify and mourn secondary losses
3. Recollect and reexperience the deceased and the relationship
   4. Review and remember realistically
   5. Revive and reexperience the feelings
4. Relinquish the old attachments to the deceased and the old assumptive world
5. Readjust to move adaptively into the new world without forgetting the old
   6. Revise the old assumptive world
   7. Develop a new relationship with the deceased
   8. Adopt new ways of being in the world
   9. Form a new identity
6. Reinvest

In all forms of complicated mourning, there are attempts to do two things: 1) to deny, repress, or avoid aspects of the loss, its pain, and the full realization of its implications for the mourner; and 2) to hold onto, and avoid relinquishing, the lost loved one. These attempts, or some variation thereof, are what cause the complications in the "R" processes of mourning.

Complicated mourning may take any one or combination of four forms: symptoms, syndromes, mental or physical disorder, or death.[1]

Complicated mourning symptoms refer to any psychological, behavioral, social, or physical symptom—alone or in combination—which in context reveals some dimension of compromise, distortion, or failure of one or more of the six "R" processes of mourning. They are of insufficient number, intensity, and duration, or of different type, than are required to meet the criteria for any of the other three forms of complicated mourning discussed below.

There are seven complicated mourning syndromes into which a constellation of complicated mourning symptoms may coalesce. They may occur independently or concurrently with one another. Only if the symptoms comprising them meet the criteria for the specific syndrome is there said to be a complicated mourning syndrome present. If only some of the symptoms are present, or there is a combination of symptoms from several of the syndromes but they fail to meet the criteria for a particular complicated mourning syndrome, then they are considered complicated mourning symptoms. The reader should be advised that a syndrome is not necessarily more pathological than a group of symptoms which clusters together but does not fit the description of one of the complicated mourning syndromes. Sometimes just a few complicated mourning symptoms—depending upon which they are—can be far more serious than the complicated mourning syndromes. With the exception of death, severity is not determined by the form of complicated mourning.

The seven syndromes of complicated mourning include three syndromes with problems in expression (i.e., absent mourning, delayed mourning and inhibited mourning); three syndromes with skewed aspects (i.e., distorted mourning of the extremely angry or guilty types, conflicted mourning, and unanticipated mourning); and the syndrome with a problem in ending (i.e., chronic mourning).

The third form that complicated mourning may take is of a diagnosable mental or physical disorder. This would include any DSM-III-R[3] diagnosis of a mental disorder or any recognized physical disorder that results from or is associated with a compromise, distortion, or failure of one or more of the six "R" processes of mourning. Death is the fourth form which complicated mourning may take. The death may be consciously chosen (i.e., suicide) or it may stem from the immediate results of a complicated mourning reaction (e.g., an automobile crash resulting from the complicated mourning symptom of driving at excessive speed) or the long-term results of a complicated mourning reaction (e.g., cirrhosis of the liver secondary to mourning-related alcoholism). The latter two types of death may or may not be subintentioned on the part of the mourner.

Generic High-Risk Factors for Complicated Mourning

Clinical and empirical evidence reveals that there are seven generic high-risk factors which can predispose any individual to have complication in mourning.[1] These can be divided into two categories: factors associated with the specific death and factors associated with antecedent and subsequent variables.

Factors associated with the death which are known especially to complicate mourning include: 1) a sudden and unanticipated death, especially when it is traumatic, violent, mutilating, or random; 2) death from an overly-lengthy illness; 3) loss of a child; and 4) the mourner's perception of preventability. Antecedent and subsequent variables that tend to complicate mourning include: 1) premorbid relationship with the deceased which has been markedly angry or ambivalent or markedly dependent; 2) the mourner's prior or concurrent mental health problems and/or unaccommodated losses and stresses; and 3) the mourner's perceived lack of social support.

To the extent that any bereaved individual is characterized by one or more of these factors, that individual can be said to be at risk for the development of complications in one or more of the six "R" processes of mourning, and hence at risk for complicated mourning.

Sociocultural and Technological Trends Exacerbating the High Risk Factors and Increasing the Prevalence of Complicated Mourning

Social change, medical advances, and shifting political realities have spawned the recent trends that have complicated healthy grief and mourning.

Social change, occurring at an increasingly rapid rate, encompasses such processes as urbanization; industrialization; increasing technicalization; secularization and deritualization (particularly the trend to omit funeral or memorial services and not to view the body); greater social mobility; social reorganization (specifically a decline in—if not a breakdown of—the nuclear family, increases in single parent and blended families, and the relative exclusion of the aged and dying); rising societal, interpersonal, and institutional violence (physical, sexual, and psychological); and unemployment, poverty, and economic problems. Consequences include social alienation; senses of personal help-

lessness and hopelessness; parental absence and neglect of children; larger societal discrepancies between the "haves" and the "have nots"; epidemic drug and alcohol abuse; physical and sexual abuse of children and those without power (e.g., women and the elderly); and availability of guns. All of these sequelae have tended to increase violence even more, to sever or severely damage the links between children and adults, and to expose individuals to more traumatic and unnatural deaths.

Medical advances have culminated in lengthier chronic illnesses, and increased age spans, altered mortality rates, and intensified bioethical dilemmas. These trends, plus those involving social change, accompany contemporary political realities of increasing incidence of terrorism, assassination, political torture, and genocide, which get played out against the ever-present possibility of ecological disaster, nuclear holocaust, and megadeath to impact dramatically and undeniably on today's mourner.[4–6]

Violence: A Particularly Malignant Trend

Any commentary on present-day trends would be negligent if it did not elaborate somewhat upon the phenomenon of violence in today's society. Violence contributes significantly to the increasing prevalence of complicated mourning, and is associated with most of its generic high-risk factors. One crime index offense occurs every two seconds in the United States, with one violent crime occurring every nineteen seconds.[7] Violent crime has risen to the extent that in April 1991 Attorney General Richard Thornburgh issued the statement that "a citizen of this country is today more likely to be the victim of a violent crime than of an automobile accident."[8] The U.S. Department of Justice estimates that five out of six of today's twelve-year-olds will become victims of violent crime during their lifetimes,[9] with estimates for the lifetime chance of becoming a victim of homicide in the United States ranging from one out of 133 to one out of 153 depending upon the source of the statistics.[10] One category of homicide—murder by juvenile—is increasing so rapidly that it is now being termed "epidemic" by psychologist and attorney Charles Ewing,[11] an authority on child perpetrators of homicide.

Other types of crime and victimization are on the rise in the United States. The National Victim Center Overview of Crime and Victimization in America[12] provides some of the horrifying statistics:

- Wife-beating results in more injuries that require medical treatment than rape, auto accidents, and muggings combined.
- More than one out of every 200 senior citizens are the victim of a violent crime each year, making a total of 155,000 elderly Americans who are attacked, robbed, assaulted, and murdered every year—435 each day.

- New York City has reported an eighty percent increase in hate-motivated crimes since 1986, with seventy percent of them perpetrated by those under age nineteen.
- One in three women will be sexually assaulted during her lifetime.
- Every forty-seven seconds a child is abused or neglected.

Certainly, society not only condones, but escalates, violence. Books, movies, music videos, and songs perpetuate the belief that violence is not merely acceptable, but exciting. Books focusing on real-life serial killers; escalating movie violence associated with anatomically precise and sexually explicit images; and music portraying hostility against women, murder, and necrophilia are routine. According to Thomas Radecki, Research Director for the National Coalition on Television Violence, by the age of 18 the average American child will have seen 200,000 violent acts on television, including 40,000 murders.[13] Children's programming now averages twenty-five violent acts per hour, which is up fifty percent from that in the early 1980s.[14] The recently popular children's movie, *Teenage Mutant Ninja Turtles,* had a total of 194 acts of violence primarily committed by the "heroes" of the film, which was the most violent film ever to be given a "PG" rating.[15] In the week of March 11, 1990, *America's Funniest Home Videos* became the highest-rated series on television. Some of the stories on that program that viewers found particularly amusing included a child getting hit in the face with a shovel, seven women falling off a bench, a man getting hit by a glider, and a child bicycling into a tree.[15] All of this provides serious concerns given the twenty-year research of Leonard Eron and L. Rowell Huesmann, who found that children who watch significant amounts of TV violence at the age of eight were consistently more likely to commit violent crimes or engage in spouse abuse at age thirty.[13] These researchers determined that heavy exposure to media violence is one of the major causes of aggressive behavior, crime, and violence in society.

Other forms of violence are increasing as well. Reports of abused and neglected children continue to rise. They reached 2.5 million in 1990, an increase of 30.7 percent since 1986, and 117 percent in the past decade.[16] One out of three girls, and one out of seven boys, are sexually abused by the time they reach eighteen.[17] In the United States, when random studies are conducted without the inclusion of high-risk groups, one in eight husbands has been physically aggressive with his wife in the preceding twelve months.[18] At least 2,000,000 women are severely and aggressively assaulted by their partners in any twelve-month period.[18] It is a myth that what has been termed "intimate violence" is confined to mentally disturbed individuals. While ten percent of offenders do sustain some form of psychopathology, ninety percent of offenders do not look any different than the "normal" individual.[19]

Sequelae of the Trends Predisposing to Complicated Mourning

As a result of all the aforementioned sociocultural and technological trends, there have been changes in three main areas which have significantly increased the prevalence of complicated mourning:

1. the types of death occurring today
2. the characteristics of personal relationships that are severed by today's deaths
3. the personality and resources of today's mourner.

Each of these adversely impacts in one or more ways upon one or more of the high-risk factors for complicated mourning, thereby increasing its prevalence.

Types of Death Occurring Today

Contemporary American society is witnessing the increase in three types of death known to be at high risk for complicated mourning: 1) sudden and unanticipated deaths, especially if they are traumatic (i.e., characterized not only by suddenness and lack of anticipation, but violence, mutilation, and destruction; preventability and/or randomness; multiple death; or the mourner's personal encounter with death;[20] 2) deaths that result from excessively lengthy chronic illnesses; and 3) deaths of children. Each of these deaths presents the survivors with issues known to compromise the "R" processes of mourning, hence each circumstance is a high-risk factor for complicated mourning.

Sudden and Unanticipated Traumatic Deaths

Sudden and unanticipated traumatic deaths stem primarily from four main causes: 1) accidents; 2) technological advances; 3) increasing rates of homicide and the escalating violence and pathology of perpetrators; and 4) higher suicide rates. Although mortality rates for children and youth in the United States have decreased since 1900, the large proportion of deaths from external causes—injuries, homicide, and suicide—distinguishes mortality at ages one to nineteen from that at other ages; with external causes of death accounting for about ten percent of the deaths of children and youth in 1900 and rising to 64 percent in 1985.[21]

Current trends reveal that "accidents"—a term covering most deaths from motor vehicle crashes, falls, poisoning, drowning, fire, suffocation, and firearms—are the leading cause of death among all persons aged one to thirty-seven and represent the fourth leading cause of death among persons of all ages.[22] On the average, there are eleven accidental deaths and approximately 1,030 disabling injuries every hour during the year.[22] Accidents are the single most common type of horrendous death for persons of any age, bringing deaths which are "premature, torturous, and without redeeming value".[23]

Technological advances simultaneously have both decreased the proportion of natural deaths that occur and increased the proportion of sudden and unanticipated traumatic deaths. For instance, substantial improvements in biomedical technology have culminated in higher survival rates from illnesses which previously would have been fatal. This leaves individuals alive longer to be susceptible to unnatural death. Additionally, the increase in unnatural death is due to greater current exposure to technology, machinery, motor vehicles, airplanes, chemicals, firearms, weapon systems, and so forth that put human beings at greater risk for unnatural death. For example, prior to the advent of the airplane, a crash of a horse and buggy could claim far fewer lives and be less mutilating to the bodies than the crash of a DC-10.

The third reason for the increase in sudden and unanticipated traumatic deaths stems from the increasing rates of homicide and the escalating violence and pathology of those who perpetrate these crimes upon others. The increase in actual homicide incidence; the rising percentage of serial killers; and the types of violence perpetrated before, during, and after the final homicidal act suggest that there are sicker individuals doing sicker things. More than ever before, homicide may be marked by cult or ritual killing, thrill killing, random killing, drive-by shootings, and accompanied by predeath torture and postdeath defilement. The increasing pathology of those who commit violent crimes may be seen as the result of the previously mentioned sociocultural trends, especially but not exclusively the individual's decreasing social connections and sense of power; fewer social prohibitions, and increasing societal violence. It reflects the increasing number of individuals with impaired psychological development, characterized often by an absent conscience, low frustration tolerance, poor impulse control, inability to delay gratification or modulate aggression, a sense of deprivation and entitlement, and notably poor attachment bonds and pathological patterns of relationships.

The fourth reason for the increase in sudden and unanticipated traumatic deaths follows from the higher suicide rates currently found in Western society. As above, these types of death appear to derive from all of the aforementioned trends contributing to complicated mourning in general.

The reader will note that most of the sudden and unanticipated traumatic deaths in this category also are preventable. Given that the perception of preventability is a high-risk factor predisposing to complicated mourning, to the extent that a mourner maintains this perception as an element in his or her mourning of the death, that individual sustains a greater chance for experiencing complications in the process.

Long-Term Chronic Illness Death

This type of death is increasing in frequency because of biomedical and technological advances that can combat disease and forestall cessation of life. Consequently, today's illnesses are longer in duration than ever before. However, it has been well-documented that there are significant problems for survivors when a loved one's terminal illness persists for too long.[24] These illnesses often present loved ones with inherent difficulties that eventually complicate their postdeath bereavement and expose them to situations and dilemmas previously unheard of when patients died sooner and/or without becoming the focus for bioethical debates around the use of machinery and the prolongation of life without quality. With the increase in the Human Immunodeficiency Virus (HIV) and Acquired Immunodeficiency Syndrome (AIDS), significant multidimensional stresses arise which engender those known to complicate mourning in anyone (e.g., anger, ambivalence, guilt, stigmatization, social disenfranchisement, problems obtaining required health care, and so forth). The fact that an individual may be positive for the HIV virus for an exceptionally long period of time prior to developing the often long-term, multiproblemic, and idiosyncratic course of their particular version of AIDS, with all of its vicissitudes, gives new meaning these days to the stresses of long-term chronic illness.

Parental Loss of a Child

In earlier years, by the time an adult child died, his or her parents would have been long deceased. Today, with increases in lifespan and advances in medical technology, parents are permitted to survive long enough to witness the deaths of the adult children they used to predecease. Clinically and empirically, it is well-known that significant problematic issues are associated with the parental loss of a child—issues which when compared to those generated by other losses appear to make this loss the most difficult with which to cope.[25] These problematic issues and complicated mourning are now visited upon older parents who remain alive to experience the death of their adult child. There is even some suggestion that additional stresses are added to the normal burdens of parental bereavement when the child is an adult in his or her own right.[26] It is a uniquely contemporary trend, therefore, that associated with all of today's deaths are a greater percentage of parents who, because of medical advancements, are alive to be placed in the high-risk situation for complicated mourning upon the death of their adult child. This is a population that can be expected to increase, and consequently swell the numbers of complicated mourners as well.

Characteristics of Personal Relationships Severed by Today's Deaths

As a consequence of societal trends, there has been an increase in conflicted and dependent relationships in our society. Both types are high-risk factors when they characterize the mourner's premorbid relationship with the deceased.[1] With more of these types of relationships than ever before, there is a relative increase in the prevalence of complicated mourning, which is predisposed to develop after the death of one with whom the mourner has had this type of bond.

In 1957, Edmond Volkart offered a classic discussion of why death in the American family tends to cause greater psychological impact than in other cultures, specifically causing the family to be uniquely vulnerable to bereavement.[6] The reasons he delineated are even more salient today, and are part of the trends already cited above. Among other trends, he noted that the limited range of interaction in the American family fosters unusually intense emotional involvement as compared to other societies, and that there is an exclusivity of relationships in the American family. Both trends breed overidentification and overdependence among family members, which in turn engender ambivalence, repressed hostility, and guilt that create greater potential for complications after the death. Adding fuel to this fire is the societal expectation that grief expression concentrates on feelings and expression of loss. There is a failure both to recognize and to provide channels for hostility, guilt, and ambivalence.

Problematic relationships are on the rise in our society for other reasons as well. Quite importantly, there is an overall increase in sexual and physical abuse of children, as well as other adults. Research repeatedly documents the malignant intrapsychic and interpersonal sequelae of abuse and victimization.[27,28] This leaves the victim susceptible to complications in mourning not only because of the myriad symptomatology and biopsychosocial issues they caused, but typically with significant amounts of the anger, ambivalence, and/or dependence known to complicate any individual's mourning. In addition, the victimization may interfere with the mourner permitting him or herself to mourn the death of the perpetrator—an often necessary task that many victims resist because of inaccurate beliefs about mourning in general and/or misconstruals of what their specifically mourning the perpetrator's death may mean.[1] This only further victimizes the person through the consequences of incomplete mourning.

These forms of victimization are not the only experiences which give rise to the conflicted and dependent relationships identified as predisposing to complicated mourning. Individuals raised in families with one or more alcoholic parents or a parent who is an adult child of an alcoholic (ACOA), or with one or more parents who are psychologically impaired, rigid in beliefs, compulsive in behaviors, codependent, absent, neglectful, or chronically ill are vulnerable too. As sociocultural trends escalate these scenarios, relationships characterized by anger, ambivalence, and dependency will become prevalent, and complicated mourning will, in turn, become more frequent.

The Personality and Resources of Today's Mourner

Current trends suggest that the personality and resources of today's mourner leave that individual compromised in mourning for three reasons. First, given the trends previously discussed, the personalities and mental health of today's mourners are often more impaired. These impaired persons—who themselves frequently sustain poor attachment bonds with their own parents because of these trends—typically effect intergenerational transmission of these deficits via the inadequate parenting provided to their own children and the unhealthy experiences those children undergo. Clinically, one sees more often these days impaired superego development, lower level personality organization, narcissistic behavior, character disorder, and poor impulse control. Given that one's personality and previous and current states of mental health are critical factors influencing any mourner's ability to address mourning successfully, a trend toward relatively more impairment in this area has implications for greater numbers of people being added to the rolls of complicated mourners.

Another liability for a mourner is the existence of unaccommodated prior or concurrent losses or stresses. In this regard, a second reason for the increased prevalence of complicated mourning comes from the presence of more loss and stress in the life of today's mourner as compared to times in the past. To the extent that contemporary sociocultural trends bring relatively more losses and stresses for a person, both prior to a given death (e.g., parents' divorce) and concomitant with it (e.g., unemployment), today's mourner is relatively more disadvantaged given his or her increased exposure to these high-risk factors.

The third reason for increased complications in mourning arises from the compromise of the mourner's resources. Disenfranchised mourning[29] is on the rise, and the consequent perceived lack of social support it stimulates is a high-risk factor for complicated mourning. It is quite evident that conditions in contemporary American society promote all three of the main reasons for social disenfranchisement during mourning, i.e., invalidation of the loss, the lost relationship, or the mourner.[29] Examples of unrecognized losses that are increasing in today's society include abortions, adoptions, the deaths of pets, and the inherent losses of those with Alzheimer's disease. Cases of the second type of disenfranchised loss that are on the increase include relationships that are not based on kin ties, or are not socially sanctioned (e.g., gay or lesbian relationships, extramarital affairs), or those that existed primarily in the past (e.g., former spouses or in-laws). Increasingly prevalent situations where the mourner is unrecognized can be found when the mourner is elderly, mentally handicapped, or a child. The more society creates, maintains, or permits individuals to be disenfranchised in their mourning, the more those individuals are at risk for complicated mourning given that disenfranchisement is so intimately linked with the high-risk factor of the mourner's perception of lack of social support.

Problems Inherent in the Mental Health Profession which Interfere with Proper Response to Complicated Mourning and to Its Escalation

There are three serious problems inherent in mental health today that interfere with the profession's response to complicated mourning and its escalation. Each one contributes to increasing the prevalence of complicated mourning either by facilitating misdiagnosis and/or hampering requisite treatment. The three problems are: 1) lack of an appropriate diagnostic category in the DSM-III-R; 2) insufficient knowledge about grief, mourning, and bereavement in general; and 3) decreased funds for and increased restrictions upon contemporary mental health services.

In the DSM-III-R, there is the lack of a diagnostic category for anything but the most basic uncomplicated grief, with the criteria even for this being significantly unrealistic for duration and symptomatology in light of today's data on uncomplicated grief and mourning. If they want to treat a mourning individual, mental health clinicians are often forced to utilize other diagnoses, many of which have clinical implications that are unacceptable. Other diagnoses that clinicians employ to justify treatment and to incorporate more fully the symptomatology of the bereaved individual frequently include one of the depressive, anxiety, or adjustment disorders; brief reactive psychosis; or one of the V code diagnoses.

The second area of problems in the mental health profession is the shocking insufficiency of knowledge about grief and bereavement in general. Mental health professionals tend, as does the general public, to have inappropriate expectations and unrealistic attitudes about grief and mourning, and to believe in and promote the myths and stereotypes known to pervade society at large. These not only do not help, but actually harm bereaved individuals given that they are used to (a) set the standards against which the bereaved individual is evaluated, (b) determine the assistance and support provided and/or judged to be needed, and (c) support unwarranted diagnoses of failure and pathology.[30] Yet, the problem is not all in *mis*information. Too many clinicians actually do not even know that they lack the requisite information they must possess if they want to treat a bereaved person successfully. Without a doubt, the majority of clinicians know an insufficient amount about uncomplicated grief and mourning; and of those who do know an adequate amount, only a fraction of them know enough about complicated mourning. Clinician lack of information and misinformation is the major cause of iatrogenesis in the treatment of grief and mourning.

An overall decrease in funds permitted and an increase in third-party payer insurance restrictions mark contemporary mental health services and constitute the third problem in the field adding to the prevalence of complicated mourning. These changes occur at a time when it not only is becoming more clearly documented that uncomplicated grief and mourning is more associated with psychiatric distress than previously recognized[31] and that it persists for longer duration,[32] but precisely when the incidence of complicated mourning is increasing and demanding more extensive treatment for higher proportions of the bereaved. Consequently, at the exact point in time that the mental health community will have more bereaved individuals with greater complicated mourning requiring treatment for longer periods of time, mental health services will be increasingly subjected to limitations, preapprovals, third-party reviews by persons ignorant of the area, short-term models, and forced usage of inappropriate diagnostic classification. This scenario demands that the mental health professional working with the bereaved find new policies, models, approaches, and treatments which are appropriate to these serious realities. Failing to do so, the future is frightening as the current system simply is not equipped to respond to the coming onslaught of complicated mourners.

The Pitfalls for Addressing Complicated Mourning Residing in the Field of Thanatology Today

It is unfortunate, but true: Thanatologists are contributing to the rising prevalence of complicated mourning as are contemporary sociocultural and technological trends and the mental health profession. While it is not in the purview of this article to discuss at length the myriad problems inherent in our own field of thanatology that contribute to complicated mourning, it must be noted:

- A significant amount of caregivers lack adequate clinical information about uncomplicated grief and mourning, e.g., the "normal" psychiatric complications of uncomplicated grief and mourning.

- Many thanatologists, in their effort to promote the naturalness of grief and mourning and to depathologize the way they construe it to have been medicalized, maintain an insufficient understanding of complicated grief and mourning.

- There is nonexistent, or at the very least woefully insufficient, assessment conducted by caregivers who assume that the grief and mourning they observe must be related exclusively to the particular death closest in time and who do not place the individual's responses within the context of his or her entire life prior to evaluating them.

- The phenomenon of "throwing the baby out with the bathwater" has occurred regarding medication in bereavement. Out of a concern that a mourner not be inappropriately medicated as had been done so often in the past, caregivers today often fail to send mourners for medication evaluations that are desperately needed, e.g., antianxiety medication following traumatic deaths.
- The research in the field has not been sufficiently longitudinal and has overfocused on certain populations (e.g., widows), leaving findings that are not generalizable over time for many types of mourners, especially complicated mourners.
- Caregivers do not always recognize that any work as a grief or mourning counselor or therapist must overlay a basic foundation of training in mental health intervention in general. While education in thanatology, good intentions, and/or previous experience with loss may be appropriate credentials for the individual facilitating uncomplicated grief and mourning (e.g., a facilitator of a mutual help group for the bereaved), this is not sufficient for that person offering counseling or therapy.
- Given that thanatology itself is a "specialty area," thanatologists often fail to recognize that the field encompasses a number of "subspecialty areas," each of which has its own data base and treatment requirements, i.e., all mourners are not alike and caregivers must recognize and respond to the differences inherent in different loss situations (e.g., loss of a child versus loss of a spouse or sudden and unanticipated death versus an expected chronic illness death).
- Clinicians working with the dying and the bereaved are subject to countertransference phenomena, stress reactions, codependency, "vicarious traumatization",[33] and burnout.

This constitutes a brief, and by no means exhaustive, listing of the types of pitfalls into which a thanatologist may fall. Each "fall" has the potential for compromising the mourning of the bereaved individual and in that regard has the potential for increasing the prevalence of complicated mourning today.

Conclusion

This article has discussed the causes and forms of complicated mourning, and has delineated the seven high-risk factors known to predispose to it. The purpose has been to illustrate how current sociocultural and technological trends are exacerbating these factors, thereby significantly increasing the prevalence of complicated mourning today. Problems both in the mental health profession and in the field of thanatology further contribute by preventing or interfering with requisite intervention. It is imperative that these grim realities be recognized in order that appropriate policies, models, approaches, and treatments be developed to respond to the individual and societal needs created by complicated mourning and its sequelae.

Notes

1. T. Rando, *Treatment of Complicated Mourning,* Research Press, Champaign, Illinois, 1993.
2. T. Rando, *Grief, Dying, and Death: Clinical Interventions for Caregivers,* Research Press, Champaign, Illinois, 1984.
3. American Psychiatric Association, *Diagnostic and Statistical Manual of Mental Disorders* (3rd ed. rev.), Washington, D.C., 1987.
4. H. Feifel, The Meaning of Death in American Society: Implications for Education, in *Death Education: Preparation for Living,* B. Green and D. Irish (eds.), Schenkman, Cambridge, Massachusetts, 1971.
5. R. Lifton, *Death in Life: Survivors of Hiroshima,* Random House, New York, 1968.
6. E. Volkart (with collaboration of S. Michael), Bereavement and Mental Health, in *Explorations in Social Psychiatry,* A. Leighton, J. Clausen, and R. Wilson (eds.), Basic Books, New York, 1957.
7. Federal Bureau of Investigation, U.S. Department of Justice, *Uniform Crime Reports for the United States,* U.S. Government Printing Office, Washington, D.C., 1990.
8. Violent Crimes up 10%, *Providence Journal,* pp. A1 and A6, April 29, 1991.
9. National Victim Center, *America Speaks Out: Citizens' Attitudes about Victims' Rights and Violence* (Executive Summary), Fort Worth, Texas, 1991.
10. Bureau of Justice Statistics Special Report, *The Risk of Violent Crime* (NCJ-97119), U.S. Department of Justice, Washington, D.C., May 1985.
11. Killing by Kids "Epidemic" Forecast, *APA Monitor,* pp. 1 and 31, April, 1991.
12. National Victim Center, *National Victim Center Overview of Crime and Victimization in America,* Fort Worth, Texas, 1991.
13. Violence in Our Culture, *Newsweek,* pp. 46–52, April 1, 1991.
14. J. Patterson and P. Kim, *The Day America Told the Truth,* Prentice Hall Press, New York, 1991.
15. National Victim Center, *Crime, Safety and You!,* 1:3, 1990.
16. Children's Defense Fund Memo on the Family Preservation Act, Washington, D.C., July 2, 1991.
17. E. Bass and L. Davis, *The Courage to Heal: A Guide for Women Survivors of Child Sexual Abuse,* Harper and Row Publishers, New York, 1988.
18. A. Brown, *"Women's Roles" and Responses to Violence by Intimates: Hard Choices for Women Living in a Violent Society,* paper presented at the conference on "Trauma and Victimization: Understanding and Healing Survivors" sponsored by the University of Connecticut Center for Professional Development, Vernon, Connecticut, September 27–28, 1991.
19. R. Gelles, *The Roots, Context, and Causes of Family Violence,* paper presented at the conference on "Trauma and Victimization: Understanding and Healing Survivors" sponsored by the University of Connecticut Center for Professional Development, Vernon, Connecticut, September 27–28, 1991.
20. T. Rando, Complications in Mourning Traumatic Death, in *Death, Dying and Bereavement,* I. Corless, B. Germino, and M. Pittman-Lindeman (eds.), Jones and Bartlett Publishers, Inc., Boston (in press).

21. L. Fingerhut and J. Kleinman, Mortality Among Children and Youth, *American Journal of Public Health, 79,* pp. 899–901, 1989.

22. National Safety Council, *Accident Facts, 1991 Edition,* Chicago, 1991.

23. M. Dixon and H. Clearwater, Accidents, in *Horrendous Death, Health, and Well-Being,* D. Leviton (ed.), Hemisphere Publishing Corporation, New York, 1991.

24. T. Rando (ed.), *Loss and Anticipatory Grief,* Lexington Books, Lexington, Massachusetts, 1986.

25. T. Rando (ed.), *Parental Loss of a Child,* Research Press, Champaign, Illinois, 1986.

26. T. Rando, Death of an Adult Child, in *Parental Loss of a Child,* T. Rando (ed.), Research Press, Champaign, Illinois, 1986.

27. C. Courtois, *Healing the Incest Wound: Adult Survivors in Therapy,* Norton, New York, 1988.

28. F. Ochberg (ed.), *Post-Traumatic Therapy and Victims of Violence,* Brunner/Mazel, New York, 1988.

29. K. Doka (ed.), *Disenfranchised Grief: Recognizing Hidden Sorrow,* Lexington Books, Lexington, Massachusetts, 1989.

30. T. Rando, *Grieving: How To Go On Living When Someone You Love Dies,* Lexington Books, Lexington, Massachusetts, 1988.

31. S. Jacobs and K. Kim, Psychiatric Complications of Bereavement, *Psychiatric Annals, 20,* pp. 314–317, 1990.

32. S. Zisook and S. Shuchter, Time Course of Spousal Bereavement, *General Hospital Psychiatry, 7,* pp. 95–100, 1985.

33. I. McCann and L. Pearlman, Vicarious Traumatization: A Framework for Understanding the Psychological Effects of Working with Victims, *Journal of Traumatic Stress, 3,* pp. 131–149, 1990.

Critical Thinking

1. Why is there likely to be an increase in complicated mourning in the future of American grieving?

2. What are the high-risk factors that can predispose an individual to complicated grieving?

3. What are the various forms of complicated mourning?

This article is adapted from a keynote address of the same name presented at the 13th Annual Conference of the Association for Death Education and Counseling, Duluth, Minnesota, April 26–28, 1991, and from the author's book, *Treatment of Complicated Mourning,* Research Press, Champaign, Illinois, 1993.

Rituals of Unburdening

MARK R. MERCURIO

Death in the newborn intensive care unit, as elsewhere, is often marked by rituals. Some, like the cadence of a code or helping parents with their grief, are included in both the formal and informal education of physicians. Among these, though perhaps not named as such, is the "unburdening" of the parents—an attempt to relieve them of misplaced guilt. A parallel ritual that is seldom taught or discussed, however, is the unburdening of the physician who has tried and failed to save a child. The unburdening of parents, typically done by the child's physician, is strikingly similar to the unburdening of the physician, done by one or more colleagues. As with so many rituals surrounding death, both may address an emotional need and provide some relief to those left behind.

A baby girl is born at 2:00 A.M. with life-threatening medical problems. The neonatology team resuscitates her and places the necessary lines and tubes. Initially her vital signs stabilize, but the honeymoon is brief. The team works for hours to reverse her downward course. The attending physician brings the parents to their daughter's bedside and tells them gently but clearly that he believes the child will probably not survive the night. They ask that everything possible be done to save her. They understand, they say, that the chance of success is low, and that even if she were to survive, she could be left with permanent disabilities. Still, they ask that everything possible be done. "How could we live with ourselves otherwise?" the father asks.

The attending watches as the neonatology fellow, almost an attending herself, expertly directs the team. He stands just behind her and off to her left, occasionally making suggestions, fine-tuning her management. He knows he is fortunate to have such an excellent group. The fellow, nurse, nurse practitioner, pediatric resident, and respiratory therapist are all experienced and skilled in their respective roles. Also, each of them has confidence in the attending's clinical judgment. As stressful as these situations can be, there is some comfort in having a veteran physician, and the clinician ultimately responsible, right there with you making sure you're doing it right—making sure you don't miss anything. This is an advantage they all share, save one.

The oxygen saturation drifts downward. Eventually the baby's heart rate begins to slow. The team initiates a code, but in truth all their efforts since the child's birth could well be described as one long code. Despite their best efforts, the situation continues to worsen. Its hopelessness seems apparent, and the fellow asks the attending how much longer they should proceed.

Acceptance seems to work its way up the ranks. The one who has the final responsibility is often the last to acknowledge that the patient will not survive. But in time the attending calls it, and efforts cease. He thanks the team and tells them they did a great job. He truthfully reassures them that they gave the baby the best chance she could have had. As the nurse gently removes the tubes and tape and machines, preparing the baby to be held, the attending sits with the parents and tells them what happened, offers condolences, answers their questions, and assures them he did everything he could.

He also unburdens them as much as possible. Parents of infants who are born sick, premature, or with congenital defects often fear they are somehow to blame. This is particularly true of mothers, who may feel they have failed in their responsibility to nurture and deliver a healthy baby. Parents often wonder what they did to cause such a catastrophe. Perhaps worse, they sometimes believe (almost always mistakenly) that they already know what they've done wrong, but are afraid to ask lest they have their theory confirmed. When their concerns are anticipated and their misplaced sense of guilt is addressed, the relief in their eyes is apparent. And then, sometimes, specific questions emerge, about having painted the apartment or missed prenatal vitamins, or something else usually unrelated to the child's death.

The attending in this case knows the ritual and understands its importance to parents. He does not need to hear the question to know it should be addressed, and so he tells the parents, "I'm so sorry this happened, but it did not happen because of anything you did or didn't do. This is absolutely not your fault. Many parents, especially moms, think it's somehow their fault when their newborn dies. It's clearly not true here. If you had done something to cause this, I'd tell you, so it wouldn't happen again. But you didn't cause this, and you couldn't have prevented it."

After more discussion, he leaves the parents and returns to the unit. There, he goes over the details of the previous night in his mind. Given the outcome, it is easy to understand why a physician would second-guess himself. There were many decision points where he might have gone another way, and of course in retrospect he may well wish he had—after all, he might think, he couldn't have done any worse. Perhaps a trial of high-frequency ventilation, which usually helps in patients like this, led in this particular case to a clinical deterioration. With the benefit of hindsight, he may wish he hadn't tried it, but it does not necessarily follow that it was a bad decision at the time he made it. He knows it is not fair to judge clinical management in retrospect, basing that judgment on information not available when the decision was made—such reasoning is not lost on him but fights with the fact that a child for whom he was responsible has died.

When a patient dies, one naturally feels sadness for the child, and for the parents. Occasionally, in cases such as this one, the physician's sadness is compounded by a fear that he might have—should have—done better. Later he may relate the story of the night to a family member or close friend, and that person may offer welcome words of comfort. But the words he most needs to hear right now are more likely to come from a respected colleague.

A more senior neonatologist, just coming in for the day, joins him at the X-ray board. She sits with him and listens as he describes the case. They go over the story, the films, and the interventions tried; left unspoken is his concern that his patient died because of something he did, or failed to do. She does not need to hear him state his insecurities to know they are there, or to know what to say. She echoes what he told the grieving parents. No, he didn't miss anything that she can see. There was nothing that he did, or failed to do, that led to the child's death. She does not see how this child could have been saved. Finally, she gets up, leaving him with one last comforting thought: "I would have handled it the same way."

He is tired. He has eight more hours to work and numerous decisions to make, some of them critical, before he goes home. Her words, in addition to alleviating his distress, may make it easier for him to focus on the patients who remain in the unit. The relief of his anxiety and the clearer focus are thus gifts not just to him, but also to those under his care. Just as his words may have left the parents more able to deal with their pain and loss, he may now be more able to deal with his ongoing responsibilities.

Had the senior neonatologist felt that he missed something truly important, their conversation would have been different, as it would not have been appropriate or helpful to lie to him. She is able to unburden him not only because he trusts her clinical judgment, but also because he trusts her to tell him the truth. But even if the conversation were different, it may still have offered some relief and could perhaps have ended with a statement like,

"That could have happened to anyone," or "I've done the same thing myself." Fortunately, in this case as in most, she was able to tell him honestly that his management was sound and that he had missed nothing of consequence.

At some point in the next several weeks the case will be reviewed at a morbidity and mortality conference. There the patient's care will be discussed, likely in greater detail and with greater scrutiny. More data, such as the results of an autopsy, may be available. The committee of neonatologists, pathologists, and radiologists may well identify things that could have been done differently—things that, if they are done differently in a future case, may lead to a different outcome. This formal process, however, is distinct from the unburdening ritual that experienced physicians sometimes share in the hours immediately following an unsuccessful attempt to save a child, when the responsible physician is the most vulnerable.

The guilt some parents feel after the death of a newborn, however misplaced, can be an emotional burden to them for years to come. Most experienced neonatologists recognize the importance of unburdening parents of this guilt. In so doing, they fulfill an old teaching about pediatric death: After the physician is finished caring for the child, he must still care for the parents. The unburdening of the physician by a trusted colleague, in contrast, is less often taught. But like so much in medicine, it is transmitted through the culture and by example, though inconsistently so. It is not always performed, is not always necessary, and one could surely argue that it is less important than the unburdening of the parents. But, when performed by a skilled and empathetic physician who observes a colleague in need, it can provide reassurance, relief, and release.

Critical Thinking

1. What is the meaning of the title "Rituals of Unburdening"?
2. How can physicians and healthcare workers ease the burden of the bereaved parent?
3. Why do parents need to hear the message "You didn't cause this, and you couldn't have prevented it."

From *Hastings Center Report*, March/April 2008, pp. 8–9. Copyright © 2008 by The Hastings Center. Reprinted by permission of the publisher and Mark Mercurio.

11 Ways to Comfort Someone Who's Grieving

If you have a friend or relative who is grieving, it can be hard to know how to console him or her. If it seems that nothing you can do or say helps, don't give up. You can't take the pain away, but your presence is more important than it seems. Accept that you can't fix the situation or make your friend or relative feel better. Instead just be present and offer hope and a positive outlook toward the future. Accept that the person's grieving will be a gradual process.

It is sometimes difficult to know what to say to a bereaved person. If you find yourself tongue-tied or uncertain of what to do in the face of someone's loss, here are some steps you might try.

1. **Name names.** Don't be afraid to mention the deceased. It won't make your friend any sadder, although it may prompt tears. It's terrible to feel that someone you love must forever be expunged from memory and conversation. (This suggestion does not apply in cultures in which mentioning the dead is taboo or bad luck, however.)

2. **Offer hope.** People who have gone through grieving often remember that it is the person who offered reassuring hope, the certainty that things will get better, who helped them make the gradual passage from pain to a renewed sense of life.

3. **Make phone calls.** Call to express your sympathy. Try to steer clear of such phrases as "It's God's will" or "It's for the best" unless the bereaved person says this first. Your friend or relative may need you even more after the first few weeks and months, when other people may stop calling.

4. **Write a note.** If you had a relationship with the deceased, try to include a warm, caring, or funny anecdote that shows how important to you he or she was. If you didn't know the deceased, offer your sympathy and assure the bereaved that he or she is in your thoughts or prayers.

5. **Help out.** Be specific when offering help. Volunteer to shop or do laundry, bring dinner, pass on information about funeral arrangements, or answer the phone. Pitch in to clean up the kitchen. A lawyer might volunteer to help with the estate. A handy person might button up the house as winter approaches.

6. **Be sensitive to differences.** People mourn and grieve in different ways. Religion plays a big role in how death is treated; so do ethnic, cultural, and family backgrounds. Avoid criticizing the funeral arrangements or memorial service. Also, try not to impose your beliefs about death on your friend.

7. **Make a date.** Ask your friend to join you for a walk or meal once a week. Be aware that weekends are often very difficult, and suggest an activity. Low-stress activities may be best: watch a video at home together versus going out to a movie. Sometimes just being there without saying much is enough—it may even be exactly what your friend wants.

8. **Listen well instead of advising.** A sympathetic ear is a wonderful thing. A friend who listens even when the same story is told with little variation is even better. Often, people work through grief and trauma by telling their story over and over. Unless you are asked for your advice, don't be quick to offer it.

9. **Express your feelings.** If you share your friend's sorrow, say so. It's even all right to blurt out that you don't know what to say. Most likely, nothing you say will turn the tide, but your sympathetic presence may make your friend feel slightly less alone. (One caveat: try not to express your feelings so emphatically that your friend has to take care of you.)

10. **Handle anger gently.** People who are grieving sometimes direct angry feelings toward the closest target. If that happens to be you, try to be understanding. That is, wait until well after

the person has cooled down before raising your concern in a nonthreatening way.

11. **Keep your promises.** If you offer to do anything, follow through. This is especially important where promises to children are involved. Losing a loved one is abandonment enough.

Critical Thinking

1. Why should one not be afraid to mention the deceased?

2. Why should one be specific when offering help?

3. Why is helping people express anger often problematic? What can you do if this becomes a problem?

From *HealthBeat*, August 24, 2010. Copyright © 2010 by Harvard University. Reprinted by permission.

Test-Your-Knowledge Form

We encourage you to photocopy and use this page as a tool to assess how the articles in *Annual Editions* expand on the information in your textbook. By reflecting on the articles you will gain enhanced text information. You can also access this useful form on a product's book support website at www.mhhe.com/cls

NAME: _____ DATE: _____

TITLE AND NUMBER OF ARTICLE: _____

BRIEFLY STATE THE MAIN IDEA OF THIS ARTICLE:

LIST THREE IMPORTANT FACTS THAT THE AUTHOR USES TO SUPPORT THE MAIN IDEA:

WHAT INFORMATION OR IDEAS DISCUSSED IN THIS ARTICLE ARE ALSO DISCUSSED IN YOUR TEXTBOOK OR OTHER READINGS THAT YOU HAVE DONE? LIST THE TEXTBOOK CHAPTERS AND PAGE NUMBERS:

LIST ANY EXAMPLES OF BIAS OR FAULTY REASONING THAT YOU FOUND IN THE ARTICLE:

LIST ANY NEW TERMS/CONCEPTS THAT WERE DISCUSSED IN THE ARTICLE, AND WRITE A SHORT DEFINITION:

We Want Your Advice

ANNUAL EDITIONS revisions depend on two major opinion sources: one is our Advisory Board, listed in the front of this volume, which works with us in scanning the thousands of articles published in the public press each year; the other is you—the person actually using the book. Please help us and the users of the next edition by completing the prepaid article rating form on this page and returning it to us. Thank you for your help!

ANNUAL EDITIONS: Dying, Death, and Bereavement 12/13

ARTICLE RATING FORM

Here is an opportunity for you to have direct input into the next revision of this volume.
We would like you to rate each of the articles listed below, using the following scale:

1. **Excellent: should definitely be retained**
2. **Above average: should probably be retained**
3. **Below average: should probably be deleted**
4. **Poor: should definitely be deleted**

Your ratings will play a vital part in the next revision.
Please mail this prepaid form to us as soon as possible.
Thanks for your help!

RATING	ARTICLE	RATING	ARTICLE
	1. Grief in the Age of Facebook		19. Why We Need Qualitative Research in Suicidology
	2. The Proliferation of Postselves in American Civic and Popular Cultures		20. A Search for Death: How the Internet Is Used as a Suicide Cookbook
	3. Roadside Memorial Policies in the United States		21. Good Mourning
	4. Brain Death Guidelines Vary at Top US Neurological Hospitals		22. When a Cherished Pet Dies
	5. Criteria for a Good Death		23. An Examination of the Potential Role of Pet Ownership, Human Social Support and Pet Attachment in the Psychological Health of Individuals Living Alone
	6. Death in Disney Films: Implications for Children's Understanding of Death		24. Veterinary Hospice: Ways to Nurture Our Pets at the End of Life
	7. Teaching Children about Death and Grief: Children Can Learn about Grief and Dying from Teachable Moments		25. What Living Wills Won't Do: The Limits of Autonomy
	8. Helping Military Kids Cope with Traumatic Death		26. When Students Kill Themselves, Colleges May Get the Blame
	9. Needs of Elderly Patients in Palliative Care		27. Cannabis Use in Long-Term Care: An Emerging Issue for Nurses
	10. End-of-Life Concerns and Care Preferences: Congruence Among Terminally Ill Elders and their Family Caregivers		28. Ethics and Life's Ending: An Exchange
	11. Dying on the Streets: Homeless Persons' Concerns and Desires about End-of-Life Care		29. I Was a Doctor Accustomed to Death, but Not His
	12. Death and Dying across Cultures		30. The Contemporary American Funeral
	13. Are They Hallucinations or Are They Real? The Spirituality of Deathbed and Near-Death Visions		31. How Different Religions Pay Their Final Respects
	14. A Spreading Appreciation for the Benefits of Hospice Care		32. Building My Father's Coffin
	15. When Death Strikes without Warning		33. Dealing with the Dead
	16. Self-Harming Behavior and Suicidality: Suicide Risk Assessment		34. The Grieving Process
	17. Effects of Race and Precipitating Event on Suicide Versus Nonsuicide Death in a College Sample		35. Disenfranchised Grief
	18. Ethical, Legal, and Practical Issues in the Control and Regulation of Suicide Promotion and Assistance over the Internet		36. Challenging the Paradigm: New Understandings of Grief
			37. Enhancing the Concept of Disenfranchised Grief
			38. We've Been Misled about How to Grieve
			39. The Increasing Prevalence of Complicated Mourning: The Onslaught Is Just Beginning
			40. Rituals of Unburdening
			41. 11 Ways to Comfort Someone Who's Grieving

ANNUAL EDITIONS: DYING, DEATH, AND BEREAVEMENT 12/13

BUSINESS REPLY MAIL
FIRST CLASS MAIL PERMIT NO. 551 DUBUQUE IA

POSTAGE WILL BE PAID BY ADDRESSEE

McGraw-Hill Contemporary Learning Series
501 BELL STREET
DUBUQUE, IA 52001

NO POSTAGE
NECESSARY
IF MAILED
IN THE
UNITED STATES

ABOUT YOU

Name

Date

Are you a teacher? ☐ A student? ☐
Your school's name

Department

Address   City   State   Zip

School telephone #

YOUR COMMENTS ARE IMPORTANT TO US!

Please fill in the following information:
For which course did you use this book?

Did you use a text with this ANNUAL EDITION? ☐ yes ☐ no
What was the title of the text?

What are your general reactions to the Annual Editions concept?

Have you read any pertinent articles recently that you think should be included in the next edition? Explain.

Are there any articles that you feel should be replaced in the next edition? Why?

Are there any World Wide Websites that you feel should be included in the next edition? Please annotate.

May we contact you for editorial input? ☐ yes ☐ no
May we quote your comments? ☐ yes ☐ no

NOTES

NOTES

NOTES

NOTES

NOTES

NOTES

NOTES

NOTES